Housing Contemporary Ireland:
Policy, Society and Shelter

HOUSING CONTEMPORARY IRELAND: POLICY, SOCIETY AND SHELTER

Edited by
Michelle Norris and Declan Redmond

INSTITUTE OF PUBLIC
ADMINISTRATION

First published 2005
Institute of Public Administration
57–61 Lansdowne Road
Dublin 4
Ireland

ISBN 1 904541 34 8

British Library Cataloguing-in-Publication Data
A catalogue record for this book is available from the British Library.

Cover design by M&J Graphics, Dublin
Typeset by Carole Lynch, Sligo
Printed in Ireland by ColourBooks Ltd, Dublin

Contents

List of Tables

List of Figures

Notes on Contributors

Michael Bannon is Professor Emeritus of Regional and Urban Planning, becoming Professor at University College Dublin. He has undertaken a wide range of planning research and has collaborated with many local and regional authorities, with several central government Departments and with the European Commission. He is author of *Metropolitan Dominance: the Challenge in Achieving Balanced Territorial Development,* the Irish input into an examination of National Urban Policies in the European Union under the Dutch EU Presidency.

Simon Brooke is a housing and social policy consultant. He worked in the areas of social housing and homelessness for many years in London and Dublin, and has extensive experience of research and evaluations in these fields. He is chair of the board of Clúid Housing Association, and lectures part-time at the Department of Social Studies, Trinity College Dublin.

Vanda Clayton is a Research Associate in the Centre for Urban and Regional Studies, Trinity College Dublin. Her doctoral research, which was completed in 2004, examined the role of housing associations in the Republic of Ireland.

Dáithí Downey is a graduate of Trinity College Dublin. His work since the early 1990s includes research and policy analysis on urban policy, access to housing and homelessness, housing systems and the economy. Over the period he has combined work as a researcher and lecturer in Irish and UK universities with policy and research consultancy work for the Combat Poverty Agency, the Homeless Agency and a number of Irish NGOs. He has published a number of reports, articles and papers on housing and urban policy as well as on homelessness. He is currently Policy Analyst with Focus Ireland, a leading Irish NGO social landlord and homeless service provider.

Tony Fahey is a sociologist and is Research Professor in the Social Policy Research Division in the Economic and Social Research Institute. His research interests include housing, living conditions, family, demography, the elderly and values and attitudes.

Eithne Fitzgerald is currently Head of Policy and Public Affairs at the National Disability Authority. A former Minister of State for Finance, she has also worked for Threshold, has lectured in social policy in both UCD and TCD, and was a member of the Housing Commission.

Yvonne Galligan is a Reader in Politics at Queen's University Belfast. Her publications include *Sharing Power: Women, Parliament, Democracy* (2005) (contributing co-editor) and *Gender Equality Indicators for Northern Ireland* (2004, co-author).

Andrew MacLaran is a Senior Lecturer in Geography and Director of the Centre for Urban and Regional Studies, Trinity College Dublin. Research interests include the social consequences of urban economic restructuring, urban housing, entrepreneurial urban planning and the impact on inner-city communities of commercial property development. He is also the editor of the *Journal of Irish Urban Studies*.

Brian Nolan is an economist. He is a Research Professor and head of the Social Policy Research Division in the Economic and Social Research Institute, Dublin.

Michelle Norris lectures in Social Policy at the School of Applied Social Science, University College Dublin. Her areas of research interest are: social housing management and estate regeneration; Traveller accommodation; tenure mixing and housing across the EU. In recent years she conducted major reviews of Irish housing policy and housing developments in the 25 EU member states, which have been published by the Stationery Office. She was Director of the Housing Unit from 2000 to 2005.

Cathal O'Connell is Senior Lecturer in Social Policy at University College Cork. His main teaching and research interests are in Irish social policy, housing policy and urban issues.

Derry O'Connell is an architect and a lecturer at the School of Geography, Planning and Environmental Policy at University College Dublin.

Eoin O'Sullivan lectures in Social Policy in the School of Social Work and Social Policy at the University of Dublin, Trinity College. Recent collaborative publications include *Crime, Punishment and the Search for Order in Ireland* (2004), *Crime Control in Ireland: The Politics of Intolerance* (2001) and *Suffer the Little Children: The Inside Story of Ireland's Industrial Schools* (1999, 2001).

Michael Punch is a lecturer at the Department of Geography, at Trinity College Dublin. His research interests are: economic geography, local development and economic renewal, uneven cities, housing, planning and community change.

Declan Redmond is a lecturer in the School of Geography, Planning and Environmental Policy at University College Dublin. He is the Programme Director of the Master of Regional and Urban Planning degree and the MSc in Planning Policy and Practice. His principal research interests revolve around issues of urban governance, social housing policy and community participation. His PhD research focused on community participation in the social housing sector and he is currently involved in projects investigating housing affordability and its impacts in the Dublin region, the role of private residents associations in the planning system and the role of entrepreneurial governance in urban change.

Mark Scott is a lecturer in the School of Geography, Planning and Environmental Policy, University College Dublin. His primary research interests focus on rural sustainable development including rural planning, housing, local development and rural governance.

Patrick Shiels is Research and Information Specialist at the Housing Unit, Dublin, and has worked on a number of projects examining housing and urban development policies and issues. He also lectures at the Institute of Auctioneers and Valuers in Ireland and holds degrees from the National University of Ireland, Maynooth and Trinity College Dublin.

David Silke is Director of the Housing Unit. His particular areas of interest are housing, older people, equality and social inclusion. He worked as a policy analyst in the National Economic and Social Forum, as a research officer in the Combat Poverty Agency and as a senior researcher in the Department of Social Security (UK). He is a graduate of University College Dublin and the London School of Economics.

Brendan Williams is a lecturer at the Department of Geography, Planning and Environmental Economics at University College Dublin. He was previously lecturer in Urban Economics and Head of Strategic Research at the Faculty of the Built Environment, Dublin Institute of Technology. His recent research has addressed the following issues: economic competitiveness of the European metropolitan areas; settlement strategies and urban regional development in Dublin; urban regeneration and future alternative policy options in Ireland and edge city development.

Nessa Winston is a lecturer in Social Policy at the School of Applied Social Science, University College Dublin. Her research interests include housing policy and migration, ethnicity and social policy. One of her recent publications, with Michelle Norris, is *Housing Policy Review 1990-2002* (2004).

1

Setting the Scene:
Transformations in Irish Housing

Declan Redmond and Michelle Norris

Introduction

For a nation somewhat obsessed with property and property rights it is
surprising that there has been a comparative dearth of published material on the
system of housing provision and housing policy in Ireland, whereas in most
other western European countries, particularly the United Kingdom, Sweden,
Denmark and the Netherlands, sophisticated housing research infrastructures
have been developed, not only in the universities but also in national and local
government and in non-governmental sectors. Recently this gap in publication
has started to be filled. For example, Norris and Winston (2004) have produced
a comprehensive overview of Irish housing policy developments over the past
decade, while in late 2004 the National Economic and Social Council (2004)
published an analysis of housing policy with a particular focus on affordability
and land policy. Despite these publications, however, it is still true to say that
the amount of original primary research on housing issues is meagre and
unbalanced. We know, for example, a good deal about social housing and the
tenants who live in this sector (Fahey, 1999), which accounts for less that 10 per
cent of all housing, but our in-depth knowledge of the owner-occupied sector,
which accounts for 80 per cent of all housing, is paltry in comparison.

This lack of information and analysis is anomalous in view of the fact that
since the early 1990s housing has become one of the central economic, social
and environmental issues in Ireland. This centrality stems directly from the
importance of housing in providing basic shelter and accommodation, its role as
a home, its role as a financial investment, its role in economic development and
its role in shaping our urban and rural environment. While these are general
attributes, they have been brought into even greater prominence in the past
decade by the extraordinary surge in housing output across the state, generated
by the economic boom and population growth. Not only have our urban centres

1

seen booms in housing development but many rural areas have also experienced the impact of high demand and supply of new housing. The boom in housing output that has occurred over the past decade is the largest and most sustained in the history of the state. Indeed, it is impressive in international terms. In 2002 the rate of new house building in Ireland was the highest in the European Union – 14.7 per 1,000 inhabitants (European Union, 2002). However, the most extraordinary and certainly the most commented upon phenomenon has been the astonishing rise in the price of housing over the past decade. For example, in the decade between 1993 and 2003 the average price of a new house in the state increased by approximately 220 per cent, and by over 280 per cent in Dublin (Department of the Environment, Heritage and Local Government, various years). General consumer price inflation increased at a fraction of this rate.

These extraordinary increases have led to a complex set of winners and losers. Those who had purchased prior to the boom could, for example, avail of the increased capital value of their dwelling and purchase a second home in Ireland or abroad; they could purchase property for investment or trade down by moving to a cheaper location and availing of the capital gain. In addition they have had significant impact on other parts of the housing system. For instance they have increased demand for private rented and social rented housing. In the case of the latter housing tenure, this has driven lengthened waiting lists, and although supply of private rented accommodation has significantly expanded, rents have also risen, thus creating affordability problems. In addition, the problems of those groups that have traditionally been marginalised in the housing system, such as homeless people, Travellers and those with specific housing needs, have been heightened by the tight house purchase and rental market, and by long waiting lists for social housing.

In that context, the purpose of this book is to present an account of key developments in the system of housing provision and in housing policy which is somewhat more detailed than that of Norris and Winston (2004) and of NESC (2004). In bringing together the leading experts on housing in Ireland, this book also aims to present the most significant of the various, often conflicting, analyses of the housing system which have been produced in recent years. Broadly, the book will examine key trends in housing provision, will trace the main policy changes and innovations of the past decade, and will attempt to evaluate the principal policy impacts. On this basis, the closing chapters of the book compare the performance of the housing system in Ireland over the past decade with that of its European Union counterparts.

The book is divided into five sections – the first three of which discuss the main housing tenures in Ireland (owner occupation, private rented accommodation and social housing), while the final two discuss housing, inequality and social exclusion and housing and the built environment. Each section is opened by a chapter which provides an overview of the particular housing issue at hand, and this is followed by two more in-depth contributions which examine a specific aspect of the issue in more depth and report on the findings of recent research. In addition, this introductory chapter provides a synopsis of some of the key housing trends and housing policies over the past decade or so, thus providing a context for the more detailed elaborations which follow.

Demand, Supply and Investment in Housing

Demand for Housing

The past decade has witnessed a sharp rise in demand for housing, the result of a combination of economic, demographic and social factors. This increased demand has, in turn, stimulated price inflation. Apart from a natural increase in population, there has been significant in-migration to Ireland which has driven the demand for housing. Table 1.1 illustrates these demographic trends. Between 1996 and 2002 the population increased by almost 300,000 and over 50 per cent of this increase was accounted for by in-migration. Bacon and Associates (1998) point out that the pattern of emigration/immigration in the late 1990s accelerated housing demand because almost half of immigrants during this period were aged between 25 and 44 years and therefore were likely to be seeking housing, while in contrast annual emigration is concentrated in the younger age group of 15-24 years who are less likely to have formed independent households.

Table 1.1: Demographic Trends which have Implications for Housing, 1981-2002

	1981	1986	1991	1996	2002
Population	3,443,405	3,540,643	3,525,719	3,626,087	3,917,336
Population Change (+/-)	N/A	+97,238	-14,925	+100,235	+291,249
Natural increase (+/-)	N/A	+169,120	+119,245	+92,035	+138,182
Net migration (+/-)	N/A	-71,883	-134,170	+8,200	+153,067
Independent households	880,000	976,000	1,029,000	Nav	1,288,000

Source: adapted from Central Statistics Office (2001b; 2002) and European Union (2002).
Note: natural increase refers to excess of births over deaths; net migration refers to immigrants minus emigrants; N/A means not applicable; Nav means not available.

The distinctive structure of the Irish population has also driven demand. Average household size in Ireland has continued to decrease and although not yet at the EU average, is heading in that direction. In 1996 average household size was 3.14 but by 2002 this had fallen to 2.94 (Central Statistics Office, 2004b). This consistent fall in household size stimulated demand for housing because, coupled with the increase in the population, it has led to an increase in the number of households. This trend is outlined in Table 1.2 which traces household change between 1996 and 2002. While the average increase in the number of households was 15 per cent the Mid-East region increased by 26 per cent and Dublin only by 11 per cent. This indicates that there have been significant changes in the spatial distribution of households, with high levels of development in the hinterland of the capital city.

Table 1.2: Number of Households, 1996-2002 ('000s)

Region	1996	2002	Change	% change
Border	124.7	142.0	17.3	+14
Dublin	343.2	379.4	36.2	+11
Mid-East	101.9	128.7	26.8	+26
Midlands	61.6	72.4	10.8	+18
Mid-West	97.2	111.4	14.2	+15
South-East	118.9	138.9	20	+17
South-West	168.9	191.3	22.4	+13
West	106.8	123.8	17	+16
State	1,123.2	1,288.0	164.8	+15

Source: Central Statistics Office, 2003.

Rapid economic growth, resulting in large-scale increases in employment, are the other main factors which have underpinned the boom in the private housing market. The past decade of housing market growth has occurred in a highly conducive economic environment, where interest rates have been historically low, financial institutions have ratcheted up their mortgage lending in response and the centre-right Fianna Fáil/Progressive Democrat government has pursued policies of low income taxation and control of inflation. Table 1.3 illustrates, dramatically, some of the key changes. Gross National Product (GNP), for example, has almost trebled in a decade. The net increase in the total labour force has been in the order of 500,000, while unemployment has decreased sharply. The combination of underlying demand for housing and the favourable economic and financial context has thus driven a sustained boom in the private market.

Table 1.3: Key Economics Changes, 1993, 2003

	1993	2003
Gross National Product (GNP)	€38,578m	€111,671m
Gross Domestic Product (GDP)	€43,240m	€134,786m
Total Labour Force (N)	1,401,000	1,899,000
Unemployed (N)	222,000	88,000

Source: Central Bank of Ireland, 2004.

Housing Supply

Figure 1.1: Dwellings built by Local Authorities and the Private Sector, 1920s-1990s

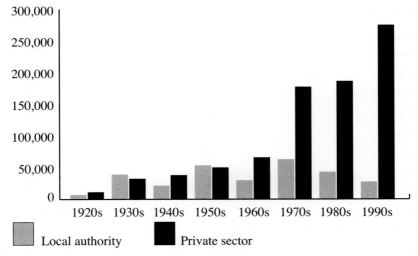

Source: Department of the Environment, Heritage and Local Government (various years), and Minister for Local Government (1964).
Note: The 1920s include the years 1923-1929 only; figures for private sector building from the 1920s to the 1950s only include dwellings built with State aid. However, the available evidence indicates that this figure probably incorporates the vast majority of private sector dwellings built from the 1930s onwards. 1990s' figures include housing association completions.

As mentioned above, increased housing demand and investment has resulted in a sustained surge in housing development since the mid-1990s. The supply of housing is traced historically in Figure 1.1. We can see that the 1970s and 1980s saw a massive increase in the supply of dwellings compared to earlier periods and this was further increased in the 1990s. It also reveals the changing balance between private and public supply. By the 1990s the private provision of housing was dominant, with social housing accounting for on average just 6 per cent of new completions in the state.

Table 1.4 outlines housing supply trends for the past decade in more detail. The supply of private housing grew rapidly during the decade. Between 1993 and 2004 the supply of private housing increased by 225 per cent. By any standards this is a remarkable level of development. For most of the period social housing supply increased at very modest rates.

Table 1.4: House Completions Nationwide, by Sector, 1993-2004

Year	Social Housing	Private Housing	Total
1993	2,090	19,301	21,391
1994	3,275	23,588	26,863
1995	3,971	26,604	30,575
1996	3,529	30,196	33,725
1997	3,388	35,454	38,842
1998	3,256	39,093	42,349
1999	3,488	43,024	46,512
2000	3,155	46,657	49,812
2001	4,875	47,727	52,602
2002	5,763	51,932	57,695
2003	6,133	62,686	68,819
2004	5,146	71,808	76,954

Source: Department of the Environment, Heritage and Local Government (various years).

It is only since 2001 that there have been significant increases in the supply of housing in this category. In Chapter 8, which sketches the history of the social housing sector, Norris explains how this increase in output has been mainly in the local authority sector. However, as Brooke and Clayton explain in Chapter 10, in recent years, there has been a growing emphasis on diversifying the sources of social housing, by encouraging increased provision by housing associations and housing co-operatives.

The consequences for this growth on the age of the housing stock are clear. Over one-fifth of the entire occupied housing stock in Ireland was built since 1991. Indeed, over 50 per cent of the State's housing stock has been built since 1971. However, these Census figures underestimate the entire housing stock as they only include occupied housing and not vacant dwellings. Thus, for example, Department of the Environment, Heritage and Local Government figures indicate that there were 260,000 housing completions in the years 1996 to 2001 but the Census identifies only 197,134 additional occupied dwellings during the same period. Some of this difference could be accounted for by obsolescence, but it is likely that the high level of production of second homes is a more significant factor. A recent comparison of the 2002 Census and housing completion figures suggests that in the inter-censal period 1996-2002 up to 70,000 of the dwellings completed were second homes or empty dwellings (McCarthy, Hughes and Woelger, 2003). This testifies, most likely, both to the general level of wealth generated during the economic boom (an issue which is examined by Fahey and Nolan in Chapter 4) and to the relatively new fashion for utilising the wealth locked up in existing housing by means of equity release products.

Investment in Housing

Table 1.5: The Economy and Investment in Housing, 1994-2004

Year	Gross National Product (GNP)	Category of Housing Investment			
		Gross Domestic Fixed Capital Formation	Capital Formation in Housing	Housing as a % of Fixed Capital	Housing as a % of GNP
	€m	€m	€m		
1994	41,785	7,674	1,694	22.1	4.1
1995	46,693	9,194	1,990	21.6	4.3
1996	51,544	11,026	2,413	21.9	4.7
1997	59,083	13,898	3,152	22.7	5.3
1998	68,161	17,341	4,139	23.9	6.1
1999	76,670	21,459	5,244	24.4	6.8
2000	88,155	25,231	6,423	25.0	7.0
2001	97,107	27,057	7,426	27.0	8.0
2002	104,474	28,983	8,802	30.0	8.0
2003	111,671	31,815	11,704	37.0	10.0
2004	122,552	36,509	15,047	41.0	12.0

Source: Department of Environment, Heritage and Local Government (various years).

The additions to the housing stock in the inter-censal period 1991-2002 has necessitated substantial financial investment and Table 1.5 details the dramatic changes in investment in housing over the past decade. Capital formation in housing increased from approximately €1.7 billion to €15 billion between 1994 and 2004 – a substantial increase in both absolute and relative terms. For example, in 1994 housing accounted for one fifth of gross domestic fixed capital formation but by 2004 it accounted for 40 per cent of such investment. Again, when we examine the relationship between housing and the economy more generally we see that in 1993 investment in housing accounted for 4 per cent of GNP but that this had trebled to 12 per cent in 2004. Thus, the impact of investment in housing on the economy has been substantial.

Table 1.6 details government expenditure on housing over the past decade. In 1994 investment was of the order of €335m but by 2003 this increased to €1,682m, representing 17 per cent of all capital formation in housing. What is noticeable from this Table, however, is that government spending on housing has only increased significantly since 2001 and has primarily gone into social housing investment. More recent policy initiatives, such as affordable housing schemes, which aim to support low-income home buyers, have seen relatively low levels of spending which is understandable, given their quite recent development, coupled with the fact that these initiatives are to a significant extent self- funded by the contributions of those who purchase the dwellings provided under their auspices.

Table 1.6: Public Expenditure on Housing, 1994-2004

Year	Local Authority Housing	Voluntary Housing	Shared Ownership	House Purchase and Improvement	Private Housing Grants	Affordable Housing (Incl Part V of the Planning and Development Act 2000)	Other	Total
	€m	€m	€m	€m	€m	€m	€m	€m
1994	199.5	34.9	56.4	24.4	33.6	0	5.1	353.9
1995	228.9	42.9	63.5	22.9	43	0	3.8	405
1996	243.7	41.9	63.5	26.2	46.6	0	5.1	427
1997	277.1	34.7	54.7	23.9	46.5	0	5.2	442.1
1998	307.5	34.3	63.7	25.3	46.9	0	6.3	484
1999	354.4	47.2	141.7	29.3	46.3	25.9	7.6	652.4
2000	521.2	91.9	149.4	38.6	59.4	5.5	11.6	877.6
2001	826.3	143.6	204.3	49.2	70.3	22.1	12.6	1,328.4
2002	999.2	165.4	200	89	80.4	50	13.1	1,597.1
2003	917.5	210.9	212	96	93.2	139	13.6	1,682.2
2004	932.9	182.6	127.8	74.8	60.3	120.7	17.9	1,517.0

Source: Department of the Environment, Heritage and Local Government (various years).

Housing Markets, Prices and Affordability

This discrepancy between the number of houses occupied and the number built over the past decade raises the question of the relationship between demand and supply and in particular the changed nature of the demand. McCarthy, Hughes and Woelger (2003) argue, for example, that housing supply in overall terms has been sufficient to meet most household growth. On the face of it, such a sustained increase in supply would imply moderate increases in house prices, with the establishment of some form of market equilibrium (Bacon and Associates, 2000). However, what has occurred has been one of the most extraordinary rises in house prices seen not only in Ireland but also in Europe. Figure 1.2 depicts the trends in new and second-hand house prices over the past decade. Nationally, for example, average new house prices increased by 185 per cent between 1996 and 2004 while second-hand house prices increased by 213 per cent over the same period. This rapid escalation in house prices has generated all manner of economic, financial, social and spatial consequences which are discussed by a number of contributors to this book.

Figure 1.2: Changes in House Prices, 1990-2004

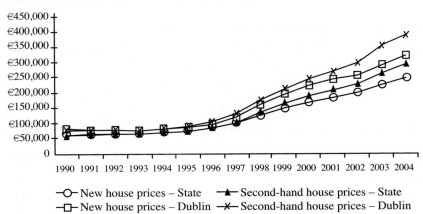

Source: Department of the Environment, Heritage and Local Government (various years).
Note: These data include both houses and apartments.

The most rapid price increases occurred in the Dublin area, where new house prices increased by 232 per cent and second-hand prices increased by 273 per cent between 1996 and 2004. As a result, average new house prices in Dublin were over 30 per cent more expensive than in other urban areas in 2004 (Department of the Environment, Heritage and Local Government, various years). While one would expect a price differential between the largest urban area in the state and the average national price, this gap has increased sharply in both absolute and relative terms. Indeed, one of the stated attractions of recent policy proposals to decentralise parts of the civil service is that Dublin-based civil servants could sell their Dublin property, make a substantial capital gain and purchase an equivalent or better property outside Dublin at a significantly reduced price.

One of the factors leading to higher house prices in Dublin relates to problems of supply in the area. What is remarkable is that in the Dublin region between 1994 and 2001, during the greatest property boom in the history of the State, house completions increased by only very moderate amounts. However, it is also clear that this undersupply in the Dublin region is being in part taken up by increased supply in the Mid-East region, where supply increased rapidly in counties Meath, Kildare and Wicklow. Between 2002 and 2004 the supply in Dublin increased rapidly, particularly in Fingal County Council area, where there has been very rapid expansion of supply in new suburban developments.

Analysis by Bacon and Associates (1998, 1999 and 2000) and by Williams, Shiels and Hughes (2002) suggests that the Dublin area has experienced major problems in increasing supply due to an infrastructure deficit, especially with regard to zoned serviced land, a key component in housing supply. In addition, however, there were problems of administration, in particular the serious shortage of professional planners in local authorities. It has also been suggested that an oligopoly exists with respect to land ownership and that developers were hoarding land and releasing it slowly, thereby keeping land prices and house prices high (Government of Ireland, 2004). These problems of land supply were reflected in the increasing share of land price as a component of new house price, with land accounting for over 40 per cent of a new house price in the Dublin region (Drudy and Punch, 2001; Central Bank of Ireland, 2003).

The Mortgage Market

The expansion of the housing market has in large part been facilitated and driven by the availability of cheap and plentiful credit. The persistence of low interest rates and the willingness of the financial institutions to be flexible in their lending policies has seen a massive expansion in the issuing of mortgage credit. Table 1.7 shows the rapid growth in the mortgage market, depicting loans paid by all lending agencies. The mortgage market for new houses increased from €0.7bn in 1994 to €7.4bn by 2004. However, it is worth noting that only 44,000 of the almost 71,000 private houses which were completed in the state in 2004 were funded by mortgages, indicating that over 27,000 dwellings were purchased without any recourse to a mortgage.

Table 1.7: Investment in Mortgages (loans paid), 1994-2004

	New Dwellings		Second-Hand Dwellings		Total	
	N	€m	N	€m	N	€m
1994	16,230	735.8	30,253	1,340.7	46,483	2,076.7
1995	19,320	936.6	27,715	1,347.6	47,035	2,284.0
1996	25,628	1,291.6	30,381	1,668.1	56,009	2,959.7
1997	28,193	1,695.5	29,708	1,893.6	57,901	3,589.1
1998	27,355	1,967.2	34,052	2,619.9	61,407	4,587.1
1999	31,359	2,776.8	39,458	3,740.1	70,817	6,516.9
2000	31,533	3,093.6	42,725	4,504.6	74,258	7,598.2
2001	29,431	3,309.2	37,355	4,354.7	66,786	7,663.9
2002	32,298	4,353.8	46,994	6,471.4	79,292	10,825.2
2003	35,292	5,398.1	49,457	8,125.7	84,749	13,523.8
2004	44,231	7,416.0	54,478	9,517.2	98,709	16,933.2

Source: Department of the Environment, Heritage and Local Government (various years).

This is an extraordinary figure and suggests that there is a large well of cash available to purchase such houses for either investment purposes or as second homes. The value of the mortgages advanced to purchase second-hand houses increased from €1.3bn to almost €9.6bn between 1994 and 2004. It is not possible to estimate the total number of transactions in the second-hand market due to the absence of any published statistics, but it is likely that a similar proportion of transactions are being funded without recourse to a mortgage.

Affordability

Inevitably, with incomes increasing at a moderate pace over this period, many commentators and political parties have argued that the rises in house prices have led to a significant affordability crisis for aspiring house purchasers, and in particular for aspirant first time buyers (Drudy, 1999). However, as Downey discusses in Chapter 3, it also true to say that the debate about affordability is a very complex one, with a variety of different measures being used to assess affordability. Affordability, in general terms, is about making a judgement regarding whether the residual income available to a household after housing costs is sufficient for what may be termed a reasonable life. As is shown by Fahey and Nolan (Chapter 4), social housing tenants in Ireland pay a very low rent, which typically accounts for less than 10 per cent of their income.

However, this measure shows us little about the sufficiency of their residual income, which may be entirely composed of welfare payments. Conversely, somebody on a high income may pay 40 per cent of his or her income on housing costs but the residual income may be more than sufficient.

Fahey and Nolan also show that private renting tenants devote a much higher proportion of their incomes to housing costs than the residents of any other tenure. Consequently, in Chapter 4, Fahey and Nolan argue that the most serious affordability problems are in the private rented sector, rather than among owner occupiers. Figure 1.3, which employs information from the consumer price index, reveals substantial increases in rents from the mid-1990s onwards. In the past two years the rises in private rents have stabilised and there is also evidence of falls in rents, particularly in Dublin (Irish Auctioneers and Valuers Institute, 2000, 2001, 2002, 2003a).

Figure 1.3: Private Rented Residential Sector Rent Inflation (% Annual Change), 1994-2004

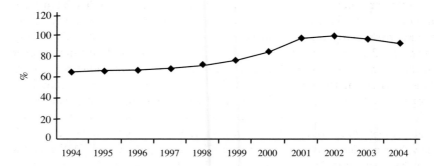

Source: Data were generated by the Central Statistics Office from the Consumer Price Index.
Note: Base December 2001 = 100.

The data analysed by Fahey and Nolan (Chapter 4) show that the proportion of income which mortgagees devote to housing costs fell slightly over the latter half of the 1990s. However, it is important to emphasise that these data encompass all home owners with a mortgage, including those who bought their homes many years ago and have paid off most of their loan, and recent first-time buyers, who own little equity in their dwelling. More recent statistics from the Quarterly Household Survey suggests that recent first-time buyers do face affordability problems (Central Statistics Office, 2004c). For example, of the 240,700 households surveyed who purchased since 1996, 24 per cent had monthly mortgage repayments in excess of €600, while just 3 per cent of those who purchased prior to 1996 had a mortgage of over €600, this being partly attributable to the age of the mortgage and also partly to the increase in house prices since 1996. However, this data set is seriously handicapped by lack of income or expenditure data which makes it impossible to compare the actual housing costs with income and thus no measurement of affordability can be made. The Irish National Survey of Housing Quality (Watson and Williams, 2003), which was conducted in 2001-2002, undertakes analysis of affordability on the basis of a sample which compares housing costs with net income. It reveals that only 6 per cent of owners with a mortgage paid over a third of net income on housing costs, compared to 11 per cent of first-time buyers. Very interestingly, all the sample households were also asked about their perception of the burden of housing costs. 11 per cent of first-time buyers, 13 per cent of owner occupiers with a mortgage, 20 per cent of private renters and 33 per cent of local authority tenants thought that housing costs were a heavy burden. These data underline the problems associated with assessing affordability simply in terms of the ratio of housing costs and incomes, which was raised above.

At the same time, Downey convincingly argues in Chapter 3 that the increase in house prices since the mid-1990s has undermined the accessibility of this tenure, particularly for households on low to moderate incomes. Historically, average industrial incomes have been a multiple of three to four times average house prices. However, by 2003 average house prices were a multiple of eight times average industrial wages nationally but up to ten times so for second-hand property in Dublin. An examination of the relationships between new house prices, the consumer price index, housebuilding costs and interest rates shows that housebuilding costs and consumer prices have increased in tandem, while new house prices have escalated (see Chapter 15, Redmond, Williams and Punch). It suggests that, as building costs have been rising at the same rate, the reasons for the rise in new house prices must be from a combination of development profits and land costs. Unfortunately, because it is almost impossible to gain easy public access to information on the price of land transactions, there is no reliable published research on this issue. There have been suggestions, including from the Central Bank, that land prices have increased in absolute and relative terms but it if this is the case, it is also reasonable to assume that some developers have reaped 'super normal' profits from the house price increases highlighted above.

Non-Market Housing, Exclusion and Inequality

Since the 1960s the social housing sector has contracted from 18 per cent to approximately 8 per cent of the national housing stock. In Chapter 8 Norris reveals that this fall in tenure share has occurred because of an absolute and relative decline in output of local authority rented dwellings and because of the extensive privatisation of the sector through a series of schemes to enable tenants to purchase their dwellings. In the past decade, local authority house building has accounted for just 6 per cent of annual total house building, whereas it averaged between 20 per cent and 30 per cent in the 1970s and 1980s. This is a result of severe cutbacks in the late 1980s during a period of fiscal crisis, which were never fully reversed, despite the advent of an economic upturn. As was mentioned earlier in this chapter, since the early 1990s government has attempted to diversify the sources of social housing, encouraging increased output by voluntary sector agencies including housing associations and co-operatives. In Chapter 10 Brooke and Clayton reveal that as yet, however, the voluntary sector has had a relatively small impact on overall housing provision, though this may increase in the coming years.

The result of these historically low levels of social housing output, coupled with population increases and the increases in house prices and private sector rents highlighted above, is a marked increase in the number of households on waiting lists for social housing. Figure 1.4 traces the increases in housing need as measured by the assessments of housing need, which local authorities carry out every three years. It reveals that the total numbers of households assessed as in need of social housing grew from 17,564 in 1991 to 48,413 in 2002. In the context of this level of growth in need the expansion in government funding for social house building outlined earlier appears modest. Although the National Development Plan provides for additional resources for social housing, the total increase in capital funding provided to this sector is not dramatic, thus confirming the hegemony of private housing provision (Government of Ireland, 1989).

In Chapter 8 Norris argues that the relative and absolute reduction in social housing tenure has also meant that the sector has become essentially a welfare housing sector. Recent research revealed that eight out of ten local authority tenants were welfare- and benefit-dependent, a figure likely to be replicated in the voluntary sector (Nolan et al, 1998, 2000). The wider societal implications of this trend are examined by Fitzgerald and Winston in Chapter 11. However, this residualisation process has also generated problems at the micro level of individual social housing estates, often related to social order, but also related to the absence of effective housing and estate management in the past. In the past decade local authorities and voluntary and co-operative housing associations have been developing housing management and estate management policies to more intensively and effectively manage their estates (Norris, 2001; Fahey (ed) 1999; Redmond and Walker, 1995; National Economic and Social Forum, 2000; Redmond, 2001). Redmond and Norris review the success of some of these measures in Chapter 9.

Figure 1.4: Changes in Social Housing Need by Category of Need, 1991-2002

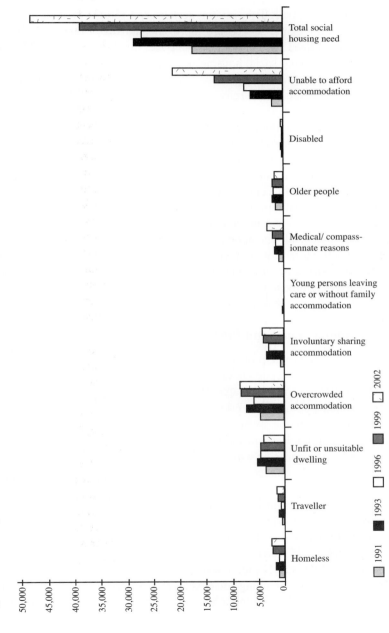

Source: Department of the Environment, Heritage and Local Government (various years)

In Chapter 11 Fitzgerald and Winston reveal that exclusion from affordable and good quality housing affects different groups to different degrees, and while such exclusion is a serious problem, there are particular and extreme forms of housing exclusion such as homelessness, and problems of providing accommodation for Travellers, asylum seekers and refugees (see also: Drudy and Punch, 2001). Some indeed are more unequal than others. While local authorities are obliged by the 1988 Housing Act to take homeless people into account when assessing social housing need, O'Sullivan reveals in Chapter 12 that providing appropriate accommodation for this group in the past has been confounded by resource scarcity and administrative and implementation complexity. However, resources are now available at a level not seen before and in Dublin, for example, there now exists an integrated policy on homelessness. With regard to Traveller accommodation, local authorities are responsible for providing appropriate accommodation. However, in Chapter 13 David Silke details how this function has often been mired in controversy, with strenuous local objections, allied to challenges generated by the mobility of Travellers. Providing accommodation for the increasing, although in absolute terms small, numbers of asylum seekers and refugees has produced a new set of problems for the authorities. Generally, temporary accommodation has been provided, but in the medium to long term it is inevitable that other solutions will be necessary. Providing appropriate accommodation solutions for these groups is a real test of government commitment to social inclusion, something which may fray in times of economic downturn.

Spatial Planning, Land and Infrastructure

The analysis of the problem of the affordability of home purchase, undertaken by Bacon in a series of reports to Government, initially focused on demand side management (Bacon and Associates, 1998, 1999, 2000). In considering options to stabilise rapidly rising house prices, the primary choices related mainly to the internal workings of the owner occupied market. For instance, there were changes in stamp duty and in the tax treatment of investors, sometimes with unintended consequences or with consequences the reverse of those intended. The reduction in stamp duty, for example, probably fuelled housing price growth, while the removal of tax incentives for landlords cut the supply of rented dwellings and contributed to rent inflation. Consequently, the thrust of the analysis by Bacon turned to supply-side responses. In broad terms, the central focus of policy since then has been to assist in increasing supply with the hope that prices would either stabilise or reduce as demand was met. One of the core elements of the supply-side response has been to seek to produce a more flexible and responsive planning and development system (see Bannon, Chapter 14). This has entailed developing a hierarchy of plans, from the national down to the local level, to give developers greater certainty. In addition to changes in the planning system, significant investment has been made in infrastructure projects such as the Serviced Land Initiative which sought to fast-track the provision of water and sewerage services to residentially zoned land.

   High house prices and affordability problems have, in part, led to the creation of a new and more complex geography of housing in Ireland. For example, the aforementioned acute supply and affordability problems in the Dublin region have led to the generation of new housing developments in a widening commuter belt around the capital, generating problems of sustainable urban and regional development as well as complex issues of urban and regional governance (See Chapter 15, Redmond, Williams and Punch). Derry O'Connell (Chapter 16) reflects on the rapidly changing pattern of urban design. The adoption of a policy in the late 1990s which promotes higher residential densities has had profound consequences for the design of housing, particularly in urban areas, where there was extensive experimentation, particularly with respect to apartment developments. Paradoxically, we have seen the development of a large amount of scattered rural housing where design standards have been heavily criticised. The demand for so-called 'one-off' rural housing has increased strongly – driven in part by the high cost of housing in towns and cities – generating controversial debates regarding the conflict between environmental sustainability and consumer choice. Mark Scott analyses this controversial issue in Chapter 17. In general terms, the policy response to the pace and scale of development has been to attempt to develop a more coherent planning response. Michael Bannon (Chapter 14) sets out the main elements of this change and outlines the attempts to develop what is termed a 'plan-led' system, from the national down to the local level.

Changing Times, Changing Policies

Compared to many other western European countries, Ireland is distinguished by its relatively high rate of home ownership. In Chapter 2, O'Connell reveals that this phenomenon can be accounted for by the high levels of private market provision (supported by longstanding and significant state investment), as well as by the impact of the longstanding policy of sales of social housing provided by local authorities to tenants, and the consequent, residual role for the social housing sector. Housing policy developments over the past decade have reinforced these trends considerably and there is now little ambiguity regarding the position of housing in Irish society; it has overwhelmingly been provided as a market good and although more recent years have seen increases in social housing supply this alters the position marginally rather than fundamentally. While this is not inherently problematic, the market, to say the least, is an imperfect mechanism for meeting a vital social need such as housing, and this has been amply demonstrated in recent years in the provision of housing in Ireland. Government policy choices have been predicated on the belief that private provision for the owner-occupied market would not only meet most housing needs, it would substantially deliver on the other policy objectives such as encouraging stable communities and facilitating the accumulation of household wealth. Of course to a degree this approach has been successful, and the private market has provided increasing numbers of new houses in the past decade.

Table 1.8 shows the changing tenure patterns in Ireland since 1946, with the rise of homeownership being the most striking trend. More recently, it reveals that the occupied housing stock has increased from over 1 million dwellings in 1991 to approximately 1.3 million in 2002, representing a net addition of approximately 260,000 in the stock. While overall the tenure structure has remained largely static, one of the interesting changes has been the revival of the private rented sector which has increased from about 84,000 to 140,000 dwellings, thereby increasing its tenure share from 8 per cent to 11 per cent. In Chapter 7, MacLaran and Williams argue that the expansion of the private rental tenure since the mid-1990s is the result of two key stimuli. First, for well over a decade, the availability of generous tax incentives for housing construction and refurbishment in 'designated areas' has stimulated a boom in output of private rented dwellings. This has been reflected primarily in the building of new apartments in large urban areas. Second, the economic growth of the past decade, coupled with increases in private house prices, has led to increased demand for private housing, and has stimulated an influx of investment from property investors who could avail of the abovementioned tax incentives and offset mortgage interest against rental income for tax purposes. Analysis by Bacon and Associates (2000) suggests that up to 25 per cent of new residential building in the mid to late 1990s was generated by investors. At the same time, however, the owner occupied sector remains dominant, accounting for 77 per cent of the stock, with social housing accounting for 7 per cent.

Table 1.8: Housing Tenure in Ireland, 1946-2002

Occupancy Status	1946	1961	1971	1981	1991	2002
Local authority rented	Nav	18.4	15.9	12.7	9.7	6.9
Private rented	42.6	17.2	10.9	8.1	7.0	11.1
Owner occupied	52.7	53.6	60.7	67.9	80.2	77.4
Other	4.7	10.8	12.5	11.2	3.0	4.6

Source: Central Statistics Office (2004b).
Note: Nav means not available.

Despite the large increases in supply over the past decade, the emergence of affordability problems, and the inability of key low to middle income groups to purchase a home, generated inevitable, and new, political and policy responses. Indeed, it could be argued that the policy reactions have been almost entirely determined by a political need to respond to problems of access to homeownership for a range of low to middle income groups. O'Connell shows in Chapter 2 that, in addition to policies to increase supply, a number of specific schemes have been introduced over the last decade aimed at helping the first-time buyer. Three affordable housing schemes have been instigated since 1999, the common element being that central government or private developers subsidise the land cost element of house prices, this being in effect state-subsidised private housing. To date, however, these schemes have had only a limited impact.

The introduction in 2000 of Part V of the Planning and Development Act is testament to the degree of policy innovation that has been attempted. A controversial and complex piece of planning legislation, it seeks to impose on private sector developers an obligation to subsidise social and affordable housing on sites they wish to develop. Paralleling UK legislation, developers are now required, as a condition of planning permission, to transfer up to 20 per cent of their sites for use as social and/or affordable housing and, crucially, to transfer the site to the state at what is termed use value, which is a fraction of the market value (See Bannon, Chapter 14). Thus, developers must transfer up to 20 per cent of the site or of the completed dwellings, or a financial equivalent of the land value, to the local planning authority. The rationale for this legislation is twofold. First, it was aimed at allowing local authorities to access development land cheaply, thereby enabling them to build social and/or affordable housing at below market cost. The new planning legislation also has a second more social aim, in that by seeking to have social housing built alongside or integrated with private market housing, levels of what the 2000 Act terms 'undue segregation between different social groups' would be diminished and social mix and social interaction would be encouraged. Thus, while the thrust of policy has been to encourage home ownership, there have been some significant attempts at policy development and innovation.

Conclusions

This introductory chapter has sought to give a broad overview of some of the key trends in housing provision over the course of the past decade. What is clear is that the high levels of new development have been remarkable and that they have had major economic, social and spatial consequences. What is perhaps less clear is the specific nature of those consequences. We are only beginning to appreciate the detailed outcomes and impacts with respect to access and affordability, for example, and our understanding of the environmental and spatial consequences is also underdeveloped. The remainder of the chapters expand in detail on some of the key trends and themes introduced here.

2

The Housing Market and Owner Occupation in Ireland

Cathal O'Connell

Introduction

One of the most defining features of the Irish housing system is its relatively high rate of owner occupation and the consequent overshadowing effect of this on other tenures. According to the 2002 Census returns the rate of owner occupation in Ireland stood at 77 per cent, while the other tenures – private renting and social housing – represented approximately 11 per cent and 7 per cent respectively (Central Statistics Office 2004b). The current imbalance in the Irish housing profile is the outcome of particular political tenure strategies pursued since the foundation of the State in the early 1920s. The pursuit of these strategies has had the effect of favouring the development of owner occupation, through a variety of both direct and indirect measures, as the preferred housing option for the majority of households in the community. The knock-on effect of this has been to constrain the size, role and effectiveness of the rental tenures in offering credible alternative housing opportunities to the population.

This chapter considers a number of themes related to the owner occupied sector in the Irish housing system. These themes can be summarised as: the direction of housing trends since the formation of the State; an overview of direct and indirect state supports for owner occupied housing, an examination of schemes which focus on enabling low-income households access owner occupation; and finally a commentary on the phenomenon of house price inflation in the Irish housing market in the 1990s and the implications of this for the housing system.

Housing Trends in Ireland

The Census of 1946 was the first to include a question regarding the tenure or 'nature of occupancy' of housing in Ireland. As is detailed in Table 1.9 in Chapter 1 of this book, the most obvious trend since that time is the growing dominance of owner occupation from just over half of all households in 1946 to nearly 80 per cent by the end of the century. In the 1946 census under 53 per cent of dwellings were classed as owner occupied and over 42 per cent were recorded as rented (Central Statistics Office, 1954). Though it was not stipulated whether these were rented from local authorities or private landlords, since the local authority sector was still in the early stages of its development, it can be assumed that most households were rented privately.

The results relating to aggregate urban areas revealed that the proportion of households renting was even more pronounced than the overall national figures. On average, over 70 per cent of urban households were returned as occupying rented accommodation. The capital city, Dublin, had a rental level of 75 per cent while Cork, Limerick and Waterford all had rental levels above 80 per cent (Central Statistics Office, 1954). Though the quality of rented accommodation ranged from the notoriously unhealthy slum tenements endured by many poorer working class households to better quality for the middle classes, the tenure did exhibit heterogeneity in catering for a wide spectrum of social groups. While these census returns suggest that renting held the dominant position in the Irish housing system at least until the 1940s, the reality was that as a tenure it was in the throes of a prolonged decline which would not ease until the end of the 1990s. Between 1946 and the next census to record nature of occupancy, in 1961, the shrinkage in private renting was exactly matched by the expansion of local authority and owner occupied housing sectors (Central Statistics Office, 1961). From the late 1960s and early 1970s onwards owner occupation embarked on a long-term growth curve but, in contrast, local authority housing reached its peak at this time and was destined to halve in size over the following decades.

The Development and Growth of Owner Occupation

The development and growth of owner occupation in Ireland evident in the census returns has arisen out of a range of legislative and policy interventions by government which to a large extent have pre-determined the housing choices of a majority of the population. These interventions can be grouped into a number of broad categories (see Table 2.1).

Firstly, there has been the development of state supports for house purchase of a direct and indirect nature. These have included grant aid assistance paid directly to purchasers, and legislative measures to provide ease of access to housing capital for persons entering the housing market.

Secondly, a range of measures have been developed to encourage the transfer of dwellings from rental tenures into owner occupation. The most notable of these has been the local authority tenant purchase scheme which enables tenants to acquire their homes at discounted rates from local authorities. Additionally, small dwellings acquisitions schemes, operated under legislation of the same name, were aimed at facilitating tenants in the private rental sector to buy out their dwellings from landlords.

Table 2.1: Categories of State Support for Owner Occupation in Ireland, Various Years

Time Frame	Category	Nature of Support	Current Status
1919-2002	Direct and Indirect Supports	Grant Aid First Time Buyers Grants	Abolished 2003
		Supplementary Grants; Improved Access to Housing Capital	Household Income Limit introduced in 1987
1919-Present	Transfer of Dwellings to Private Ownership	Local Authority Tenant Purchase Scheme	Permanent since 1988
		Small Dwellings Acquisitions Acts	Curtailed 1987
1970s-Present	Fiscal Treatment of Owner Occupation	Local Authority Rates on Residential Property	Abolished 1977
		Property Taxes	Abolished 1994
		Capital Gains Tax	Note levied on Residential property
		Mortgage Interest Tax Relief	Curtailed since late 1980s
1984-Present	Targeted Supports for Low-Income Households	Surrender Grant Scheme	Available 1984-1987
		Local Authority Affordable Housing Scheme	Established in 1999
		Mortgage Allowance Scheme	Established in 1991
		Shared Ownership Scheme	Established in 1991
		Local Authority Loans for Home Purchase and Improvement	Established in 1991
2000-Present	Measures under Part V Planning and Development Act, 2000	Affordable Housing under Part V Planning and Development Act, 2000	Established in 2000

Thirdly, there has been a number of fiscal supports for owner occupation which have induced households into the sector and encouraged them to remain. Noteworthy among these have been tax relief on mortgage interest, the abolition of local authority rates on domestic dwellings and the abolition of property taxes.

Finally, there is evidence of a shift in emphasis from the mid-1980s onwards from generic supports for owner occupation to a more targeted approach aimed specifically at assisting low-income households. This policy has entailed a range of local authority delivered schemes including the shared ownership scheme, mortgage allowance and mortgage subsidy schemes and affordable housing initiatives.

When combined, these interventions and policy measures have had the long-term effect of shaping the context within which housing choices in the Irish system are made and constitute a significant cluster of advantages for owner occupation over the other tenures. The dominance of owner occupation is a reflection therefore of the rational behaviour of households in the face of particular policy biases. In the discussion which follows a more detailed examination of how the different categories of support for owner occupation have evolved is undertaken.

Direct and Indirect Supports for Owner Occupation

Grant Aid for House Purchase

The provision of state support for the private provision of housing predates the inception of the independent Irish State in 1922 and persists as a policy characteristic to the present day. Financial aid for the provision of houses by private persons was first introduced in Ireland under the Housing (Ireland) Act of 1919. Following independence in 1922 the tenure preferences of the new Free State government were signified in early housing legislation which placed a strong emphasis on supporting private provision by individuals. The first housing act, passed in 1924, set the legislative tone for the following decade and at the core of this was the subsidy for private dwellings for better off households. Subsidies were offered for dwellings of between three and five rooms with an area between 520 and 1,000 square feet, or up to 1,500 square feet for civil servants! The act provided a grant of £250,000 to subsidise the building of 3,000 dwellings and a further £50,000 for the rehabilitation of existing houses. Further housing acts passed between 1925 and 1929 maintained the thrust of the 1924 Act. Throughout the 1920s there was little official attention given to the appalling slum conditions endured by poor households, on the assumption that a greater supply of private housing would lead to a trickle-down effect which would ultimately benefit the poor.

Additional incentives to owner occupation were offered under the first housing legislation of the Fianna Fáil government which took office in 1932.

Though its 1932 Housing (Financial and Miscellaneous) Provisions Act is popularly remembered as the measure which began the 'housing drive' against the urban slums, it contained in equal measure financial assistance to promote private house building. For urban house building, grants of £50 per house were offered to individuals and public utility societies and in rural areas grants of between £40 and £80 (depending on rateable valuation) were offered to farmers and agricultural labourers. Public utility societies were entitled to avail of grant aid for the purpose of erecting houses for the working classes, though in practice they tended to build for sale to the general public and often acted as intermediaries between builders and house buyers.

Up to March 1947 a total of 34,816 dwellings had been erected with state aid by private individuals and public utility societies. Almost 24,000 of these were built in rural areas by farmers who had access to cost-free, or cheap sites on which to erect dwellings. Five counties – Dublin, Cork, Kerry, Mayo and Galway – accounted for 13,000 of the total number of houses built in rural areas. The remainder were in urban areas, mainly in Dublin and Cork (Department of Local Government and Public Health, various years). In overall terms, given the time span in question of almost 25 years, the level of output was extremely modest, averaging under 1,300 houses per annum, though it must be acknowledged that World War II curtailed building for almost a decade from the late 1930s. The housing legislation of the fledgling state can be remembered more for establishing the principle of state-aided private provision than for the actual volume of dwellings constructed.

From the late 1940s onwards the momentum towards growing state support for owner occupation gathered pace. The Housing White Paper: *A Review of Past Operations and Immediate Requirements* (Minister for Local Government, 1948) highlighted what it identified as the disadvantaged position of private building in comparison to that of local authorities. The commentary of the White Paper suggested that urban middle income households were not accessing the owner occupier sector in sufficiently large numbers and were continuing to rent privately often in physically deteriorating conditions, reflecting the effects of rent control legislation dating from World War I. In contrast, at the bottom end of the private rented market, working class households were gradually being decanted from insanitary slums and tenements to newly constructed local authority housing built under the subsidy provisions of the housing legislation of the early 1930s. To redress this situation the White Paper recommended that direct assistance to potential urban home-owners should be improved:

> The government decided that the foregoing scheme of grants was inadequate in the altered circumstances of the post war period. Building costs have risen far above 1939

levels, the demand for materials and skilled labour has outstripped supply, and the consequence has been that the middle income group are finding it increasingly difficult to command a share of the resources of the building industry commensurate with their urgent housing needs.

(Minister for Local Government, 1948: 20)

The White Paper was followed by the Housing (Amendment) Act of 1948 which enhanced direct financial aids to persons building and acquiring private dwellings from their own means. Grants of up to £275 were offered to private persons and, in order to encourage the growth of self-sufficiency, higher grants of £285 were offered to public utility societies. Supplementary grants were aimed at households with an annual income of less that £832. Additional indexation of incentives provided for by the 1956 Housing (Amendment) Act sealed the tenure options for lower middle and middle-income households and signalled the institutionalisation of owner occupation as the dominant housing tenure. All but the poorest households would be directed into state-subsidised owner occupation and from an official standpoint private house building and nation building were synonymous. This sentiment was clearly articulated by Taoiseach John A. Costello (cited in Daly, 1997: 348) who in an address to Dublin builders stated:

The best way we can insure (*sic*) that each person is a good citizen is to give everyone a stake in the country and the way in which we can do that is to give him his own home. No matter what it costs, that is good business nationally and socially.

In terms of impact, the housing legislation of the late 1940s and 1950s began a growth pattern and created a framework of financial assistance which was to continue unabated throughout the following decades. By the time the 1956 Housing Act was enacted only 150 private dwellings per annum were being constructed without State aid. Between 1949 and 1964 a total of 73,659 dwellings were constructed and, of these, 54,000 were built with the direct assistance of state grants, loans administered by the local authorities or other grants (Department of Local Government and Public Heath, various years). By the early 1960s such was the range of grants and incentives on offer, combined with direct and indirect subsidies, that almost 30 per cent of the cost of a standard suburban house could be recouped by the purchaser. For example a house costing £3,000 would benefit from a state grant of £275, supplementary grant of £275, rates remission of £281, stamp duty reduction of £50, resulting in a total subsidy of £891.

A particular feature of housing policy of this era is the ongoing analysis of how existing measures could be modified to maintain the appeal of owner occupation over the other (in particular local authority housing) tenures. The government White Paper *Housing in the '70's* is a case in point (Department of Local Government, 1969). Policy modifications arising out of this document explicitly set out to consolidate owner occupation as the most financially and arguably socially attractive housing option for the majority of households. The White Paper argued that the grant and subsidy system which operated throughout the 1960s had in fact still led some households to favour local authority renting rather than private ownership. This opinion was formed on the basis of comparison between the subsidy treatment of local authority houses and privately built dwellings and clearly pitches the role of owner occupation as the preferred tenure and local authority housing as the residual one when it states:

> the disparity between assistance available for each new local authority house and most new private houses is very marked. The size of the disparity, in fact, tends to defeat one of the principal purposes of the grant scheme – which is to help persons who would otherwise have to seek a local authority house to provide houses for themselves.
>
> (Department of Local Government, 1969: 35)

In the 1970s and 1980s the supports for first-time buyers were improved to eliminate any ambivalence of this nature. By the early 1980s new entrants to the housing market could avail of a first-time buyers grant of £2,000 (first introduced as £1,000 in 1977), a mortgage interest subsidy of £3,000 (subsequently replaced by a £2,250 builders grant, itself abolished in 1988), and for a period in the late 1980s local authority tenants who surrendered their dwellings could also avail of a special £5,000 surrender grant. The generosity of these direct supports is borne out by the fact that a standard new suburban house in the mid-1980s cost in the region of £35,000 of which up to £10,000 could be secured by purchasers through availing of grants and subsidies. By any analysis therefore it is clear that the over-riding priority of housing policy in the decades since the inception of the State was the promotion of owner occupation and this was achieved via a heavy emphasis on direct and indirect financial supports.

Improving Access to Housing Capital

While the growing demand for owner occupied housing generated its own momentum for continued preferential treatment of the tenure by way of direct aids, the matter of an adequate and accessible supply of housing capital was soon to present itself as a potential constraint to this growth. This prompted a series of legislative reforms to open up new sources of housing finance especially to households of modest means. The 1956 Housing Act offered new incentives to owner occupiers by doubling the loan limit to £2,000 for houses purchased under loans granted through the Small Dwellings Acquisition Acts and by offering grants of £275 for new and reconstructed homes for private ownership. This had come on top of the Housing (Amendment) Act of 1950 under which first-time buyers automatically qualified for grants and were no longer required to have contracts signed with builders prior to grant approval, a measure which allowed purchasers to negotiate better terms with house builders.

Under the Small Dwellings Acquisition Acts households entering the cheaper end of the housing market could secure mortgages on very attractive terms from local authorities, most of whom raised funds for such purposes from the Local Loans Fund, apart from Cork and Dublin who were initially precluded from access to this source of funds and raised money through their own stock issues. The Local Loans Fund was established in 1935 as a source of housing capital for local authorities. Under this arrangement the Minister for Local Government borrowed on behalf of the Fund and made advances to local authorities. This provided a more attractive alternative to borrowing commercially from the banks who charged higher interest rates and had shorter repayment periods. When the Small Dwellings Acquisitions Act was first passed in 1899 its intention was to assist tenants who wished to buy out the interest in their homes from private landlords. However, take-up rates of the measure were extremely modest, to the point that a government commission was set up in 1927 to investigate the reasons for this and in the 1940s the remit of the original act was altered to permit borrowing for the purposes of buying newly built dwellings (Town Tenants Commission, 1927).

When Small Dwellings Acquisitions Act loans were combined with first-time buyers grants, rates remissions and the local supplementary grants frequently given by local authorities, potential buyers could see themselves on the housing ladder by having to raise no more than a modest deposit. Despite problems with the operation of the legislation in Dublin city, where stock issues proved unattractive to investors, the importance of the scheme nationally in embedding owner occupation cannot be overstated. Its operation provided the foundation upon which the Irish house construction industry was built for subsequent decades and advances under the legislation grew consistently until the middle of the 1970s. In essence the Small Dwellings Acquisitions Act loan system became the most widely used mechanism employed by the State to bolster State-subsidised owner occupation and to create a situation where policy on this tenure and broader housing policy became synonymous.

The ready accessibility of housing capital and consequent growth in building under the Small Dwellings Acquisitions Act almost became a victim of its own success, such was the insatiable appetite for new homes. By the late 1950s the government was in the peculiar position of actively promoting owner occupation but at the same time feeling increasingly uneasy at the persistent breaches of spending limits by local authorities under the Small Dwellings Acquisitions Acts, a situation which threatened to precipitate a crisis in government funding of local authorities. These circumstances dictated that other actors, in addition to the State, were required to facilitate the expansion of the sector by providing additional sources of housing capital. Daly (1997) notes that in the late 1950s the Minister for Local Government, Pa O'Donnell, was so concerned with the level of spending by local authorities on Small Dwellings Acquisitions Act loans that he felt alternative sources of capital for house purchase would have to be found in order to alleviate the pressure on the Local Loans Fund. This alternative source of finance was to come in the form of capital from the building societies – a previously under-utilised resource. Although restrictions on building societies' lending practices have been eased under the Building Societies Act, 1942, limits were only raised from 66 per cent of the amount secured to societies through borrowings of up to 75 per cent. In practice this had little effect in enticing households to take out mortgages as most potential borrowers still found the gap between the mortgage limit and the cost of a house too wide.

This was in marked contrast to the conditions attaching to Small Dwellings Acquisitions Act loans where 90 per cent of the dwelling cost could be borrowed and then supplemented with other incentives. Building society mortgages accordingly remained under-utilised while Small Dwellings Acquisitions Act loan approvals grew consistently. It was not until the late 1950s when further alterations were made to the building societies' regulations, and the government decided to impose restrictions on access to Small Dwellings Acquisitions Act loans through imposing income ceilings on applicants, that building societies emerged as more active providers of housing finance. Under the terms of the Building Societies Act, 1956, from that year onwards building societies were permitted to offer mortgages of 95 per cent over thirty-five years, to applicants who had been granted a mortgage guarantee from a local authority. The *Second Programme for Economic Expansion* (Government of Ireland, 1964: 275) notes:

> This expansion of availability of housing capital coincided with the state strategy to modernise the Irish economy. Economic growth was viewed as an optimal context for the expansion of owner occupation, a housing objective specifically noted in the Programmes for Economic Expansion. As the Second Programme noted, 'with increases in prosperity, more persons can now buy their homes, government policy will favour the provision of houses for owner occupation'.

The combination of economic modernisation, which occurred in the context of growing urbanisation, plus an extremely generous fiscal regime of grants and incentives, produced the desired effects in terms of owner occupation. The size of the sector grew by 10 per cent between 1961 and 1971, from 59.8 per cent of housing stock to 68.8 per cent. By the late 1960s therefore there were two principal sources of capital for households entering the Irish housing market. Those on modest incomes, but who were nevertheless disqualified from local authority housing, could avail of Small Dwellings Acquisitions Act loans from local authorities and from 1950 to the end of the 1960s over 64,000 local authority mortgages were issued. These were later supplemented by the provision of income related Housing Finance Agency loans in 1982 which were 'designed to assist persons of low or modest income to acquire a private house and so reduce demand for local authority housing' (Department of the Environment, 1985: 32).

Higher income households whose means were above the qualification thresholds for local authority loans were directed towards the rapidly expanding building societies. Between 1960 and 1975 membership of building societies grew from 30,000 to 150,000 and mortgage advances increased from £4 million to almost £80 million during the period (Registrar of Friendly Societies, various years).

Transfer of Rented Dwellings to Owner Occupation

Tenant Purchase of Local Authority Houses

The range of direct and indirect measures discussed above have played a major role in shaping the tenure choices of households entering the housing market. The use of means testing has limited access to local authority and other social housing and strong incentives to private ownership have boosted ownership levels among modest and middle income groups. These measures have been complemented by direct strategies to boost ownership which involve the direct transfer of dwellings from the rental to the privately owned sector. Two main instruments have been deployed for this purpose – in the case of the local authority sector, the tenant purchase scheme, and in the case of private renting the Small Dwellings Acquisitions Act in its original form. The policy could accurately be described as one of the most sustained and long running programmes of privatisation ever undertaken by the State in Ireland.

The facility of allowing tenants to buy out their dwellings from local authority landlords, popularly known as tenant purchase, has been on the Irish statute books since before the State was founded. Under Section 12 of the Housing (Ireland) Act, 1919 certain local authority tenants could buy their homes. However, that measure was not widely availed of. The new state pursued the policy with enthusiasm and in the mid-1930s tenant purchase was offered in rural areas under the Labourers Act, 1936 as a final instalment in the drawn-out process of rural land reform, and from the mid-1960s in urban areas under the Housing Act of 1966. The scale of success of rural tenant purchase was such that by 1964 around 80 per cent of the 87,000 cottages built by local authorities since the 1880s had been sold on to their occupants. In overall terms in the course of its implementation, especially since its extension to urban areas, the policy of tenant purchase has swelled the ranks of owner occupation by approximately 230,000 dwellings.

Extending tenant purchase to urban areas was essentially a political tenure strategy to expand the rate of owner occupation. Daly (1997) notes that officials at the Department of Local Government, highly conscious of the rental shortage facing urban local authorities during the 1960s, were rightfully concerned with the long- and short-term implications of depleting the stock of rental dwellings in cities and towns. These concerns however were over-ridden by the political appeal of tenant purchase as a novel and apparently cost effective route to owner occupation which was by now well embedded as the most favoured tenure in official housing policy. From the first urban scheme in the 1960s the incentives offered under tenant purchase schemes were gradually improved to entice tenants into owner occupation.

After it was initially introduced in 1966, tenant purchase got off to a relatively slow start. This was mainly because up to 1973 the incentives to purchase were relatively modest. Under a new scheme introduced in 1973 more generous terms were introduced. A discount of 3 per cent per on the sale price for each year of residence subject to a maximum of 30 per cent in urban areas and 45 per cent in rural areas was offered. The sale price before discount was calculated as being the historical construction cost updated by the consumer price index (Department of Local Government, 1973). This resulted in very modest sales prices as the consumer price index was increasing over time at a rate less than the rate of increase of house prices. In addition to these discounts a grant equivalent to that available to first-time house buyers was offered to tenant purchasers as was a grant equivalent to the value of rates remission on offer to first-time buyers. A tenant deciding to avail of the scheme could also borrow up to 100 per cent of the eventual cost of the dwelling from the local authority at a fixed rate of interest over a period of thirty years under the Small Dwellings Acquisition Act. This was repayable either on a weekly or monthly basis. Finally, in keeping with how other house buyers were treated, tenant purchasers who borrowed from local authorities could avail of tax relief on the interest element of local authority loans. The net result for many tenants was that, after discounts and allowances were accounted for, the actual cost of acquiring a dwelling was often 50 per cent or more below its market value.

The onset of a recession in the Irish housing market prompted the introduction of a new tenant purchase scheme in 1986. The taper in tenant purchasing is reflected in the gradual decline in sales from the beginning of the

1980s onwards to the extent that by 1986 total sales amounted to only 533 dwellings. The drop in house prices caused by the recession meant that the appeal of tenant purchase was lessened for many tenants as the gross price of the house was calculated by updating the historical construction cost by the consumer price index. Prior to the recession in house prices this formula was sufficient to ensure that the net sale price would be substantially less than the market value of the dwelling, thus ensuring an incentive for tenants to opt for the scheme. In the recession, with falling house price values it was often the case that the sale price calculated under the scheme was higher than the current market value of the dwelling, thus offering no incentive for tenants to buy their dwellings. To counter the effects of falling house values the 1986 scheme determined that the gross price of the dwelling could be calculated on the basis of its market value where this was less than the original cost as updated by the consumer price index. Such was the level of political attachment to tenant purchase that whenever market conditions threatened to undermine its appeal to tenants, the State was prepared to modify the terms on offer in the form of more generous discounts to maintain sales. Between 1973 and 1987 a total of 93,000 dwellings were built. However, in the same period local authorities sold off a total of 67,200 (Department of the Environment, Heritage and Local Government, various years).

The evolution of tenant purchase policy was to peak under the scheme announced in 1988 which offered highly favourable terms and established tenant purchase as a permanent option for tenants. Among other incentives, it offered tenants discounts from between 40 per cent and 100 per cent of the cost of the dwelling, depending on their years of residence. Local authorities were exhorted to adopt a 'hard sell' approach to the scheme, with the government highlighting the disparity between local authority rent revenues and housing management cost by pointing out that they spent £72 million per annum in management and maintenance costs but only collected £39 million in rents. This formula conveniently ignored the implicit costs of the heavily discounted sale of housing assets, the subsidised rents which tenants enjoyed during their tenancies and the accumulated maintenance costs which had been invested in dwellings over the course of their rental period. Arising out of the 1988 scheme alone a total of 18,000 dwellings were sold and as the 1988 Housing Act established tenant purchase as a permanent option for local authority tenants its reverberations have been felt ever since. In the years following the 1988 scheme sales easily outstripped building rates – for instance in 1990 and 1991 a total of 1,003 and 1,180 houses were built by local authorities while in the same years 5,600 and 3,143 respectively were sold off to tenants.

Such has been the popularity of tenant purchase with local authority tenants that large tracts of state built housing have now been transferred into private ownership, many of which have been sold on subsequently for large capital gains with no provision of claw-back of profits for the state. Though there has been little by way of empirical analysis of the fiscal impact of tenant purchase, the accumulated costs to the state must by definition have been substantial given that the outstanding capital debts on dwellings sold to tenants remain the responsibility of the state. In analysing the subsidy effects of tenant purchase the National Economic and Social Council (NESC) (1988: 40) noted that:

> the encouragement for tenants to purchase their homes, built at public expense, for far less than their market value may have acted to create a two tiered system. The more fortunate who are able to afford to buy their homes, are possibly receiving a greater State subsidy than those who continue to rent.

In a subsequent analysis of the discount levels offered to tenant purchasers the Lord Mayor's Commission on Housing in Dublin estimated that the average discount on the market value of dwellings sold to tenants ranged from 56 per cent in 1989 to 65 per cent in 1992 (Dublin Corporation, 1993).

In recent years the rate of sales to local authority tenants has slowed considerably and its contribution to the owner occupier sector has diminished. There are probably a multiplicity of reasons for this but foremost among them is that all those who want to or can afford to have by now availed of the option to become owners. Given the strongly residual tendency now exhibited by local authority housing it is likely that all of the most attractive and desirable stock has been privatised and local authorities are increasingly left to manage the least popular stock in areas where tenants are unwilling to take a leap of faith and opt to buy. Nonetheless these very recent experiences do not detract from the phenomenal and largely under-analysed role tenant purchase has played in widening access to owner occupation. As a strategy to expand the tenure to low-income households it has been an overwhelming success but at major, and as yet uncalculated, cost to the public purse which has been compounded by the even higher price of denuding the local authority rented sector of huge segments of its most valuable asset –namely desirable rental stock.

Fiscal Supports for Owner Occupation

The third category of measures examined concerns supports of a fiscal nature designed to entice households into the sector and encourage them to remain. In the discussion which follows a number of these will be looked at including: mortgage interest tax relief, the removal of fiscal disincentives such as local authority rates on domestic dwellings, the abolition of property taxes and the exemption from capital gains taxes of the proceeds of domestic property sales.

Local Authority Rates on Residential Dwellings

One outcome of the expansion of owner occupation by virtue of its preferential treatment in the housing system has been an increasing sense of its political significance. This is most clearly reflected in an implicit tendency to frame overall housing policy in terms of what is good or bad for the tenure. A case in point was the abolition of local rates on domestic dwellings as part of the populist general election package in 1977. This represented a serious body blow to the financial independence of local authorities and essentially deprived them of any independent revenue source. While hugely popular (and largely responsible for a landslide general election victory of the Fianna Fáil Party) this measure signalled that owner occupation was to be viewed as largely immune from liability within the tax code, at either local or national level.

Residential Property Taxes (RTP)

The abolition of rates on domestic dwellings in 1977 was complemented by a marked political reluctance to apply property taxes in any meaningful form. Despite the scope represented by property tax as a means of broadening the tax base and encouraging more efficient consumption of the national housing stock (and as a potential device of keeping house prices in check), such a tax has never been energetically applied since it was first introduced in 1983. When modest amendments to the property tax code were mooted in 1994 a major campaign of opposition occurred. This was despite the fact that under the proposals, which combined the excess of household income over £25,000 and property values above £75,000 as the determining criteria, only a tiny minority of high income households would become liable for RTP. This was indicated in the increase in households assessed for RTP from 15,000 in 1993 to 38,000 (out of a national total of around 900,000 households) in 1994 and a consequent growth in the tax receipts from £8.9 million to £14.5 million (Office of the Revenue Commissioners, various years). Commenting on the popular outrage which greeted the proposals the Economic and Social Research Institute (1993: 31) observed, 'in the context of a total budget package which reduces the average tax burden for the majority of households and at a time when the housing costs of most mortgage payers have been drastically reduced by the fall in interest rates, this relatively trivial extension of a minor tax has been widely perceived as a major net imposition on a broad segment of society'.

Until it was finally abolished in 1997 property tax was a diluted and weak source of revenue which never enjoyed fulsome political support. When it did appear to be modestly gathering momentum as a source of revenue, during the early 1990s, after adjustments to qualification thresholds, it was abolished, so its stabilising potential on house prices remains undetermined. Testifying to the limited scope of property tax, the maximum sums gathered in any given year were extremely modest. For example, in 1996 it contributed just £13.3 million (€18.2 million) to state tax revenues arising from 21,500 assessments. The highest number of households assessed for RTP was 38,132 in 1994 (yielding £14.5 million). By 2002, five years after abolition in 1997 the residual yield was just €827,000 though various calculations at how much a property tax/ imputed income tax could yield made in the mid-1990s estimated amounts varying from £130 million to £400 million, sums which could have been multiplied several times over in the context of subsequent house price inflation.

Mortgage Interest Tax Relief

Mortgage interest tax relief (MITR) has been another important source of fiscal support for owner occupiers. Though it has been scaled back in recent years it has represented a significant financial advantage and incentive to house buyers since its introduction. According as lending for owner occupation grew, in the context of rising interest rates between the late 1970s and the mid-1990s, the cost to the exchequer of MITR grew rapidly, from £25 million in 1981 to £150 million by 1986. Restrictions on the value of reliefs were introduced progressively during the 1990s and the value of tax relief fell back from a high of £164 million in 1995 to €158 million in the year 2000 (Office of the Revenue Commissioners, various years).

There are also a number of other important indirect subsidies built into the tax code which benefit the owner occupier sector. Since the abolition of Schedule A of the Income Tax Acts in 1969 there has been no tax liability on imputed income (i.e. what a household would have paid on rent for the dwelling it occupies) which accrues to owner occupiers. The abolition of Schedule A tax was undertaken, according to the Commission on Taxation, not 'on the grounds of principle but rather was due to the fact that it was a convenient and cheap method of giving tax relief'(Commission on Taxation 1982: 134). Nor is there any liability for capital gains taxes on profits accruing out of the sale of principal residences. Both of these concessions significantly enhance the relative appeal of owner occupation within the tax system and contrast particularly with the treatment of households which rent privately. Private renters must pay rent, which the home owner does not, and they are only entitled to receive minimal tax relief on these. Such contrasting treatments add to the perception that what is good for owner occupation makes for intrinsically sound housing policy despite the inequities caused between households in different sectors and the real cost to the national finances of funding concessions in the form of taxes foregone.

Targeted Support for Low-Income Households

The final aspect of policy support for owner occupation to be examined concerns assistance to low-income households entering the owner occupied sector. The gradual development of these supports is noteworthy because they signify a shift in emphasis in the nature of state support for the tenure and though owner occupation remains the preferred sector in policy terms, the era of universal unconditional supports is now tempered by a more targeted approach which has seen many of the established concessions mentioned in the course of this chapter rolled back. Recent notable examples of this shift in policy include restrictions on the mortgage interest tax relief and the abolition of the first-time buyers grant, although many of the favourable tax treatments remain in place.

A number of schemes can be identified as promoting owner occupation among low-income households including: the local authority affordable housing scheme, the mortgage subsidy scheme; the mortgage allowance scheme, the shared ownership scheme and the local authority loans scheme for home purchase and improvement.

Local Authority Affordable Housing Scheme

The local authority affordable housing scheme was introduced in 1999 and provides for the building of new houses by local authorities in areas where house prices have created an affordability gap for lower income house purchasers. The houses constructed under the scheme are sold to applicants whose income (subject to a multiple of 2.5) is €79,359 or less. Households with an income of less that €25,000 can qualify for a mortgage subsidy ranging from €2,250 to €1,300 annually. Houses are offered for sale to first-time purchasers at cost price. A total of 882 dwellings were built during 2002 with a further 1,907 under construction at the end of the year. Fingal County Council was the largest single producer of houses under the scheme in 2002 with an output of 267 dwellings, while other urban areas built a combined total of 128. In early 2003 in Cork two schemes of 78 and 52 affordable houses have come on the market while in Dublin a scheme of 120 affordable houses within a private development of 720 dwellings has been sold (Department of the Environment, Heritage and Local Government, various years).

The Mortgage Allowance Scheme

The Mortgage Allowance Scheme provides tenants of local authority houses, tenant purchasers and tenants of voluntary housing with assistance of €11,428 over a five-year period towards purchasing a private dwelling with the aid of a mortgage. Until late 2002 this allowance could be supplemented by a first-time buyers grant in the case of a new dwelling. Under the terms of the scheme the rented dwelling must be surrendered to the local authority by the tenant and though this scheme is broadly based on the same principle of the £5,000 Surrender Grant of the mid-1980s its overall effects are extremely low key. As an illustration of the difficulties low-income households are experiencing in accessing the private market, transactions under this scheme have seriously tapered, from already low levels. In 1996, 268 dwellings were surrendered by tenants moving into owner occupation. However, by the year 2000 this had shrunk to just 93 (Department of the Environment, Heritage and Local Government, various years).

The Shared Ownership Scheme

The shared ownership scheme was introduced under the *Plan for Social Housing* (Department of the Environment, 1991) and under its terms the local authority and the individual purchaser jointly acquire a dwelling. Under the terms of the scheme the house purchaser acquires one half of the equity, by way of a local authority housing loan and the local authority buys the other half. At the end of the purchase period the householder buys out the equity held by the local authority and assumes full ownership of the dwelling. The overall contribution of shared ownership is extremely modest, and in 2000 it accounted for 1,200 transactions at a total cost of £107m (€136m). In part this is explained by the reluctance of purchasers to opt into the scheme on the grounds that unless they act swiftly to purchase the local authority's equity in the dwelling, it can spread the costs of home ownership over a long period. A further factor is the apparent lack of enthusiasm for the scheme among house vendors who have concerns that drawn-out administrative procedures can hinder the speedy closure of sales.

Another aspect of the poor take-up rates relates to the rising house prices which have occurred since the mid-1990s. The maximum loan granted under the scheme is €127,000 (£100,000) which effectively puts a lot of housing outside the reach of many qualified applicants as there are simply not enough affordable and suitable dwellings available in that price range. It has also been suggested that take-up rates of the scheme reflect the enthusiasm of local authorities in promoting it. For instance Offaly County Council, a relatively small local authority in the midland region, accounted for 400 transactions out of a national total of 1,611 in 2001 (Department of the Environment, Heritage and Local Government, various years). Households with an income of less than €25,000 can qualify for annual assistance, ranging from €2,250 to €1,300 under the mortgage subsidy scheme available to shared ownership home buyers.

Local Authority Loans for Home Purchase and Improvement

Local authority loans have been a source of housing finance since the end of the nineteenth century and under the Small Dwellings Acquisition Act proved to be the main vehicle in supporting owner occupation for households of modest means. As was noted earlier, during the 1960s and 1970s after the Small Dwellings Acquisitions Act system was focused on low-income borrowers the scheme proved to be the engine driving the major expansion of owner occupation. By the 1970s local authority loans accounted for over one third of all mortgage finance and one half of value. Their role continued until the mid-1980s when they still accounted for a quarter of all house lending. New restrictions on access to local authority loans signalled a major reduction in number of loans issued. From 1987 onwards applications were only considered from persons who could not secure a loan from a commercial lender. This slide is apparent from the number of approvals which fell from 2.1 per cent of the housing market to 0.1 per cent in 2001.

The local authority loans scheme is open to individuals who are unable to get a mortgage from a commercial lender in order to purchase or build a dwelling. This scheme testifies to the commitment of the State to ensuring that owner occupation extends as far down the income ladder as possible. However, the extremely modest income limits of circa €31,700 (£25,000) for a single income household and €37,500 (£32,00) plus the effects of house price inflation in recent years have meant that this scheme is barely registering in statistical terms. The maximum loan available in 2001 was just €130,000, yet the average house price that year was over €190,000 – thus there exists a wide gulf between house prices and loan levels of offer. In the period since 1997, when serious house price inflation took hold in the Irish housing market, to 2001, the number of loans paid has fallen from 259 to 155, though the value of loans rose from €7.2 million (£5.7) during this period to €10.7 (£8.3) which is a clear testament to the effects of house price inflation (Department of the Environment, Heritage and Local Government, various years).

Housing Affordability and House Price Inflation

House Price Inflation in the 1990s

The long and largely untroubled growth trajectory of owner occupation in Ireland was overshadowed from the mid-1990s by a sustained period of house price inflation. From the late 1990s house prices rose by double digit figures, peaking in 1998 with a rise of 16 per cent and settling at around 11 per cent per annum between 2000 and 2003. Such price growth raised unprecedented issues relating to affordability and access to the tenure. The current phase of price rises can be traced to 1997, when the average price of a new house nationally in 1997 was just below €100,000. By the middle of 2003 this price had risen to nearly €215,000. An important consequence of this is that for the first time ever in the history of the Irish State many of those who traditionally formed the backbone of the owner occupier market, namely first-time buyers and middle income households, are finding it increasingly more difficult to gain a foothold on the housing ladder. Many can only do so through borrowing substantially larger mortgages over longer periods than has traditionally been the norm or by supplementing borrowings with assistance from sources such as parents and relatives and many financial institutions now offer facilities whereby parents can release portions of the equity in their homes to assist their children get a foot on the housing ladder. Despite the escalating prices and questions about the affordability of dwellings, private housing output has attained record levels as demand continued to outstrip supply. In 2002 a record 57,000 dwellings were constructed in Ireland, while output for 2003 could reach over 65,000, though some observers have estimated that as many as 72,000 of all new houses built (269,000) between 1996 and 2002 were second homes (McCarthy, Hughes and Woelger, 2003).

As is discussed in more depth by Redmond and Norris in Chapter 1 of this book, a number of factors contributed to the increase in house prices. These included changes in demographic patterns and household formations, economic growth (in particular growth in employment); increases in disposable income facilitated by lower direct taxes; low mortgage interest rates resulting from European Monetary Union, investor and speculative activity in the housing market, the controlled release of serviced developed land, increases in the price of land for housing development, and demand for housing generated by returning emigrants and immigration. In an effort to address the effects of rising prices the government set in train a series of initiatives which extended from 1998 to 2000 based on a series of reports compiled by Bacon and Associates Economic Consultants. Over the course of the reports a range of proposals were suggested to address supply side constraints on the capacity of the housing system to respond to demand for houses. The first Bacon Report – *An Economic Assessment of Recent House Price Developments* – proposed a range of measures aimed at improving housing supply. These proposals can be broadly categorised as measures of a planning, land use and infrastructural nature such as the serviced land initiative, capital gains taxes on the proceeds of the sale of development land and better resourcing of planning functions of local authorities (Bacon and Associates, 1998).

The second group were of a fiscal nature and included measures to rebalance the burden of taxes and stamp duty on residential properties towards individual house buyers and away from investors through exemption from stamp duty of new owner occupied dwellings and changes to stamp duty rates for houses within particular price bands. Thirdly, there were proposals specifically aimed at low-income purchasers who qualified for local authority schemes. These included revised income limits for the local authority shared ownership scheme, lower rent levels on the local authority equity of dwellings under the shared ownership scheme, and finally efforts were to be made to encourage private sector shared ownership schemes through financial institutions. The government subsequently published a policy document entitled *Action on*

House Prices to give effect to the Bacon proposals (Department of the Environment and Local Government, 1998a). Bacon and Associates were commissioned to produce a second report in March 1999. This concluded that though the measures outlined in the first report had a moderating effect on house price inflation, problems of affordability and access remained (Bacon and Associates, 1999). Arising out of the second report the Government announced a second initiative, the *Action on the Housing Market* (Department of the Environment and Local Government, 1999a), which proposed investment in sewage facilities under the Serviced Land Initiative to aid the release of development land, especially in North County Dublin where 16,000 new dwellings could be provided. It also proposed an examination of the potential use for housing of lands in state ownership, better geographical balance of economic activity and population distribution through the National Development Plan, the formulation of a National Spatial Development Strategy, and the advent of measures to encourage construction of higher density housing developments.

A third report by Bacon *et al* was published in June 2000. This highlighted an ongoing imbalance between supply and demand for private housing and pointed out that anticipation of perceptions of further price increases were fuelling demand and creating continued instability in the housing market. It also argued that speculators were continuing to play a significant part in the market, often by purchasing dwellings for short-term capital gains rather than as long-term investments (Bacon and Associates, 2000). It was followed by another government policy statement entitled *Action on Housing* (Department of the Environment and Local Government, 2000a) which outlined a series of supply side measures such as strategic development zones for housing, focusing on the removal of infrastructure constraints to housing provision such as transportation, water supply and sewage, greater investment in planning services and higher residential densities. On the demand side a revised schedule of stamp duties on residential dwellings was announced and an anti-speculator property tax was announced.

The Planning and Development Act, 2000 (Part V)

In an effort to address the problem of affordability and also to alleviate the spatial segregation which has come to characterise the Irish housing system, Part V of the Planning and Development Act, 2000 required that all new private developments of four houses or more set aside 20 per cent of dwellings for social and affordable housing. In practice, developers have tended to allocate the minimum 5 per cent of dwellings to social housing and 15 per cent to affordable housing. Inevitably a measure such as this one which obliges developers to set aside the profit motive for social and planning considerations has provoked some opposition. A court case challenging the constitutionality of the measure was rejected in 2001. In 2002 the Irish Home Builders Association claimed that the measure was slowing down the supply of new homes and that it made the planning process more bureaucratic and cumbersome, leading to a fall in planning applications (Irish Home Builders Association, 1999). Developers have also suggested that a more effective application of Part V would be to earmark specific sites in county development plans for social and affordable housing, to acquire land on the open market (rather than the existing requirement of using only existing zoned land) for such schemes and to undertake public/private partnerships using local authority land banks (Norris, 2004).

By late 2002 it appeared that the lobbying efforts of builders had the desired effects with the government announcing amendments to the Planning and Development Act. Under these amendments a range of options were provided by which the original obligations contained in Part V could be renegotiated between builders and local authorities. The new arrangements allowed for land, houses or sites to be provided at alternative locations, land exchanges between developers and authorities or payments to local authorities funds to provide social and affordable housing. The amendments also provided for the removal of the provision under the original act which set time limits on the duration of planning permissions. This measure was aimed at preventing the planning permission from running out on an estimated 44,000 houses in 2001 and a further 30,000 in 2003. In order to avail of this measure developers and builders were required to pay local authorities a levy (which could not be passed onto house purchasers), as a contribution to social housing programmes.

A notable aspect of the Part V provision from a policy point of view concerns the income limits for determining whether a household is qualified or not. The 2000 Act specified that eligibility to purchase affordable dwellings is limited to persons in need of accommodation and whose income would not be adequate to meet the payments of a mortgage on a suitable dwelling, because such payments would exceed 35 per cent of their net annual income. In the case of dual income households half the net income of the second earner must also be taken into account in determining eligibility. Local authorities calculate limits by reference to local first-time buyer prices, which are invariably higher in urban areas, leading to the possibility of people on relatively high incomes qualifying to buy in those areas.

In this context it could be argued that the affordable housing measure marks a reversal of the trend of targeting assistance to low-income house buyers which had been developing since the mid-1980s. Many of the households who meet the qualifying criteria for this variant of affordable housing such as teachers, nurses and civil servants could be described as key workers – ironically the traditional base of mass owner occupation. While their incomes place them above the thresholds for local authority affordable housing schemes the sustained house price inflation which occurred during the latter half of the 1990s has priced many of them out of the mainstream market and thus made them reliant on the subsidies offered under Part V to gain access. Though the numbers availing of Part V affordable housing remain low the scheme symbolises the transforming nature of owner occupation in Ireland. After decades of occupying a pre-eminent and preferred position owner occupation is exhibiting serious structural limits in either expanding further, or in responding to the housing needs of an increasing segment of its traditional client group.

Conclusion

This chapter has sought to chart the historical development of owner occupied housing in Ireland in the context of policy interventions by the State in the housing market. Broadly speaking the sector experienced a period of sustained expansion from the 1940s to the very recent past on the basis of a variety of direct and indirect state supports, policies of privatisation of state housing, and benign local and national tax regimes relating to residential property. From the mid-1980s there was a departure from the unconditional support of the tenure by the state to a more targeted approach which focused assistance on low-income households. Since the mid-1990s, however, this targeted approach has come under pressure as many middle-income groups, traditionally the mainstay of the tenure, were confronted by rising house prices. This has stimulated new government schemes devised to ease the burden of affordability.

It would therefore appear to be the case that if the long-standing official preference for owner occupation is to be maintained, the strategy of broadly based supports, which characterised policy until the mid-1980s, will have to re-emerge in the place of the focused initiatives of recent years. If this does not happen, and present political and economic policies suggest it is less rather than more likely to occur, it appears that the long-standing political preference for owner occupation will, in practice if not in principle, taper out. In more practical terms it will mean that the assumptions Irish households make about housing choices will have to be reappraised with many, by necessity if not by choice, having to explore rental options. There is evidence that this trend may already be taking root. The most recent census figures, relating to 2002, suggest that the size of the owner occupied sector has fallen marginally – with a corresponding growth in the size of the private rental tenure. While this sector has experienced something of a revival in recent years, in terms of its size, and the quality of accommodation, the regulatory infrastructure has until very recently been rudimentary and underdeveloped. Thus, owner occupation is likely to remain the dominant tenure, and by virtue of the standing it holds in policy and cultural terms, the tenure the majority of the population will continue to aspire to for some time to come. However, the changed policy circumstances and ongoing affordability issues within the Irish housing market are likely to mean that converting these aspirations into tangible bricks-and-mortar realities could prove increasingly more difficult for a growing number of Irish households in the low and middle income brackets.

3

Access Denied? The Challenge of Affordability for Sustainable Access to Housing

Dáithí Downey

Introduction

Access to owner occupation in Ireland is no longer available for a growing number of households who are priced out of the market. Instead they must rely on an insecure private and residual social rental sector that lacks sufficient housing stock to meet growing housing need. *Force majure* they remain domiciled in the parental or family home. These households are disparate and different with unequal resources, but all have a housing need. Singularly the one issue that has come to connect them and access to the tenure to which they aspire is the market affordability of housing. Affordability is the critical issue determining the question of access to housing in Irish society. For those who cannot afford, access is denied.

Although the Irish housing market is now in uncharted waters in terms of house prices and affordability, new risks and future potential penalties are now becoming clear. Over the period of the current house price boom, international equity markets have bust and stock markets have fallen, yet Irish house prices continue to rise. While recovery in international economic growth remains a considerable way off eurozone interest rates are likely to be kept low to encourage investment. As the Irish economy is not immune from these developments the threat of an unstable house price bubble emerging cannot be dismissed. Internal shocks also cannot be discounted. In sum, while the rewards of Irish owner occupation remain high, the penalties associated with how Irish housing is changing are now catching up.

This chapter explores the relationship between housing affordability and housing access in today's housing market. Success and failure in Irish housing policy pivots on whether this relationship is positive or negative. The chapter begins with a comment on how the issue of affordability has become an inter-tenure problem that connects penalties and rewards across the housing system and how these can determine access to housing in Irish society. By illustrating changes in housing output, the chapter will detail the anatomy of the Irish house price boom within the context of Ireland's entry to the euro and the fiscal treatment of housing as an asset.

The chapter then turns to an investigation of market affordability in private housing and explores the usefulness of different indicators before presenting a critique of their use. The economics of housing affordability is considered with reference to entry to owner occupation. Changes in who is accessing private housing, and how first-time buyers are meeting the affordability challenge, are examined. The chapter explores the risks, rewards and penalties arising for different households in housing need. Lastly, the challenge posed by affordability to sustainable access to housing for the first-time buyer and the social housing tenant is considered within the context of the risk of future further market failure.

Affordability and Access to Housing

Affordability issues to accessing housing are becoming more and more established as a feature of the Irish housing system. It remains to be seen if all current affordability issues become permanent features of the Irish housing system. Nevertheless, affordability issues – however they might be defined – are today's yardsticks to measure rewards and penalties connecting across the Irish housing system to determine housing access for households with unequal resources and different abilities to pay. Furthermore, affordability issues relating to housing costs and housing access are becoming increasingly established as an inter-tenure concern within the Irish housing system. How has affordability come to connect these issues?

In straightforward or orthodox economic terms, accessing private housing in Ireland as an investor or home owner continues to carry an overwhelming number of important financial rewards. Rising house prices generate manifold rewards for the majority of home owners in terms of a general wealth effect. This wealth effect describes a period of rising positive sentiment and consumer confidence expressed in terms of growing consumer expenditure that in turn adds to economic growth and greater capital formation in housing. Under-supply of housing over this period ensures these rewards are extended and strengthened as house prices climb steeply and capital gains are large enough to trigger growth in speculative investment.

As this scenario unfolded over the 1990s in Ireland, penalties arose for a range of households and individuals with a housing need. For example, supply-side shortages deepened the penalty of high and rising house prices for aspiring owner-occupiers. The employed, solvent first-time buyer (FTB) maintained a positive relationship to the housing market, but found opportunities to purchase housing restricted by the rising price barrier. Quickly, the established pathways to owner occupation for lower income households (such as shared ownership and affordable housing schemes provided by local authorities and examined by O'Connell in Chapter 2) became limited to households on income significantly above average earnings and capable of servicing a substantial mortgage.

Affordability constraints and price barriers to accessing owner-occupation subsequently led to a significant transfer of housing need to the rental housing sector. This housing need is problematic, containing as it does two distinct compositions of demand. In the first instance are employed households with an effective, but postponed demand for private housing, who rent privately. Secondly, there are the low-income, often welfare dependent households with little or no effective demand (that is they will never afford entry to owner occupation) who must rely on state housing income support to rent privately, while awaiting an assessment of their housing need and the allocation of a social tenancy. Both compositions of demand represent two-thirds and one-third of the private rented sector respectively.

Large year-on-year increases in housing costs due to rental inflation have led to a crowding-out effect, impacting most on private tenant households with marginal incomes. These households are forced to quit tenancies and choose cheaper and lesser quality accommodation in order to reduce their rental costs (Downey and DeVilly, 1999). For such households the risk of homelessness is high. Access to social rental housing is also directly affected by issues in the private house market. Under recent market conditions asset price inflation for housing can be seen as a cause of inflation in the cost of development land. In parallel, house building and general construction costs have risen. These have had an adverse effect on improved access to social housing by leading to a lesser rate of output than required for over 48,000 households on local-authority housing waiting lists. This is despite recent increases in capital expenditure on social housing. Affordability is therefore an inter-tenure concern, connecting issues of access to housing across private and rental tenures and illustrating the rewards and penalties associated with achieving access to housing or having access denied.

Irish Housing: Trends and Changes in Output and Provision

There are a number of discernible trends in Irish housing output. To begin with, since 1997 there has been a significant increase in the rate of housing completions nationally. Completions rose from 38,842 units in 1997 to 46,512 in 1999 and a record 52,602 by 2001. Recent data available for 2003 indicate the numbers of new houses completed, at 68,819 units, to be up 19 per cent on

2002. The greatest proportion of this output has been private housing. In 1997 just over 91 per cent of all output was private housing. The dominance of detached and semi-detached new housing in the Dublin region is nearing an end, yet it remains the case that higher-density apartment developments have not filled the supply-side deficit. Williams, Shiels and Hughes (2002) found that there remains a significant shortfall of 10,000 units per annum fewer than are required in the greater Dublin region, which includes the surrounding counties of Wicklow, Kildare and Meath. The predicted result is that there will be no decrease in house prices generally in Dublin in the foreseeable future.

Notably, the role of Dublin's effective housing demand in pulling up the national rate of house price inflation cannot be underestimated. Over 30 per cent of the national population live in the greater Dublin region. While the national rate of new housing output improved to an estimated 68,000 units in 2003, property industry research suggests that the actual percentage of new housing built in Dublin during this year was less than 21 per cent of this overall national output (Gunne Residential, 2004). Under-supply continues to generate higher price inflation than would be the case if supply were approaching demand in the Dublin region.

Figure 3.1: Trends in Capital Formation in Irish Housing, 1975-2002

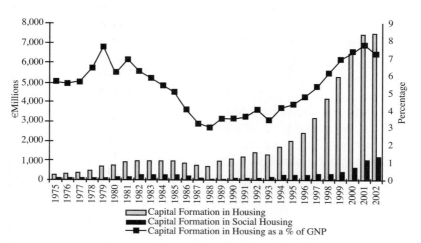

Source: Department of the Environment, Heritage and Local Government (various years).

In contrast, as Norris examines in more detail in Chapter 8 of this book, Irish social housing output has remained residual over the decade to 2000. In real terms, and despite consistent growth in assessed housing need over the period, the relative position of social housing output deteriorated rather than improved.

In 1992, new completions of social housing nationally were just above 9 per cent of total housing output. With the exception of the year 1994, between 1992 and 1997 this output fell back to closer to 8 per cent annually. In the latter half of the 1990s, the situation deteriorated further so that output fell to 7.6 per cent in 1998, 7.4 per cent in 1999 and reached a nadir in 2000 of 6.3 per cent of total output. As Figure 3.1 illustrates, public capital investment in social housing as a proportion of overall capital formation in all housing fell significantly over the 1990s and is today below previous rates of investment achieved during the 1970s and 1980s.

In contrast and despite reduced capital investment in social housing, overall capital formation in Irish housing as a percentage of gross national product (GNP) continues to rise from a low level in 1993 of 3.4 per cent to 7.2 per cent in 2002. This recovery in the rate of capital formation in housing is not due to public investment strategies in social housing and related infrastructure, but rather is a result of meeting the spiralling cost of entry to owner occupation. Trends in social housing investment have recently begun to reverse somewhat, primarily as government policy seeks to respond to growth in assessed housing need. Recent investment may represent a reversal in the previous fortunes of social housing. Nonetheless, over the period of the 1990s and up to 2002, social housing in Ireland never accounted for more than one in ten dwellings completed and on many occasions was less than that.

Irish Housing: Trends and Changes in House Prices

The progress of asset price inflation in the private housing market remains a dominant influence over the nature of housing policy development. House price inflation has a direct relationship to both monetary and fiscal policy regimes operating in Ireland since the adoption of the euro as national currency. In the first instance, downward trends of European Central Bank (ECB) interest rates combined with pro-cyclical national budgets over the period from 1998 to 2001 to ensure that during a period of supply-side constraint, strengthening effective demand for housing resulted in exaggerated price inflation. Figure 3.2 shows how the period to 2001 is characterised by a steep rate of price inflation.

The wider economy's macroeconomic links with the housing market are further illustrated by the impact of changes in the international economic environment since 2001. The openness of the Irish economy, its small size and the importance of trade and international investment to economic growth and development ensured that the global economic downturn of 2001 impacted the Irish housing market. In particular, the high-tech downturn in the USA that reduced foreign direct investment (FDI) in Irish-based multinational production combined with a crisis in global stock market equity values to reduce investment and employment, and interrupted the rise since the mid-1990s in net disposable income. The era of the so-called 'Celtic Tiger' was over. In addition, government changes to the fiscal treatment of housing as an investment also affected the rate of asset price inflation. Consequently, house prices fluctuated throughout 2001 and both new and second-hand prices fell during the final half of that year. Nonetheless, the rate of price inflation picked up again in 2002, quickly cancelling out whatever improvements were made to general market affordability for new entrants to private housing in 2001.

Figure 3.2: Change in National Average House Prices for Whole Country and Dublin, 1976 – Quarter 3, 2003 (Nominal Values)

Source: Department of the Environment, Heritage and Local Government (various years).

There are a number of factors behind this u-turn. First, Budget 2002 once again reversed direction on the tax treatment of housing as an investment and restored the ability of investors to offset interest payments against rental income. Stamp duty was also reduced. Secondly, with equity markets continuing to lose value and an opportunity to capitalise on 2001's downward pressure on prices, investors responded to budgetary changes and quickly returned to the housing market. Finally, in response to the economic slowdown, eurozone interest rates were reduced and the cost of borrowing fell, prompting increased market activity from new entrant investors and first-time buyers (FTBs).

This ensured that in spite of prevailing economic conditions and a weakening in other private-sector credit growth, 2002 recorded a surge in residential mortgage borrowing. Industry estimates suggested that one in four residential mortgages were being advanced to investors while the Department of the Environment, Heritage and Local Government *Housing Statistics Bulletin* for

Quarter 1, 2002, indicated that two out of every three new houses were being bought by investors, not owner occupiers (Department of the Environment, Heritage and Local Government, various years). Effective demand for housing continued to outstrip supply in 2002, and increased competition for the use-value of housing between investors and owners meant house prices resumed their upward trajectory, albeit at a somewhat more moderate rate than before.

Over 2002, second-hand house prices increased nationally by 16 per cent, and by 20 per cent for Dublin. Despite the increased rate of completions in 2002, prices for new housing rose by 7 per cent nationally and by 9 per cent for Dublin (Permanent TSB and ESRI, 2002). Official data for the third quarter of 2003 found that the average price of a new house was €225,356 nationally and €295,158 in Dublin. The average price of a second-hand house was €266,444 nationally and €350,603 in Dublin (Department of the Environment, Heritage and Local Government, various years).

Nominal values in house price inflation over the period since 1996 indicate a rate of inflation that is unsustainable and may be economically unstable over the medium to long term. To reveal the underlying trends we can calculate real values that take account of annual consumer price inflation and thereby give a better indication of the true extent of the wealth effect accruing to home owners over a longer time period. Real values for the annual percentage change of house price inflation for Dublin and nationally since 1977 are shown in Figures 3.3 and 3.4 respectively. These charts illustrate how high rates of consumer inflation negatively impacted on the real rate of house price growth in the 1980s and again in the early 1990s. These trends were thrown into sharp and sustained reverse over the period of the Celtic Tiger economy that witnessed unprecedented rates of real house price inflation.

The period 1999 to 2001 saw the annual house price inflation rate drop back. However, the overall rate of price growth remained very much in the positive zone in real terms, with double digit price inflation becoming re-established again in 2003. With house prices at such record high levels in real terms, the issue of the market affordability for new entrants to owner occupation began to move up the political agenda and government commissioned an investigation into affordability and price trends in Irish housing (Bacon, 1998). As a result of this study, new light was thrown on how market affordability in Irish housing was understood, defined and measured by financial institutions. The next section investigates this further by taking a critical look at the use and usefulness of these measures when calculating risk and decision-making on providing mortgage finance to fund access to private housing.

Investigating Market Affordability in Private Housing

There are a number of alternative (sometimes competing) methods used for investigating and measuring the market affordability of private housing. They include indices based on ratios of housing expenditure-to-income, on advance-to-income and debt-service costs-to-income, and the ratio of house prices-to-earnings (Downey, 1997; 1998).

Figure 3.3: Change in Annual National Percentage Rate of House Price Inflation (Real Values) 1977 – Quarter 3, 2003

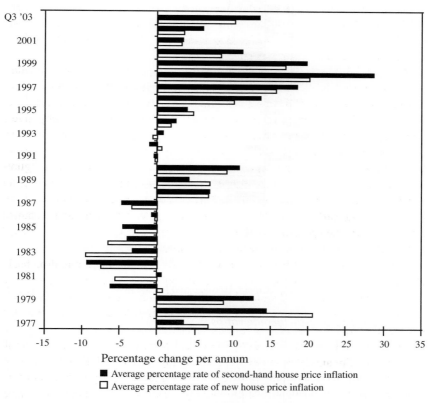

Source: Department of the Environment, Heritage and Local Government (various years).

Figure 3.4: Change in Annual Dublin Average Percentage Rate of House Price Inflation (Real Values) 1977 – Quarter 3, 2003

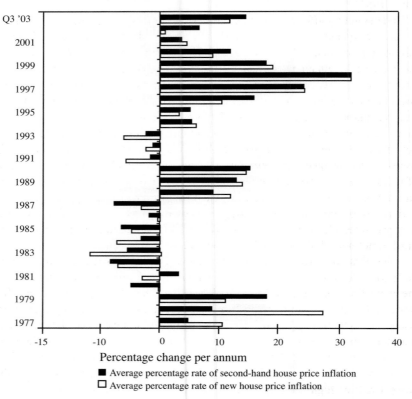

Percentage change per annum

■ Average percentage rate of second-hand house price inflation
□ Average percentage rate of new house price inflation

Source: Department of the Environment, Heritage and Local Government (various years).

Housing Expenditure-to-Income ratios

At the level of day-to-day practice and decision-making, a number of assumptions regarding the amount any given household can afford to pay to obtain housing have become established as expenditure-to-income rules-of-thumb among Irish financial institutions. For example, a household is said to have a housing affordability problem when it pays more than a certain percentage of its income to obtain adequate and appropriate housing. Leaving aside the consideration of what adequate and appropriate housing might be, this formulation of affordability originates in studies of household budgets. The origins of housing expenditure-to-income rules-of-thumb are generally attributed to the work of Ernst Engel and Herman Schwabe, two prominent nineteenth-century German statisticians who formulated the earliest known 'laws' about the relationship between incomes and categories of household expenditures (also see Allen and Bowley, 1935; Zimmerman, 1936; Feins and Lane, 1981).

Understanding affordability as a measure of housing costs relative to income is commonly used to generate a sliding scale rule-of-thumb about how to minimise risk when selling mortgage finance to different households. However, the manner in which it is used to adjudicate regarding access to mortgage finance for different categories of borrowers remains critical to house purchase decision-making during the current period of house price inflation, as well as to positive market sentiment. At the beginning of the house price boom, the financial industry rule-of-thumb stated that monthly mortgage repayments must not exceed 33 per cent of gross monthly salary (Finnegan, 1997). Today this measure has changed and now only if a household spends more than one-third of its total *net* income on rent or mortgage repayments is it considered to have an affordability problem. This adjusted rule-of-thumb is 'an approximate, but widely used indicator of housing affordability. Lending institutions, for instance, often check whether mortgage repayments would exceed roughly one-third of net household income' (Watson and Williams, 2003).

Using this approach Watson and Williams (2003) investigated and analysed 2001 Irish Census data on housing costs relative to income as a key indicator of the current market affordability of Irish housing. Their findings were somewhat startling for many commentators who consider market affordability a problem issue in Irish housing. The analysis found that over 90 per cent of all households who are purchasing or renting in Ireland spend less than one-third of their net household income on rent or mortgage payments, with only 9 per cent spending more than one-third of net income. However, the study also found that the current risk of high housing costs is greatest for younger households (25 per cent) and the elderly living alone as 'empty nesters' (14 per cent) as well as lone parents with dependent children (17 per cent) and households in the lowest income categories. Today, one fifth of the lowest income group in Ireland pay more than one-third of their income on rent or mortgage payments. The risk of high housing costs was also found to be larger in Dublin (12 per cent) and the Border and Mid West region urban areas (14 per cent) than elsewhere. Finally, among house purchasers, the risk of high housing costs for those who purchased over the five-year period to 2001 was much higher than those who had purchased earlier. This finding reflects the risk position or exposure of recent buyers to housing costs that are significantly higher than the norm for Irish owner occupation.

However, measuring affordability using financial industry rules-of-thumb can be said to be based on not much more than generalised assumptions about the amount that average households 'tend to' or 'ought to' pay for housing, without ever specifying which households are being averaged or how this normative 'ought' statement is derived and calculated. In essence what has occurred over time is the translation of observations about what some households were spending on housing into assumptions about what they 'ought' to be spending, based on market assessments of risk and the strength of prudential concerns among mortgage finance and other credit institutions, banks and building societies.

House Price-to-Earnings Ratio

The ratio of house price-to-earnings is a basic measure of the market affordability of housing, the market use of which reflects the fact that there is often an intuitive link made between house prices and earnings. It is assumed that any increase in house prices that takes the ratio above its long-term average is likely to be unsustainable. Conversely, when house prices fall below this multiple of earnings a future recovery in house prices is assumed to ensue. Oswald (2002) argues that the stable ratio of house prices to earnings is 4:1 and that ratios above this will adjust downwards over the economic cycle. Downwards adjustment in prices can be rapid and significant enough in size to generate negative equity. Figure 3.5 indicates how, for a range of different categories of Irish employment since 1997, this ratio is significantly above the sustainable long-term ratio of 4:1.

Advance-to-Income and Debt-Service Income Ratios

These are perhaps the most commonly used measures of market affordability as they take account of the amount that may be borrowed (or advanced to income) under mortgage finance lending criteria, as well as the cost to household income of servicing this debt over the period borrowed. This indicator is also more sophisticated as it has a direct relationship to an important aspect of the user cost of capital in housing – mortgage interest rates. The government-commissioned Bacon (1998) study on house prices relied on this approach to measuring affordability. Indices were calculated on the basis of the following affordability ratio:

<u>(1) Annual Mortgage Service Cost</u>
(2) Net After Tax Income

where:
(1) Annual Mortgage Service Cost = Annual Mortgage Cost for a 90% Mortgage on a new house, and:
(2) Net After Tax Income = (Gross Income)-(Income Tax)-(PRSI and Levies) + (Mortgage Interest Tax Relief)

Notwithstanding the robust calculations on market affordability presented by Bacon (1998), this measure of affordability is the simple function of a contingent relationship between house prices, income levels and mortgage interest rates. All of these indicators have changed significantly during the Irish economic boom of the late 1990s and into the new millennium. Indeed the contingent nature of this relationship was recognised by Bacon (1998) who concluded that the influence of house price increases over the period 1994-1997 produced a subsequent decrease in affordability as measured through his index. This was despite the mitigating influence of historically low interest rates and the buffer of reductions in personal taxation over this period that would otherwise have led to improved general housing affordability rates.

Figure 3.5: House Price to Earnings Ratio for Different Categories of Employment, 1995 – Quarter 3, 2003

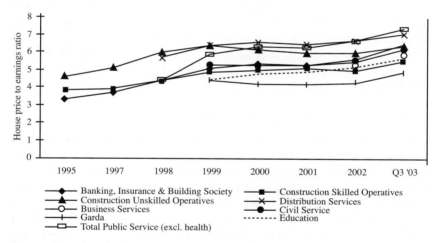

Source: Central Statistics Office (2001b) and Department of the Environment, Heritage and Local Government (various years).

Using Market Affordability Indicators: Reliability and Validity Issues

The market use of the above range of indicators to assess affordability decision-making on house purchase, to determine affordability 'risk', as well as measure and describe affordability positions and trends for different categories of borrowers can be questioned on the basis of their overall reliability and validity. For example, Table 3.1 shows a typology of uses to which the housing expenditure-to-income ratios are put. These can be separated into two categories.

Table 3.1 Housing Expenditure-to-Income Ratio: Six Uses of the Percent of Income Rule-of-Thumb

1. DESCRIPTION	describe a typical household's housing expenditure
2. ANALYSIS	analyse trends, compare different household types
3. ADMINISTRATION	administer rules defining who can access housing subsidies
4. DEFINITION	define housing need for public policy purposes
5. PREDICTION	predict ability to pay the rent or mortgage
6. SELECTION	select households for a rental unit or mortgage

Source: Hulchanski (1995).

One category contains the first three uses of this ratio – 'description', 'analyses' and 'administration'. These uses are valid and helpful measures of market affordability when calculated correctly. The second category contains the final three uses – 'definition', 'prediction' and 'selection'. In contrast, these uses are arguably invalid because the ratio fails to measure what it claims to be measuring, even if the statistical techniques used are properly executed. Why can this claim be made? Firstly, the conceptualisation of the income part of the ratio is faulty. This point is strongly supported by Hulchanski (1995) who argues that the definition of what household income is and what is meant by income is crucial. Because this ratio relies on the easiest to measure form of income – money or cash income from the formal market economy – the ratio can fail to be a true measure of affordability. It effectively ignores other sources of support, both cash and non-cash, by which households meet their needs. Indeed, there are at least five economic spheres by which households can obtain cash and non-cash resources (see Table 3.2).

Table 3.2: Five Economic Spheres from which Households Obtain Income

The Domestic Economy	economy internal to the household, e.g. income from siblings and offspring
The Informal Economy	income from the extended family and close acquaintances
The Social Economy	neighbourhood and community-based groups and agencies
The Market Economy	the formal marketplace for labour
The State Economy	government welfare entitlements

Source: Hulchanski and Michalski (1994); also see Davis and Dhooge (1993) for strategies on how households obtain increased income to deal with mortgage default and arrears.

This convenient measure of income simplifies too far, to the point that it does not reflect the reality of most households. In other words, housing-to-income approaches to market affordability are open to the charge that they are fundamentally flawed. Stone (1990: 50-51) argues that the housing expenditure-to-income ratio definition of affordability is inadequate in a 'logically sound' way:

> Any attempt to reduce affordability of housing to a single percentage of income – no matter how low or high – simply does not correspond to the reality of fundamental and obvious differences among households. Even attempts to establish a few prototypical groups and have somewhat different percentages for each, or to set up narrow ranges in order to recognise some differences, fail to grapple in a logically sound way with the range of variation households really can afford to pay.

Baer (1976: 383-384), in a study of housing indicators, goes further and argues that ratios that impose the same standard for all households are fundamentally 'unrealistic':

> Given the variety of circumstances facing different households, rules of thumb about the percent of income to be devoted to housing can be extremely misleading in individual cases and therefore in aggregate as well ... a maximum rent-income ratio for one kind of household may not be appropriate for another, and imposing the same standard for all households is unrealistic.

Lastly, it is important to realise that advance-to-income and debt-service affordability indices generally do not fully measure trends in the market affordability of owner occupation over time. Rather these indices should only be taken as indicators of the situation facing a particular category of aspiring borrower at one point in time. They represent a snapshot 'cash-flow' concept of market affordability which cannot be relied upon to signal clearly whether households are likely to exercise a decision in favour or against home ownership at any one time. In addition, the interpretative value of advance-to-income and debt-service affordability ratios are severely limited by the assumptions they must make regarding the levels and definition of income, the price value of the property, the rate of interest charged on mortgage finance and the maximum income multipliers and loan-to-value ratios applied by lending institutions.

New approaches to measuring market affordability are therefore needed. A comprehensive measure should seek to provide information about the relative desirability of owner occupation by taking into account those factors which shape the individuals' choice between different tenure options and the perceived cost of opting for owner occupation now rather than at some later date. This would increase the validity and reliability of an indicator's usefulness.

Entry to Owner Occupation: The Economics of Housing Affordability

Entry to Irish owner occupation is influenced by the monetary policy and decision-making of the European Central Bank on lowering or raising interest rates, as much as it can be by domestic factors. The relationship between income, house price and the cost of borrowing confirms the strength of the influence of eurozone monetary policy. Tracing the relationship between falling interest rates and rising house prices, as is done in Table 1.5 in Chapter 1 of this volume, illustrates the impact of the adoption of the euro as national currency. From 1999, the anticipated rate of decline in interest rates is realised upon the full launch of the new currency. Together with improving average earnings until early in 2001, market affordability ratios for most categories of borrowers are improved. This was opposite to the trend in affordability for the previous three years, especially for new entrants.

Nonetheless, affordability related decisions to purchase, or not to purchase, a property are complex ones likely to be influenced by a plethora of other related expectations regarding house price movements, career and salary prospects, assumptions about future interest rates, inflation rates, tax rates, taxation and fiscal supports for owner occupation and so forth. Of all the factors that influence decision-making, house price expectations are likely to loom the largest. For example, Banks *et al* (2003) compared the UK and US housing markets and investigated the differences in households' decisions about whether or not to buy housing at various stages in individual households' lives. This study concluded that the greater volatility of the UK's housing market is a feature that explains why people buy houses sooner in their lives compared to the US. This is because there is no other means of hedging against further increases in house prices, except to buy housing itself. Arguably, this finding also applies to the Irish private housing market.

In the mind of the owner occupier considering trading up, but also of the first-time buyer, the capital-gearing effect involved due to the expectation of even modest appreciation in capital values will offset concerns regarding the ongoing overhead and maintenance costs associated with owner occupation. In other words, as long as housing remains an investment with a high rate of return, mortgage finance allows a household to 'gear-up' their investment returns in housing compared to other non-geared assets. Equally, when house prices fall, a highly geared buyer will experience a greater negative rate of return.

How does borrowing with a mortgage 'gear up' these returns? Barker (2003) offers a clear example upon which the following is based. Suppose we have a new entrant to owner-occupation, the first time buyer (FTB), purchasing a €300,000 house that will incur transactions costs of 6 per cent (i.e. total cost to buyer is €318,000). With 20 per cent house price inflation, and an implicit income of 4 per cent as imputed rent (home owners pay no rent), maintenance costs of 2 per cent, and even adding in a property tax of 1 per cent, this investment results in an annual return of €63,000 (€60,000 capital appreciation plus €12,000 saving in rent, minus €9,000 in maintenance costs and tax) on the €300,000 investment. This is a 19.8 per cent return.

Typically, our FTB will access mortgage finance to buy a house. In this case, s/he borrows €270,000 (90 per cent loan-to-value) at a variable interest of 5 per cent. This means our FTB invests only €48,000 (€318,000 minus €270,000) and will receive a return on that sum. Take nominal house price inflation again to be 20 per cent and our FTB's return is €49,000 (€64,000 minus €13,500 interest repayable on loan) after year one of ownership, a rate of return on the original investment of 103.1 per cent. This is one of the primary reasons why demand in Ireland for private housing remains so strong despite the period of rapid price growth since the mid-1990s. It is that the rate of return on owning property is high and the risk of highly geared borrowing (i.e. large mortgages) is less due to low interest rates.

It may be appropriate, therefore, that future assessments of affordability adopt an approach based on the housing user cost of capital – an approach which factors in anticipated house price rises. In other words, it measures the direct costs of property ownership while acknowledging that house price inflation offsets these costs over time. A simplified version of the real user cost of capital in housing (UCC) is defined by Barker (2003: 29) as:

$$UCC = [R + M + TR = T - \Delta PH^e/PH] \ PH/P$$

where

R	=	nominal interest rate, adjusted for any mortgage interest tax relief,
M	=	maintenance costs as a percentage of value,
TR	=	transactions costs as a percentage of value,
T	=	property tax as a percentage of value,
PH	=	index of second-hand house prices,
P	=	index of general consumer goods, and
$\Delta PH^e/PH$	=	expected rate of change of house prices.

When house price inflation more than offsets the direct costs of home ownership, speculative behaviour in investment is triggered. House price bubbles can emerge as demand significantly overwhelms the supply of what remains an intrinsically inelastic good that has a long supply-side response time, and is directly affected by issues of land costs, construction industry capacity and cost, taxation and planning among other factors. However, in terms of market affordability, calculating the user cost of capital shows how the real cost of home ownership varies according to both the level and change in house prices. That is, the real cost of home ownership falls when the rate of house price inflation rises, as the return on the house price offsets the cost of interest payments and the other costs on the property.

Recent calculations by the ESRI based on their *HERMES* macro-model of the Irish housing market indicates the user cost of new housing falling steadily since 1992 (for full details on the *HERMES* model see Murphy and Brereton (2001). Duffy (2002) provides a detailed description of the Irish housing market). In short, while new houses are highly priced, they are relatively cheap to live in because of low interest rates and expected capital gains. Other research by Bergin *et al* (2003) forecasts that user-cost will continue to underpin demand in the Irish housing market until 2005 at least. It should be noted that the absence in Ireland of local taxation of housing and payments for services that are standard internationally contribute to the relatively low cost of owner occupation. Today the challenge to potential entrants to owner occupation is the cost of entry, not necessarily the cost of staying there.

Access to Owner Occupation: Market Affordability, Fragmentation and Polarisation

High house prices represent a barrier to new entrants eager to enter owner occupation and get a foot on the property ladder. However, high expected rates of capital gain and robust revenue yields (in the form of rents) also attract investors and speculators. Investment and speculation in housing drives change in the composition of net effective demand and has introduced greater market fragmentation as developers respond to separate types of demand arising from investors and aspiring owner occupiers. While little detail is known of Irish property investment patterns, McCarthy, Hughes and Woelger (2003:3) have argued that these 'unquantified elements in the dynamics of housing demand require closer examination'. Their 2003 study found that new household formation for the six years to 2003 accounted for only 61 per cent of new house completions. In 2003, it was likely to account for less than 50 per cent of house completions. They conclude that currently up to one third of Irish housing output is to satisfy demand for second homes and investment properties – a conclusion that has far-reaching implications for current government housing investment strategy to 2006 under the *National Development Plan 2000-2006* (NDP) (Government of Ireland, 2000a). The mid-term evaluation of the NDP found the problems of Irish housing require special attention and the adoption of appropriate policy measures to lessen the impact of the housing market on the wider economic competitiveness of the Irish economy (FitzGerald *et al* 2003).

So, what has been happening for the aspiring first-time buyer in the face of investor activity? Using data on the numbers of approved mortgages for new housing and the number of approved grants for new housing, Figure 3.6 shows how the percentage of FTBs entering the new house market since 1981 has changed from a position of dominance in the 1980s to one of lesser influence today. With the current house price boom underway by late 1996, the percentage of FTBs purchasing new housing fell from a mid-1990s high of almost half the market (47.3 per cent) to a low of below one-third of the market (28.9 per cent) in 1999. From 1999 until early 2001, the falling cost of borrowing and changes in the residential mortgage market triggered an improved position for FTBs. However, despite downward price movements throughout 2001, deterioration in the prevailing economic climate interrupted growth in average earnings and combined with rising house building costs, construction industry and consumer price inflation to reduce market affordability again. At the end of 2002, FTBs represented only 29.1 per cent of the share of the new house market.

Figure 3.6: Changes in the First-Time Buyer's Percentage Share of the New House Market, 1981 – Quarter 4, 2002

□ Percentage share of market (new houses, countrywide)

Source: Department of the Environment, Heritage and Local Government (various years).

Notably, in November 2002 government announced the abolition of the new house grant scheme for first-time buyers (Norris and Winston, 2004). This caused only a moderate reaction beyond those directly affected (i.e. purchasers agreeing contracts at the time). The rationale leading to the abolition of this subvention to the price of new housing was an increasingly established view that new house prices adjusted upwards to take account of the value of the grant. In other words, the grant represented a gain to property developers more than to purchasers – particularly so during the prolonged period of asset price inflation and supply-side constraints apparent since the mid-1990s. Notwithstanding this, it is arguable that the abolition of the new housing grant was a cost-cutting measure, rather than an indication of government's intention to move towards a tenure-neutral fiscal treatment of housing as an asset. This view is supported by the fact that other tax and subsidy arrangements underpinning investment in housing for rental purposes remain in place, as do reduced rates of capital gains tax and an absence of local taxation or rates levied on residential property.

At the start of the new millennium, not only can we now trace a qualitative change in the type of household entering owner occupation, we can see how these changes have become quickly established as norms or new realities. Entry is becoming increasingly polarised among different groups in Irish society who would traditionally aspire to home ownership, but who are not equally able to overcome the price barrier. For example, the socio-economic characteristics of borrowers have altered significantly as a consequence of house price inflation. Since the mid-1990s, approximately one in two borrowers is a professional manager or employer, while the proportion of salaried, non-manual employees has fallen from one in four to approximately one in ten of all borrowers. This can be interpreted as a reflection of changes in the Irish labour market over the period but also represents a real change in the composition of net effective demand for private housing. Borrowers employed in skilled and semi-skilled occupations have maintained a position of one in three of all borrowers over the period.

The extent of change is further illustrated by the transformation in the range of incomes required for the purchase of housing. The income range of borrowers on combined incomes (two-person household) in the Dublin housing market has increased significantly. Similarly, the range of loans borrowed has also changed. In 1997, 3 per cent of all repayments paid in Dublin were on loans above €190,000 and 7 per cent of repayments were on loans of between €127,000 and €190,000. By 2002, this situation had changed dramatically with the percentage of loans above €200,000 and between €145,000 and €200,000 rising to 26.2 and 32.4 per cent respectively.

Trends in the Dublin region also indicate that the percentage of borrowers for new housing who are already in owner-occupation fell from 52.2 per cent in

1997 to 38.6 per cent by the end of 2002. The percentage that entered owner-occupation from the parental home fluctuated at around one in three of all borrowers for new housing for the same period. First-time buyers originating in the privately rented sector fluctuated at around one in four of all borrowers. For second-hand housing in Dublin, trends indicate that two-thirds of borrowers were home owners in 2000, falling back to 60 per cent for 2002. Purchasers of second-hand housing residing in the parental home fell to 13.9 per cent by 2000, before increasing to 16 per cent in 2002.

First-time buyers now opt for longer mortgage repayment periods (up to 30 or 35 years) as well as seeking the maximum loan possible under changed and more flexible eligibility criteria that allow multiples of up to 4.5 times the primary household income to be borrowed. Recent changes to lending multipliers and eligibility criteria for the calculation of income have raised questions over the prudential nature of credit institutions' lending practices, prompting the Irish Central Bank to insist on a set of stress tests being applied to a borrower's ability to make repayments.

Significantly, increased equity in private housing generated by consistent asset price inflation is targeted by financial institutions offering new equity-release and mortgage re-financing products. While not unique in themselves, these products are new to the Irish market and are offered as a means of overcoming the price hurdle facing FTBs by means of an inter-generational transfer of housing wealth in the form of a parental gift or loan. Market research by Gunne Residential and ICS Building Society (2002) in Dublin found that one in five Irish parents now underwrite their children's attempts at house purchase by providing a gift (or loan) to the value of €75,000 or more. Specifically, the research found that for all FTBs in Dublin earning under €40,000 nearly three quarters (71 per cent) obtained parental or third-party assistance, nearly half (46 per cent) were given between €20,000 and €35,000 and over a quarter received a gift of between €35,000 and €50,000. This so-called untapped equity in the Irish housing market is estimated at €75 billion and the recent phenomenon of the parental gift acted as a precursor to the arrival of new products dedicated to the release of equity for this purpose (Downey, 2003).

New financial products ensure that for certain aspiring FTBs the issue of accessing home ownership is less problematic than before. Nevertheless, they are selective in their impact. Not having a positive familial relationship, or not having parents/guardians with an equity value to spare will mean not having access to a parental gift or loan of any kind or size. A more prudential concern is that the parental gift is actually more of an intergenerational debt transfer than anything else, one that increases risk and deepens the impact of default or payment interruption. Equity release and the parental gift will also generate further upward pressure in house price inflation as more money becomes available to purchase what remains a scarce asset, particularly in Dublin. The marketing of these products has also led to criticism that FTBs will not seek to save independently for their deposit and that overall reliance on parental support is not economically or socially desirable in relation to independent household formation. In brief, the emergence of the Irish stay-at-home 'perma-kid' who has postponed entry into owner occupation and/or has ceased to aspire to owner occupation due to current price barriers is becoming a middle-Ireland concern, particularly in terms of their expenditure and consumption patterns and the absence of savings or investment.

Accessing Irish Housing: New Risks, Greater Rewards and Bigger Penalties?

Access to housing, via the market and the social rental system is now established as a critical issue of Irish social and economic policy. The concept of access tends however to be reduced to one of house price and cost rather than a focus on the inequities of the housing system and the lack of equality of outcome for households with high housing need but low or weak net effective demand due to their inability to pay. The risk facing poor households is one of deepening social exclusion due to inadequate, inappropriate, poor quality but expensive private rented accommodation. Their reward is the possible future allocation of a social tenancy on the proviso that they register their housing need with a local authority and subsequently satisfy the tri-annual assessment of housing need, but also that investment to produce the required social housing is made on time and is maintained. The penalty they face if social housing is not available and accessible is one of long-term housing poverty, associated ill health and potentially long periods of homelessness in emergency accommodation, hostels, night shelters or as rough sleepers.

The risks and penalties faced by owner-occupiers have also become more evident, as too have the rewards. However, in 2004 the Irish housing market faces serious problems that threaten wider economic growth and even social stability. We know that with supply constrained, many households invest in housing as an asset to garner profit from rental yields and capital gains and also as a form of pension. Equally, many first-time buyers push their solvency to the limits to borrow the capital required to get a foot on the property ladder lest they become priced out of home ownership. Now it appears that the price of our housing has created debt levels that leave the economy and individuals vulnerable to shocks (Central Bank of Ireland, 2003). Also, there is growing concern that as many as 15,000 of the new houses built in 2003 and purchased by investors as popular 'buy-to-let' schemes are unlikely to produce required rental yield (McCarthy, Hughes and Woelger, 2003). In effect, these dwellings may be surplus to rental demand and if sold off rapidly, could spike the price 'bubble' which a number of commentators believe exists in the Irish housing market.

Previously, shocks to the Irish housing market have tended to be externally influenced and caused by rapid interest rate rises, as occurred in the early 1990s. However, eurozone entry has diminished the likelihood of large interest rate movements. Today, a shock is just as likely to emerge directly from the mainstream Irish economy in the form of unemployment, interruptions in income growth and a rising cost of living. This risk is becoming more established even at a time when projections for housing completions suggest an output rate that will begin to balance supply and demand for private housing and may lead to a broad market equilibrium.

House price indices show that while prices eased slightly for new housing in 2003, house price growth was still strong for existing second-hand homes. We may now be witnessing the transfer of a price bubble in new housing up the housing chain to older, larger properties in established residential urban areas. The recently increased rate of counter-urbanisation and urban sprawl in Ireland – a direct result of affordability issues in accessing private housing – is now a risk in itself, particularly in the greater Dublin region. If the housing market is moving towards equilibrium, it may be in the outer-urban housing estates, suburbs and Dublin commuter towns, where development land is available at lower prices, that supply eventually outstrips demand, pushing down prices, and adding further to established penalties of long commuting ties, shortages of childcare and pressure on social resources and capabilities. Future downward price movements are not unrealistic risks for new greenfield, counter-urban residential areas.

But just what is a house price bubble, do we have one and if so will it burst? If it does, will all regional and sub-markets be equally affected? These are the big questions of the Irish housing market, especially as house price increases have overcome their slight fall in 2001 and rebounded upwards again despite the fact that the economic boom of the 'Celtic Tiger' is well and truly over. A recent European Central Bank (2003) report investigating structural factors in EU housing markets found that real house prices in most EU countries follow long cycles around a moderate upward trend and that since 1980 price cycles have often lasted more than 10 years. House price changes of more than 10 per cent in real terms either up or down are taken to represent a boom or bust. Booms were found to be more frequent than busts since 1980, especially in the euro area and are typically followed by prolonged periods of very low growth or even of decline in house prices.

The ECB also found that sluggish responses to increased demand means house prices will tend to overshoot their long-term trend for considerable periods of time. Furthermore, this overshoot can be prolonged by the role of interest rates and the impact of inflation on real interest rates. Differences in business cycles emerge, triggering changes in contractual arrangements of housing credit systems as well as changes in land prices and availability. Such a scenario is likely to amplify the effects of any macro-economic shock to house price growth such as reduced economic growth, lower job prospects and increasing unemployment.

This scenario looks unnervingly familiar to us, but if we really do have a price bubble, will it burst or will there be a so-called soft landing? Helbling and Terrones (2003) traced asset price booms and busts in the post-war period for 19 industrial countries including Ireland. They state that, in principle, a bubble exists when the price for an asset exceeds its fundamental price by a large margin. Their analysis found that housing price busts were slightly less frequent than equity price crashes, that in 14 countries (including Ireland) where there had been real house price growth between 1970 and 2002 there were 20 housing price crashes recorded compared to 25 equity price crashes. To qualify as a bust, house prices had to contract by 14 per cent in real terms, whereas for equity values the rate was 37 per cent.

Overall, Helbling and Terrones (2003) suggest that their findings correspond roughly to one house price bust in a country every 20 years that will last for about 4 years and involve a price decline of approximately 30 per cent. One in four house price booms will end in bust and these can be highly synchronised across countries, especially in times of recession. Over the period to 2002, housing busts involved much smaller price declines (compared to equities) but the effects on economic output are twice as large and the slowdown after a housing price bust also lasts twice as long. Accordingly, the last big Irish house price boom peaked in the second quarter of 1979, troughed in the first quarter of 1986 and ended in a bust. It took four years for a subsequent price recovery to occur. House prices then peaked in the third quarter of 1990 only to trough in the second quarter of 1991, peak in quarter one of 1992 and trough again in the first quarter of 1993. There was no house price bust in the early 1990s. However, the price boom ongoing since then is unprecedented and means that Ireland will be heading close to 20 years since the last bust in 1986, at a rate of house price inflation that is the highest on record.

Conclusion

The rewards of accessing home ownership in straightforward economic terms continue to be very positive. The rate of return on property (via capital gains and rents) is high while the cost of borrowing is low. Additionally, the fiscal treatment of housing as an asset in Ireland is favourable, not punitive. There is no tax on imputed income and there is an absence of generalised taxation on ownership of multiple properties or of local taxation of housing to pay for services. Access to mortgage credit is now easier than before and the lending institutions operate increasingly flexible lending criteria as well as supplying new equity release schemes to established mortgaged housing. These products allow funds to be used to purchase and invest in new housing for the household or for a family member – as well as to purchase other consumer items or durables such as foreign holidays or new cars. This is the real wealth effect of being in a position of ownership of housing in Ireland.

Now however the risks of home ownership are also greater than before. There is a risk that a price bubble emerges and is spiked. Interruptions to the rates of income growth, over-borrowing and over-indebtedness all pose risks to house price stability and mortgage repayment schedules. Arrears and repossessions would have a downward influence on prices. Wider social penalties abound if, in order to satisfy housing demand, Ireland continues to allow rates of counter-urbanisation and urban sprawl that are unsustainable. It is something of an unenviable trade off for many households with ability to access private housing – locate in a peripheral greenfield development where prices are lower than central urban residential areas, or risk losing their current opportunity to get a foothold in owner occupation due to continued price inflation. The threat of 'access denied' becoming a default response to an individual or household's attempts to enter owner occupation is arguably a greater push to overcome entry barriers by using all available means. Not so much as entry at *all* costs as entry at *any* cost.

Now there also appears the potential threat of a double whammy to new entrants locating in outer urban developments. These new peripheral residential areas, especially those of the Eastern region, may also be adversely affected by any soft landing that brings a supply–demand equilibrium and an end to rampant price inflation, and that in turn triggers a profit take by investors eager to unload property while prices remain positive. If prices are to fall back under such circumstances it will disproportionately affect those areas where development is most recent and mostly speculative, where location is still in its infancy and place making is nascent if underway at all. The 'location, location, location' mantra that describes the economic and social value placed on the residential geography of Irish housing may only ensure that some new housing loses open market value in the foreseeable future while other older housing continues to rise in value.

Lastly, inter-tenure connections are becoming increasingly apparent in the Irish housing system. They may yet transform housing affordability from a house price issue that can temporarily deny access to certain households into an issue of almost permanent exclusion from housing for low-income and poor households with no ability to pay to access owner occupation. The immediate risks of denied access to some aspiring home owners should not appear as equal to the scenario faced by growing numbers of Irish households in housing need, with poor or no effective housing demand who must wait on a laggard system of social housing to play catch-up in terms of output and access. Unmet housing need and the risk of homelessness is the immediate penalty for poor households. Irregular and uncertain access to housing is something familiar to the household on a social housing waiting list. It is now a risk increasingly familiar to the aspiring home owner in Ireland for whom access is denied because housing is unaffordable.

4

Housing Expenditures, Housing Poverty and Housing Wealth: Irish Home Owners in Comparative Context[1]

Tony Fahey and Brian Nolan

Introduction

With the arrival of economic boom in Ireland from 1994 onwards, housing has surfaced both as a social policy and macro-economic concern. The social policy concern is that housing demand, fuelled by rising incomes, low interest rates and demographic growth, has raced ahead of supply and has given rise to house price increases, affordability pressures, unavailability of accommodation for marginal groups, and new inequalities in the distribution of housing assets and housing costs. The macro-economic concern is that housing has become an area of infrastructural deficit which acts as a drag on wider economic expansion.

Our concern here is with the social policy perspective, with reference especially to its bearing on the owner-occupied sector. Our main purpose is to present information which provides a context for present social policy debates about owner-occupied housing. This purpose is prompted by the view that such debates have not been sufficiently informed with knowledge of the details of current housing patterns in Ireland. Given recent concerns about house price rises and consequent pressures on affordability, we focus on the effects of house purchase costs on living standards in the owner-occupied sector, viewed in comparison with other tenures in Ireland and with other EU countries. We assess the implications of household expenditures on house purchase for social inequality, with particular reference to inequalities over the life cycle and across income categories. We also take account of the wealth effects of changing house values. The conclusion draws some policy implications arising from the findings.

Data and Concepts

Data for the paper are drawn from three main sources. The first is the Household Budget Surveys (HBS) carried out in 1973, 1980, 1987, 1994-95 and 1999-2000. This is a rich and under-utilised source of information on many aspects of housing. It enables us to trace the evolution of housing expenditures in Ireland from the early 1970s up to 2000. The second is the European Community Household Panel (ECHP) survey which provides harmonised data on housing expenditures and housing conditions for EU countries. The ECHP is a panel survey carried annually since 1994, though with less than complete coverage of housing variables for all the EU countries in each year (for general details on the ECHP, see Watson 2003). Here we focus on data from the 1996 wave of the ECHP as this wave contains the most comprehensive country coverage of the housing variables (though even in this year one EU country – Sweden – is not included in the data). The third source is the Living in Ireland survey for the year 2000. This is the Irish component of the ECHP but because it is available for a more recent year than the combined ECHP, we draw on it as a separate data source here. It contains information on aspects of Irish housing not covered in other sources, especially in connection with housing assets and housing quality. We also make use of the 1994 Living in Ireland survey for comparative purposes.

The concept of housing expenditures which is central to our analysis is defined in simple terms. In principle it relates to all recurrent direct expenditures which households incur in order to access and sustain their housing accommodation (such as expenditure on maintenance and insurance). In practice, we focus mainly here on expenditures on access and refer only briefly to maintenance and insurance costs. Given that our main interest is in home ownership, we concentrate on mortgage payments by home purchasers, though we set these alongside rent payments by tenants (in both the private and social housing sectors) for comparative purposes. In the case of mortgage payments, no distinction is drawn between the consumption component and the asset acquisition component of expenditures (i.e. between interest payments and repayments of principal). Nor is there any attempt to factor in the opportunity cost of capital as an element of housing costs for home owners. A focus on housing costs rather than housing expenditures would be necessary for many areas of economic and social policy analysis. However, our view here is that much can be learned from a simpler and less data-demanding approach, and that is what is offered here.

Trends in Housing Expenditure

As examined in the Introduction to this volume, the history of tenure patterns over the second half of the twentieth century was dominated by the growth of owner occupation, both in absolute and relative terms. The home-ownership rate rose continuously from the 1940s to the 1980s, but plateaued at just under 80 per cent in the 1990s. This was in a context where the number of occupied housing units almost doubled, from 662,600 in 1946 to almost 1.3 million in 2002. A sharp increase in the use of mortgage financing as a way of accessing housing occurred in the 1970s and 1980s. In 1971, just 22 per cent of Irish households, about 161,000 in number, had mortgages; by 1991, 41 per cent – more than 413,000 households – did so. By 2002, the proportion with mortgages remained at 41 per cent, but the numbers involved had risen to almost 530,000. The heavy reliance on mortgage financing as a way of entering owner occupation is indicated by the fact that of the new homes built for owner occupation between 1988 and 1998, 80 per cent were carrying a mortgage in 1998 (calculated from Table 7, Central Statistics Office 2000).

We now turn to an examination of housing expenditures costs associated with house purchase, focusing on the period covered by Household Budget Survey data, that is, from 1973 to 1999-2000. Table 4.1 below sets out the full data on which this analysis will be based.

Before examining the evolution of mortgage expenditures, both in itself and in comparison to expenditures on rent, it is worth noting briefly how other housing expenditures as recorded in the Household Budget Surveys have changed over this period. Today, the category of 'other housing expenditures' used in Table 4.1 consists mainly of house insurance, repairs and maintenance, and accounts for just under 3 per cent of total household expenditure among home owners (whether with or without a mortgage) and under 1 per cent among social and private renters. These percentages have remained relatively stable since 1981. However, for home owners 'other housing expenditures' showed a substantial fall between 1973 and 1981. This was due to the abolition of domestic rates in 1978, a measure which significantly reduced the burden of housing costs on home owners and eliminated the main form of taxation on residential property which existed at that time. Though a residential property tax was introduced in 1984, it was levied on a much smaller proportion of households than had previously been subject to domestic rates, and in any event was abolished in 1994. Thus, after 1977, taxation of residential property is notable for its absence from housing expenditures for Irish households.

Table 4.1: Trends in Housing Cost Indicators by Housing Tenure, 1973-2000

		1973	1980	1987	1994-95	1999-2000	Per cent change 1973-2000
Outright owner:							
Mortgage payments	€	0	0	0	0	0	0
Other housing expenditures	€	14.93	9.77	14.13	12.31	14.30	-4
Total household expenditure	€	339.61	379.89	352.87	378.77	480.41	41
Mortgage as per cent of total		0	0	0	0	0	0
Other as per cent of total	%	4.40	2.57	4.00	3.25	2.98	-32
Persons per household	No.	3.71	3.42	3.07	2.86	2.68	-28
Tot. equivalised hhold exp.	€	176.32	205.42	201.39	223.97	293.46	66
Owner with mortgage:							
Mortgage payments	€	28.71	45.44	51.78	65.19	73.79	157
Other housing expenditures	€	23.56	15.79	13.00	16.85	22.37	-5
Total household expenditure	€	404.10	577.12	526.59	625.89	767.40	90
Mortgage as per cent of total	%	7.1	7.9	9.8	10.4	9.6	35
Other as per cent of total	%	5.83	2.74	2.47	2.69	2.92	-50
Persons per household	No.	4.56	4.41	4.15	3.95	3.76	-18
Tot. equivalised hhold exp.	€	189.24	274.82	258.49	314.92	395.76	109
Social renters:							
Rent	€	21.55	15.31	14.63	19.10	22.69	5
Other housing expenditures	€	3.09	2.17	2.41	2.58	3.04	-2
Total household expenditure	€	289.31	326.72	252.06	252.63	306.99	6
Rent as per cent of total	%	7.4	4.7	5.8	7.6	7.4	0
Other as per cent of total	%	1.1	0.7	1.0	1.0	1.0	-9
Persons per household	No.	4.89	4.36	3.89	3.44	3.15	-36
Tot. equivalised hhold exp.	€	130.83	156.47	127.80	136.21	172.97	32
Private renters:							
Rent	€	35.14	39.48	45.25	80.26	126.30	259
Other housing expenditures	€	2.75	5.87	6.21	1.53	4.97	81
Total household expenditure	€	280.54	372.00	360.98	423.72	601.93	115
Rent as per cent of total	%	12.5	10.6	12.5	18.9	21.0	68
Other as per cent of total	%	1.0	1.6	1.7	0.4	0.8	-20
Persons per household	No.	3.02	2.40	2.45	2.45	2.66	-12
Tot. equivalised hhold exp.	€	161.43	240.12	230.62	270.70	369.07	129

Sources: Central Statistics Office, 1977, 1984, 1989, 1997, 2001a
Note: Prices are expressed in constant 2000 terms (CPI deflator). 'Other housing expenditures' consist of local authority charges, house insurance, repairs and

decorations. Domestic rates are included in other housing expenditures for owners (with and without mortgages) in 1973. Rates were abolished in 1977 and do not figure in the data subsequently. Total equivalised household expenditure = total household expenditure divided by the square root of the number of persons per household.

Total Household Expenditure

Figure 4.1 places changing levels of rent and mortgage payments for Irish households since 1973 in context by outlining the growth in households' total current financial resources. Total household expenditure (expressed in constant euros at 2000 prices) is the measure of financial resources used here (this measure is used in preference to household income since it is available from the HBS and is usually regarded as less liable to under-reporting in survey data). The graph shows that following a marked real increase in household expenditure during the 1970s, a slight decline set in during the 1980s, followed by a strong and sustained recovery after 1987.

Figure 4.1: Total Weekly Household Expenditure by Housing Tenure, 1973-2000

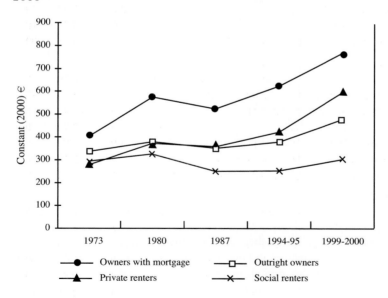

Source: Table 4.1

The overall effect was that, in general, real household expenditure grew substantially over the period 1973 to 1999-2000. The level of growth differed sharply by tenure, ranging from a 115 per cent increase among private renters to a 6 per cent increase among social renters. In consequence, inequalities in household expenditure widened dramatically across tenures. In 1973, for example, household expenditure among owners with a mortgage was 1.4 times that of social renters, while by 1999-2000, it was 2.5 times that of social renters. Private renters improved their relative position especially dramatically. In 1973, their household expenditure was lowest of all the tenure categories, marginally below that of social renters. By 1999-2000, it had risen to almost double that of social renters and was also substantially higher than that of outright owners.

Figure 4.2. Total Weekly Equivalised Household Expenditure by Housing Tenure, 1973-2000

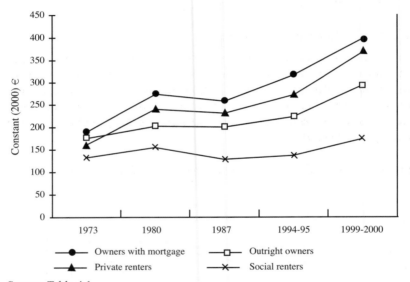

Source: Table 4.1
Note: Equivalised household expenditure = household expenditure/square root of household size.

Household expenditure data on their own tell only part of the story since they do not take account of changes in household size. As household size generally tended to decline over this period, increases in individual consumption were even greater than gross household expenditure trends would suggest. In addition, decline in household size was unevenly spread across the tenures: the decline was smallest among private renters and largest among social renters. In consequence, if one adjusts household expenditure to take account of household size (to arrive at 'equivalised' household expenditure), somewhat different comparative rates of increase in expenditure emerge across tenures (Table 4.2

and Figure 4.2; the adjustment for household size used here is arrived at by dividing total household expenditure by the square root of the number of persons in the household). The relative position of social renters is most affected by this adjustment as they had the largest decline (36 per cent) in household size over the period. Where they register an increase of only 6 per cent in non-equivalised household expenditure over the period 1973-2000, they register a 32 per cent increase in equivalised household expenditure. Private renters register an increase of 129 per cent in equivalised household expenditure compared to a non-equivalised increase of 115 per cent. Viewed in these terms, the widening of inequalities in equivalised household expenditure between tenure categories is still present and is quite strong but is somewhat less extreme than it appears when non-equivalised household income is looked at.

Expenditure on Mortgages and Rents

We now come to trends in mortgage and rent expenditures over time. Since outright owners have no such expenditures, the comparisons across tenures reduce to three categories – owners with a mortgage (who have mortgage expenditures) and both private and social renters (who have rent expenditures). Figure 4.3 shows the trend in absolute real mortgage/rent expenditures for these three categories since 1973.

Figure 4.3: Weekly Rent/Mortgage Payments by Housing Tenure, 1973-2000

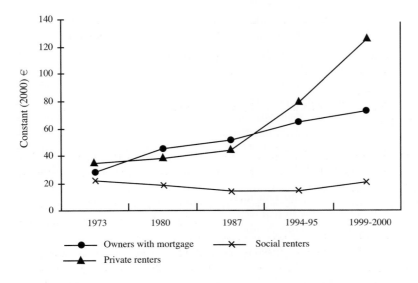

Source: Table 4.1

The most striking change occurred not among home purchasers but among private renters. Their rent expenditures increased only slightly between 1973 and 1987 but thenceforth rose sharply. By 1999-2000, private rents (at an average of €126 per week) were 2.8 times greater than they had been in 1987 (when they had averaged €45 per week in constant 2000 money terms). It is notable here that this rapid increase was well underway in advance of the housing shortage and house price boom which occurred from 1994 onwards. It did, however, coincide with the expansion of the SWA rent allowance scheme referred to earlier. It is beyond our scope here to try to assess whether or to what degree the availability of rent allowances contributed to these rent rises (and there probably was a circular element to the causality in that rising rents caused rent allowances to grow). Aggregating up from Household Budget Survey data, we can estimate that the total annual rent bill for private tenants in 1999 was of the order of €719 million. Annual public expenditure on rent allowances in 1999 was just under €130 million (£100.5 million), which was about 18 per cent of the total rent bill. Thus, had rent allowances been entirely absent, the total available to tenants to pay private rents would have declined by one-fifth at most (and possibly by less if tenants were able to provide replacement funds from other sources, including their own resources). In consequence, it would seem that rent allowances represented too small a share of the total private rent bill to be seen as a major *direct* cause of rent rises. This is not to rule out the possibility of indirect effects, such as, for example, might arise from an incentive effect on young adults to leave home and set up independent households in private rented accommodation who otherwise would have continued to live with their parents. Nevertheless, one would hesitate to attribute anything more than a secondary role to SWA rent allowances as a causal influence on the rapid increases in private rents during the 1990s.

Owners with a mortgage also registered an increase (in this case in connection with mortgage payments) but the increase was smaller and more evenly spread over time than was the case for private renters. It is not notable that the upward trend was not intensified by the house price boom after 1994-95. In fact the increase between 1994-95 and 1999-2000 (at €9 per week, or 13.8 per cent) was *less* than it was in the period between 1987 and 1994-95 (€13 per week, or 25 per cent).

Among social renters, no real increase occurred – average social housing rents were about the same in real terms in 1999-2000 as they had been in 1973, and in fact had fallen considerably below those levels in the intervening decades.

Figure 4.4 shows the trend in rent/mortgage payments as a percentage of total household expenditure. Here again, the most striking changes are seen to have

occurred among private renters. The share of their total household expenditure
going on rent fell between 1973 and 1980 and rose back to the levels of 1973
by 1987. It then experienced a rapid increase, rising from 12.5 per cent of
household expenditure in 1987 to 18.9 per cent in 1994-95 and then to 21 per
cent by 1999-2000.

*Figure 4.4: Weekly/Rent Mortgage Payments as a Percentage of Total
Housing Expenditure, 1973-2000*

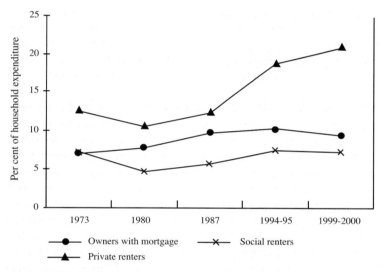

Source: Table 4.1

Among owners with a mortgage, the share of household expenditure absorbed
by mortgage payments rose during the 1970s and 1980s. However, echoing the
disjunction with house price trends noted above, this share peaked at 10.4 per
cent in 1994-95 and thenceforth fell slightly, declining to 9.6 per cent by 1999-
2000. It is worth comparing the shape of this trend with two trends which curves
represent the dominant influences on mortgage payment levels, namely interest
rates (Figure 4.5) and house price increases (Figure 4.6). This comparison
suggests that the trend for mortgage expenditures over time is closer in shape to
that for real interest rates than for house price rises. In particular, the peaking in
mortgage payments as a percentage of household expenditure in 1994-95
coincided with a peak in real interest rates at that time, while its subsequent
slight fall-off followed a fall in interest rates and ran directly counter to the
boom in house prices. These overall trends and influences on mortgage
payments undoubtedly mask sharply different experiences for different

categories of mortgage holders, particularly as between new entrants to the housing market and those with older mortgages, but nevertheless the relatively slight impact of recent house price rises on overall housing expenditures is striking.

Figure 4.5: Mortgage Interest Rates and Inflation (Consumer Price Index), 1965-2001

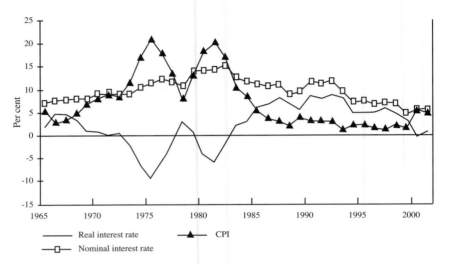

Sources: National Economic and Social Council 1977, p. 94; Central Bank of Ireland Quarterly Bulletin (various); and data supplied by the Central Statistics Office.

Social renters experienced the most favourable trend in housing expenditures over the period. For them, the share of household expenditure going on rent declined sharply during the 1970s, falling below 5 per cent in 1980. Thenceforth, it rose slowly to peak at 7.6 per cent in 1994-95 and showed a marginal decline (to 7.4 per cent) in 1999-2000. The overall trend was such that the share of household expenditure going on rent among social renters was the same in 1999-2000 as it had been in 1973.

Figure 4.6: Trends in House Prices, 1970-2000

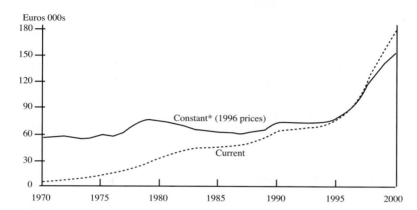

* Adjusted by Consumer Price Index. The price series makes no adjustment for quality and includes both new and second-hand house prices
Sources: Department of the Environment, Heritage and Local Government (various years), and data supplied by the Central Statistics Office.

European Comparisons
We now attempt to locate Irish housing expenditures in international perspective by means of comparisons of tenure patterns and housing expenditures across 14 EU countries in 1996. As mentioned earlier, the data used here are drawn from the 1996 ECHP.

As in our account of the Irish case on its own, the first step is to obtain an overview of tenure patterns in the countries concerned. As Table 4.2 shows, Ireland, along with Spain, had the highest level of home ownership in the EU as it was in 1996. However, if we focus on the percentage of homes that are owned outright, the Irish position, at 42 per cent, was fifth in the table, below the four southern European countries (Greece, Spain, Italy and Portugal). As a counterpart to this, the Irish percentage of homes owned with a mortgage was fourth highest in the table, below Denmark, the Netherlands and the UK. An alternative measure of the significance of mortgage holding is given by the data on aggregate residential mortgage debt in each country as a percentage of GDP. Again, this shows Ireland occupying something close to a middle position for EU countries. The countries with the highest burden of mortgage debt – Denmark and the Netherlands – have low levels of overall home ownership but reasonably high levels of ownership with a mortgage compared to other countries.

Table 4.3 gives details on housing expenditures (i.e. monthly rent and mortgage payments) as a share of net household income across the 14 EU countries, referring mainly to 1996 but including updated data for Ireland in 2000. This table shows that, averaged out over all households (row 1), the level of housing expenditures in the EU varied widely, lying below 7 per cent in the southern European countries (Italy, Greece, Spain and Portugal) and above 20 per cent in Denmark and the Netherlands. In the case of Ireland, the data included from the LII 2000 show that, allowing for measurement and sampling error, the differences in expenditure levels between 1996 and 2000 are slight. This confirms the picture for Ireland of stability in mortgage payments as a share of household expenditure which was drawn from Household Budget Survey (HBS) data just outlined, though it understates the rise in rents which emerged strongly from HBS data.

Table 4.2: Tenure Patterns and Mortgage Debt in 14 European Union Countries

	All	Owner With mortgage	Owner Without mortgage	Social renter	Private renter	Rent free	Residential mortgage debt as % of GDP, 1998
			% of households				
Spain	80.8	18.8	62.1	0.8	12.0	6.4	24
Ireland	80.3	38.1	42.3	11.0	6.4	2.2	33*
Greece	75.9	7.0	68.9	0.2	21.0	2.9	7
Italy	73.2	10.9	62.3	5.7	13.4	7.6	8
Belgium	73.2	32.2	40.9	7.0	17.3	2.5	25
Lu'bourg	70.1	35.5	34.6	2.9	23.6	3.4	
UK	68.3	41.5	26.8	23.1	6.9	1.7	57
Portugal	66.3	14.4	51.9	3.7	20.1	9.9	35
Finland	64.5	27.4	37.2	17.0	16.2	2.3	30
France	53.3	24.4	29.0	16.8	24.1	5.8	21
Denmark	52.5	45.5	7.1	27.5	19.4	0.6	69
Austria	50.4	20.0	30.4	19.9	23.0	6.7	5
Netherlands	49.0	41.7	7.3	42.1	7.8	1.1	65
Germany	40.2	18.6	21.6	12.5	43.2	4.1	53

Source: ECHP 1996, OECD 2001/European Mortgage Federation.

Table 4.3: Housing Expenditures (Rent and Mortgage) for Households in 14 European Union Countries, 1996

Mean rent/mortgage expenditure as % of net monthly income:	Ger	Dk	Nl	Be	Lu	Fr	UK	Irl 1996	Irl 2000	It	Gr	Sp	Pt	Au	Fin
1 For all households	19	26	23	13	14	17	18	9	8	7	7	7	6	12	19
2 Excluding those with no housing costs	25	28	25	22	22	27	26	17	15	23	24	21	16	19	32
3 For owners with mortgage	22	23	22	21	22	23	18	18	14	24	11	24	24	15	26
4 For renters	26	33	27	24	23	29	37	15	17	22	28	17	12	20	36
5 – private renters	26	30	26	26	24	29	34	24	24	24	28	18	14	21	36
6 – social renters	25	36	27	20	15	28	38	10	9	16	19	8	3	19	37
7 For owners with mortgage, age-group 25-39	26	26	23	23	23	27	20	24		24	28	21	22	20	33

Sources: European Community Household Panel 1996; Living in Ireland Survey 2000.

As Figure 4.7 shows, the level of housing expenditures across countries is strongly influenced by the proportion of households who own their homes outright, that is, by the proportion who have zero housing expenditures in our present terms. Ireland's position in this graph as far as housing expenditures are concerned is close to what would be predicted by its level of outright home ownership.

However, even if we discount those with zero rent/mortgage expenditures, it emerges from Table 4.3 (row 2) that rent/mortgage expenditures averaged out over those who have such expenditures were still relatively low in Ireland in 1996 and remained so up to 2000. Indeed, at 16.7 per cent of net income, they were almost the lowest in the EU (only Portugal was lower at 16.4 per cent). This lowness arose in part because mortgage payments among owners with a mortgage, relative to household income, were reasonably small by EU standards (row 3). Another significant contributor was the low level of rents for social renters (row 6) – at 9.5 per cent of income, these are well below the level for most EU countries, particularly those such as the UK, Denmark and the Netherlands with large social housing sectors. Only in the case of private renters did housing expenditures in Ireland, at 24.3 per cent of private renters' income, close the gap with most other countries in the EU.

Figure 4.7: Relationship Between Outright Home Ownership Rates and Average Housing Expenditures by Country in the European Union, 1996

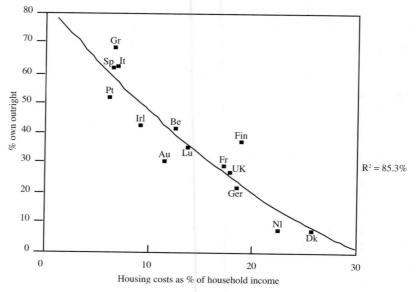

Source: Tables 4.1 and 4.2.

Note: refers only to those countries which were EU members in 1996.

It is also worth noting from Table 4.3 that a large social housing sector does not imply lower housing expenditures. In fact, the three countries with the largest social housing sectors – Netherlands, the UK, and Denmark – also have particularly high rent expenditures for social housing tenants (row 6). Furthermore, social and private rents track each other closely – where one is high, so is the other. Finally, in most countries (Spain and Portugal being the only two exceptions) mortgage payments cost less, relative to household income, than do private rents (rows 3 and 5, Table 4.3). This point is significant since house purchase is normally thought to cost more than private renting: it entails both asset acquisition (represented by repayment of mortgage principal) as well as 'rent' for the use of capital (represented by interest payments), where tenants pay rent only. Yet, the most common situation in the EU (including Ireland) is that tenants in the private sector pay a larger share of their income on rent than purchasers do on mortgage payments.

Punch's chapter in this volume refers to the important role of SWA rent allowances in private rental housing in Ireland. This leads on to a question about the comparative significance of housing allowances expenditures across Europe. In most countries, housing allowances include state cash payments for both rents and mortgage repayments (as is the case in Ireland, though mortgage allowances are much less significant in Ireland than rent allowances). Table 4.4 indicates that housing allowances exist in all the 14 countries but vary widely in significance. They are received by 1 per cent or less of households in Belgium, Luxembourg, Italy, Greece, Spain and Portugal but by about one-fifth of households in Denmark, France, the UK and Finland. They are particularly important for renters in the UK, of whom over half receive housing allowances and for whom housing allowances account for over a quarter of household income. Similar proportions of tenants in Finland receive housing allowances, but the level of payments involved are much smaller, accounting for about one-eighth of household income for recipients on average. France and Denmark are two other countries where housing allowances are widely received by tenants.

Housing Expenditures and Affordability

We have already seen that, overall, expenditures on house purchase by Irish households are moderate by EU standards, even taking account of the large house price increases of the second half of the 1990s. However, this overall low spend is an average of different experiences for different tenure categories and possibly also for different sub-groups within tenure categories. An obvious contrast in this regard arises between outright owners and social renters on the one hand (who have either zero or uniformly low rent/mortgage expenditures) and owners with a mortgage and private renters on the other hand (who have higher and differentiated levels of housing expenditures). Focusing on the latter

Table 4.4: Housing Allowances: Households in Receipt and Significance for Household Income in 14 European Union Countries, 1996

	Ger	Dk	Nl	Be	Lu	Fr	UK	Irl	It	Gr	Sp	Pt	Au	Fin
% of households in receipt:														
per cent all households	4.2	21.8	6.1	0.8	12.9	20.4	17.0	1.7	0.6	0.9	1.0	0.3	5.4	22.3
per cent owners	1.4	3.9	2.4	0.5	17.3	8.3	2.1	0.4	0.6	0.3	0.7	0.2	5.3	6.7
per cent renters	6.5	42.2	9.9	2.0	3.3	38.7	52.4	8.0	0.7	2.9	3.8	1.0	6.3	53.9
Housing allowances as % of net annual income:														
– for all recipients	11.4	12.8	10.0	8.6	5.4	10.0	26.6	18.0	13.1	6.6	10.3	14.0	6.6	12.1
– for owner recipients	5.0	6.3	6.9	1.9	5.2	6.4	15.5	7.7	11.1	3.0	8.3	2.5	2.6	5.5
– for renter recipients	12.4	13.4	10.8	13.4	8.7	11.0	27.6	20.2	19.8	8.0	12.5	19.5	10.5	13.6
– private renters	12.2	10.7	5.0	24.9	15.2	11.3	33.0	20.2	16.7	7.9	13.0	19.5	11.6	14.7
– public renters	12.1	14.4	11.0	8.8	7.1	10.7	26.8		26.0	9.7	3.8		9.9	13.1

Source: European Consumer Household Panel 1996.

two groups, one means of identifying those who are likely to be suffering affordability pressures is to specify an affordability threshold for rent and mortgage expenditures and count the numbers above that threshold. Affordability thresholds as defined in housing policy in a number of countries are usually in the range 25-30 per cent of gross household income, though the precise income concept used varies and the types of households defined as liable to affordability pressures are usually limited to those on the lower reaches of the income ladder (see Landt and Bray 1997 for the approaches used in Australia, the United States and Canada). Here we focus on 35 per cent of household expenditure as a relevant threshold as it echoes the threshold of 35 per cent of net household income used to define eligibility for 'affordable housing' in recent legislation (cf. Planning and Development Act, 2000).

Figure 4.8: Percentage of Owners with Mortgage and Private Renters who have High* Mortgage/Rent Expenditures

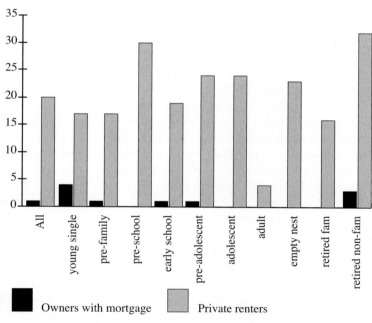

* High = 35 per cent of household expenditure or higher
Source: Household Budget Survey 1999-2000 microdata

Figure 4.8 shows the proportions of owners with a mortgage and private renters whose rent or mortgage expenditures are 35 per cent of household expenditure or higher. The classification by family cycle stage is introduced in this graph to help identify those house purchasers likely to be recent entrants into the housing market and thus most likely to have high mortgage expenditures. As we might have expected from data already looked at, private renters are far more likely than home purchasers to exceed the affordability threshold defined here. In 1999-2000, 20 per cent of private renters had housing expenditures above the affordability threshold, compared to 1 per cent of house purchasers. In absolute terms, this equates to approximately 20-25,000 private rented households compared to approximately 4-5,000 owners with a mortgage. Looking at the proportions above the threshold across the stages of the family cycle, owners with a mortgage who were in the earliest stage of the cycle (households headed by a young single person) had a higher proportion exceeding the affordability threshold than those in most other stages, but even this proportion amounted only to 4 per cent and was far below the level of both private renters as a whole and of private renters in the young single family cycle stage. (The numbers of both private renters and mortgage holders who were in the later stages of the family cycle were small, so that the affordability measures in Figure 4.8 are based on small sample numbers and should be interpreted with caution.)

Housing Expenditures by Life Cycle Stage

We now turn to a closer examination of the distributional consequences of housing expenditures in Ireland. To do so, we first look at the distribution across the life cycle, relying on the Household Budget Survey data. Table 4.5 shows the way housing expenditures vary across stages of the life cycle, using a 10-category grouping of households from 'young single' through to 'retired'. We see that rent or mortgage expenditures as a percentage of total household expenditure are at their peak in the young single stage, at 17 per cent. The burden remains significant in the 'married pre-family', 'pre-school' and 'early school' stages, at 11 to 13 per cent of total expenditure, but then declines quite rapidly and is only 6 per cent for the 'adolescent' stage, falling as low as 1 per cent for those in the 'retired' stage. This pattern reflects first of all the fact that private renting is much more common in the 'young single' stage than subsequently, with almost half those households in that tenure. Owner occupation is much more common among the 'married pre-family' and early school stages, but at least 60 per cent have a mortgage and these spend about 15 per cent of their total expenditure on mortgage repayments. Moving through the other stages, the proportion of outright owners rises and even among those who do have mortgage debt repayments constitutes a declining proportion of total expenditure. So stage in the life cycle is a critical influence on housing expenditures.

Table 4.5: Housing Expenditure by Family Cycle Stage, 1994

					Family cycle stage					
	Young single	Married pre-family	Pre-school	Early school	Pre-adolescent	Adolescent	Adult	Empty nest	Retired family	Retired non-fam
Mean age of reference person (years)	30.2	33.3	32.0	35.4	40.0	46.4	47.5	60.4	73.9	74.5
per cent of population	4.1	2.4	7	11.3	14.9	23.5	25.4	3.9	3.1	4.4
Rent/mortgage as % of household expenditure	16.69	13.70	13.05	10.77	8.47	5.65	2.51	3.37	0.96	4.10
Tenure: % own outright	21	13.7	14.8	17.4	26.9	35.7	55.9	63.3	86.8	74.5
% own with mortgage	20.8	67.7	61.5	60.7	54.5	50.1	34.1	26.3	7.5	4.3
% public rent	4.7	2.3	10	17.1	14.9	12.4	7.9	5.3	3.1	13.4
% private rent	48.2	14.5	11.8	4.3	2.7	1.5	1.8	3.5	1.8	3.9
Owners with mortgage:										
Mortgage payments as % of household expend.	19.3	15.1	15.8	13.8	12.2	9.1	5.7	7.9	6.7	9.0
Weekly amounts (€)	74.22	82.39	80.05	71.50	59.54	49.97	35.67	31.15	17.05	14.20

Source: Household Budget Survey 1994-95 micro-data.

Family cycle definitions: *Young single* – household head aged under 45, no children; *Married pre-family* – couple, wife aged under 45, no children; *Pre-school* – head with eldest resident child (ERC) aged 0-4 years; *Early school* – head with ERC aged 5-9 years; *Preadolescent* – head with ERC aged 10-14; *Adolescent* – head with ERC aged 15-19 years; *Adult* – head with ERC aged 20 years plus; *Empty nest* – couple, wife aged 45-64, no resident children; *Retired family* – couple, wife aged 65 years plus, no resident children; *Retired non-family* – head aged 65 years plus, no resident spouse or children

Housing Expenditures and Poverty

Housing expenditures could clearly have major implications for a household's living standards and whether it experiences poverty. At a given income level, a household expending one-quarter of its income on housing expenditures will be in a very different situation to one facing little or no housing cost. The outright home-owner avoids rent and mortgage payments entirely, and needs less income to achieve a given standard of consumption than those who have rent or mortgages to pay. Thus the distribution of housing tenure and housing expenditures may well have a direct impact on social inequalities in terms of current living standards and the risk of poverty in particular (see also Fahey *et al,* 2004a; Fahey, 2003). This section seeks to assess the scale and patterning of that impact on poverty. The more indirect but important relationship between social inequalities and housing in terms of wealth-holding will be explored in the next section. For both purposes we now employ data from the Living in Ireland household surveys carried out by the ESRI, rather than the Household Budget Survey. The Living in Ireland surveys have provided the basis for regular monitoring of the extent and nature of poverty, so it is helpful to start from that base in assessing the role of housing expenditures, while they also obtained information on house values and mortgages which allow for analysis of housing wealth.

The most commonly employed measure of poverty in developed countries is based on comparison of household income with an income threshold, often derived as a proportion of average income in the country in question. An indication of the likely impact of differing housing expenditures on the risk of poverty can be got by employing this approach, but using income after housing expenditures have been incurred – that is, income net of housing costs. In this approach the term 'housing cost' is widely used to refer to housing expenditures, even though, strictly speaking, the terms 'cost' and 'expenditure' are usually used to refer to somewhat different concepts; in this section of the paper, we use the term 'housing costs' where elsewhere we use the more accurate term 'housing expenditure' (for a full conceptual discussion, see Fahey *et al*, 2004b). This is done in Table 4.6, distinguishing different tenure types. The 'before housing costs' figure is the relative income poverty rate as conventionally calculated, the percentage of households with (equivalised) disposable incomes below 60 per cent of median equivalised disposable income in the sample.[2] The 'after housing costs' poverty rate is arrived at by subtracting rent/mortgage costs from household incomes, recalculating the 60 per cent of median poverty line, and seeing which households now have incomes less their housing cost below this new threshold.

Table 4.6: Percentage of Persons Below 60 per cent of Median Income Before and After Housing Costs by Tenure, LII Survey 2000

Tenure	Poverty rate (% below 60 per cent of median income)	
	Before housing costs	After housing costs
Owner of private housing without mortgage	24.3	19.7
Owner of private housing with mortgage	11.4	13.0
Owner of (former) public housing with no mortgage	27.8	21.4
Owner of (former) public housing with mortgage	22.5	24.6
Renter of private housing	19.2	27.5
Renter of public housing	62.2	60.8
All households	22.1	21.3

Looking first at the relative income poverty rate as conventionally measured, i.e. before housing costs, we see that this varies substantially across tenure types. The poverty rate is lowest for those in private housing and paying a mortgage, at only 11 per cent – half the figure for the sample as a whole. About one-quarter of those in houses owned outright are below the 60 per cent threshold, with little difference between those in houses purchased from local authorities versus privately. Turning to those in rented housing, there is a very sharp divergence between those renting private sector housing, where about one in five are below the threshold, and those renting in the public sector where the figure is not far short of two-thirds. So private sector renters do not seem at higher risk than the average, but public sectors renters certainly do – and it is relatively to public but not private renters that owner-occupiers appear advantaged.

Those poverty rates take no account of differences across the groups in the housing costs they incur. Simply subtracting housing costs from income and assessing living standards and poverty status in terms of 'income after housing costs' is undoubtedly a crude approach, since it ignores the fact that people on a similar income may simply make different choices about how much to spend on housing versus other goods and services: higher housing costs may be associated with higher quality housing. However, it does give some indication of the potential scale of the overall impact of housing costs on poverty and how different types of household are affected. For this reason, the UK for example regularly produces such statistics on the numbers below average income both before and after housing costs – in effect assuming that neither gives the full picture and that the truth probably lies somewhere in between.

We see from Table 4.6 that taking housing costs into account in this way makes very little difference to the overall number falling below the relative income threshold. This corresponds to the results of a similar 'before versus after housing costs' comparison carried out with data from the household survey undertaken by the ESRI in 1987 and reported in Callan *et al* (1989). The gap between overall relative income poverty rates before and after housing costs is by contrast substantial in Britain, with the after housing costs figure (with the 60 per cent of median threshold) as much as six percentage points higher than the more conventional before housing costs measure (United Kingdom, Department of Work and Pensions 2002). This reflects in particular the much greater importance of housing-related transfers in the UK, and helps explain the prominence given to the issue and to the treatment of housing costs in measuring poverty there. Housing-related social security transfers account for almost one-quarter of total social security spending in Britain, compared with about 3 per cent in Ireland. Including such benefits in household income while taking no account of corresponding housing costs, as conventional in measuring poverty elsewhere, is thus seen as particularly problematic in the UK.

Returning to Table 4.6 we also see that focusing on income after housing costs makes little difference to the very high poverty rate of public renters, which is still over 60 per cent. This is unsurprising given that we saw earlier that housing costs are in fact relatively low for that group. The fact that their poverty risk is so much higher than other households is attributable to their socio-economic and demographic profile, and indeed to the fact that it is disadvantaged households which are likely to find themselves in an increasingly residualised public rented sector. The differences between the other tenure categories in relative income poverty rates are however somewhat reduced when we focus on income after housing costs. As might be expected, the largest impact is on private renters since housing costs account for such a large share of their incomes: their poverty rate rises from 19 to 28 per cent. The absence of housing costs means the position of outright owners (both of private and formerly public housing) improves, and they now have about 20 per cent below the relative income threshold. On the other hand the poverty rate rises for those in owner-occupied housing with a mortgage, but this impact turns out to be marginal for those in private housing. Their poverty rate goes up by only 1.5 percentage points and at 13 per cent is still well below average. While this group has significant housing costs, most are clearly not on incomes in the vicinity of the 60 per cent threshold, so the shift from income before to after housing costs makes little difference to their poverty rate.

Shifting from before to after housing costs thus makes effectively no difference to the overall numbers falling below relative income poverty lines, and has quite a limited impact on the pattern of risk across tenure categories – which is where we would expect any impact to be most obvious. It is not surprising then to find that the effect on the variation in risk across types of households distinguished in other ways, notably by household composition type or labour force status, is also quite limited. This can be seen by comparing income poverty risk after housing costs by household composition type and labour force status with the corresponding figures using income before housing costs presented in Nolan *et al* (2003). The profile of poverty risk is generally very similar. However, focusing on income after housing costs does produce an increase in income poverty risk for certain groups, notably lone parent households (53 per cent versus 47 per cent) and those headed by an unemployed person (54 per cent versus 51 per cent). On the other hand that risk falls for households comprising two adults with no children (20 per cent versus 26 per cent) and those headed by a retired person (27 per cent versus 33 per cent).

Perhaps the most striking difference is in the position of the elderly. Table 4.7 shows that there is little difference in the proportion of children of working-age adults falling below the income threshold before or after housing costs. The percentage of persons aged 65 or more below such a threshold is however 34 per cent using the income after housing costs, compared with 43 per cent with the conventional income measure. With women having a higher probability of being in that situation than men, this means that the percentage of women aged 65 or over below the income threshold falls from 49 per cent before housing costs to 41 per cent after housing costs.

Table 4.7: Percentage of Persons Below 60 per cent Median Income Poverty Line Before and After Housing Costs by Age, Living in Ireland Survey 2000

	Before housing costs %	After housing costs %
Adults	21.0	19.7
Aged 18-64	16.9	17.1
Aged 65 or more	43.3	33.9
Children (aged under 18)	24.9	25.5

These changes in risk profile reflect the composition of the groups who are below the income threshold after housing costs but above it before housing costs and vice versa, which comprise 7 per cent and 8 per cent of persons below these lines respectively. If we focus on those who are below after but not before housing costs as a group which might be 'missed' by conventional income poverty measures, they are predominantly young (71 per cent are in households where the reference person is aged 35 or less and only 2 per cent in ones where he or she is aged 65 or over), and in the work force rather than retired. About one in three of this group are in rented accommodation, well above the national average, but this still means that two-thirds are owner-occupiers with mortgage costs.

Support for the notion that this group should not be ignored is provided by their subjective assessments of their housing costs. Households in the survey were asked whether they would say that their total housing costs – rent, mortgage, repairs, and utilities – were 'a heavy burden', 'somewhat of a burden' or 'no burden at all'. We can first contrast the households above the 60 per cent relative income threshold both before and after housing costs, where only 12 per cent said these costs were a heavy burden, with those below that threshold both before and after housing, where 28 per cent gave that response. Against that background we find that 16 per cent of those below the threshold before but above it after housing costs said they represented a heavy burden, whereas more than one-third of those below the threshold after housing costs but above it before gave that response.

At least some of the latter do clearly face particular problems in relation to housing costs, and we can see the extent to which this has an impact on their capacity to meet other needs by using direct information on deprivation levels also obtained in the Living in Ireland surveys. We focus at this stage on items such as a telephone, a car, central heating, leisure activities, and an annual holiday – a set of nine items capturing what in previous work we have labelled 'secondary deprivation' (see Nolan and Whelan 1996 for a detailed discussion). The mean score on a summary deprivation scale based on these items of the group below the 60 per cent income threshold after but not before housing costs, at 0.64, is almost as high as the 0.70 seen for those below the threshold both before and after housing costs. Those below before but not after these costs, by contrast, have a lower mean score of 0.41.

Table 4.8 reveals, however, that among all those falling below the 60 per cent income threshold after deducting housing costs the reported levels of secondary deprivation vary substantially by tenure. We see that, among this group as a whole, the position of owner-occupiers of private housing – whether with or without mortgages to service – is relatively favourable. Their mean secondary deprivation scores are only half those of households who have purchased or are purchasing local authority housing. Those currently renting local authority housing have mean scores that are much higher again, but the really distinctive group are those in private sector rental housing. Their mean deprivation score, at almost 1.9, is about five times that of the owner occupiers below the income threshold.

These results firmly point our attention towards those on low income in private rented accommodation as a group to be concerned about. They also serve to illustrate the more general points that we have emphasised repeatedly in previous work, about the hazards of relying on income on its own in measuring poverty and the value of taking directly-observed levels of deprivation into account. Poverty is widely conceptualised in terms of exclusion from the life of society due to lack of resources, and so involves various forms of what that society would regard as serious deprivation (Townsend 1970). A definition of poverty in these terms has been enshrined in the National Anti-Poverty Strategy (Government of Ireland, 1997a, 2003a). Simply seeing that someone is below a relative income poverty line is not enough to be sure he/she is experiencing such deprivation, as is clear from analyses of data for Ireland (see especially Nolan and Whelan, 1996) and other EU countries (Whelan *et al*, 2001; Layte *et al*, 2001). In that context direct non-monetary measures of deprivation can provide a valuable complementary source of information. A measure of poverty developed at the ESRI identifies those both below relative income poverty lines and experiencing 'basic' deprivation – in terms of a set of items including inability to afford items relating to food, clothing and heating – as experiencing generalised deprivation due to lack of resources. This 'consistent' poverty measure provides the basis for the global poverty reduction target in the National Anti-Poverty Strategy.

Table 4.8: Mean Secondary Deprivation Score for Persons Below 60 per cent Median Income Poverty Line After Housing Costs by Tenure, Living in Ireland Survey 2000

Tenure	Mean
Owner occupier without mortgage	0.36
Owner occupier with mortgage	0.31
Local authority tenant purchaser without mortgage	0.66
Local authority tenant purchaser with mortgage	0.64
Local authority renter	1.19
Private renter	1.87

It is therefore of interest to also look at whether taking housing costs directly into account makes any difference to the extent or profile of poverty using this measure. The percentage of persons in consistent poverty, that is below 70 per cent of median equivalised disposable income and experiencing basic deprivation, was 5.5 per cent in the 2000 Living in Ireland Survey. If we replace the income element of this measure by income after housing costs, that figure turns out to be almost identical at 5.7 per cent. The impact on the risk profile of different types of households and persons is then unsurprisingly also very small. The risk for those aged 65 or over does decline once again, but only from 6.6 per cent to 6 per cent, with the figure for elderly women falling from 8.5 per cent to 7.5 per cent. The position of large families and households headed by an employee correspondingly worsen slightly. Overall, though, taking housing costs into account in this way has even less impact on the consistent poverty measure than on measures based on income alone. This is hardly surprising, since the non-monetary deprivation indicators element of the consistent poverty measure should itself help to capture situations where particularly high housing costs leave households unable to meet basic needs in other areas.

The Distribution of Housing Wealth

We now turn from poverty to the broader question of the impact of home ownership and escalating house prices in Ireland on the distribution of wealth. Once again we rely on data from the Living in Ireland Survey, which is particularly valuable in that it seeks *inter alia* the respondent's (and the survey interviewer's) estimate of the market value of the house, as well as information about the mortgage, if any, which allows the level of debt outstanding to be estimated. This means that both the gross value of the housing asset and its net value after deducting housing debt can be derived. A detailed discussion of what is involved in deriving such estimates and of results relating to 1987 is given in Nolan (1991), which also looks at other forms of wealth-holding along with housing. Here, however, our focus is solely on housing.

We first present some results based on the 2000 Living in Ireland Survey, to give an up-to-date picture of current patterns of wealth holding in the form of housing. We use the household as the unit of analysis. About 78 per cent of all households in that survey had some *net* housing wealth – in other words, all but a very small minority (about 2 per cent of all households) of those in owner occupied housing had houses thought to be worth more than their estimated outstanding debt. Table 4.9 shows the pattern of owner occupation and the distribution of housing wealth by the (equivalent) income quintile in which the household is located. We see that the level of home ownership is extremely high throughout the income distribution. Towards the top of the income distribution the percentage in owner occupation approaches 90 per cent, but even for the bottom quintile it is almost 70 per cent. The average house value for those who are owner occupiers is also quite high even in the lowest income quintile, with a mean gross house value of €128,000 which is half the mean house value for owner occupiers in the top income quintile of €244,000. When mortgage debt is deducted, the mean net house value in the bottom quintile is reduced only marginally, to €124,000, while that at the top is reduced more substantially to €206,000. Owner occupiers in the bottom quintile now have on average 60 per cent of the net value for the top quintile.

Table 4.9: Housing Wealth by Income Quintile of Households, LII Sample 2000

Income quintile	% of total equivalised income	% owner occupier	Mean house values of owner occupiers (€ 000s)		Net value as % of gross	% of total housing wealth
			Gross	Net		
Bottom	7.3	69.6	128.3	124.1	96.7	15.2
2	11.3	80.6	138.2	130.6	94.5	16.1
3	17.0	87.3	169.1	156.0	92.3	19.2
4	23.8	88.7	218.9	198.1	90.5	24.3
Top	40.7	87.0	244.0	205.7	84.3	25.3

The variation in home ownership rates and in the net asset which the house represents combines to produce the distribution of housing wealth by (equivalent) income quintile also shown in the table. We see that the bottom income quintile has 15 per cent of total net housing wealth, while the top income quintile has 25 per cent. While unequal, this is rather closer to a uniform distribution across the income quintiles than we see for income itself, where the bottom quintile has only 7.3 per cent of total disposable income and the top quintile has 41 per cent. In other words, some of those on relatively low incomes are much less disadvantaged with respect to housing wealth, even though they have a somewhat smaller share of housing wealth than they ought to in strict proportional terms. In thinking about social inequalities more generally, then, it is important to have a comprehensive picture going beyond the distribution of income to incorporate housing wealth (and indeed other forms of wealth holding beyond the scope of this paper).

Table 4.10 shows the distribution of housing wealth by the age of the household reference person. This helps throw light on the relationship between housing wealth and income, in that it brings out the links between income and housing patterns on the one hand and life cycle stage on the other. Young households (those headed by a person aged under 35) have a bigger share of income than of housing wealth: they have over 25 per cent of total income but only 14 per cent of net housing wealth. Elderly households are in the opposite situation. Those aged 65-74 have 11 per cent of income compared to 15 per cent of housing wealth, while those aged 75 and over have 7 per cent of income and 11 per cent of housing wealth. For households in the intermediate age-ranges (ages 35 to 64) there is less divergence between their shares of income and of housing wealth, but even here there is a slight tendency for the balance between income and housing wealth to shift in favour of housing wealth as age increases. These patterns indicate, in other words, that housing wealth tends to accumulate as age increases, whereas income does not, at least when it comes to the divide between active working life and retirement. Housing wealth thus offsets to a certain degree the inequalities in current income because it is most concentrated on the elderly, who have low incomes, and least concentrated on younger people, who have higher incomes.

Table 4.10: Housing Wealth by Age, LII Sample 2000

Age group	% of total equivalised income	% owner occupier	Mean house values of owner occupiers (€ 000s)		Net value as % of gross	% of total housing wealth
			Gross	Net		
Under 35	25.4	56.7	164.9	109.3	66	14.1
35-44	20.0	86.9	186.3	158.4	85	19.4
45-54	21.7	88.0	206.7	189.1	92	23.9
55-64	15.0	88.5	175.8	172.2	98	16.8
65-74	10.7	95.0	181.2	180.8	100	14.7
75 and over	7.3	91.1	161.9	160.6	99	11.0

It is worth noting the factors which account for the relatively low level of housing wealth among the younger households (those aged under 35). First, though their level of home ownership is high by international standards (57 per cent), it is substantially lower than that of older age-groups. Second, their houses on average are worth less than those of all the other age-groups except those aged 75 and over. This may indicate the prevalence of relatively low-cost starter homes among younger households. Third, younger households have higher levels of mortgage debt on the houses they own – they own on average only 66 per cent of the equity, compared to virtually 100 per cent equity ownership among the elderly. It might be thought that 66 per cent equity ownership is quite high among household heads aged under 35, since they would not be old enough to have cleared a significant proportion of mortgage debt (keeping in mind the fact that the capital amortisation is slight in the early years of a mortgage). However, the house price boom of 1995-2000 is significant in this context since it dramatically altered loan to value ratios among existing mortgage holders (and outright owners), thus bestowing them with large windfall gains in equity values.

It is particularly useful in that context to be able to make a direct comparison between the distribution of housing wealth in 2000 and corresponding results derived in exactly the same way from the 1994 Living in Ireland Survey, before the house price boom got underway. The proportion of all households with some net wealth in the form of housing in 1994 was slightly lower than in 2000, at 76 per cent, reflecting the marginally lower level of owner occupation. Comparing the figures for 1994 in Table 4.11 with those for 2000 in Table 8 shows however that the increase in home ownership over the intervening period was concentrated towards the bottom of the income distribution. The percentage of households in the bottom quintile who were owner occupiers rose from 64 per cent to 70 per cent, whereas in the top two quintiles it was already close to 90 per cent in 1994 and had not risen further by 2000. On the other hand, the mean net value of the housing asset did rise slightly less rapidly towards the bottom of the income distribution, by about 218 per cent in nominal terms, compared with about 225 per cent for quintiles 3 and 5 and 253 per cent for the fourth quintile.

Table 4.11: Housing Wealth by Income Quintile of Households, LII Sample 1994

Income quintile	% owner occupier	Mean net house values of owner occupiers	% of total housing wealth
Bottom	63.6	39,000	15.7
2	73.7	41,200	16.6
3	84.6	48,100	19.4
4	90.2	56,100	22.6
Top	88.5	63,400	25.6

So these factors worked in opposite directions in terms of the overall spread of housing wealth over the income distribution, and the result was that there was little change in that distribution between 1994 and 2000. The share of total net housing wealth going to the bottom two quintiles of the income distribution fell by 1 per cent, but the overall picture is one of remarkable stability.

Conclusion

This chapter has argued that in spite of the rise in house prices faced by home purchasers in Ireland since the mid-1990s, the greatest affordability pressures have arisen in the private rented sector. Private tenants have been faced with sharp increases in private rents, both in absolute terms and relative to household income. Among house purchasers, by contrast, mortgage expenditures relative to total household income have remained more or less stable. This is so because a combination of rising incomes and falling interest rates have counter-balanced the effect of rising house prices on the burdensomeness of mortgage payments for home purchasers. Affordability problems in the Irish housing system, therefore, are less a feature of the home purchase sector than public discussion of house prices in Ireland would lead one to expect. This is reflected in the poverty pressures associated with housing costs. House purchasers for the most part are not poor, and even though their house purchase costs may be high in some cases, they are rarely high enough to cause the households concerned to slip into poverty. Low-income households in the private rented sector, by contrast, suffer greatest financial strain as a result of their housing costs. Those in the social rented sector are also generally in poor material circumstances, but because their rents are so low in real terms, their housing costs do not greatly add to their burdens.

In looking at these issues, we should not assume that the exceptional rate of increase in house prices in Ireland has led to exceptional levels of housing expenditure for householders. In fact, Irish households on average spend less on rent and mortgages than most EU countries – only the southern European countries (Greece, Italy, Spain and Portugal) have lower average household expenditures on these items. Even those households in Ireland which have mortgages are no more burdened by mortgage payments, relative to household resources, than their counterparts in other EU countries. Again, the key issue is that house *prices* are only one contributor to housing costs and the affordability of house purchase. Other equally important factors are interest rates, the availability of credit and the level of disposable income, all of which have moved in positive directions for Irish householders over the past ten years.

When we look at the distribution of housing wealth, we find that it has a somewhat progressive effect when set against the distribution of income: many of those on low incomes (among whom the elderly are especially prominent) have a relatively large share of housing wealth, while those on high incomes (among whom are included many younger households) have a lower share of housing wealth than their income position would lead one to expect. These patterns were not greatly altered by the house price boom of the 1990s. One cannot say that housing wealth is more equally distributed than income. Housing wealth, in fact, is more *unequally* distributed than income – all households have at least some income while something over 20 per cent of households own no housing wealth. However, the two axes of inequality cut across each other. In general, housing wealth favours the elderly, while income inequalities favour younger households, and in combination the two offset each other to a considerable degree.

The implications of these findings for policy require careful consideration. To simply point to the central messages here, it is clear that discussions of affordability should take much greater account of the private rented sector. The burdens associated with owner-occupation are not as severe as often suggested and are sharply concentrated among a relatively small sub-set of all owner-occupiers. At the same time, owner-occupied housing acts as a key form of wealth-holding. Seeking to improve the lot of those who are facing serious difficulty with their housing expenditures should not be confused with generalised benefits for owner occupiers, nor directed simply at easing the route into owner occupation.

5

The Private Rented Sector

Yvonne Galligan

Introduction

Until the 1990s the policy preferences operating to support home ownership in Ireland led to private rented accommodation declining in importance as a housing sector, comprising less than one tenth of all housing provision at the beginning of this decade. Since then, a combination of demographic change and economic prosperity, along with a shortage of housing for ownership, resulted in an upward demand for private rental accommodation. The traditional profile of the sector as a tenure for long-term poor households, students and others requiring temporary accommodation was augmented in the last decade by relatively well-off households seeking temporary accommodation on the way to home-owning, and the expansion of this sector to meet this demand was also fuelled by generous tax incentives. This was not the only pressure on the limited rented stock. In addition, cutbacks in local authority housing provision forced local councils to meet their housing obligations to low-income families through the private rental sector. In the mid-1990s, policy initiatives arising from a series of housing reviews designed to assist home ownership (Bacon and Associates, 1998, 1999, 2000) intentionally discouraged investors from the market and further reduced the potential stock of rented accommodation.

Thus, although the private rented sector in Ireland is often categorised as a marginal tenure, trends in the sector in the last decade have seen it become the focus of policy attention where three main sets of interests with varying degrees of power interact to secure their interests. The key concern of government in relation to this sector is enabling the free market to operate with minimal regulation while granting tenants modest protection from exploitation by unscrupulous landlords. For landlords, minimal regulation of their activities in conditions conducive to maximum investment return is their preferred policy environment and they have campaigned to secure this condition. For tenants, of critical importance is the availability of quality and affordable accommodation with security of tenure.

These competing perspectives came to the fore in the closing decade of the twentieth century, and despite the publication of a comprehensive report on the sector by a government-sponsored Commission in 2000, little has changed for any of these groups (Commission on the Private Rented Residential Sector, 2000). This chapter aims to explore the many aspects of the private rented tenure in order to understand the dynamics of the sector. It begins by presenting an overview of the private rented residential sector over time. It examines the size of this sector in relation to other tenures and assesses the role the sector is called on to play in the housing system. This is followed by a discussion of the social composition of landlords and tenants, and by a review of the main investment incentives open to landlords. A further section analyses the key elements of the sector that give rise to polarised debates – security of tenure, rent-setting and landlord-tenant relationships. Before concluding, some attention is given to the report of the Commission on the private rented sector and the chapter closes with a general review of the sector as a whole.

The Private Rented Sector: Comparative Trends

It is clear that the private rented sector has been in decline as a source of accommodation provision for over forty years. As explained in Chapters 1 and 2 of this volume, census returns indicate that since 1961 the tenure has reduced by more than half, due in large measure to a consistent preference for owner occupation. However, primarily because of the impact of a variety of tax incentive schemes in operation since 1986, the sector has experienced something of a revival. Between 1996 and 2002 the private rented sector increased from 8 to 11 per cent of the housing stock.

When compared with the stock of private rental accommodation in most of the other 25 European Union member states the level of private renting in Ireland is below the EU average of 17 per cent. However Figure 5.1 below reveals that this average figure disguises wide variations – in the mostly western European countries which were EU members prior to 2005 a much larger proportion of the population rent their homes in the private rented sector, while in the new, mostly central and eastern European EU members, levels of private renting are much lower than in Ireland. In other countries outside of the European Union, with similar administrative and legal structures to that of Ireland (Australia, Canada, New Zealand) the size of the private rental sector in all is at least double that of Ireland. The relatively large size of the sector in Australia, Canada and New Zealand is related to the marginal role of social housing: thus the private rented sector is a major source of accommodation for those unable or unwilling to become home owners (Commission on the Private Rented Residential Sector, 2000).

Given the very divergent political ideologies underpinning the principles of housing provision across Europe, it is quite difficult to extrapolate genuine comparisons with the Irish case, especially in the context of housing provision for low-income households. Pertinent to understanding the profile and standing of the private rented tenure is the operation of the housing market over time and the nature and impact of policy decisions taken at critical moments in the market. The impulses currently shaping Irish policy in private rental provision appear to be similar to those of Australia where, according to Wulff and Maher (1998: 84):

Figure 5.1: Percentage of Dwellings which are Private Rented in European Union Member States and Applicants for Membership, Various Years

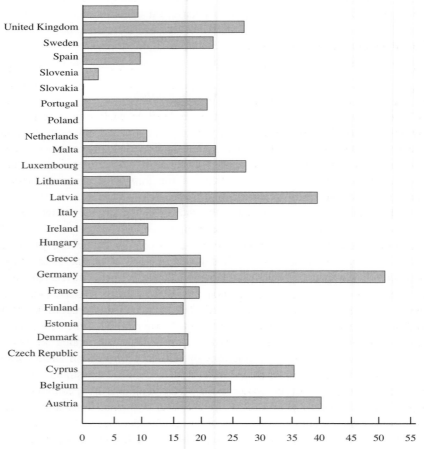

Source: Norris and Shiels (2004).

Note: data for Malta refer to 1995; data for Finland refer to 1999; data for Cyprus refer to 2000; data for Denmark refer to 2003; data for all other countries refer to 2001 or 1002.

The private rented sector [is] becoming a tenure of increasing importance as house-buying rates in early adulthood declines, public housing waiting lists grow to well beyond supply capacity and demographic projections indicate an increase in the number of single-adult households.

Important as these trends are for situating private renting in Ireland in an overall comparative context and in terms of the Irish housing system, they reveal little about the tenure – how it works, the age and nature of the accommodation in the sector, the socio-economic characteristics of landlords and tenants and the relative balance of power between them. The tenure serves diverse accommodation needs not addressed in the owner-occupied or public and social rental tenures. These issues are examined below.

Social Profile of Tenants and Landlords

Impressionistic evidence and statistics on particular categories of tenants suggest a changing role for private renting in recent years. In addition to meeting the needs of long-standing renters, of house movers, and of students (who in Ireland are generally housed in the mainstream private rented sector, rather than in dedicated accommodation), it appears that private renting currently meets four novel or greatly expanded categories of household demand: providing housing of last resort; as an interim solution to those on the way to home ownership; as a tenure of choice and finally as a source of flexible accommodation for a mobile workforce.

A major role of the private rented sector today is in meeting the housing needs of low-income households who cannot otherwise obtain or afford accommodation. As Redmond and Norris discuss in Chapter 1, the growing demand for local authority housing from the early 1990s on has outstripped the modest improvements in local authority new build and refurbishment, resulting in increases in the numbers on local authority waiting lists (Norris and Winston, 2004). The private rented tenure is called upon to make up the shortfall in local authority provision (Fahey and Watson, 1995; Norris and Winston, 2004). This social housing role entails the provision of private rented accommodation for households dependent on social welfare or government training schemes who are not priority categories for public rented allocation. The result is that private renting contains disproportionate numbers of single-person households on unemployment benefit or assistance, households on lone parents allowance, asylum seekers and de-institutionalised persons. The demand in this category is swollen by those who for a variety of reasons find themselves unable to access or retain their home in the public rented or owner occupied tenures, e.g. low- to middle-income persons leaving the family home after marriage breakdown. Approximately 40 per cent of privately renting households depend on rent supplement to assist with their housing costs, a calculation based on 60,000 households receiving rent supplement in 2003 as a percentage of the approximately 142,000 households in the private rented sector (Department of Social and Family Affairs, various years).

The private rented sector increasingly is also used as a 'stepping stone' for middle-income households saving for a deposit on a house (although as the section on rents below makes clear, escalating rents makes this strategy increasingly problematic). A combination of house price inflation since 1995 and centralised wage controls has generated an 'affordability gap' between average earnings and average new and second-hand house prices. Combined with an increase in the number of newly forming households, swollen by record levels of net inward migration, this has generated a reliance on the private rented sector by middle income households priced out of the new homes market (Downey, 1998). This role is set to expand if the affordability gap between average incomes and rising house prices is symptomatic of an historic upwards adjustment in the cost of Irish housing. Such an adjustment would shift the new homes market towards a continental model of deferral of house purchase until later in the household life cycle.

Private renting may be an attractive housing option, in the short term, for those who prefer the inherent economic advantages of rented accommodation (principally its relatively low entry and exit costs, freedom from commitments to maintenance, and liquidity of savings) over its inherent economic disadvantages (principally that mere use rather than actual ownership of the accommodation is secured by rental payments, that increased capital values accrue to the owner rather than to the user, and that rental payments tend to reflect current rather than historic capital values). Although income tax relief for employed tenants was introduced for the first time in the Finance Act, 1995, home owners still fare considerably better tax-wise than those who live in the private rented sector (Bacon and Associates, 1998).

The tenure may also be the social housing choice of many low-income households: up to 25 per cent of households on local authority waiting lists may prefer private to public renting, if conditions were improved in the former (Fahey and Watson, 1995). Changing attitudes towards apartment and inner city living have helped to increase demand for private rented units of this type and location (Floyd et al, 1996). This choice-based demand for private renting has been underpinned by rising incomes of the beneficiaries of the current economic expansion, for whom the economic disadvantages of the tenure will be less of a disincentive. Furthermore, with increasing longevity, older home owners may be attracted to renting secure and smaller homes, in the process freeing up the capital invested in their former homes. Another factor at work in the demand for private rented accommodation may be the decline in average household size and a resulting demand for smaller housing units, many of which are available in the private rented sector (Review Group on the Role of Supplementary Welfare Allowance in Relation to Housing, 1995). Finally, private renting offers housing flexibility to mobile workers. If the consensus amongst labour market analysts is correct, then flexible labour markets will increasingly require flexible housing markets, in which private renting will play a major role.

These broad characteristics of the housing need filled by the private rental sector in Ireland fits the profile of private renting in other countries. In addition, tenants tend to be relatively youthful, with four of five renters being under thirty-five years. Moreover, the sector is dominated by one- and two-person adult households and finally the average income of rental tenants is below the average income for the country as a whole. Taken together with statistics on household composition in the sector, the dominant profile of private renting appears as a tenure of transition in early to mid adulthood, with few long-term renters. On a comparative basis, the proportion of adult/s with dependent children in private renting in Ireland (28 per cent) is similar to that in Australia (28 per cent), with Canada having a higher proportion of families with children in the sector (34 per cent) and the UK with proportionally fewer (18 per cent) families with children in private renting (Commission on the Private Rented Residential Sector, 2000).

The expansion in the sector, from 81,400 households in 1991 to 142,000 households in 2002, indicates a dramatic increase in the number of privately renting households, and an increase (albeit not necessarily a proportionate one) in the quantity of housing available to rent.[1] This trend is corroborated by media reports of the experience of estate agents and of mortgage financiers, who prior to the abolition of mortgage interest tax relief for landlords, were reporting that approximately 30 per cent of new build was being purchased by private residential landlords (Bacon and Associates, 1998).

Evaluation of the motivations of Irish landlords remains speculative. It is unclear what percentage of landlords are 'accidental' investors who may have entered the business through inheritance etc., or 'intentional' investors whose reasons for being in the business are purely financial. Within the category of 'intentional' landlord, the financial motives can vary from short-term speculation (dependent on housing asset appreciation) to more medium-term investment interests (e.g. as a provision for college-going children or for a pension) to a long-term business orientation. The picture of private renting as primarily a small-scale business is borne out by data from the register of landlords compiled by local authorities and aggregated by the Department of the Environment, Heritage and Local Government. For example, these figures show that in 2003, approximately 27,000 private rented units registered were owned by 17,500 landlords (Department of the Environment, Heritage and Local

Government, various years). Another factor which has increased investment, although not a quantifiable one, is the degree to which home owners who have considerable equity in their property have availed of it to purchase and become landlords.

Irish landlords are for the most part individual investors owning a small number of rental properties often managed in their spare time. These small investor landlords came into the sector in the 1990s as a result of Section 23 and 27 tax incentives and the majority had only one property for letting. Other types of landlords such as professional individual landlords, commercial landlords, resident landlords and accidental landlords constitute the remainder. The dominance of small personal or individual landlords, for whom property rental is a sideline venture, is similar to the pattern of landlord-holding in England and Australia (Crook and Kemp, 1996). Unlike tenants, such landlords are in their prime working years, are middle-aged and have an above-average income, enabling their purchase of rental property.

The Development of the Private Rented Sector, 1922-2000
Investment and Fiscal Incentives

Historically, tax and other fiscal policies reinforced the desirability of home ownership while security of tenure along with an affordable rent attracted low-income households into local authority housing. By contrast, no subsidies were available to (uncontrolled) private tenants (Blackwell, 1988a) so that the after-tax housing costs of comparable households were typically greater for private renters than for home buyers. In terms of the choice between local authority and private rented accommodation, it was clear that households fortunate to obtain council housing were in a more advantageous position than those in the private rented sector. The security of tenure and stability of rents on offer from local authorities, as well as the route into home ownership afforded by successive 'right to buy' offers, historically meant that the balance of advantage lay decisively with public renting for eligible households.

Apart from the mortgage tax relief available to all house-purchasers (owner occupiers as well as landlords), no financial measures were taken to increase the supply of private rented accommodation for most of the twentieth century. It was only in 1981 that incentives to landlords (for both new build and refurbishment) were introduced in Section 23 of the Finance Act. However, Section 23 had a very limited impact until they were incorporated into the Urban Renewal Schemes, which commenced in 1986. One result of the fiscal and general policy neglect of the supply side of private renting was that widespread tenure transfer appears to have occurred in the uncontrolled rental sector, particularly in Georgian or Victorian houses in multiple occupation.

Legislation regulating rent levels and security of tenure in the private rented sector was introduced during World War 1 to control opportunistic rent increases at a time of housing shortage (O'Brien and Dillon, 1982). In the inflexible form in which it was introduced, rent control gave guarantees both of affordability and stability of housing costs and of security of tenure to households, at the cost of creating profitability problems for controlled landlords. This discouragement of existing and potential landlords often resulted in tenure transfer when the accommodation became vacant. However, all new lettings, and certain categories of existing lettings, were decontrolled in 1960 under the Rent Restrictions Act, 1960 (O'Brien and Dillon, 1982: 13). At the beginning of the 1990s, households in the controlled sector accounted for approximately 12 per cent of all private rented households, and 1 per cent of private households overall (Rent Tribunal, various years).

The other changes in private rented policy which did occur in this period were usually either *ad hoc* and reactive (e.g. much of the changes were driven by court decisions about controlled tenancies and by judicial interpretation of landlord-tenant law), or were minimalist in the extreme. This climate of policy uncertainty may have discouraged the supply of private rented accommodation by increasing the perceived risk of investment in the sector. Another manifestation of the policy neglect of the sector has been its anomalous tax treatment *vis-à-vis* other businesses. For example, privately rented property does not qualify for business relief from capital acquisitions tax, which constitutes an impediment to the transfer of a letting business within a family (Commission on the Private Rented Residential Sector, 2000).

An increased policy focus on the supply of private rented housing emerged in the 1990s. Of particular importance here were the Department of the Environment (1991, 1995b) housing policy statements of the early 1990s – *A Plan for Social Housing* (1991) and *Social Housing – The Way Ahead* (1995). Whilst these resulted in certain minimum standards and registration requirements with which landlords had to comply, they were offset by various financial incentives for landlords. These incentives centred principally, but not solely, on a capital expenditure-based tax relief. The principal tax incentive for landlords is popularly known as 'Section 23' relief after the relevant section in the 1981 Finance Act, which introduced these reliefs. This tax incentive was initially introduced on a modest basis in 1981 with the aim of stimulating both investment in private residential accommodation in particular and the construction industry in general. 'Section 23' relief was made more geographically focused in the 1986 Urban Renewal Act in order to serve as an instrument of urban renewal in nine 'designated areas' in the five cities of Dublin, Cork, Galway, Limerick, and Waterford. The urban renewal schemes were extended in subsequent years to designated areas in the majority of the major towns. Significant investment was not generated by 'Section 23' urban renewal schemes until the 1990s (Department of the Environment, 1996b; Department of the Environment and Local Government, 1997b).

Tax relief was available for expenditures incurred on the construction, conversion or refurbishment of rented residential property. The tax relief was in the form of a deduction of (a percentage of) the capital expenditures incurred (in the case of construction, net of site cost) from the rental income from either the accommodation itself or any other Irish rental income. The tax relief was available to the landlord, whether this was the builder/developer who retained ownership for rental purposes or the first buyer of the premises. It was a condition that the property be let for a period of ten years from the first letting. However, the overall increase in rental units in the 1990s far outstripped new build under Section 23, and thus owed more to investors buying accommodation to rent on the basis of house price inflation, high tenant demand and availability and cost of borrowing, than to the impact of the urban renewal schemes.

Other policy measures whose introduction encouraged supply included tax relief on wear and tear of fixtures and fittings, introduced for landlords for the first time in the Finance Act, 1997. This relief was in addition to the already existing provision for tax-deduction of landlords' management expenses. Reductions in capital gains tax from 40 per cent to 20 per cent in 1997 indirectly advantaged landlords and made investment in private renting an attractive proposition. Among other factors that positively impacted on the supply of privately rented homes in the last decade was house price inflation, which enhanced the attractiveness of residential property investment, leading to many equity-rich households investing their money in rental properties. This trend was further fuelled by an historically low interest rate environment that made loans available on very attractive terms. In addition, a buoyant demand for housing, stemming from increased numbers at work, rising incomes amongst certain occupational categories, and increased inward migration, outstripped both record levels of private new build and continuing low levels of social housing new build (Bacon and Associates, 1998; 1999).

However, in the context of widespread disquiet at the perceived role of prospective landlords in 'crowding out' first-time buyers, driving up property prices and creating fears of a speculative 'bubble', the government moved in 1998 to discourage new investment in private rented accommodation (Department of the Environment and Local Government, 1998a). The main action taken was the removal of deductability of interest on borrowings undertaken for new investment in residential property against rental income for personal income tax purposes. This policy was reversed in 2000 and 2001 and resulted in investor landlords returned to the housing market.

Issues in the Private Rented Sector

The operation of the private rented residential sector is framed by a body of legislation that defines the respective rights and obligations of landlords and tenants. Until the reform of this legalisation by the Residential Tenancies Act, 2004 which is examined later in this chapter, three related aspects of the legislative regime for the private rented sector proved particularly problematic. These are: security of tenure for tenants, rent setting practices and mechanisms for resolving disputes between landlords and tenants.

Historically, lack of security of tenure was the greatest single reason preventing many households from viewing the private rented sector as a desirable form of housing tenure. However, any discussion of security of tenure must differentiate between two types of households: those in the formerly rent-controlled sector and those in uncontrolled rented accommodation. A much greater degree of security attaches to those dwellings whose rents are essentially controlled by the provisions of the Housing Act of 1982. The Act applies to dwellings whose rents were previously controlled under the Rents Restrictions Act, 1960 and 1967. In 1982 the High Court ruled that sections of the Rent Restrictions Act were unconstitutional. This decision was appealed to the Supreme Court, which upheld the decision of the High Court. As a result of this, the government was obliged to introduce the Housing Act of 1982. The Act provides a degree of security for existing tenants and mechanisms by which rents can be reviewed. There were 10,916 such dwellings registered at the end of 1987 (Curry 1998).

Very little research has been carried out on the experiences of these tenants. Concerns expressed by voluntary housing organisations such as Threshold, indicate that the current major issues facing these tenants are:

- Failure by landlords to carry out repairs on the premises. This reluctance is linked to the uncertainty of arrangements after 2002 when the rent control legislation is due for review
- Uncertainty over the status of the inheritance of tenancies in the post-2002 situation
- The fact that the vast majority of tenancies fall under The Housing (Miscellaneous Provisions) Act, 1992. These tenancies can be governed by a lease binding the landlord and tenant to an agreed term or can be weekly or monthly periodic tenancies depending on the frequency of rent payments. In the case of all tenancies, however, a minimum written notice to quit of 28 days applies to both landlords and tenants.

Despite the overall paucity of available research, all of the completed studies have graphically illustrated the impact of the lack of security on private rented tenants. The 1982 study *Private Rented: the Forgotten Sector* provided the first comprehensive analysis of the effects of non-security of tenure on tenants' lives (O'Brien and Dillon, 1982). Security of tenure remains a serious and outstanding concern of tenants twenty years later. Up until the recent enactment of the Residential Tenancies Act, 2004, a tenant had to be in continuous possession of a dwelling for 20 years before he/she acquired a right to a 35-year lease under the Landlord and Tenant (Amendment) Act of 1980. This fact put private renters at a considerable disadvantage relative to householders in other tenures where payment of mortgage or local authority rent ensures security of tenure. A recent national attitude survey revealed that 63 per cent of tenants believed insecurity of tenure was a disadvantage of the private rented sector (Guerin, 1999). At the same time, an oft-cited advantage of the sector is its flexibility in meeting the needs of labour market mobility. While the new Residential Tenancies Act, 2004 does improve security of tenure, at least theoretically, it remains to be seen whether this will in fact be the case, or whether landlords will find ways to circumvent its provisions.

In essence, fear of losing accommodation forced tenants to desist from informing a local authority of a landlord's non-compliance with the Housing Miscellaneous Provisions Act of 1992 and subsequent regulations, which cover minimum standards, rent books and registration of landlords. Such a reluctance is all the more acute where there is a high demand for accommodation, as has been the situation until recently, particularly in the lower end of the market. Again, the new legislation sets out to change this situation but it is only through effective implementation that significant change will be seen. Combat Poverty Agency research found that one-third of respondents to its survey had been living in their present accommodation for less than a year (Guerin, 1999). This finding is similar to a 1994 survey of recipients of rent supplement in Cork, which found that 34 per cent of respondents had been living in the same accommodation for less than a year (Guerin, 1994). Both reports cited the lack of security of tenure as well as poor housing standards as explanatory factors for this phenomenon.

A lack of affordable housing has created pressures on an overstretched rental market where increasing rents have tracked increases in house prices and resulted in lengthening local authority housing lists (Drudy, 1999). The Labour Party Housing Commission summarised the affordability problem as follows:

> Rental increases of 20-25 per cent are not uncommon and related problems include overcrowding due to unaffordable rents, reduced savings capacity, and reduced household budget for other needs, housing debt problems, worsening poverty, greater vulnerability to homelessness and low quality housing conditions (Drudy, 1999: 29)

The Labour Party Commission, in common with other commentators, pointed out that the 'arrival' of mid- and high-income groups in the sector, who would be expected to buy in normal conditions, had placed great pressures on the sector as a whole, squeezing out the low-income and marginal groups traditionally dependent on the low end of the private rented sector (Drudy, 1999).

The escalation of rents also constricted the housing choices available to low-income tenants. Depending on the market rate prevailing locally, rent supplement allowances were not always sufficient to fully cover rents over a certain level. In effect this means a substantial section of the available supply of good quality accommodation was beyond the means of many rent supplement tenants. Severe unemployment and poverty traps were also found to be associated with the rent supplement scheme. The effect of the income clawback mechanism often deterred claimants from taking up employment because this would result in a loss of the supplement. This situation was recognised in the Report of the Inter-Departmental Committee on the transfer of rent supplement to the local authorities (Department of the Environment and Local Government, 1999b).

Landlords point to increased costs of compliance with regulations made under the Housing Act, 1992, in particular the minimum standards regulations and the unit registration fee. Furthermore, new investment in the sector requires increased rental income to cover higher entry costs, whilst existing landlords point to the operation of market forces leading to substantial rent increases being charged to tenants to recoup maintenance and refurbishment costs. The introduction both of private rented reforms and of measures to discourage house price inflation has led to quite different and contested prognoses for private renting. For example, in the context of the long-term decline of the sector and of impressionistic evidence of more recent tenure transfer through gentrification, fears have been expressed about the present health and future viability of the lower end of the private rental market.

All of the research suggests that access to accommodation is becoming an increasing problem for low-income tenants, particularly those on rent supplement. Extreme difficulties are becoming apparent for rent supplement tenants with children. The Combat Poverty Agency found that 52 per cent of tenants reported a high level of difficulty in getting a landlord who would accept tenants on rent supplement (Guerin, 1999). In research conducted by Isis, an analysis of the experiences of a sub-sample of 44 lone parents found that 32 or 72 per cent had been refused accommodation on the grounds of their being lone parents (Isis Research, 1998). However, such selectivity may be perfectly rational from the landlord's point of view, given that families with children cause more wear and tear on accommodation than do adult tenants.

The inadequate supply of low-cost private rented accommodation, particularly in the large urban areas, has been referred to as the 'crowding out effect' whereby new entrants to the tenure from the prime first-time buyer point of origin are increasing the competition for quality budget accommodation in the private rented sector (Downey, 1998). This effect has implications right through the private rented sector with its most graphic manifestation in the rise of the numbers of homeless people. A profile of people using Cork Simon's emergency shelter in 1998 directly attributes the lack of accommodation to an increase in numbers. The report goes on to argue that although fewer people are coming to the shelter from rent supplement accommodation, this is directly attributable to its decline in availability (Cork Simon, 1999).

Insecurity of tenure is crucial to understanding the nature of the traditional relationship between landlord and tenant in Ireland. The unbalanced nature of the relationship fundamentally alters the expectation of actual provision of services that tenants can legally expect their landlord to supply. Although tenants and landlords are entitled to a statutory minimum period of notice to quit, there is evidence that some landlords are not adhering to this requirement either by creating 'temporary convenience lettings' or by simply ignoring it entirely. There is very little research available which could give an indication of the scale of this problem. Some snapshot evidence is available from Threshold in the form of its annual reports. For example, in 1996 there were 1,935 queries dealing with notice to quit in their Dublin office, 504 cases in the Cork office and 421 cases in their Galway office. Landlords also have legitimate grievances relating to tenants 'overholding' after the expiry of a notice to quit period. In these cases, court proceedings to secure eviction may take a number of months, with landlords both losing out on rental income and usually having to pay their legal costs.

Under the 1992 Act, tenants are entitled to a rent book from their landlord. There is some evidence to suggest that many landlords are supplying their tenants with rent books, but this is not a widespread practice. Half of the 125 rent supplement tenants surveyed in the 1999 Combat Poverty Agency Report did not have a rent book (Guerin, 1999: 74). In many instances the absence of a rent book indicates provision of inferior quality accommodation. Again, the 1999 Combat Poverty Agency Report found that for rent supplement tenants there is still considerable evidence of physically unfit accommodation, particularly in relation to bedsits (Guerin, 1999). This study also found that nearly one third of respondents had disputes with landlords concerning repairs to the accommodation. Problems of lack of space were identified by the study conducted on behalf of Dublin Inner City Partnership in 1998. This study found from a study of 126 rent supplement tenants that although 41 per cent of respondents had children, only 13.5 per cent were living in the housing type most usually associated with a family, the two- or three-bedroom house (Isis Research, 1998).

Difficulties continue to exist with regard to the illegal retention of deposits by landlords. The 1998 Dublin Inner City Partnership Study found that only 20 per cent of a sample of 126 rent supplement tenants were in a position to get back their deposit for former accommodation and carry it over to current accommodation. The main difficulty with deposit retention continues to be the lack of a mechanism where deposits can be held by an independent third party who can adjudicate on the extent of the forfeiture of deposits in cases of dispute. Loss of deposit can imply enormous financial consequences for many tenants when a deposit can be a multiple of current monthly rents. Dispute resolution is another contentious area in private renting, revealing the imbalance in relationships between landlords and tenants, especially low-income renters.

The Commission on the Private Rented Residential Sector

The issues discussed above highlight the dilemmas within private renting, particularly as they pertain to low-income households. In the light of pressures on the sector during the 1990s and lobbying by non-governmental organisations concerned with housing issues the government established a commission to investigate the sector and produce legislative and taxation proposals addressing the main policy concerns outlined above. The Commission was composed of landlord and tenant interests, student representatives, members of the legal, accounting and auctioneering professions, property investment specialists and representatives from relevant government ministries. In detail, the Commission's brief was 'To examine the working of the landlord and tenant relationship in respect of residential tenancies in the private rented sector and to make such recommendations, including changes to the law, as the Commission considers proper, equitable and feasible with a view to:

- improving the security of tenure of tenants in the occupation of their dwellings
- maintaining a fair and reasonable balance between the respective rights and obligations of landlords and existing and future tenants
- increasing investment in, and the supply of, residential accommodation for renting, including the removal of any identified constraints to the development of the sector, and to report to the Minister for Housing and Urban Renewal by 1 June 2000 (Commission on the Private Rented Residential Sector, 2000: 1).

The overall ambition was to devise a set of fair and workable recommendations that would improve conditions for tenants and landlords in the sector. In working to its brief, the commission examined research on the sector, considered position papers and submissions from a wide range of interests, held a seminar addressed by independent experts and engaged in extensive internal discussions. It produced its findings with detailed suggestions for reform on 14 July 2000 (Commission on the Private Rented Residential Sector, 2000).

The report contained an overview of the private rented sector along with the demographic and economic factors influencing demand and supply of private rented accommodation. It identified the high demand for accommodation and the need to increase the supply of housing to meet this demand as the single most important factor influencing the housing market across all sectors. It also identified the relationship between underlying fiscal and infrastructural patterns (such as the low cost of mortgage servicing, investor interest in residential housing and the relatively scarce supply of social housing) and the increased attention on the private rental sector as a source of accommodation while the housing market regained stability. However, the report also pointed out that investigation into the characteristics of the Irish private rented sector was hampered by a dearth of information in a number of key areas – investment trends and yields, patterns of ownership, nature of the housing stock in the tenure and profiles of landlords and tenants.

A comparison was drawn between the Irish sector and private renting in other countries which highlighted the pattern of legislative reform of private renting provisions, addressing in particular the balance between the competing demands of tenant security of tenure and landlord right of repossession. This investigation also brought to the fore two divergent models of governance in the sector – minimal state regulation in some countries contrasting with active government oversight of tenant rights, rent setting and dispute adjudication in other instances. This discussion was followed by a detailed analysis of the legal and regulatory framework governing the operation of private residential renting in Ireland. The legal relationship between landlords and tenants was examined as was compliance and enforcement of registration regulations. An interesting point to emerge from this analysis is that there are no legal barriers preventing landlords from granting leases of up to 20 years to tenants with an agreed basis for rent reviews as part of the lease. On the other hand, the report identified deficiencies in the operation of the Landlord and Tenant (Amendment) Act, 1980 leading to a reduction in the security of tenure afforded to tenants.

The contested issues of rent regulation, affordability, and security of tenure were also addressed in the report. Rent control models were subject to critical scrutiny, with advantages and disadvantages argued at length. A majority of the Commission favoured rents being determined by the open market and also agreed that excessive profit-taking should be curbed. The basis for defining a 'market rent' was identified in existing legislation, while there was also agreement that rent increases should take place on an annual basis during a tenancy. The report supported a minimal level of security of tenure for tenants while mindful of the need to keep landlords in the market. It suggested tax credits as a mechanism for targeting assistance to low- and middle-income earners in private rented accommodation to alleviate affordability problems in a context where rents were set at open market levels.

Consideration of the taxation framework for landlords and tenants was guided by the extent to which the Commission viewed proposals as contributing to increasing the supply of rented accommodation while avoiding or minimising distortions in the wider housing market. The report comes down on the side of the provision and management of rental property as a business in order to encourage a professional approach by landlords. It also concluded that the outcome of targeted tax incentives should be to increase the overall supply of accommodation rather than displacing demand from the home-owning sector. Consequently, it suggested that renting should be subject to a tax code similar to that applying to other business activities. In this context it also suggested a reduction in the 9 per cent stamp duty to facilitate investment in rental accommodation. It also made a case for the extension of tax relief (Section 23) to those providing rental housing for specific groups with priority accommodation needs – persons with disabilities, low-income households and others – and argued for the extension of incentives for student accommodation provision. In keeping with the aim of professionalising the sector, the report recommended that availing of tax incentives or reliefs will require landlords to comply with the regulatory controls applicable in the sector.

The Commission made a series of recommendations on the central issues of dispute resolution, security of tenure, and rent-setting. With regard to dispute resolution, it sought the establishment of a statutory Private Residential Tenancies Board to deal with various forms of disputes between tenants and landlords. This board was also seen as having a function in advising government in policy in the sector, developing model lease arrangements and guidelines for best practice in landlord and tenant relationships. On security of tenure, it sought leases of up to four years to be granted to tenants with a six-month continuous tenancy, and devised explicit conditions that sought to balance the competing rights of landlords and tenants. On rent-setting, it recommended open market rents to be set at the beginning of a tenancy and subject to annual review. It suggested the use of tax credits as a mechanism for supporting low-income households with rental payments. With regard to investment incentives, it recommended the continuation of Section 23 and Section 50 (student housing) provisions, while also addressing landlordism as a professional occupation through the granting of tax reliefs for expenses in the same manner as for other forms of business. On registration of rental property, the Commission was of the view that this needed urgent attention by local authorities, and in addition suggested amending the registration requirements to make the process less cumbersome. It also suggested registration with a rental tenancies board. Finally, it suggested that tenants in former rent-controlled dwellings should have a transitional period of 5 years to claim a lease of up to 35 years, with market rents applying after that 5-year period.

The Residential Tenancies Act, 2004

The report made a genuine effort to address the many difficulties in the private rented sector. Reconciling the divergent interests represented on the Commission was not always possible, as evidenced by the series of dissenting views published in the report. However, it did bring about some level of consensus around a number of the critical issues confronting the sector. The Commission recommendations were accepted in large measure by government and many were enacted in the Residential Tenancies Act of 2004.

Passed in the summer of 2004, the Act officially commenced on 1 September, 2004. On paper at least, the provisions of the Act will fundamentally alter landlord-tenant relationships for the better. The Act sets out standard obligations on the part of both the tenant and the landlord irrespective of whether there is a lease or other written agreement. With respect to rent, landlords may not charge more than the open market rate, rent reviews are to be limited to once a year only and tenants are to be given 28 days notice of such reviews. While there may be an assumption that such reviews will be upward only, the Act also allows tenants to seek a review of the rent if they think it is above the going market rate. Perhaps one of the most controversial aspects of the changes to the landlord-tenant relationship introduced by the Act relates to security of tenure. Under the new provisions, security of tenure will be based on four-year cycles. While landlords will be able to terminate a tenancy within the first six months without giving any reasons, once the tenancy has exceeded six months they will only be able to end the tenancy in the following three and a half years for certain specified reasons. Such reasons include, understandably, situations where the tenants have not complied with the conditions of the tenancy. However, more controversially, they include situations where the landlord requires the dwelling for themselves or a family member or where they intend to refurbish the dwelling. Such options may be open to abuse. Assuming the tenancy goes to its full four years, at the end of that cycle a new tenancy will commence on the same basis as just described. So, a tenant who has rented for four years and who wishes to remain in the dwelling effectively starts a new four-year cycle. Alternatively, the landlord can start a new tenancy with different tenants.

As this chapter has made clear, there are all manner of potential disputes that can arise between landlords and tenants. While the Act seeks to create a more certain framework for relationships, inevitably disputes will arise. Instead of seeking redress in the courts, the Act places the Private Residential Tenancies Board on a statutory footing, although the board has been in operation since 2001. The board will deal with disputes such as: deposit refunds; breaches of tenancy obligations; lease terms; termination of tenancies; market rent; rent arrears and complaints by neighbours regarding tenant behaviour (Department of Environment, Heritage and Local Government, 2004a). The purpose of the

Board is to avoid expensive and lengthy legal battles and may involve either mediation or adjudication or a public hearing by a three-person tenancy tribunal. Furthermore, the registration of tenancies by landlords, which had been the responsibility of the local authorities will, from September 2004, be the responsibility of the board. Registration by landlords of tenancies to date has been poor, but it seems that the board will seek to enforce registration to a much greater degree, with landlords facing fines of up to €3,000 or up to six months in prison. All of these changes mark a major change in the private rented sector and should, in theory, lead to better conditions for tenants and more certainty for landlords. However, it will be necessary to monitor the impacts of the changes to evaluate the long-term success or otherwise of the changes.

In another major change to the private rented sector, the Department of the Environment, Heritage and Local Government plans to make fundamental changes to the Supplementary Welfare Allowance rent supplement (Norris and Winston, 2004). It is envisaged that, in future, households in receipt of rent supplement for over 18 months will be accommodated by local authorities and will not receive a direct rent supplement. The proposal is that local authorities will provide accommodation for this group by means of long-term lease arrangements with particular landlords. This system is to be phased in on a pilot basis in 2005, but once it is implemented, rent supplement will be utilised only as a short-term income and housing support.

Conclusion

Ireland's comparatively high level of home ownership – a trend sustained with the growing urbanisation of the economy and society from the 1960s onwards – relegated private renting to a marginal role in housing provision and also mitigated against major reforms of the private rented sector. Legislative initiatives directed at private renting concentrated on opening the sector to market forces and were accompanied by piecemeal implementation of minimalist tenant protections. Not surprisingly, private renting became a tenure of 'last resort' for families and individuals unable to access either home ownership or social housing and a tenure of transition for younger households. Concerns about security of tenure, rent affordability and the quality of accommodation deterred households from considering private renting on a medium- or long-term basis. Tax treatment, investment return, the acquisition and maintenance of an illiquid asset deterred large-scale investors from private renting, leaving the sector to part-time or 'occasional' landlords. The confluence of long-term demographic and social changes, with a rise in economic prosperity in the 1990s, along with a decline in local authority housing and an inadequate supply of affordable private homes, led to a strong demand for private rented accommodation. Tax reliefs such as Section 23 prompted a significant investment in new rental dwellings which in turn raised rents as investors sought to recoup the cost of their outlay. Multiple occupancies in single houses declined while apartment-style accommodation and 'gentrification' became a strong feature of the sector. The tenant profile and the nature of rental accommodation became more varied, and tenant expectations regarding time in private renting began to lengthen.

However, as the underlying policy framework governing the operation of the sector had not changed, issues of landlord and tenant rights and obligations came to the fore. In response, a government commission sought to reform the regulatory framework on private renting and produced a comprehensive analysis of the sector. It recommended the establishment of a private residential tenancies board to resolve disputes between landlords and tenants, an improvement in security of tenure, a mechanism for encouraging affordable rents and reform of the tax code for the owners of private rental properties. The Commission recommendations were accepted and acted upon by government, leading to initiation of a comprehensive legislative review of private renting, incorporating these long-overdue policy reforms, and has now been enacted in the Residential Tenancies Act, 2004. The Victorian basis for governance of the private rented sector has finally been replaced by a system of administration that seeks to balance the interests of government, landlords and tenants in a modern policy framework.

6

Uneven Development and the Private Rental Market: Problems and Prospects for Low-Income Households

Michael Punch

Introduction

The problem of housing access for disadvantaged social groups raises important analytical questions, not just because of the human implications but also because this issue is tangled up with a number of critical questions of political economy. It is perhaps unsurprising, therefore, that the issue has generated a measure of public and academic debate at various junctures, as well as, occasionally, innovative practical interventions in the housing system. Most obviously, such interventions have involved the construction of a considerable planning apparatus and public housing system in top-down fashion to engage in, respectively, regulation of the worst defects of the market and private capital and direct provision of accommodation in a non-market fashion. Meanwhile, alternative possibilities have continuously been imagined and sometimes implemented from the bottom-up, as people have sought their own solutions to the struggle for shelter through sweat equity, squatter movements and shanty-town development. Such grassroots interventions have seen the most impoverished and disempowered people producing their own residential space, in some cases, such as in many Latin American cities, becoming major agents of urbanisation in the process. These various state and grassroots practices constitute important responses to the problems of housing (and related services) created by uneven development over many decades (Castells, 1983).

In industrialised societies, however, a significant proportion of disadvantaged and marginalised households have always depended on accessing accommodation at the low-end of the rental market from private landlords. As a result, an enduring analytical and political question has revolved around the problems poorer households face in the private rental sector, as well as the insights such experiences provide about the relations between housing, socio-spatial structure and uneven development.

The aim of this chapter is to provide some insight into these issues and ideas by attempting a conceptual and practical exploration of the experiences of low-income households in the Irish privately rented sector. As a context, the chapter introduces some basic ideas about inequality, housing markets and public intervention. The intention is to attempt a more carefully theorised approach to the question before proceeding to examine some practical aspects of the private rental system as a low-income housing model in Ireland. This includes a discussion of inequality in the sector and increasing government reliance on it to meet social needs in the context of neoliberal policy tendencies. It concludes by summarising some concerns with the current approach and considering some possible alternative futures, drawing on the diverse positions advocated in a number of important reports produced in recent years and some alternative overseas models.

Uneven Development and Housing

The housing problems associated with low-income households raise complex analytical questions, linking many aspects of political economy. For example, the very existence of 'low-income households' reflects a particular kind of social relation and deeper problems of uneven economic power. The fact that such households may find themselves facing problems of vulnerability, displacement or homelessness also raises general concerns over the links between housing and the economy, including critical questions about commodification,[1] welfare and social reproduction. The following attempts a basic conceptualisation of the territory in order to provide a necessary theoretical context for the empirical discussion which follows.

To begin with, there are interconnections between housing systems, class structure and the relations and processes of economic development. The problem is also simultaneously entangled with the broader imperative to ensure the reproduction of a suitably healthy and quiescent work force to serve the labour-power requirements of production. However, tensions immediately arise as industrial capital's interest in a low-rent solution to the problem (thereby reducing labour costs for private industry) contradicts the entirely opposite interest of property capital in maximising the returns from investment in the built environment. Caught somewhere in the middle, workers on low pay and those marginal to the formal economy struggle to find reasonable accommodation and are periodically faced with housing shortages and its attendant social problems (overcrowding, poor conditions, ill health, homelessness, etc).

These immediate problems signal some of the complexity of the issues. However, a broader conception of uneven development is needed to theorise fully the problematic of low-income housing in a rental market. This approach highlights how the 'primary' circuits of the economy (that is, standard production, exchange and consumption activities within manufacturing and service industries) are subject to periodic crises of 'overaccumulation' (surpluses of labour and capital lying side by side), as reflected in economic stagnation and unemployment. This leads to the related process of 'creative destruction', whereby capital flows out of sectors and regions that yield low rates of profit in order to reinvest more profitably elsewhere. The de-industrialisation of many inner cities in North America and Europe since the 1970s reflected one side of this process, the other being the movement of capital to peripheral countries in search of cheaper factors of production (labour, land) and the resultant construction of a new international division of labour (see, for instance, CDP, 1977; Frobel *et al*, 1980; Bluestone and Harrison, 1982, 1988; Hobsbawm, 1995; Massey, 1995).

These temporal waves of development have differential (uneven) impacts or implications across various social and spatial positions, as evidenced in social class differences and marginalisation, regional and urban inequalities, patterns of de-/re-industrialisation and regional boom/bust cycles. In turn, these uneven rhythms and patterns of development generate everyday disparities between winning and losing groups, as reflected in differentials in incomes and economic opportunities (including labour-market trajectories) and a whole gamut of social inequalities (educational, health, housing, etc). In short, there is a simultaneous 'equalisation' and 'differentiation' of the levels and conditions of development, as general processes produce local variations, with uneven implications for different people and places (Smith, 1984).

At a different scale (urban, local), the 'secondary' economic circuits of the property market (including the production of residential space) also unfold in an uneven manner. Capital flows through the built environment in search of profitable opportunities, in the process creating some of the necessary 'use-values' for social production and the reproduction of labour power. However, capital may equally be withdrawn, moving elsewhere to take advantage of better potential returns, again a process of creative destruction, reflected in the uneven rhythms and patterns of investment and disinvestment. Periods of investment drought can generate environmental problems of decay and dereliction and social problems linked to housing shortages and obsolescence. However, periods of investment gluts can also generate tensions such as displacement, exclusion and (somewhat paradoxically) rapid price inflation. The general pattern is that earlier processes of under-development or disinvestment generate a 'rent gap' in 'devalued' locations (Smith, 1996), that is, a gap between the existing and the potential ground rent. This is then exploited at a later stage through large-scale and sometimes cataclysmic reinvestment (Jacobs, 1961), or the invasion of low-value by high-value (or high-priced, more accurately) uses (Ravetz, 1980). In many well-known cases, these processes have led to the gentrification of whole areas, involving the middle-class recolonisation of formerly working-class quarters.

The problem can be clarified by considering the possible strategies which can be deployed to restore or increase the rate of profit in the built environment at any given location (MacLaran, 1993). First, the intensity of use can be increased (e.g. by building higher or turning a single accommodation unit into a dozen bedsits). Second, a higher grade of user can be sought (e.g. by 're-imaging' bedsits as studios and seeking high-income tenants). Third, the function can be changed (e.g. from residential to commercial), though this may depend on securing a favourable rezoning decision (a public action which can in itself also provide an opportunity for considerable capital accumulation in speculative land markets).

The key differential in all of these conceptions is economic power. In a 'free' market situation, a competitive struggle for housing ensues, leaving those on lower incomes (who are disadvantaged in the primary economic circuits, being unable to access well-paid or secure economic opportunities and subject to un- or under-employment) with few (or no) housing options. This is reflected in the lived experience of vulnerability, poor conditions, unaffordability and homelessness. In this way, the problem of low-income housing connects with the 'unevenness' of economic power, which is rooted in the broader structures and processes of economy and society:

> The differential use of space by capital in pursuit of profit creates a mosaic of inequality at all geographic scales from the global to the local. At the metropolitan level, the outcome of this process of uneven development is manifested starkly in the poverty, powerlessness and polarisation of disadvantaged residents (Pacione, 1990: 193).

The analysis can be brought further by considering the dichotomous role 'housing' is given as both a commodity for investment and a social good. The commodification of any good implies it is given both a use-value and an exchange value. The former relates to its real practical purpose, qualitative essence, and material or symbolic worth, such as providing shelter, security, a sense of place, etc. The latter refers to the expected return on investment – the rate of profit it is hoped to extract – and as such is purely quantitative and abstract or phantom-like, lacking any qualitative character whatsoever. There is an immediate tension, at least in theory, between the imperative of maximising the return on investment and securing necessary use-values such as food or shelter, in line with socially accepted standards, as well as other less fundamental needs (or 'wants', more correctly). This highlights a number of structurally contradictory interests, such as those of landowners, landlords, financiers, investment funds, tenants and, as noted above, industrial capital, for whom high and escalating ground rents are also detrimental. Of particular note here, however, is the relation between the imperative to maximise returns in a profit market (although this may not necessarily be the motive of all landlords) and the accommodation needs of poorer residents. In a commodity market, one can secure exactly as many use values as can be paid for, but on a low or insecure income, this may not amount to much, with detrimental implications for levels of well-being, including access to housing. Thus, there is an important distinction between the social concept of 'need' and the economic concept of 'demand' which pertains to market systems of exchange and distribution. People have a universal 'need' for housing, regardless of social status or income. However, this need cannot be translated into an effective demand in a housing market unless the household has sufficient income to compete for what can be a relatively scarce resource in some situations. Accordingly, there is no necessary equation between *demand* and *need* in a market situation; indeed, much need may remain unmet, while at least some effective demand may have nothing to do with need, deriving instead from a desire for multiple home ownership or capital gains (Hickey *et al*, 2002).

The Logic of State Intervention

The foregoing captures some critical aspects of the socio-economic base upon which a whole raft of interventions, even an entire planning system, have been constructed in the public realm. The problems of inequality and the limits of the market follow from processes of uneven development, producing many complex social and environmental conflicts, pressures and occasional crises. This has led to a necessary intervention by the state in order (depending on the theoretical stance one favours) to reform the system, improve the lot of the most disadvantaged and promote a more socially just development trajectory or to manage recurrent crises of capital and ensure that the conditions for social production and reproduction are maintained. However, the level and nature of intervention and the kinds of policies devised and adopted have varied over time and space.

Whatever the theoretical explanation, state intervention has also become an important dimension of contemporary housing systems, and some consideration of its variable role must also be part of the analysis of low-income rental provision. Interestingly, it was concerns regarding this exact question which underlay the construction of a planning system in British towns from the late nineteenth century (see Hall, 1996 for a lively account). For a lengthy period, the housing of poorer people was largely left to the market, and a combination of low industrial wages and the concentration of burgeoning working-class populations in the urban areas generated a considerable housing crisis in most industrial cities, as well as related fears regarding health, disease and the threat of insurrection. Overcrowded slums, the actions of unscrupulous private landlords and the inactions of municipal authorities (despite the provision of some powers under various public health acts) ensured the problems intensified steadily. Numerous social studies and commissions, notably the Royal Commission on the Housing of the Working Classes, provided impetus for stronger public intervention in housing markets. However, in some instances, grassroots opposition proved more effective in focusing minds and prompting strong public intervention. Notably, the Glasgow rent strike of 1915 mobilised 20,000 working-class households with the tacit approval of industrial capital for whom the housing shortage meant upward pressure on wages and intensified class struggle. Rent control was implemented immediately (Rents and Mortgage Interest Restriction Act, 1915), and the Housing and Town Planning Act of 1919 mandated and resourced local governments to build housing for workers (Castells, 1983).

In this manner, housing policy and planning (and the politicisation of the housing question) emerged from engagement with some of the worst manifestations of uneven development in the urban system, particularly the poverty and ill-health of industrial cities and the problems deriving from low wages and housing shortages. The nature and level of engagement has varied historically (interventionism becoming much more radical through the new-town programmes in Britain, for instance) and geographically (across different welfare regimes such as those of Sweden, Germany or Britain). The resultant housing models and the experiences of low-income households in finding accommodation have also varied considerably in line with these differences in the degree of intervention and in the nature of policies for renting, private or social ownership, land acquisition, regulation of the market and other concerns.

The Irish Housing System

The Irish rental system has been substantially realigned over many decades, which is important to recognise in examining the 'place' of private renting as a low-income tenure. Historically, private landlords played a sizable role in providing accommodation for low-income households. This included the urban tenement housing of the nineteenth and early twentieth century, most notably in Dublin. Homes to a generally impoverished if diverse population of casual labourers and their families, unemployed and other disadvantaged and disempowered residents, these have an unhappy history and reputation due to the social and health implications of overcrowding, poor sanitation and upkeep. The social life of the tenements has been well recorded (Kearns, 1994), but an analysis of the political economy of these urban forms could be equally instructive, revealing much about the historical geography of housing and poverty in the city. For example, one interesting line of enquiry concerns the coalition of local authority neglect of its duties as a regulatory body and the private interests which benefited from urban social misery. As Aalen (1992, p. 296) notes of the period 1850 to 1921 in Dublin:

> Speculation in tenement ownership was a profitable venture. Owners were of varied class and occupation but the majority were small business men, the same class that dominated the corporation. Indeed in the early twentieth century and before, tenement slum landlords were well represented on the corporation and their presence there may well have inhibited the application of strict sanitary controls and explain why the corporation was never hostile to or strongly critical of tenement owners.

However, as in Britain, the corporation turned increasingly to direct municipal provision rather than regulation of private landlords as a solution to the housing shortages and health hazards associated with the slums. Public housing was initiated with Dublin Corporation's first project in 1887 at Barrack (now Benburb) Street, but the focus later turned to suburban projects such as Inchicore in 1912 (Aalen, 1992). The early part of the twentieth century saw a considerable expansion in local-authority housing nationally, and by the mid-1940s, public provision had eclipsed the private sector as the principal source of housing (Blackwell, 1988a). Over the same period, general disinvestment on the part of private capital in housing for rent also had an important impact, while slum clearance policies and the decline in unfurnished and rent-controlled dwellings also hastened the shrinkage of the private rental system (O'Brien and Dillon, 1982). These changes signalled a considerable restructuring of tenures: the decline of private rental housing and the emergence of large-scale public intervention.

More recent decades have seen further change through disinvestment in both the social and private rental sectors, while private housing for ownership has been given a position of considerable dominance. A number of policy factors have underpinned both these periods of restructuring, notably the long-running and vigorous practice of privatising the local authority stock (leading to its ultimate commodification) and a whole raft of fiscal and other public supports, which have been provided on a general basis (that is, without means-testing) to promote the ideology of private ownership (Guerin, 1999). These include the abolition of rates (1978), the failure to maintain a property tax to capture imputed income from owner occupancy (a short-lived property tax introduced in 1984 was removed in 1994), the absence of a capital gains tax on sale of principal residence and the availability of mortgage interest relief (Drudy and Punch, 2001).

By contrast, policies towards the private rented sector have largely been more *laissez-faire*, and the decline of private renting has been marked, at least up until various tax incentive schemes from the 1980s onwards (Section 23/27 and urban renewal schemes) began to stimulate new investment. From a position of considerable dominance in the early part of the century, by the mid-twentieth century only 25 per cent of households were in this sector. The decline continued for a number of decades, the sector stabilising at about 10 per cent from the late 1970s until the 1990s. Between 1991 and 2002, the sector expanded again, almost doubling in size to 141,500 dwellings, or just over 11 per cent of all dwellings. Moreover, rent control was abolished in Ireland in 1982 and no regulation of rents has existed thereafter. The effective regulation of standards has also remained largely a foreign practice, despite the introduction of mandatory rent books, minimum notice to quit (one month) and minimum standards of accommodation in 1992. The problem lies in part in a failure to enforce these regulations and in part in a high level of non-compliance with the registration requirements on the part of landlords.

A Private Rented Tenancies Board was established in 2001, the first practical change implemented from the recommendations of the Commission on the Private Rented Residential Sector (2000), while the final legislation to formalise this new system was enacted in 2004. Although this marks a welcome policy change, there are concerns and critiques of the legislation, particularly with regard to the experiences of people on low incomes. Concerns include the conditional provisions on security of tenure and the absence of rent regulation (the central concept of the legislation is that of a 'market rent'). These concerns were presaged in the debates over the report of the Commission (the basis for the legislation). Threshold (the national housing advice and research agency) entered a number of reservations into the Commission's final report, including the view that the proposals on security of tenure, regulation and affordability will neither lead to a fundamental reform nor be of substantial benefit to tenants. Indeed, the failure to address the frequency and size of rent increases and resultant affordability problems effectively undermines the concessions on tenure security. These and other concerns (notably the failure to date to ensure that landlords comply with registration requirements) need to be addressed, but it is to be hoped that once the new system is up and running, it will at least begin the task of modernising the Irish rental system.

Social rental, meanwhile, has been increasingly marginalised to a welfare role, being increasingly only available (on a means-test basis) to the poorest and most disadvantaged people. The sector was particularly under-developed at the end of the last century, local authority completions falling to only 768 in 1989, while national output in the 1990s remained low, even as levels of need rose precipitously.

These various trends are well covered in other chapters of this book and need not be revisited here in great detail (see also: Blackwell, 1988a; Fraser, 1996; Fahey (ed), 1999; Drudy and Punch, 2001, 2002; Redmond, 2001). The important point is the nature of the rental component within the contemporary housing system, which has resulted from these various phases of tenure restructuring. Critically, it can be argued that recent changes have been underpinned by an effective (if seldom acknowledged) neo-liberal philosophy.[2] Officially, Irish housing policies are informed by two guiding principles: the use-value concern of ensuring every household has access to affordable housing of good standard and an ideological concern with encouraging home ownership as an end in itself. Interestingly, it seems that this latter emphasis is a more recent addition, as the former policy alone appeared in the 1969 White Paper on housing (Blackwell, 1988b). However, as noted above, the promotion of private ownership has become the dominant political concern. This translates into a typically neo-liberal support for the commodification of this vital social good, whereby exchange value interests (investment, capital gains) are privileged over use-value concerns (general housing access, shelter, home, community, etc). The debate on the desirability of this ideological bias has scarcely started and there has, as yet, been little consideration of possible alternatives. That there are alternatives can be seen from brief consideration of some important perspectives from comparative housing studies.

Comparative Perspectives on Irish Housing

In a number of respects, the Irish case now presents a classic example of what has been termed a 'dualist' housing system in the international literature. The concept derives from Kemeny's (1995) seminal work on comparative housing studies, in which the variable 'structuring of forms of tenure' is seen as central to understanding the striking differences between housing systems in a number of countries. A typological distinction is identified between 'dualist' and 'unitary' systems, primarily based on contrasting policies towards rental housing, particularly the role afforded non-profit provision and social renting. In dualist systems, a 'profit-driven market' is kept apart from an effective 'command economy' in social housing. Non-profit provision is suppressed, but maintained as a residual safety net for the casualties of the profit market, which is itself protected from any competition from non-profit providers. In effect, 'getting into home ownership at all costs' is promoted and heavily supported as the most rational (or 'natural') economic decision, while rental options are downgraded to temporary or secondary roles and therefore become perceived as somewhat unsatisfactory options. A social housing stock is maintained, but only for the most marginalised. Kemeny identifies Britain, Australia and New Zealand as typical examples of dualist housing systems. The main features in

Irish housing noted above, particularly the tenure restructuring carried out over a number of decades, provide a strong argument for now including Ireland in this group. It can be further argued that such policies have been a factor in deepening inequality and social division (Drudy and Punch, 2002), as dualist systems tend to promote segregation as well as clear winners and losers. For example, while some enjoy the capital gains and speculative returns in housing and land during boom times, others are faced with a crisis of housing poverty and exclusion.

In a unitary system, by contrast, a 'social market' is allowed to evolve, involving both profit- and non-profit provision for general needs (Kemeny, 1995: 4). Cost rental models of housing are encouraged, and over the long term, these can better meet a range of needs by exploiting the benefits of rent pooling across a mature stock. This approach can go some way to resolving the tensions between exchange-value and use-value interests by opening up profit markets to competition from non-profit providers. It is argued that this can ensure effective tenure choice, de-stigmatise social housing and improve the housing options open to people regardless of income or social status. Kemeny identifies a number of housing systems that typify unitary systems, namely Sweden, the Netherlands, Germany and Switzerland (see also Davidson, 1999).

These various policy biases and restructuring tendencies have important social and community effects with implications for the experiences of low-income households in the private rental sector. The following sections look more carefully at two critical issues in this regard: inequality and the increasing reliance on private renting as a social-housing solution in the context of a dualist system since the 1980s.

Inequality in the Private Rental Sector

A duality in Irish housing conditions, reflective of broader social inequalities and disparities in economic power, has long been noted (Blackwell, 1988b). On the one hand, many households have access to accommodation and related services of reasonable quality, while some have been able to realise significant capital gains as investors in second properties and speculation in land. On the other hand, many households on low incomes are faced with the everyday reality of overcrowding, insecurity, exclusion and other problems. Indeed, for some disadvantaged households, conditions have actually deteriorated further through recent years of housing shortage and many others have seen little improvement in their housing experiences. These are the contradictions of recent years – a housing boom for some is a crisis for others – as reflected in the trends in escalating property and land prices alongside increasing housing poverty, need and homelessness. In cities and towns, many disadvantaged households are also affected by urban inequalities, having limited access to additional use values (or 'positive externalities') within their neighbourhoods, such as amenities and public and commercial services.

In this regard, examination of the private rental sector is revealing, as it presents a microcosm of these uneven realities in housing and in Irish society more generally. At one end, private renting is typified by high-grade accommodation occupied in the main by high-income households from upper-middle class or élite groups (such as visiting delegates from multinational corporations). The mid-part of the sector is largely occupied by middle-class, salaried workers, who also have considerable social-class advantages, as reflected in labour-market and educational trajectories. These include a considerable (and in recent years rapidly increasing) proportion of younger households who have had to postpone becoming homeowners due to the affordability problems created by rampant house-price escalation over recent years.

At the lower end, a different set of realities prevails, as low-income and disadvantaged households with limited job opportunities (being faced with low-paid work, unemployment or outright marginalisation) are most prevalent, while problems of relatively high rents for low-quality dwellings and insecurity are commonplace. Economic hardship can also translate into a personal housing crisis when faced with rent hikes and possible homelessness. Such problems have long been reported (O'Brien and Dillon, 1982), but progress has been slow, and familiar housing problems continue to affect many people.

Data on household income and tenures provide some evidence of the nature of social inequalities across tenures as well as the disparities within the private rental sector itself. Table 6.1 examines evidence in the relative income situation across the different tenures since 1973. The national average is set at 100 for each year, allowing the relative average income in each tenure to be compared. This reveals some striking trends, perhaps most dramatically the continuous and considerable decline in the relative income position of tenants renting from local authorities. The trends are typical of the tenure restructuring outlined above, whereby social renting has been steadily residualised to a welfare role. The most striking change in private rental is its opposite trajectory in recent years, recording a significant increase in the average relative income of households in this sector. This is reflective of trends in housing over recent years, as higher income households are increasingly turning to this sector (both by being obliged to as tenants and as small-landlord investors, seeking rental income and capital growth) due to house price movements, while urban renewal policies have generated significant investment in apartments targeted at the upper rental market.

Table 6.1: Index of Average Disposable Income by Household Tenure, 1973-2000

	Owned outright	Mortgaged	Private rental	Local authority rental	Rent free	State
1973	100.6	119.8	83.1	85.7	61.6	100.0
1980	91.6	126.1	87.4	73.4	69.1	100.0
1987	91.0	127.6	91.8	64.6	68.5	100.0
1994-95	88.2	129.7	87.1	57.0	84.5	100.0
1999-2000	87.1	127.5	101.2	55.6	83.1	100.0

Source: Central Statistics Office, 1977, 1984, 1989, 1997 2001a.

Figure 6.1: Households in Each Tenure by Income Quartile, 1999-2000

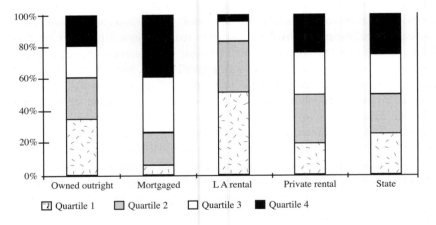

Source: generated by the Central Statistics Office from the 1999/2000 Household Budget Survey.

These average income figures are useful in tracking general trends. However, given the widening patterns in social inequality revealed by successive household budget surveys, it is necessary to look beyond the median to get a more accurate picture. Figure 6.1 provides a simple view of the connection between differentials in economic power and tenure in the Irish housing system. The entire population is grouped into four quartiles according to income (quartile 1 representing the poorest 25 per cent of households, quartile 4 the richest). It is then possible to examine the 'social structure' of each tenure, as reflected in the relative dominance of upper, upper-middle, lower-middle and lower income groups. For instance, as would be expected, those in home ownership (mortgaged) are overwhelmingly from the upper income or upper-middle income categories. The exact opposite situation prevails in local-authority housing, with over 52 per cent of households in the lowest income quartile. The situation with regard to outright home ownership is also interesting in that 35 per cent of households are in the lowest income quartile. Many of these are elderly households who may be described as 'asset-rich, income-poor'. The private rental sector, meanwhile, is strikingly close to the national situation, providing some support for the notion that it is a microcosm for inequality and housing in the country more generally. Just over 19 per cent of households in the sector are in the lowest income quartile, while almost 25 per cent are in the top quartile. Households in the middle quartiles make up almost 56 per cent of the sector.

There is also evidence (Central Statistics Office, 2001a) that housing expenditure (taking account of rent and water charges, mortgage repayments, house insurance and repairs and decorations) absorbs a much higher proportion of the household budget in the private rental sector than other tenures. On average, over 30 per cent of the weekly budget of private renting households from the lowest quartile goes on rent, compared to a national average housing expenditure of 9.6 per cent. In the lower-middle quartile of the private rental sector, an average of 25 per cent of the household budget goes on rent, while the average figure for the upper middle and upper quartiles is, respectively, 20 and 18 per cent.

Further evidence as to the social structure of the private-rental sector can be derived by examining the economic status of households in each quartile. This is set out in Table 6.2. It provides better insight as to the variable social predicament facing households with differential incomes within the private rental sector. The 19 per cent of households renting in the market who fall into the lowest income quartile are in the main economically inactive (retired or otherwise marginal to the labour force). Just over a quarter are unemployed, while just over 15 per cent are at work (low-wage workers). The balance between marginalised, unemployed and employed is reversed in the other quartiles. A considerable majority (86.5 per cent) of private rental households falling in the upper income quartile are dual earners. The above provides evidence for the fact that while one cohort of households relying on the private rental sector for housing are either low-paid workers, unemployed, elderly or otherwise marginalised, others are economically advantaged, being on high incomes and in many cases possessing dual sources of income.

Table 6.2: Private Renting Households by Income Quartile and Economic Status (%), 1999-2000

	Quartile 1	Quartile 2	Quartile 3	Quartile 4	Nationwide
At work: One person	15.0	59.1	38.3	9.4	34.7
One or more	0.7	12.7	52.6	86.5	35.8
Unemployed	25.1	6.8	0.4	0.0	4.2
Economically Inactive: Pension	18.7	3.5	0.0	0.0	14.9
Other marginal	40.5	17.9	8.7	4.1	10.5
Total	100.0	100.0	100.0	100.0	100.0

Source: generated by the Central Statistics Office from the 1999/2000 Household Budget Survey.

The well-documented (and politically well-represented) difficulties facing first-time buyers in the context of escalating house and land prices also have inter-tenure effects, with important ramifications for low-income renters. The rapid increase in housing costs through the late 1990s – between 1994 and March 2003, the average new house price for which loans were approved for the country as a whole increased by 210 per cent from €72,732 to €225,356 (Drudy and Punch, 2004) – meant that middle-class households have increasingly had to postpone purchasing, many of them becoming long-term renters instead.[3] This has created extra pressure at the upper- and mid-points of the rental market. One important resultant tendency is what has been well described as a 'crowding-out' effect, as the transfer of housing demand from home ownership to private renting has led to diminishing accessibility for disadvantaged households (Downey, 1998, 2003).

At the same time, the boom in house prices has also created an incentive for landlords in possession of houses in multiple occupancy (HMOs), traditionally the only affordable option in this sector for poorer households, to realise the capital value of their asset by de-tenanting, converting and selling the property into owner occupancy. The process at work is essentially one of 'gentrification', as historic patterns of disinvestment in low-grade properties (being rented out for many years as cheap but poor quality residential units) is reversed and the considerable 'rent gap' (the gap between historic and potential ground rents) is exploited by upgrading the use (flats become apartments) or converting and selling for ownership. Further pressures derive from the accumulation imperative, which demands that any residential investment produce a satisfactory rental yield above the cost of servicing the mortgage. As a result, rental levels have generally tracked the boom in house prices, generating in the same movement windfalls for those in a position to exploit the enhanced exchange-value potential in a tight market and a real housing crisis for poorer households. Finally, a further unintended source of pressure on the traditional cheaper options is the implementation of (necessary but basic) regulations for minimum standards, which also have the unfortunate potential side effect of reducing the only accessible and affordable accommodation open to poorer households in the market. The problem of inequality is such that people on lower incomes are restricted in the amount of use-values they can secure in a profit market, which means they generally cannot afford much in the way of minimum standards.

These tendencies are also reflected in income trends within the private rental sector (Figure 6.2). In the mid-1990s, tenants were predominantly from the lowest income quartile (over 31 per cent), while less than 19 per cent were from the upper quartile. The 'crowding-out' effect is reflected in the fact that by the end of the decade, most tenants were from the two highest income quartiles, including over 24 per cent in the highest.

Figure 6.2: Private Renting Households by Income Quartile, 1994-95 and 1999-2000

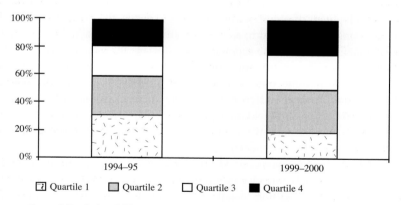

Source: Central Statistics Office, 1997, 2001a.

Increasing pressures for tenants at the lower end of the private rental market are confirmed by a recent survey of landlords in Dublin city (Memery and Kerrins, 2000a). Of particular relevance, this research highlighted that much of the 1990s growth in the sector has been in apartments, while the remaining HMOs, that is, traditional flats and bedsits, tend to be owned by long-standing landlords rather than new investors. This is important given that HMOs are generally more affordable for low-income households, elderly, unemployed and other disadvantaged groups. The research also suggests that continuing rent hikes were likely into the future, as 50 per cent of landlords felt they required rental increases (of over 10 per cent in most cases) to meet their exchange-value expectations. The research indicated the most 'desirable' profile for a prospective tenant from a landlord's perspective is someone in employment possessing good references. Moreover, only 7 per cent noted difficulty in finding their 'ideal' tenant, highlighting further the increasing difficulties facing low-income groups competing for accommodation in this sector.

These various issues relating to inequality, commodification and the increasing pressures on disadvantaged households struggling to compete for rental accommodation in the profit market are central problems of Irish housing, yet have attracted minimal policy consideration, at least in comparison to that afforded home owners and first-time buyers. Such problems derive from conditions of uneven economic power and the contradictions between exchange and use-value interests, which leave such tenants 'squeezed between their own economic weakness and a shrinking supply of adequate accommodation' (Blackwell, 1988b: 184).

Private Rental as Social Housing

As a partial consequence of tenure restructuring in the 1990s, particularly the under-development of social housing relative to needs, the private rental sector has increasingly been turned to as an alternative source of social housing. This has been facilitated under the supplementary welfare allowance (SWA) scheme, which is now an important policy approach to low-income housing provision. The SWA, which came into operation on 1 July 1977 to replace the home assistance service, was designed to provide income support to households whose means are insufficient to meet their needs. The rent and mortgage supplement component of SWA, which also provides basic income maintenance, mortgage supplements, heating and diet supplements, exceptional needs and urgent needs payments and the back-to-school clothing and footwear scheme, was originally intended as a source of short-term assistance, e.g. while seeking employment, to help people meet the cost of renting. However, this model has taken on, in ad-hoc fashion, a broader more deeply embedded social role in the housing system: 'Originally, SWA rent supplement was designed as a residual means of income support to provide immediate and short-term assistance with unmet needs. Nonetheless it has become, almost by default, a mainstream housing income support' (Guerin, 1999: 83).

This is borne out by the striking escalation in expenditure on the scheme, as well as the fact that a majority of households receiving rent supplements have been on the scheme for more than 12 months. In a recent study of SWA recipients, over 12 per cent of respondents had been receiving rent supplements at their present accommodation for over four years (Guerin, 1999). Moreover, it is estimated that one-third of all private rented households are receiving rent supplement (Fahey and Watson, 1995; Guerin, 1999). Although it has clearly become a mainstream social housing model, the SWA is weakly situated within the rubric of housing policy, being funded by the Department of Social and Family Affairs and administered by the health boards through their community welfare service. Furthermore, its intended role has not been clearly articulated, and it represents in some senses a disjointed response to low-income housing needs, particularly since many of those dependent on it do not feature in the assessments of housing needs (Fahey and Watson, 1995; Guerin, 1999).

Nevertheless, positive as well as negative features of this approach have been identified. Most importantly it offers a relatively rapid response to housing need once it is established, at least in comparison to the lengthy waits increasingly typical of local authority housing. Furthermore, it is the *only* housing option open to many marginalised people, such as single-person households, who often have difficulty accessing public waiting lists, despite being on a low income and in real need. A further positive is that accommodation available is often in relatively accessible locations in urban areas, e.g. inner city, inner suburbs.

A number of problems are immediately apparent, however. The quality of accommodation has tended to be modest in general and quite poor in some instances, although this will vary from area to area depending on the practices of the relevant community welfare officer (many aspects of the SWA scheme are applied on a discretionary basis). Despite this, the cost of accommodation being subsidised under the scheme has increased considerably over the years (see below). Prospective recipients of this income support must first establish a tenancy, and they may experience considerable difficulty in doing so. This also leaves people open to the possibility of discrimination. Although this housing option is often seen as affording greater choice, at least in comparison to the residualised social rental system, in reality disadvantaged households may struggle to access suitable accommodation, particularly during times of scarcity. Guerin's (1999) study, for instance, shows that choice in accommodation was limited, 42 per cent of respondents describing their dwelling as 'all that was available', while for 17 per cent it was simply the 'cheapest available'.

Also of relevance here is the finding that 66 per cent experienced some difficulty in finding a landlord who would accept SWA (including 52 per cent who had a high level of difficulty). Further difficulties are likely to arise from a decision at the end of 2002 to increase tenant contributions to the rent, i.e. from their social welfare payment from €6 to €12 per week and to limit the maximum rent allowable in different geographic areas, e.g. a limit of €107 per week was set for single people in Dublin. Moreover, it is difficult to know how people in many difficult situations coped with recent policy changes (introduced in the 2003 budget and subsequently abolished in 2004) that disqualify households from SWA unless they have a tenancy for at least six months. Although there is no doubt that changes in the system are needed as the commentary below clarifies, it is unfortunate that concrete policies for restricting access to financial supports are being pushed through rapidly in the absence of the development of any obvious housing alternatives, such as social housing, non-profit rental, housing benefits or other systems. Austerity measures to curb demand have been seized upon, but moves to increase the supply and accessibility of affordable rental housing are as yet sadly lacking, raising considerable concerns about the social implications for low-income and vulnerable people.

Bearing these considerations in mind, the following offers a picture of trends in this approach to social housing, drawing on the most recent data available from the Department of Social and Family Affairs. Expenditure on rent supplements has increased remarkably over the last decade. At the end of the 1980s, annual expenditure stood at less than €8 million; that has since grown to almost €332 million, or more than 42 times the 1989 level (Table 6.3). Reliable statistics are not available on the number of recipients before June 1999, when this information was computerised, making it difficult to account for the sizeable rate of increase in the early 1990s, i.e. to what degree these are attributable to extra recipients or the increasing cost of accommodation. However, it is important to note that the considerable absolute increase in annual expenditure since 1999 – almost €204 million or 160 per cent – appears to reflect considerable increases in the market rent, as recipient demand over the same period only increased by 43 per cent, from 42,000 to 60,000 claimants.[4] Moreover, the average expenditure per claimant increased by 83 per cent over the same period. These trends provide support for the contention that the system tends to underwrite rent inflation in the low end of the sector, possibly for sub-standard accommodation in some cases:

> It is now a serious contention that SWA rent supplementation is guaranteeing and underwriting minimum market rents for poor, unregulated accommodation. This contributes to an open-ended and spiraling cost that has become increasingly irrational in terms of best value for money, and which at the same time does little to ensure quality and choice of accommodation for recipients (Guerin, 1999: 83).

The problem of enforcing standards, decreasing accessibility is also relevant here – there would be an obvious case for not providing public support for any sub-standard accommodation, yet this has the problem of reducing further the accessible stock (recipients still have to compete for accommodation in the first instance before receiving rent allowances). This also raises the concerns that there may be abuses of market power, in that the availability of supplements may underpin rent escalation in the lower end, where the uneven economic power which prevails between the owners of property and poorer households desperate for accommodation leads to predictable results. Obviously, this problem has prompted some of the policy departures noted above; however, while the limited policy response may curb further inflation of the SWA cost to the exchequer, the most likely outcome for tenants, in the absence of alternative affordable rental options, is further hardship.

Table 6.3: Expenditure on Supplementary Welfare Allowance Rent Supplements, 1989-2003

Year	Expenditure (€m)	Annual change (% increase)
1989	7.8	-
1990	10.9	39.7
1991	18.3	67.9
1992	29.2	59.6
1993	49.1	68.2
1994	56.9	15.9
1995	69.5	22.1
1996	79.5	14.4
1997	95.6	20.3
1998	111.6	16.7
1999	127.7	14.4
2000	150.7	18.0
2001	179.4	19.0
2002	252.2	40.6
2003	331.5	31.4

Sources: Department of the Environment and Local Government, 1999b; Department of Social and Family Affairs, various years.

That the SWA-PRS system has, almost in ad-hoc fashion, become a mainstream social housing option is borne out by the duration of individual claims. Two-thirds of households have been relying on supplements for more than six months, with a majority receiving the supplement for over one year (see Figure 6.4). This includes 13,500 households (or 22.5 per cent of the total) who have been claiming SWA rent supplements for over two years. Further research would be required to ascertain how many of those renting for less than 6 months during 2003 are likely to become long-term dependants. However, earlier studies indicate two dominant case types – those who remain on the scheme for relatively short periods (the original function of the scheme was for just this kind of claimant) and a relatively stable group of long-term claimants, whose duration and age profile is increasing (Department of the Environment and Local Government, 1999b). In other words, there is no doubt that for many people on low incomes, subsidised private rental accommodation has become their long-term, if not permanent, housing tenure.

Figure 6.3: Households in Receipt of Supplementary Welfare Allowance Rent Supplement by Duration of Claim, 2003

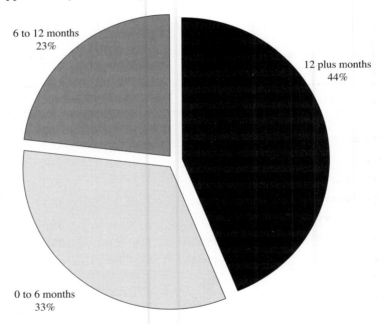

Source: Department of Social, Community and Family Affairs, various years.

The system is also increasingly meeting the needs of a range of age groups. In 2003, 42 per cent of recipients were 35 or older (Table 6.4), a slight increase over a figure of 39 per cent in 1994 (Fahey and Watson, 1995). The proportion under 25 has declined from 26 per cent in 1994 to 20 per cent in 2003.

Table 6.4: Number of Recipients of Supplementary Welfare Allowance Rent Supplement by Age Group, 2003

Age group	Number	%
Under 25	12,253	20.4
25-34	22,658	37.8
35-59	21,155	35.3
60 plus	3,910	6.5
Total	59,976	100.0

Source: Department of Social, Community and Family Affairs, various years.

Table 6.5: Households in Receipt of Supplementary Welfare Allowance Rent Supplement by Income Source (%), 2003

Income Source	%
One-parent family payment	21.6
Disability benefit/allowance	12.3
Long-term unemployment assistance	11.9
Short-term unemployment assistance	8.4
Unemployment benefit	5.9
Supplementary welfare allowance*	23.6
Employment support services	6.3
Pensions**	5.2
Other	4.9
Total	100.0

*Includes approximately 4,800 asylum seekers
**Includes old-age, widows/widowers' and invalidity pensions
Source: Department of Social, Community and Family Affairs, various years.

One important operational feature of SWA is that people in full-time employment or education are excluded. Some recipients are involved in training schemes of some kind, but most are wholly dependent on some form of social welfare support. The economic status of recipients in 2003 is shown in Table 6.5. The two most important categories are the unemployed and those receiving direct payments, also under SWA – including asylum seekers. Lone parents comprise the third largest category, followed by those with disabilities and people on employment support services – including Back to Work Allowance, Community Employment, Back to Education Allowance, VTOS and FÁS. However, perhaps the most important point emerging from these data is the diversity of social predicaments facing tenants in subsidised private rental accommodation.

It is clear from the above that subsidised accommodation in the private rented sector has, almost by default, become a significant alternative social housing model to direct provision by local authorities or housing associations. While retaining the original aim of providing a relatively accessible (compared to local authority housing, for which there is usually a waiting period), short-term housing option, it has taken on a much more substantial role as a permanent housing solution for marginalised people on low incomes. There are concerns about the quality and appropriateness of the accommodation available, as well as the possibility that the rent supplements may underpin rent increases across a housing stock of variable quality.

It should finally be noted that alternative models of low-income private rental housing are also being pursued and there have been further important policy departures implemented or signalled in recent months (2003-04). As noted above, recent measures have already been introduced to discourage/limit demand for SWA rental support (rent caps, the requirement that new recipients must have established at least a six-month tenancy). In July 2004, a new long-term accommodation initiative for rent supplement tenants was announced by the government, whereby local authorities will now assume responsibility for meeting the long-term housing needs of people dependent on SWA for 18 months or longer, while the existing scheme will focus on meeting short-term income-maintenance needs. In practice, it is envisaged that this will see greater engagement between local authorities and the private rented sector, including long-term public-private partnership arrangements to meet social needs. It remains to be seen how effectively the local authorities will be able to take on this expanded housing/administrative role, what kinds of agreements and deals are reached with private landlords, the overall cost-benefit of this new approach, as well as the social outcomes for poorer households.

Policy Implications and Considerations

It is evident that concerns exist regarding the efficacy of the current rental market as a source of housing for low-income and disadvantaged households. This reflects a much more general problematic of uneven development and the commodification of housing, and the tenure focus of this chapter should not cloud this important theoretical and contextual setting. Specific issues highlighted in the foregoing include the persistence of a very weak rental sector – profit and non-profit – in the Irish housing system and consequent problems of long waiting times or de-prioritisation in the ring-fenced social sector or exclusion and unaffordability in the market sector, pressures which are worsened during 'boom' cycles in the larger ownership market. The immediate implications for disadvantaged households reliant on the rental market include inadequate housing, unaffordability and vulnerability to homelessness.

What are the broader policy implications of this analysis? Various commentators have mapped some possible future directions to respond to the main concerns, ranging from reform to radical change. These include long-term calls for adequate regulation and enforcement of such regulations (O'Brien and Dillon, 1982), as well as the need for targeted incentives, for the provision of low-income rental options. Measures have been suggested for neutral policies across the ownership and rental sectors. This would entail addressing the imbalanced fiscal situation, which strongly promotes the ownership market with a raft of measures (Drudy and Punch, 2001), and the variations in the operation of rent supplement and the income-related rent system which applies to most social housing tenancies (Blackwell, 1988a; McCashin, 2000). This includes the need to coordinate the two systems, notably by moving the administration of the former from the health boards to the local authorities (Department of the Environment, 1995b; Department of the Environment and Local Government, 1999b). The need for rent regulation has also been espoused, perhaps within a statutory framework governing rent increases (such as a rent indexing structure), which is likely to have success in sustaining both supply and demand (McCashin, 2000). These are all important points, which would make a difference for low-income households and deserve further attention. However, Blackwell's (1988a, p: 280) conclusion regarding the future of the profit rental system as a low-income housing option still rings true and suggests that rather more is needed:

> On balance, the only place in the private rented sector for State intervention is the lower end of the market. There is little justification in market failure or equity grounds for tax breaks aimed at the upper end of the market. The prospect facing the lower end is further shrinkage. The enforcement of the regulations, recommended above, will probably add further to the shrinkage but that will be a price that will have to be paid. Consequent on any housing benefit, there would need to be a monitoring of the impact on rents to ensure that landlords do not gain all or most of the benefit … The best which the State can do is ensure an orderly retreat in this segment of the market and encourage housing associations and local authorities to fill the gap.

What then is to be done? Any number of social and environmental problems across all of the sectors – unmet need, homelessness, unaffordability, overcrowding, unsustainable commuter patterns, and so on – highlight the urgent need to foster a much more robust rental sector. This could greatly improve accessibility, regardless of social class, as well as enhance choice and flexibility in the housing system. Besides these social arguments, broader economic imperatives also underline the need for such a move, given the structural realities of global capitalism, including the increasing uncertainty and vulnerability introduced to labour markets and the rise of a low-wage service sector under conditions of flexible accumulation (Bluestone and Harrison, 1988; Harvey, 1990, 2000; Castells, 1996; Maclennan and Pryce, 1996). Yet, rental provision and affordability have not received due policy attention, these concerns being markedly de-prioritised in favour of traditional middle-class concerns with affordable ownership.

The rental component, in the broadest sense, of the housing sector is one area for action and change, which emerges strongly from the foregoing. In view of the serious social and environmental consequences of the existing situation and the fact that these problems have festered for many years, it may be time to embark on a new round of tenure restructuring. The objectives of such a course of action would include improving housing access and choice for those most disadvantaged by broader processes of uneven development in the primary and secondary sectors of the economy, increasing and diversifying the rental stock (and competition in the rental market), reducing the stigma currently attached to housing provided outside of the profit market and increasing flexibility in the housing system.

This will require nothing less than a fundamental reorientation of policy, moving away from the 'ceaseless pushing up of owner occupation' (Blackwell, 1988b), re-prioritising instead social and private rental options, and the long-standing underlying central principle of general access, affordability and quality. This would require greatly expanded non-profit activity in rental housing (involving, for example, local authorities, housing associations, co-operatives, community groups, mutual associations, etc.), providing for general needs on a cost-rent basis. This would provide fresh competition, particularly towards the lower end of the market, thereby improving accessibility, affordability and choice for low-income groups. The rent pooling potential across a mature stock, whereby the total rental income available from higher-grade units and from a large, mature stock cross-subsidises lower rents (or rental subsidies) for poorer households as well as investment in maintenance and new build, would in due course make social provision rational and sustainable, without stigmatising social groups by confinement to a marginalised social sector. Although beyond the focus of this chapter, the cost of expanding a non-profit sector must also be taken into consideration, including the issues of escalating land prices (McNulty, 2002).

A unified housing benefit scheme could take the place of a differential rents scheme and limited subsidies for low-income households in the profit market.

Such a scheme would be means tested but would be available to those at work, unemployed and those marginal to the labour force. Both dimensions of these changes – in provision and income support – are necessary, since achieving a greatly diversified and de-stigmatised rental system is central to its success. There are potential benefits beyond improving housing options for low-income groups and lessening inequality in the housing system. Increased choice in the rental sector will be of general benefit, promoting rational options (beyond displacement to far-flung commuter belts) for workers in urban areas, thereby offering a partial solution at least to the continuing urban housing crisis and related problems of unsustainable commuter patterns and lifestyles.

Although tenure restructuring of this kind would be a departure in terms of Irish housing policy, in a sense there is nothing radical in these proposals, most of these ideas having long been examined and advocated in one form or another by various commentators here and abroad (e.g. Blackwell, 1988a; Downey, 1998; Drudy, 1999; MacLaran, 2001). In essence, these departures would involve a move from a dualist to a unitary rental system constructed in a social market, wherein 'the economy is not seen as a sheltered preserve for unrestrained profit-taking but should be exposed to direct competition from non-profit organisations' (Kemeny, 1995). Ironically, such an approach is founded on the principle of increasing competition and choice in the housing system. This throws an interesting light on the contradictory logic of the neo-liberal ideologies underpinning dualist housing policies, which refer to the principles of competition and freedom, while supporting a profit market protected from competition and a command economy in social housing accessible only to the most marginalised.

Throughout this chapter, a number of socio-environmental problems, conflicts and contradictions with regard to the general processes of uneven development, commodification and state intervention in housing were highlighted, raising particular questions about the realities faced by low-income households within the private rental market. The seriousness and persistence of these concerns suggest the need to consider possibilities for engaging in a new round of tenure restructuring in order to re-prioritise both rental housing and the underlying use-value principle of general access to affordable and good-quality housing, regardless of social status or income.

7

Urban Renewal and the Private Rented Sector

Andrew MacLaran and Brendan Williams

Introduction

An analysis of the change from private renting of residential accommodation as the dominant form of tenure in nineteenth-century Dublin to a position, in 1991, where fewer than 8 per cent of households rented privately indicates that economic, social and policy issues influenced the decline. Increased incomes, coupled with access to long-term finance, facilitated by the growth of the building society movement, secured access to private home ownership to an expanding middle-income class. This process expanded eventually to most classes of society as ownership became both the market norm and the objective of government policy (Commission on the Private Rented Residential Sector, 2000).

The two world wars saw emergency legislation introduced to control rents in the residential sector and give security of tenure. Such restrictions diminished the economic returns available from the sector and provide a partial explanation of the sector's decline. Under various social housing initiatives, particularly from the 1930s to the 1970s, the development of state-subsidised social housing created an important alternative to private renting to comprise a significant portion of Dublin's housing stock. Due to shortages of housing and lobbying by industry, political intervention supporting the housing development process became a political priority from the 1960s. As O'Connell describes in Chapter 2, financial support for home ownership, mainly through tax allowances and grants to purchasers, provided a strong impetus to householders to move as quickly as possible into owner occupation. Privately-rented accommodation became a residual segment of the market, serving groups for whom the commonly preferred longer-term options of owner occupation or social housing were either unattainable or not relevant.

Policy Interventions in the Privately-Rented Sector

The 1970s had been a context in which residential lettings had failed to provide a sufficient economic return to attract investment interest. Indeed, landlords typically sought to escape from the sector, either by selling properties to sitting tenants or, when they became vacant, to owner occupiers. Those with controlled tenancies, where rents commonly failed even to cover maintenance costs, let alone provide a reasonable return on the investment embodied in the property, were in a particularly invidious position. Desperate to extricate themselves from a situation in which they were effectively providing a substantial and continuous subsidy to their tenants, many landlords even allowed properties to deteriorate to the extent that demolition became necessary. This at least permitted some investment value to be recouped in the form of the price of the redevelopment site (Baker and O'Brien, 1979).

The Report of the Commission on the Privately-Rented Sector (2000) analysed the decline of the sector over the period from 1946 to 1991. It found that nationally the proportion of households renting privately shrank from 26.1 per cent in 1946 to 8 per cent in 1991. In terms of absolute numbers, this represented a decline from 173,000 in 1946 to 81,400 in 1991. The greatest decline occurred in the period 1946-1961, when economic stagnation and unemployment caused significant emigration from Ireland, resulting in a reduced demand for the development of privately-rented accommodation. Instead, growth occurred in socially-provided rental housing and the subsidised owner-occupied sector.

As the privately-rented sector declined, the demand for such accommodation was met in the 1950s and 1960s either by means of temporary lettings of surplus residential space by private householders (digs or lodgings) or by the conversion of larger old dwellings to multiple occupancy. In Dublin, this occasioned the widespread conversion of inner-suburban housing in areas such as Ranelagh and Rathmines into 'flatlands'. The introduction of planning legislation in 1963 allowed the continuation of existing functions and levels of occupation which predated the legislation, giving rise to the concept of so called 'Pre'63' multiple occupation units as a long-term feature in the Dublin property market. Widespread concern regarding the condition of many of these dwellings and the levels of tax compliance by owners led governments in the 1980s and 1990s to consider alternative ways of providing more suitable privately-rented accommodation. Demand for private lettings intensified as a result of economic growth and an expansion of employment in the Dublin region by 150,000 in the 1990s (Williams and Shiels, 2002). Addressing the needs of an increasingly mobile and economically prosperous population proved a major stimulus to the development of the apartment market during the decade.

Information on the quality and standards of privately-rented accommodation is limited. Regulatory authorities' returns on enforcement of standard regulations indicate that in 1996, 814 of the 3,846 dwellings failed to comply with the minimum standards stipulated in the regulations. In 1997, authorities inspected 1,902 dwellings which did not meet regulatory standards and this figure rose to 2,710 sub-standard dwellings in 1998 (Commission on the Privately-Rented Residential Sector, 2000). However, as a considerable portion of the privately rented stock was built in the last twenty years it is likely that these dwellings meet minimum standards and that problems of sub-standard buildings relate primarily to the older stock.

Recent Housing Policy Interventions and the Privately-Rented Sector

Throughout the 1990s, rapid population and economic growth was not matched by increased housing provision in the Greater Dublin Area (GDA). Resulting demand produced significant price increases and placed pressure on an already overburdened private rental market. Government action to ease such pressures concentrated on the problems of the first-time house purchaser and expanded to include measures affecting the whole market. Three substantial packages of measures resulted. These three initiatives, which represent evolving government responses, were based upon economic assessments and subsequent reviews carried out for Government by Bacon and Associates (1998, 1999, 2000), often referred to as the Bacon Reports.

The measures introduced were *Action on House Prices* 1998, *Action on the Housing Market* in March 1999 and *Action on Housing* in June 2000, and were legislated for in the Finance Acts of the relevant and subsequent years (Department of the Environment and Local Government, 1998a; 1999a; 2000a). In the absence of any standardised empirical evidence or data on rental levels in the privately-rented sector, the impact of the various initiatives is difficult to establish. Indeed the rapidly changing and sometimes contradictory policy responses and reversals over a relatively short period show the policies to be short-term and reactive rather than strategic in nature.

Of particular importance for the privately-rented sector was the 1998 package of measures which aimed to use fiscal policies to manage demand. A main aim was to reduce the role that property investors played in the market in order to stabilise supply and demand relationships and thereby assist first-time buyers. In 1999, the focus of policy was to boost supply by promoting increased residential densities and other measures, while in 2000, the focus remained on maximising housing output through additional taxation changes. The following were the principal changes from this period affecting the privately-rented sector.

Capital Expenditure Relief for Landlords

Changes in respect of this tax relief, commonly described as Section 23/27 relief, occurred in 1998 as part of the new urban renewal policies. This relief was extended in 1999 under Section 50 of the Finance Act to the provision of student accommodation and, in 2000, to Living Over The Shop schemes. An additional scheme related to investors in rented residential units at Park and Ride facilities was also introduced in 1999. All such reliefs are currently due to expire in 2006.

Tax Relief regarding Interest on Borrowings

Relief on the interest on borrowed monies used to purchase, improve or repair residential property from which an investor derived a rental income was removed in 1998. This was intended to favour first-time purchasers competing with investors for scarce supply. Following considerable industry pressure and the fears that investors might withdraw from the market, the relief was restored in the Finance Act, 2002. The restored relief can be used as a deductible item in calculating tax on rental income.

Stamp Duty

General stamp duty rates affecting second-hand housing was altered in 1998 and stamp duty was introduced for the purchase of new houses or apartments for non-owner occupiers. In the 2000 initiative, provision was made for the introduction of a flat-rate stamp duty rate of 9 per cent for investors.

Capital Gains Tax

The December 1997 budget reduced the rate of capital gains tax from 40 per cent to 20 per cent. This applies to rented property and development land and is intended to increase the supply of residential development.

The continuation of rental increases and house price inflation from 1998 to the present (2004) indicates that the affordability issue remains critical despite government actions. General criticisms are that demand management measures, including attempts to deflect investor demand, are unlikely to succeed in a market where large supply deficiencies remain (Williams, 2001). Equally, support for purchasers, such as assisted loans or grants, have been absorbed into the market at higher price levels. The complex inter-tenure nature of the market means that the use of selective tax-based interventions may actually cause further market distortions rather than a successful outcome (Williams, 2001). It is only when supply measures take effect that the market is likely finally to level off, with prices for rented residential property stabilising at high levels.

Urban Renewal and the Privately-Rented Sector in Dublin

Aside from the general policies explained above, urban renewal policies have played a significant role in the development of the modern privately-rented sector, particularly in Dublin. Structural factors, including the influence of changing technologies on employment, resulted in the economic and physical decline of Dublin. Diseconomies associated with high land prices contributed to the decline of the central area as the focus of residential and industry development shifted towards the suburbs in the 1960s and 1970s, with an economically marginalised population remaining in the inner-city. As Dublin entered the 1980s, it was evident to policy makers and others that there was a need for reurbanisation and to encourage new generations of city dwellers, whether owners or renters, to return to rehabilitated areas.

Public policies throughout the 1960s and 1970s aspired toward urban renewal, whereas many policies and initiatives contributed to urban blight. Housing policies involved replacing unfit city housing with a newly-built stock at outer-urban locations. Such clearance, allied with extensive city road proposals, resulted in development stagnation and dereliction. Residential rent control legislation, enacted during the world wars and never repealed, froze rentals at levels below that required to maintain property. These controls, affecting a large number of older city properties, was ended by legislation in 1992, with final expiration of such controls in 2002. The result of such policies was that by the 1980s large areas of the inner city were vacant and derelict. Investment and development activity in the residential sector was dormant and the classic inner-city problem of deprivation and development stagnation prevailed. The existence of under-utilised social and physical infrastructure made regeneration based upon residential redevelopment a logical option. However, weak market demand and risks associated with procuring finance for such development meant that renewal remained merely a possibility.

The case for state intervention to stimulate the market process of inner-urban change and minimise emerging problems was clear by the 1980s. The commitment of large-scale public financial resources to address the problem was not considered feasible due to the poor state of public finances. The option of stimulating residential and commercial development through the use of preferential tax incentives in designated areas was chosen. The Urban Renewal Act of 1986 and relevant provisions of the Finance Acts made available incentives to encourage the development of residential units in designated areas. Areas of main cities and towns were designated for such preferential tax incentives. The aim of such interventions was to revitalise areas which, in the absence of such interventions, were likely to remain undeveloped and to stimulate investment in the construction industry and expand employment in the short term.

Local authorities and specially established single-purpose state agencies (Dublin Docklands Development Authority, Temple Bar Properties and Ballymun Regeneration Ltd.) administered the programmes which included the physical redevelopment of lands and properties previously owned by the public sector. In the period to 1991, commercial development dominated urban renewal. A slump in office demand and the emergence of strong residential demand altered the trend towards residential and several thousand units were completed over the next five years. The substantial increases in population for designated areas of Dublin are evidenced by the large population increases in population for city wards such as North City and the Quays districts over census periods 1991 to 2002. Urban renewal policies have evolved over time away from simply achieving development on derelict sites. The newer more holistic approach is represented in the structured programmes for Integrated Area Plans (IAPs) introduced in the 1998 Urban Renewal Guidelines. The role of taxation incentives has now been altered from a blanket provision to one of using incentives including taxation relief as a support for specific catalyst projects where proven barriers to development exist. The emphasis has now moved away from a simplistic boosting of development activity in designated areas towards a new approach aiming to achieve integrated development in a sustainable manner. Tax incentives continue to play a contributory role in urban and town renewal schemes. The lasting impact of tax-based urban renewal development on the privately-rented sector can be seen in that a large part of the city's privately-rented stock now comprises apartment developments built with the aid of tax incentives.

Urban Renewal Incentives

Over recent decades, the general principles of public policy towards the privately-rented sector can be seen as principally supply-orientated. This involved a twin approach. First, there was a general avoidance of the imposition of stringent regulatory measures which might discourage the supply of such accommodation. The second element involved the provision of generous tax incentives for private investors in accommodation for renting. From the 1980s, the availability of fiscal incentives for residential landlords transformed the investment context and acted as a significant stimulus to development for the privately-rented sector. As mentioned above, the principal fiscal incentive for investors in new residential development was introduced as Section 23 of the Finance Act, 1981. These provisions expired in 1984 but were subsequently re-introduced by Sections 27-29 of the Finance Act, 1988. These created special tax allowances for investors in order to encourage the construction of apartments and, in the later Act, small houses for rent. The provisions allowed the costs of properties, net of site value, or the costs of converting buildings into flats, to be deducted from landlords' rental income from all sources until the tax allowance was used up. This mechanism effectively reduced considerably the real purchase price of such investment properties. Qualifying properties had to fall within specified size ranges, amounting to 30-90 sq.m. (323-968 sq. ft.) in the case of apartments and 35-125 sq.m. (377-1,345 sq. ft.) for houses. They had to be rented out for a minimum of ten years. If a qualifying investment were disposed of within ten years, there was provision for a clawing back of the allowances. However, the purchaser or new investor would subsequently be entitled to claim relief on these clawed-back allowances.

Urban Renewal Impacts

The financial incentives engendered a surge of apartment construction from the early 1980s and a significant expansion in the volume of properties available at the middle to upper range of the lettings market. As the reliefs applicable to Section 23/27 properties were available generally throughout the city, the locations preferred by landlords availing of the Section 23/27-type incentives during the 1980s were predominantly of an inner-suburban character, notably in areas such as Ballsbridge, Ranelagh and Rathmines. These were perceived as relatively low-risk locations, typified by strong demand by tenants and as having reasonable prospects of rental growth and capital appreciation. In contrast, in those inner-city areas where little private-sector residential development had taken place during the twentieth century, the incentives managed to induce little interest.

However, from the late 1980s, developers began to test the marketability of new locations, tentatively directing their attention towards inner-city sites. In 1989, a scheme of 36 townhouses in Ringsend sold out within three hours of release. Half sold within the first hour. Somewhat surprisingly given its location, a quarter of the units were sold for owner occupation. By the time of the release of the second phase of units of apartments, duplexes and townhouses in 1991, 70 of the 85 units that were sold in the first week following the launch were purchased by owner occupiers. This was to mark a major trend for the following decade in which landlords, often availing of Section 23/27-type allowances, were obliged thereafter increasingly to compete with individuals purchasing for owner occupation. From the 1992 Finance Act onwards, tax-reliefs for investors in rented residential accommodation became linked to Urban Renewal Initiatives and only available in areas designated under the Urban Renewal Schemes. Henceforth, the financial incentives available to landlords were to become an integral component of urban renewal policy. This contributed significantly to a geographical refocusing of apartment developments during the 1990s and a growing predominance of inner-city locations over suburban sites.

In Dublin, the timing at which the refocusing of financial incentives for investors occurred was particularly significant. Early urban renewal developments had been dominated by speculative office schemes but, by 1992, these had generated a significant oversupply of office space in the Designated

Areas (MacLaran and Hamilton Osborne King, 1993; Williams, 1997). Development interests therefore became increasingly willing to refocus their initiatives on the emerging opportunities provided by the city-centre apartment sector. The support of public agencies, including Dublin City Council whose efforts to encourage living in the city centre involved the sale of suitable development sites at significantly discounted prices, was of considerable importance in facilitating development.

Furthermore, as rising rates of car ownership and car-based commuting created increasing levels of traffic congestion in the city, proximity to the central area became a strong marketing feature and the schemes sold well, not only to landlords but to young middle-class owner occupiers. By early 1997, some 6,000 dwellings had been developed in Dublin's Designated Areas, with a further 2,700 units located on inner-city sites lacking such incentives (MacLaran, 1996; MacLaran *et al,* 1994; MacLaran *et al,* 1995; MacLaran and Floyd, 1996).

The limited available research (MacLaran and Floyd, 1996) into the changing balance between the purchase of such dwellings by landlords and owner occupiers suggests that a majority (54 per cent) of the units taken up in the earlier inner-city developments were bought by landlords. Clearly, the availability of Section 23/27-type allowances proved a sufficient incentive to encourage landlords to undertake a pioneering investment interest in such marginal locations. Thus, the residential investment market provided an important private-sector impetus for urban renewal. However, as urban renewal schemes became better established, the gradually-renewing physical fabric and slowly changing social character of the inner-city increasingly attracted the interest of potential owner occupiers who also became more willing to take on the investment risk in these locations. By 1995, owner occupiers were purchasing over 70 per cent of the units being released in new schemes and, by 1996, they comprised a majority (57.3 per cent) of households in the stock of inner-city new residential developments (MacLaran and Floyd, 1996).

The provision of financial incentives for landlords to acquire and lease out residential properties clearly revealed a considerable underlying latent demand for good quality rental units among young-adult age groups. Hitherto, private renting had been virtually synonymous with the occupancy of flats and bed-sitting accommodation in subdivided eighteenth- or nineteenth-century buildings, frequently ill-provided with facilities and often suffering from damp. However, the creation of a new stock of purpose-built apartments proved highly attractive to a younger generation which had sharply differing ideas about urban living from those of their parents. More sceptical than their parents of the advertising industry's eulogies extolling suburban living, for a generation with weakened ties to religious practice and postponed plans for child rearing, the merits of being 'close to schools and churches' seemed less relevant. The lure of the central-city outstripped the attractions of suburban 'monotonia', bereft of amenities relevant to the urban-oriented culture of a younger generation. In time, perhaps, the established advantages of suburbia for family rearing would reassert themselves. Meanwhile, much real living had to be accomplished, especially as attitudes to sexual activity became transformed, engendering a desire to free oneself from the shackles of parental control. Imitating the lifestyles depicted in the international media of films, television and new lifestyle magazines, the image-package of city life was seductive. This emergent culture of new city living was itself adopted and refined by the advertising industry and used in marketing new inner-city residential developments, a noteworthy example being the image of a besuited business-person commuting to work by water jet-ski from the redeveloped Custom House Docks. It is arguable that such a latent demand had actually been long present but that it had failed to elicit a response in supply due to the high risks associated with initiating central-city residential development for a middle class which had progressively abandoned the inner city during the course of the previous century. The financial incentives changed the economic calculations both for developers and landlords, providing a substantial inducement to landlords willing to take on such a pioneering investment role.

Moreover, following the economic difficulties of the previous seven years which had been characterised by high rates of unemployment and large-scale emigration, the economic upturn from the late 1980s was to usher in a decade of rapid economic expansion. This created growing employment and rising incomes which enabled the previously latent demand for inner-city dwellings to be transformed into an effective demand backed by the enhanced spending-power of the young. By the mid-1990s, a review of Government policies on urban renewal contributed to a further geographical limitation of the incentives to areas incorporated within Integrated Area Plans and catalyst projects noted in the Urban Renewal Guidelines 1998. A related initiative which also continues to use Section 23/27-type incentives is the 'Living Over The Shop Scheme'. This encourages the refurbishment and redevelopment of run-down commercial streets in Dublin. In addition, Section 50 of the Finance Act, 1999 made Section 23/27-type tax reliefs available for investors in student accommodation provided it complies with specified conditions. This has resulted in significant development activity in this sub-sector of the privately-rented market.

Profile of Households Accommodated in Urban Renewal Properties

As this chapter is concerned with private-sector tenancy, it is apposite here to examine the characteristics of the tenant households which were being accommodated in inner-city developments. Due to the paucity of recent research, it is obliged to restrict itself to the findings of work carried out in the mid 1990s (MacLaran, 1996; MacLaran *et al*, 1994; MacLaran *et al*, 1995; MacLaran and Floyd, 1996). However, these data do provide a useful indication of the character of the demand for accommodation that the incentives had assisted in meeting. Nevertheless, it should also be borne in mind that although most inner-city residential developments would have qualified for Section 23/27-type incentives for investors, this was not universally the case after their restriction in 1991 to the Designated Areas. Unfortunately, the available data do not permit a comparison between the social character of the tenants of properties whose landlords did avail of incentives and those who did not. However, there is little to suggest that there might have existed major differences between the two sub-groups.

The research completed in the mid-1990s indicated that the vast majority (97 per cent) of residents were adults aged between 18 and 44 years (See Figure 7.1). Children aged 17 or under and middle-aged and elderly adults were virtually absent. The accommodation attracted a high proportion (47 per cent) of young-adult tenants aged between 18 and 25 years, with the bulk of the remainder (49 per cent) being aged between 26 and 44. As might be expected from the fact that access to mortgage credit is more feasible for older individuals, this age distribution was rather younger than that encountered among owner occupiers in the same developments, as the 26-44 age group accounted for 71 per cent of owners.

Figure 7.1: Ages of Owners and Renters Accommodated in Urban Renewal Properties in Dublin, 1995 (Percentages)

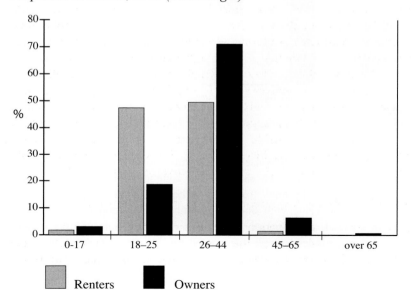

These contrasts in household type between tenants and owners were reflected in differences in the number of persons resident in each household as indicated in Figure 7.2. With a greater tendency for tenant household to occupy larger properties than did owner occupiers, thereby enabling them to divide the (albeit somewhat higher) rent over a greater number of residents, tenant households were found to be significantly larger than their owner-occupied counterparts. Whereas 85 per cent of tenant households had two or more persons resident, some 57 per cent of owner-occupied households comprised a single person only. Thus, the average household size among tenants was 2.29, whereas among owner occupiers it amounted to 1.51.

Figure 7.2: Size of Households Accommodated in Urban Renewal Properties in Dublin, 1995 (Percentages)

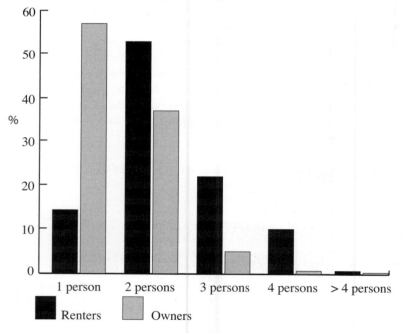

The most frequently occurring household type among tenants was that of unrelated individuals in employment who shared the accommodation, which comprised around 44 per cent of the total. 'Couples' without children formed the second largest group (28 per cent), with single-person household accounting for only 31 per cent. In contrast, single-person households comprised some 55 per cent of owner occupiers, childless couples accounted for 21 per cent, while unrelated individuals in employment who shared the property comprised just 12 per cent.

An indication of the social status of tenants was revealed by the high levels of educational attainment characterising the new residents. Among tenants, over 82 per cent possessed a degree or professional qualification, a proportion which was higher even than that prevailing among the owner occupiers (71 per cent). These suggestions that the incoming population was sharply differentiated from the indigenous population of the inner city were confirmed by an examination of the profile of occupational categories occupied by the new residents illustrated in Figure 7.3. Around 60 per cent of tenants were engaged in the higher echelons of the labour market (professions, company owners and directors, managers and administration), of which over 50 per cent occupied professional grades. There was also a significant representation of third-level students, who accounted for over 12 per cent of the tenant population.

Figure 7.3: Types of Households Accommodated in Urban Renewal Properties in Dublin, 1995 (Percentages)

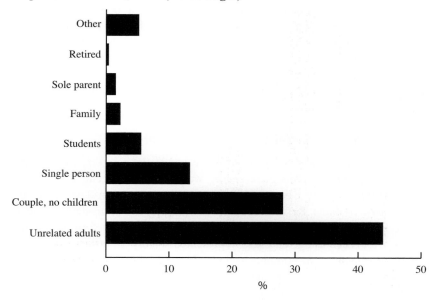

Incomers tended to have few ties to the locality, fewer than 14 per cent having been drawn from the inner city and even fewer (11 per cent) having relatives in the area. Few tenants (9 per cent) reported having made friendships among the established community. Indeed, the potential for long-term community building tended to be minimised by the high annual turnover rate among tenancies, with over 80 per cent of tenant households vacating their accommodation annually. Thus, in broad terms, the new residential developments in inner Dublin had catered primarily for a youthful middle-class population which possessed few previous residential, family or friendship ties to the area. Insofar as considerable public financial subsidy had underpinned a significant proportion of the residential development which had taken place in the inner city since 1980, the subsidies to investors had effectively underpinned a process of gentrification which bore little relevance to the accommodation requirements of the indigenous communities. Indeed, in that the schemes had contributed to an expanding market for the development of high-status residential projects in areas of the city which had remained relatively untouched by the pressures of twentieth-century property development, the subsidies sometimes created new problems for the existing inner-city communities. In many instances, sites in local authority ownership that had been assembled for the construction of much needed social housing were sold to private developers for apartment construction.

More generally, by encouraging private-sector redevelopment in marginal areas, the incentives contributed to land-price inflation and the upgrading of land uses through redevelopment, notably the displacement by apartment schemes of low-grade economic functions which had previously provided employment for inner-city residents. Moreover, the large-scale importing of higher-status social groups enabled the local authority to point to falling unemployment rates as evidence of the success of urban regeneration. This was despite arguments that such impacts tend to be indicators attributable to a dilution process rather than the measure of real improvements in conditions for the established community.

Recent Private Residential Market Trends: 2000-2004

During 2000, the average level of rent increased by 19 per cent, while over a longer period, average rents increased by well over 50 per cent, from around €600 per month for a 1-bed apartment to €900 between August 1998 and January 2002 (Gunne Residential, 2002). This created a substantial rise in income for landlords at a time when their outgoings in the form of interest charges were decreasing, and also represented a very significant degree of capital appreciation. The stimulus to the residential lettings sector provided by fiscal incentives, together with the strong market returns provided by residential lettings, seems to have encouraged a large number of new investors to enter the sector. A survey of landlords and tenants conducted by Gunne Residential (2002) revealed that only 15 per cent of landlords had been investing in residential property for more than 10 years and that 62 per cent had been involved in the sector for less than 3 years. The survey also pointed to the high degree of fragmentation of ownership, with 54 per cent of landlords owning just one property and a further 23 per cent having two or three lettings. During the first half of 2003, 29 per cent of all residential sales were to investors (Sherry FitzGerald, 2003).

More recent work by Kelly and MacLaran (2004) has provided evidence of a dramatic rise in capital values of inner-city properties during the period 1995-2003. They based their calculations on the Trinity College Centre for Urban and Regional Studies database of launch prices of apartment developments that were completed in the inner city during 1995. Apartments which returned to the market in late 2003 were at prices which had more than trebled during the intervening period, marked by increases of between 202 and 363 per cent. Such growth greatly outpaced the rise in the Consumer Price Index, which rose by 25 per cent during the period, or the rise in earnings, which increased by 43 per cent.

Kelly and MacLaran (2004) have also reviewed the contribution of private-sector residential development in the renewal of central Dublin and evaluated the impact on the social geography of the inner city. The research revealed that in addition to the 7,730 residential units developed in the city between 1989 and March 1996 (MacLaran and Floyd, 1996), some 8,769 units had subsequently been completed by late November 2003 and that 2,485 were under construction. Furthermore, live planning permissions existed for an additional 4,962 units, with applications having been lodged for another 2,277. The research also showed the impact of such development to have been considerable. Between 1991 and 2002, the number of private permanent households resident in the 40 inner-city wards in Dublin City Council's operational area increased from 31,555 to 97,257, its population expanding by over 29,800 persons, from 84,055 to 112,076. Meanwhile, the remaining wards in the city actually lost population, their aggregate population dropping from 393,334 to 383,705. Five inner-city wards (North City, Rotunda A, Royal Exchange A, St Kevin's and Merchant's Quay B) registered a population increase of over 1,500 persons, while a further 7 increased by over 1,000 residents. The inner 40 wards thereby increased its proportion of the City Borough's population from 18 to 23 per cent.

Significant changes in residential tenures also occurred in the inner-city, notably with regard to private renting, Table 1 revealing the major expansion in the scale of private-sector furnished lettings between 1991 and 2002. During this period, its significance rose from slightly under 25 per cent of the total to almost 36 per cent. Meanwhile, the local-authority rental sector dropped from almost one third of the total (32 per cent) to just 18 per cent, and although the absolute number of owner-occupying households increased, its proportionate significance reduced from 35.4 per cent to 32 per cent. The latter, involving an increase in owner occupation subject to mortgage and a decline in the number of outright owners, reflects an influx of a younger population of buyers, of both newly developed buildings and older properties which previous residents owned outright.

Table 7.1: Housing Tenure in Central Dublin, 1991, 2002

	1991 N	2002 N
Owner occupation (Outright)	6,688	6,060
Owner occupation (Mortgaged)	4,493	7,879
Purchasing from local authority	663	1,950
Local authority renting	10,233	8,111
Private renting, unfurnished	2,121	2,318
Private renting, furnished	5,611	13,272
Rent free	576	629
Not stated	1,170	3,330

Source: Central Statistics Office, 1996, 2004b.

Major changes in the social composition of the population of the Inner-40 Wards also took place between 1991 and 2002 (Kelly and MacLaran, 2004). The number of two-person households increased dramatically, from 7,650 to 14,216 households. In age structure, there was a significant rise in the proportion of the population aged between 25 and 44 years, the group which had been shown in the mid-1990s to predominate in the new residential developments (MacLaran *et al*, 1995). In 1991, this age group had accounted for 28 per cent of the residents whereas, in 2002, it comprised over 40 per cent. The representation of Social Classes 1 and 2, broadly the professional, managerial and proprietorial grades, rose from 14.3 per cent to 25.4 per cent. Particularly noteworthy was the change in the social class of the 25-44 year-old age cohort. Between 1991 and 2002, the number of young residents in Social Classes 1 and 2 rose from 5,075 to 17,578, their proportionate share of that age cohort increasing from 21.5 per cent to 39 per cent. These changes were further emphasised by the fact that the number of residents with third-level education or possessing a professional qualification rose from 6,581 in 1991 to 27,090 in 2002.

Evaluation and Future Directions

While the special incentives in place since 1981 have played a major role in achieving the stated objectives of improving the supply and quality of privately-rented accommodation, general taxation policy is a major influence on investment trends. The generally favourable tax treatment of residential property investors, following the Finance Act of 2002, represented a reversal of previous measures which had attempted to favour purchases by owner occupiers over investors. The reintroduction of interest relief as an allowable tax deduction for landlords, combined with allowances and deductions in respect of expenditures on fixtures and fittings and other costs, makes this form of investment very attractive for potential investors (Cronin, 2002). These provisions became particularly attractive in the light of the concerns of investors concerning the performance of alternative investment media, e.g. equities and bonds.

On balance, therefore, despite the planned expiration of various special incentives schemes in 2006, fiscal policy remains supportive of investment in the privately-rented residential sector. In addition, as Galligan describes in more detail in Chapter 5, as the privately-rented sector has grown in recent years, the need for adequate regulation of the sector has been recognised. The Report of the Commission on the Privately-rented Residential Sector (2000) has provided the basis for recent government actions in the area, including the establishment of the Private Rented Tenancies Board and the introduction of the Residential Tenancies Act, 2004. It is evident from the Report of the Commission and subsequent public debate that such proposals will continue to generate considerable discussion and opposition. Reform in respect of the private housing market and its regulations will thus remain a difficult and contentious area in the years to come.

8

Social Housing

Michelle Norris

Introduction

The foundations of social housing provision in the Republic of Ireland can be traced back to the mid-1800s. At this time, in many European countries there was growing concern about the housing conditions of the low-income population – inspired by a range of interests including: philanthropists and social reformers; the emerging labour movement and a belief that housing conditions in urban slums were creating public health problems, impeding economic efficiency and fostering social unrest. This concern led to the creation of systems of State-subsidised housing for rent to low-income and disadvantaged groups which is know as social housing (Pooley, 1992). Ireland was no different in this regard, with the important caveat that its status as part of the United Kingdom until 1922, meant that the early development of its social housing was shaped by UK legislation, which has bequeathed both countries an atypical system of social housing provision in the wider European context (Harloe, 1995). In addition, the distinctive political concerns of Ireland at that time meant that the early development of social housing in this country also has some unusual features which differentiate it from Britain, and have influenced its evolution over the long term (Fahey, 1998b).

This chapter sketches the most significant trends in the development of the social housing provision in this country from the mid-1800s, until the contemporary period. The opening part of the chapter examines the early housing legislation; explains how it shaped the system of social housing provision and assesses the contribution which social housing providers made to addressing housing need in urban and rural areas. In the second part of the chapter, a more in-depth examination of the development of the social housing sector during the last two decades is presented. This section concentrates on efforts to diversify the methods of providing social housing and the increasing focus on the part of central government on qualitative issues such as efficient housing management and the regeneration of difficult-to-let social rented estates, in addition to its traditional quantitative concern of ensuring that supply of social housing matches need. On the basis of this discussion, the concluding comments to the chapter quantify the achievements of the social housing sector in Ireland and identify some of the key questions facing the sector at the current time.

Foundation and Municipalisation: 1880-1922

The foundations of social housing provision in urban areas in both Britain and Ireland lie in two policy developments – the gradual extension of slum clearance legislation throughout the latter half of the nineteenth century which empowered local authorities to identify, close and clear unfit dwellings, and in legislation requiring the licensing and inspection of common lodging houses, beginning with the Common Lodging Houses Act, 1851, which established the principle of State involvement in enforcing minimum housing standards. The advent of State subsidisation of housing provision to ensure higher standards was a logical extension of these provisions. Subsidies of this type were originally introduced in Ireland under the 1866 Labouring Classes (Lodging Houses and Dwellings) Act, which provided low-cost public loans over 40 years to private companies and urban local authorities, for up to half the cost of a housing scheme. Although this initial housing legislation produced relatively modest outcomes, social house building increased significantly under its successor – the 1875 Artisans and Labourers Dwellings Improvement Act, which provided low cost public loans to the larger urban local authorities for the clearance of unsanitary sites, which could then be used for new house building.

The majority of output under the early social housing legislation was not by local authorities. In fact, the 1875 Act allowed local authorities to build dwellings only if no alternative provider could be found. Instead most social rented dwellings were provided by a range of non-statutory agencies which can be organised into three categories. These are: philanthropic bodies such as the Guinness Trust (now called the Iveagh Trust), which was founded in 1890; semi-philanthropic organisations such as the Cork and the Dublin Artisans' Dwellings Company, which were run as a business paying a modest dividend of between 4 and 5 per cent to shareholders and industrialists such as the Malcolmson family of Portlaw Co. Waterford who built rented housing for their workers (Aalen, 1985, 1990; Keohane, 2002; Hunt, 2000). Not surprisingly in view of the industrial underdevelopment of the country at this time, the number of dwellings provided by this third source was relatively modest. However, with the aid of the low-cost loans provided under the housing legislation, together with grant aid from Dublin City Council, philanthropic and semi-philanthropic organisations had built 4,500 dwellings, accounting for approximately 15 per cent of Dublin's housing stock, by the outbreak of World War I (Fraser, 1996).

These dwellings were generally high density in design, they took the form of either flats such as the Iveagh buildings in Dublin's south inner city which was built by the Iveagh Trust, or of terraced housing such as Oxmanstown Road in the Stoneybatter area of Dublin's north inner city which was built by the Dublin Artisans' Dwellings Company.

In contrast, local authority provision in towns and cities was slower to get off the ground. Ireland's first urban local authority housing scheme was completed in 1879 by Waterford City Council in Green Street, Ballybricken, but Fraser (1996) estimates that urban authorities completed a total of only 570 dwellings in the decade which followed. As Figure 8.1 demonstrates, urban local authority housing output began to increase after the introduction of the 1890 Housing of the Working Classes Act, which provided for more attractive central government loans, and for the first time allowed social house building on green field sites to meet general housing need, as well as in slum clearance areas. It expanded significantly after the 1908 Housing Act, which introduced even better loan terms and established an Irish Housing Fund which provided the first direct exchequer subsidy for urban housing, and, in contrast to the norm in countries such as Germany, Denmark and Sweden, from this period onwards local authorities took over from non-statutory bodies as the main providers of social housing for rent in Ireland (Harloe, 1995).

Figure 8.1: Local Authority Dwellings Built Under the Housing of the Working Classes Acts and the Labourers Acts, 1887-1918

Source: Minister for Local Government (1964).

In the case of the semi-philanthropic companies the reasons for this turn of events are straightforward – the pre-World War I economic slump rendered it uneconomic for the main providers including the Dublin Artisans' Dwellings Company to continue building (Aalen, 1985). The story of why a larger philanthropic housing movement did not emerge in Ireland at this stage is more complex, however. Power (1993: 321) emphasises that the Artisans' Dwellings Company and the Iveagh Trust were founded by Protestant industrialists (although neither organisation had either sectarian or proselytising motives), and argues that '… it was inevitable therefore that Dublin Corporation, with its Catholic voters and Nationalist councillors would feel forced to do something about the problems of the very poor'. On the other hand, Fraser's (1996) account of the period stresses that these religious divisions frustrated the development of a philanthropic housing movement large enough to resolve the chronic housing problems of Ireland's urban poor, and that the semi-philanthropic housing providers concentrated on housing the better-off sections of the working class such as skilled artisans and tradespeople. Thus, he argues that the increasingly more generous housing subsidies introduced during the late 1800s and early 1900s allowed urban local authorities to build dwellings of high standard at lower rents, which encouraged them to expand their housing provision to meet the needs of the poorest sections of society. Either way, as Mullins *et al* (2003) explain, from the early twentieth century onwards, non-statutory social housing providers were 'crowded out' by expanding local authority output.

An unusual aspect of the early development of local authority housing in Ireland in comparison with Britain and most other Western European countries is the emphasis which was placed on provision for low-income workers in rural areas. Initiatives in this regard began with the, largely unsuccessful, Dwellings for the Labouring Classes (Ireland) Act, 1860, which allowed landlords to borrow from the Public Works Loans Commission to build cottages for their tenants and expanded following the introduction of a series of increasingly more radical rural housing schemes which granted significantly more generous subsidies than those available in urban areas, starting with the Labourers (Ireland) Act, 1883 (as amended in 1885), which subsidised local authorities to provide housing for rent to farm labourers. As revealed by Figure 8.1, this initiative, together with the 1886 Labourers Act, which extended housing eligibility to anyone working part-time as an agricultural labourer, resulted in the completion of 3,191 labourers cottages in 1890 alone by rural local authorities. Output over the following decade averaged at 700 dwellings per year, but it rose again as a result of the Labourers (Ireland) Act, 1906 which established a dedicated Labourers Cottage Fund to provide low-interest loans for rural local authority house building, and more significantly, sanctioned that 36 per cent of the loan payments would be met by central government.

Fahey (1998b) links the advent and expansion of the labourers cottage programme with the campaign for the redistribution of land from landlords to tenant farmers which was one of the main preoccupations of Parnell's Irish Parliamentary Party during the late nineteenth and early twentieth centuries. He characterises the labourers cottage programme as a 'consolation prize' for the farm labourers who were excluded from the process of land reform, but were numerous enough to warrant the attention of the Irish Parliamentary Party. His argument in this regard is supported by the fact that each of the Labourers Acts referred to above was introduced immediately following a Land Act which provided subsidised loans to allow tenant farmers to purchase their farms, and subsidies for house building under the Labourers Acts were strikingly similar to the land purchase subsidies.

The combination of World War I, the 1916 Rising and the War of Independence obstructed any further significant development of local authority housing in the pre-independence period. However, by the foundation of the State, the structure of the social housing sector for much of the rest of the century had already been determined in the sense that local authorities, rather than the non-statutory agencies, would be the dominant providers. Furthermore, the combination of the various Housing of the Working Classes Acts and the Labourers Acts bequeathed the infant Irish State a very sizeable local authority housing stock, albeit one which the 1913 Dublin housing inquiry revealed to be grossly inadequate to meet the needs of the urban poor (Housing Inquiry, 1914). By 1914, Irish local authorities had completed approximately 44,701 dwellings, in comparison with only 24,000 council dwellings built in Great Britain during the same period (Fraser, 1996; Malpass and Murie, 1999). However, only 8,063 of the Irish local authority dwellings built by 1914 were in urban areas, in contrast to Britain where the comparable figure is 98 per cent of output (Department of Local Government, various years; Fraser, 1996).

Slum Clearance and Tenant Purchase, 1922-1960

In the years immediately following independence housing remained at the top of the agenda of the new administration, but the focus of government attention moved from social to private housing. Admittedly additional funding was made available to the social housing sector in the early 1920s under the auspices of the 'Million Pound Scheme' which, as its name implies, generated one million pounds for urban local authority house building from a mixture of central government funds, local authority rates and short-term bank loans. The scheme achieved an immediate response, and Figure 8.2 below reveals that, by 1924, it had resulted in the construction of 959 new dwellings. From the architectural and planning perspective the most significant development built under the auspices of the scheme was at Marino in Dublin where 1,262 houses were constructed in an innovative design, influenced by the British 'Garden City' architectural movement which endeavoured to combine the virtues of urban and rural life by building suburbs with layouts akin to traditional country villages and ample green space (McManus, 2002).

However, the subsidies proffered under the scheme proved to be exceptional for the time, as legislative developments in 1924 revealed that private rather than social housing was the primary concern of the new Cumann na nGaedheal government. The Housing (Building Facilities) Act, 1924 introduced substantial subsidies for private house building, which covered approximately one sixth of the usual building cost at the time (Roche, 1982). As Figure 8.2 illustrates, these grants triggered a dramatic increase in private building, and the vast majority of new private dwellings built after 1924 availed of the grants (Minister for Local Government, 1964). In contrast, local authorities' social house building programme was reined in as central government proved unwilling to continue the programme of long-term subsidisation of local authority house building initiated under the 1906 Labourers (Ireland) Act and the 1908 Housing Act, or even to treat local authority housing more favourably than private construction. Instead, the Housing (Building Facilitates) (Amendment) Act, 1924 offered amounts similar to private grants for urban local authority house building, although the 1925 Housing Act tilted the balance in favour of local authorities by reducing the private grants while maintaining the standard grant level for urban local authority housing and extending this subsidy to include labourers cottage schemes.

Figure 8.2: Local Authority Dwellings Built Under the Housing of the Working Classes Acts and the Labourers Acts, and Private Dwellings Built with State Aid, 1923-1960

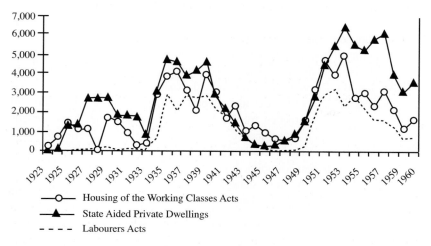

Source: Minister for Local Government (1964).

Difficulties in raising bank loans combined with the high cost of this source of finance inhibited local authorities from undertaking large-scale building programmes during the second half of the 1920s, however, and output only began to increase significantly in 1929, when the government decided to restore the practice, suspended since 1922, of providing local authorities with low-interest State loans for house building. As a result, output of urban local authority dwellings rose to 1,789 in 1929, although building under the Labourers Acts remained low and only 385 dwellings were completed by rural local authorities between 1923 and 1930. Output from the latter source was not a major cause for concern as housing need in rural areas had diminished as a result of earlier labourers cottage building programmes. However, even this expanded level of output proved insufficient to meet housing need in the towns and cities. A survey of housing need in urban local authority areas undertaken by Government in 1929 found that relatively little progress had been made in clearing the slums and addressing housing need among the poorest households and as a result some 40,000 new dwellings were required in these areas. McManus's (2002) detailed study of housing in Dublin between 1910 and 1940 reveals that, as well as inadequate housing output, the situation related to concerns on the part of the local authorities about generating adequate revenue income and minimising outgoings in order to meet loan charges, as a consequence of which most of the local authority dwellings built in Dublin during the 1920s were allocated to relatively affluent working-class families, and/or as in the case of the aforementioned estate at Marino were sold to tenants soon after completion.

The findings of the 1929 survey spurred government into radical action and the result was the Housing (Miscellaneous Provisions) Act which replaced the slum clearance provisions of the Housing of the Working Classes Act, 1890 with new, more effective procedures and also replaced the policy of State assistance to public house building by means of lump sum grants that had prevailed throughout the 1920s, with annual subsidies towards loan charges, which Roche (1982: 224) assesses as ' … generous for those depression times'. Although the 1931 Act laid the foundation for the radical expansion of local authority house building over the rest of the decade, several of its provisions never came into effect. They were superseded by the Housing (Financial and Miscellaneous Provisions) Act, 1932, introduced by the first Fianna Fáil government which took office that year. The 1932 Act further increased the central government subsidies to loan charges for public house building introduced by its predecessor and provided for even more generous subsidies in the case of dwellings constructed for households displaced by slum clearance programmes, together with subsidies for private house building.

O'Connell (1994) argues that the particular mix of subsidies introduced by the 1932 Act played a key role in determining the long-term role of social housing in Ireland – the majority of the population would be housed by the expanding private sector with the help of state subsidies, while the refocusing of subsidies to local authorities on slum clearance meant that they would in future concentrate their efforts on housing the poorest section of society. In the short term, however, as Figure 8.2 above demonstrates, these subsidies also resulted in a marked increase in local authority house building. Output under the Housing of the Working Classes Acts rose to a pre-World War II high in 1936 when 4,215 dwellings were completed and building of Labourers Acts schemes was also revived and peaked in 1939 which saw the completion of 2,867 rural dwellings. A total of 48,875 local authority rented dwellings were constructed between 1933 and 1943, as compared to the 9,994 units completed in the previous decade. Although local authority output began to slow in the late 1930s and early 1940s as a result of government concerns about capital expenditure and the impact of World War II, in comparison with private-sector output during the war years it still remained relatively buoyant. In fact, 1933 to 1943 was the only decade in the history of the State in which house building by the local authority sector exceeded private-sector output.

Some one third of the local authority rented dwellings built during the 1930s and 1940s was constructed by Dublin City Council as part of a massive inner-city slum clearance programme. Since the Council first became involved in social house building a lively debate had raged in architectural and political circles in Ireland concerning the propriety of suburban or urban locations for social housing. Most of the units built by the Council in the 1920s were standard houses. However, Herbert Simms who worked as City Architect during the 1930s and 1940s, was a proponent of urban locations for social housing, and as a result a large proportion of the dwellings constructed during his tenure were located in inner-city areas, including: Hanover Street, Cook Street, Chancery Street and Townsend Street (McManus, 2002). These dwellings were generally four-storey blocks of flats, the perimeter of which followed the existing street pattern with communal courtyards at the rear which provided access, play space, clothes drying areas and storage. From the 1940s Dublin City Council redirected its efforts to suburban housing development but the estates it constructed during this time such as Crumlin, Donnycarney, Cabra and Ballyfermot bore little resemblance to the garden suburbs advocated in the 1920s. They were large in size, relatively low density and of similar, monotonous design with little or no landscaping.

As O'Connell examines in more detail in Chapter 2 of this volume, from the perspective of local authority housing, the 1930s are also notable for the introduction of a universal right of purchase for tenants of labourers cottages, replacing the previous system whereby local authorities could, at their own discretion, apply to the central government to establish sale schemes. This reform was initiated on the recommendation of a commission of enquiry on the subject which reported in 1933, and legislated for in the 1936 Labourers Act, which obliged all county councils to sell their labourers cottages using a system of annuity payments which were set at a generous discount from the original rent. Like many other distinctive aspects of housing policy in this country, the impetus behind the introduction of rural tenant purchase, three decades before this scheme was extended to include urban tenants, and some 45 years before the British government introduced a similar universal right to buy for all council tenants, lies in the land reform movement. Fahey (1998b) argues that the de Valera government was finally forced to concede to the sale of labourers cottages – after many years of lobbying from tenants, because its 1933 Land Act had made significant reductions in the annuities payable by tenant farmers who had purchased their holdings. Furthermore, he contends that the way in which 'land reform continued to influence the substance of housing policy ... gave Irish public housing a character that in some respects was unique in Europe' (Fahey, 1998b: 10). As mentioned earlier in this chapter, the influence of land reform during the nineteenth century had conferred the Irish social housing system with a uniquely rural character, but in the twentieth century, the land reform inspired advent of tenant purchase would contribute in the long run to the reduction of the social rented stock in this country to a low level, in comparison with most other northern European countries (Harloe, 1995). As this scheme was initially confined to labourers cottages, this contraction impacted first on rural areas. By 1964 approximately 80 per cent of the 86,931 labourers cottages built by that date had been tenant purchased, whereas only 6,393 urban dwellings had been sold by then (Minister for Local Government, 1964).

Despite this high level of sales, however, in absolute terms the number of local authority rented dwellings did not decline during the next decade, as the rate of new building remained high. The 1948 White Paper *Housing: A Review of Past Operations and Immediate Requirements* estimated that 100,000 new dwellings were needed – 60,000 of which should be provided by local authorities and 40,000 by the private sector (Department of Local Government, 1948). In order to achieve this, the 1948 Housing (Amendment) Act further increased central government subsidies for local authority house building. As a result, local authority output increased more than tenfold between 1948 and 1954, and although it fell back somewhat towards the end of the 1950s, output for the 10 years 1950 to 1959 totalled 52,767 dwellings – more than double what had been achieved during the previous decade. Notwithstanding this impressive level of construction, however, in relative terms the share of total housing output contributed by local authorities fell in the 1950s. This is because, contrary to the predictions of the 1948 White Paper, private building increased even faster than public sector output. By the time local authorities had reached their target of 60,000 new dwellings in 1963, just over 68,000 private sector dwellings had been completed – over twice as many as had been envisaged in 1948. This development, which was largely a consequence of a series of Housing Acts offering ever higher subsidies to private builders, marked the start of a long-term trend which has not only persisted, but has accelerated in the decades since the 1950s.

Modernisation and Decline, 1961-1979

In common with wider Irish society and the economy, during the 1960s the local authority housing service modernised in a number of respects. For instance, housing law was reformed, rationalised and updated and local authorities began to utilise modern building techniques in their housing developments. More significantly, during the 1960s and 1970s the local authority rented tenure began to contract in size, and it became apparent that local authorities would play a more modest role in housing the population of modern Ireland than they had in the past.

The rationalisation of the public housing legislation was achieved at a single stroke by means of the 1966 Housing Act. This act replaced more than fifty earlier legislative provisions with a simple statement of powers enabling housing authorities to deal with unfit dwellings and districts within their operational areas; requiring them to assess local housing needs regularly; to devise a programme of building dwellings for people unable to adequately house themselves on this basis; to allocate these dwellings according to a scheme of letting priorities which should give preference to households in greatest need of housing and enabling them to manage these dwellings and to sell them to tenants. Indeed such is the extensive scope of the Act that to this day, most aspects of local authority housing administration still fall under its remit and it is referred to in the subsequent housing legislation as the 'Principal Act'. The 1966 Act also had an important modernising function, as it encompassed all levels of local government and thus marked the end of the tradition of separate legislation governing urban and rural public housing which had prevailed since the 1800s.

However, this aspect of the Act is not as innovative as it ostensibly appears. Rather it is the culmination of a thirty-year trend whereby new housing laws tended to make identical provisions for urban and rural areas, the extent of which was such that by 1966 only three significant outstanding differences between the two codes remained for the Housing Act to abolish. These are: the lack of a universal right of purchase for urban tenants, minor divergences in land acquisition procedure and procedures for the repossession of dwellings (Minister for Local Government, 1964). As well as rationalising and modernising the public housing legislation, the 1966 Act instituted a number of reforms to local authority housing management, the most important of which relate to rent setting. The Act empowered the Minister to regulate the rents levied on local authority dwellings and since 1967 all local authority housing rents in Ireland have been calculated on the basis of the tenant's household income – an arrangement which is colloquially termed 'differential rents'.

Another interesting reform introduced in the 1966 Housing Act is the provision of additional state subsidy to housing authorities constructing blocks of flats of six or more storeys. This subsidy was part of a series of initiatives introduced by central government during the 1960s and 1970s to encourage the use of modern building techniques, which, it was envisaged, would help to rapidly expand housing output to meet the demand created by the growing population and the economic boom at that time (Minister for Local Government, 1964). Many of the housing schemes constructed using these modern methods were built by local authorities. A semi-prefabricated or 'system' building technique was used in the construction of mixed estates of houses and three-storey flats at Mayfield, the Glen and Togher for Cork City Council, while Dublin City Council employed a similar system of pre-cast concrete panels to build Ireland's only high-rise estate at Ballymun and a lower-rise version at St Michael's Estate, Inchicore (Power, 2000).

In comparative terms, Irish local authorities' embrace of modern building methods was belated – these techniques were in common use in other European countries since the end of World War II, especially among exponents of the modernist architectural movement. Furthermore, it was short lived; ironically Ballymun was completed in 1969 just seven months before the collapse of the Ronan Point tower block in London signalled the beginning of the end of the high-rise experiment in Europe. However, Dunleavy (1981) argues that in the public imagination these system-built public sector dwellings have assumed an importance disproportionate to their modest numbers. In many European countries, the unpopularity of high-rise estates among tenants, and the well-publicised structural problems of many system-built dwellings, have contributed to the 'delegitimation' of the social rented tenure as a whole – in the popular imagination local authority housing was no longer seen as the best solution to poor housing conditions, and it was increasingly seen as the cause of them. As well as problems related to design and construction, the image of social housing was also undermined by negative media attention and by a series of studies, inspired by the so-called 'rediscovery of poverty' in the social sciences during the 1970s, which found that poverty and social problems were increasingly concentrated in this tenure and highlighted the intractability of these problems (for instance, Reynolds, 1986). Barlow and Duncan (1988) relate the stigmatisation of the local authority rented sector to the wider growth of 'tenurism' in Britain at this time, as housing tenure became associated with other social phenomena and a causal relationship was increasingly assumed between the two. This concept demonstrates that the increasingly negative image of the social rented sector in recent decades has implications not only for public policy relating to the tenure but also for its occupants. The people who live in social rented accommodation are often as stigmatised as the estates in which they live.

Figure 8.3: Local Authority Dwellings and Private Dwellings Completed and Local Authority Dwellings Sold to Tenants, 1960-1979

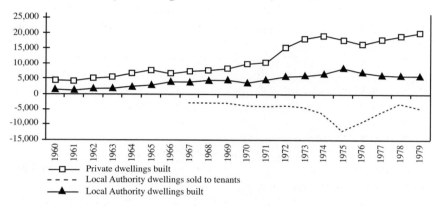

Source: Department of Local Government (various years) and Department of the Environment, Heritage and Local Government (various years).

Note: No figures are available on sales before 1967; figures from 1967 to 1970 include both Labourers Act dwellings sold and all dwellings sold under the 1966 Housing Act; figures from 1970 onwards include dwellings sold under the 1966 Housing Act, only. Details of dwellings which were sold in urban areas at the discretion of local authorities after the enactment of the 1966 Housing Act are not included in this graph; therefore it slightly underestimates the true level of sales.

Finally, as alluded to above, between 1961 and 1971 the percentage of the national housing stock rented from local authorities fell from 18.4 per cent to 15.9 per cent and it would fall further to 12.7 per cent by 1981 (Central Statistics Office, 2004b). As Figure 8.3 demonstrates, to some extent this phenomenon is due to the continued fall in the relative contribution of public sector building to total housing output during these decades. Although the local authority housing output rose during the 1960s and 1970s, private sector completions grew at a much faster rate. Another significant factor in the decline of the tenure is the steady rise in number of sales of dwellings to tenants after the 1966 Housing Act extended the tenant purchase scheme to urban local authority housing. At this stage tenant purchasers were offered a reduction on the market value of the dwelling for every year of residency, subject to a maximum discount of 30 per cent in urban areas and 45 per cent in rural areas. Figure 8.3 also highlights a sharp rise in tenant purchase sales between 1973 and 1979, to the extent that they outstripped new building, which was due to the introduction of additional discounts for tenant purchasers in the former year (Foras Forbartha, 1978).

Residualisation, Regeneration, Diversification, 1980-Present

The last two decades have, more than any other since the foundation of the State, been characterised by radical change in the social housing sector. The title of this section encapsulates the key developments during this turbulent period as the residualisation of the tenure, coupled with efforts to regenerate it and to diversity the methods of social housing provision.

Residualisation refers to the tendency for the social housing sector '… to cater for an increased proportion of deprived people and to cater more exclusively for this group' (Lee and Murie, 1997: 7). The concept was initially devised as a result of the aforementioned growing interest among housing researchers in the late 1970s, to explain the increasing level of poverty in this tenure in the UK which, until the 1940s, had been dominated by skilled manual workers and lower middle class families (Malpass, 1990). In contrast to their British counterparts, apart from a brief period in the 1920s, Irish local authorities have generally charged low rents and let to disadvantaged groups (Fraser, 1996; McManus, 2002). Therefore it is reasonable to assume that the local authority rented tenure in this country has always been more or less residualised. However, in common with the UK, the available evidence indicates that the level of residualisation of local authority housing in Ireland has worsened considerably over the last two decades.

This evidence is presented in Table 8.1, which demonstrates that, between 1987 and 1994, the number of local authority tenant households with incomes below 60 per cent of the national average grew from 59.1 per cent to 74.6 per cent. Nolan and Whelan (1999) report that this process of residualisation was particularly acute in urban areas. The proportion of urban local authority tenants with incomes below 60 per cent of average rose from 53.2 per cent in 1987 to 77.2 per cent in 1994, whereas the equivalent figures for their rural counterparts are 63.9 per cent and 71.2 per cent respectively. Additional research by Murray and Norris (2002) on Dublin City Council tenant households indicates that this trend continued during the latter half of the 1990s. They found that in 2001 73.1 per cent of Dublin City Council tenant households had incomes below 60 per cent of average, as compared to 27.2 per cent of the general Irish population.

Table 8.1: Income Poverty Among Households by Tenure, 1987, 1994

	% of Households with Incomes Below 40% of Average		% of Households with Incomes Below 60% of Average	
	1987	1994	1987	1994
Owned outright	16.8	18.1	30.0	37.8
Owned with a mortgage	6.7	8.7	2.5	14.6
Local Authority tenant purchased	17.8	21.8	27.5	41.6
Local Authority rented	37.4	49.8	59.1	74.6
Other rented	14.4	15.1	27.7	34.0
All households	17.0	18.8	29.1	34.6

Source: adapted from Nolan, Whelan and Williams (1998).

The research on residualisation relates its development to either or both of the following issues: the broader socio-economic environment of the time, and housing policy and social housing management, although there is no consensus in the literature as to the relative import of these different issues (Malpass, 1990).

In relation to the former of the two, Nolan and Whelan's (1999) analysis indicates that the economic crisis of the 1980s had a strong negative impact on Irish local authority tenants, who they reveal as likely to have low educational attainment, work in unskilled manual jobs, be headed by a single parent or a pensioner and therefore were at high risk of social security dependence and of poverty. By contrast, Murray and Norris's (2002) research on Dublin City Council tenants concludes that in addition to the socio-demographic characteristics of these households, residualisation patterns can be also explained by the characteristics of the neighbourhoods in which they live. Specifically, they highlight the lower levels of income poverty amongst tenant households living in inner-city areas which accommodate a mixed-income population and contain a large number of amenities and employment opportunities, and the higher level of income poverty amongst tenants living in large local authority estates on the periphery of the city which are dominated by low-income households.

In relation to housing policy, Forrest and Murie's (1983) research in the UK identifies the relative size of the local authority rented tenure as a key cause of residualisation and as Figure 8.4 below demonstrates, in Ireland, the period since 1980 has seen dramatic change in this regard. From the mid-1980s, the number of new local authority dwellings built fell steadily, to a post-World War II low in 1989 when only 768 units were completed. In the face of a marked increase in waiting lists in social housing, which rose from 17,564 households in 1991 to 48,413 households in 2002, local authority housing output increased steadily throughout the 1990s, reaching a high of 5,074 dwellings in 2002 (Department of the Environment, Heritage and Local Government, various years). However, it has remained well below 10 per cent of total new house construction, which is significantly lower than in the period 1930 to 1980 when local authority house building comprised an average of 20 per cent to 30 per cent of total output (Fahey and O'Connell, 1999). Low levels of building reduced the number of dwellings available for letting, and because local authority dwellings are allocated on the basis of need, it is reasonable to assume that only the most disadvantaged households have secured tenancies during the last 20 years.

Figure 8.4: Local Authority and Voluntary and Co-operative Dwellings Acquired and Completed and Local Authority Dwellings Sold to Tenants, 1980-2002

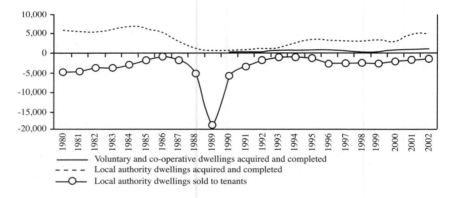

Source: Department of the Environment, Heritage and Local Government (various years). Note: data on voluntary and co-operative dwellings completed prior to 1990 are not available.

Figure 8.4 also reveals that the level of tenant purchase of dwellings increased substantially between 1987 and 1991, spurred on by extra discounts for buyers introduced in 1986 and 1988. This trend is important because sales have a twofold residualising effect. By reducing the number of dwellings available for letting they stimulate an influx of disadvantaged people into the tenure. Furthermore, as Table 8.1 above demonstrates, because tenant purchasers tend to be wealthier than public renting households (although they are still poorer than other owner occupiers) sales also promote an exodus of better-off households.

In addition, the process of residualisation was exacerbated by the advent of the '£5,000 Surrender Grant' scheme in October 1984. This scheme, which allocated €6,349 to local authority tenants and tenant purchasers who were prepared to surrender their dwelling and to buy a home in the private sector, was intended to free up dwellings for letting without incurring the cost of new building. Blackwell (1988a) reports that by the time the scheme was abolished in March 1987 a total of 7,700 surrender grants were paid out – accounting for 6.5 per cent of the entire public renting population at the time. A study of the effects of the grant in the Dublin area, which was carried out by the housing advice agency Threshold (1987), confirms that practically 100 per cent of the families who took advantage of the scheme were in employment, and the residualising effects associated with the departure of these households from public sector estates were compounded by the fact that many of those who moved into the dwellings vacated under the scheme, e.g. lone parents or single unemployed men, were at high risk of poverty.

On a more positive note, by the mid-1980s growing central government concern about social problems and poor living conditions in residualised local authority sector estates inspired the instigation of a number of measures intended to regenerate these areas, mainly by means of refurbishing the built environment. Irish developments in this regard reflect similar initiatives in several other EU member states. Power (1999: 147-148) points out that France, Germany and Denmark all launched 'estate regeneration' programmes between 1978 and 1987 involving: '… renewed intervention to restore physical, financial, organisational and social viability to mass estates' in the social rented sector. The in-depth *Investigation of Difficult to Let Housing* carried out by the British Department of the Environment in the late 1970s inspired a veritable 'alphabet soup' of social housing estate regeneration schemes, starting with the Priority Estates project (PEP) which was established in 1979 and soon joined by programmes such as Estate Action (EA) and the Housing Action Trusts (HATs) (Burbridge, *et al* 1981; Power, 1987; Pinto, 1993; Evans and Long, 2000). In many European countries, including Ireland, the increased prioritisation of investment in the regeneration of existing social rented estates was paralleled by retrenchment in output of new social rented dwellings, which in turn corresponded with the delegitimation and stigmatisation of the tenure highlighted earlier in this chapter.

The first of the Irish estate improvement schemes, the Remedial Works Scheme, was established in 1985. It funds improvements to dwellings and to public space in run-down estates, and targets in particular estates built before 1940 and the system-built estates of the 1960s and 1970s which were mentioned earlier in this chapter. Remedial Works funding has been exploited with considerable enthusiasm by local authorities, and in the period 1985-1999 a total of 16,520 local authority dwellings, accounting for approximately 16.6 per cent of the current national public housing stock, were refurbished under its auspices (Norris, 2001). In the mid-1990s Dublin City Council also developed an Area Regeneration Programme. This involves the once-off upgrading of high density older housing complexes in various locations around the city and is linked to the development of robust arrangements for estate management. It is primarily directed at flat complexes in the inner city and is co-funded by the City Council and central government (Norris and Winston, 2004).

In more recent years efforts have also been made to attract private sector funding for regeneration projects, by making investment in designated local authority estates eligible for tax relief under the 1998 Urban Renewal Act. The best known application of this mechanism in practice is in Ballymun, where Dublin City Council has set up a designated company called Ballymun Regeneration Ltd, which is tasked with planning for and managing the demolition of all of the tower blocks and their replacement with conventional housing and low-rise apartments, organised around a new town centre, which will contain private rented dwellings, social rented dwellings provided by voluntary and co-operative bodies, shops, offices and a hotel (see Ballymun Regeneration Ltd, 1998a and 1998b). The rebuilding of the local authority dwellings and the provision of other social housing in the estate will be funded directly by central government, but it is envisaged that most of the town centre will be developed by the private sector. In addition, Dublin City Council has recently announced plans to regenerate Fatima Mansions and several other inner-city flats complexes using a public-private partnership arrangement whereby a developer will demolish the existing social housing and construct replacement social rented dwellings coupled with units for sale to home owners and private landlords.

By the 1990s the attention of policy makers shifted from the regeneration of individual local authority estates, to the reform and renewal of the entire local authority housing service, and indeed of the social rented tenure in general. The advent of this new policy agenda was first signalled in the 1991 housing White Paper – *A Plan for Social Housing* (Department of the Environment, 1991). This policy statement differed significantly from the housing white papers which preceded it – the latter were mainly concerned with estimating the numbers of people in need of social housing and making provision for this demand to be met, principally by means of local authority building, whereas the former presented a strategic analysis of all potential methods of accommodating low-income households by the private sector, local authorities and the voluntary and co-operative sector. Furthermore, on the basis of this analysis, *A Plan for Social Housing* proposed a number of reforms to mechanisms for housing these groups which, it admitted, 'imply significant changes in the traditional role played by local authorities' (Department of the Environment, 1991: 30).

The most significant of the changes identified in *A Plan for Social Housing* involved widening the traditional role of the local authority housing service to include '…. a new facilitating and promotional role aimed at improving and speeding up access to housing' (Department of the Environment, 1991: 30). In order to enable local authorities achieve this *A Plan for Social Housing* announced a series of new measures which local authorities can utilise to enable low- to middle-income households to buy a home of their own as an alternative to renting from a social landlord. In addition, it emphasises that a key aspect of this new enabling role will be encouraging higher levels of building by voluntary housing associations and co-operatives. As was mentioned earlier in this chapter, agencies of this type had built a large number of dwellings in the late nineteenth century, but for a number of reasons they did not emerge as major social housing providers for most of the twentieth century. However, as Figure 8.4 above demonstrates, this began to change in the early 1990s when voluntary and co-operative housing output, particularly of accommodation for special needs groups such as elderly, disabled or homeless people began to increase substantially. Mullins *et al* (2003) link this revival to the establishment of the capital assistance scheme in 1984. This was the first dedicated funding scheme for voluntary and co-operative housing providers and previous to its establishment these organisations were funded by local and central government on an ad-hoc basis.

A Plan for Social Housing announced an increase in the limits for funding under the capital assistance scheme; the introduction of new arrangements to fund the provision of communal facilities in voluntary and co-operative estates and the establishment of a capital loan and subsidy scheme, which provides an ongoing management and maintenance allowance to these organisations for each dwelling provided, together with capital funding towards the costs of construction. In order to qualify for this funding the Housing (Miscellaneous Provisions) Act, 1992 requires voluntary and co-operative housing providers to gain approved status from the Department of the Environment, Heritage and Local Government. Brooke (2001:12) reports that the Capital Assistance Scheme '… is used primarily although by no means exclusively for special needs housing' for people who require additional supports in addition to housing, while the Capital Loan and Subsidy Scheme is used mainly for general needs housing for those who have no additional support needs apart from housing. As is outlined in Figure 8.4 above, as a result of these reforms voluntary and co-operative social housing output increased further during the late 1990s, with output under the Capital Loan and Subsidy Scheme growing especially quickly.

As well as examining alternative social housing providers, *A Plan for Social Housing* also cast a critical eye over the quality of the service provided by local authorities to their own tenants. For instance, it raises a number of concerns about the management and maintenance of local authority estates, making the point that the quality of these services must be improved if public investment in public house building and refurbishment is to be protected. A more detailed analysis of the standard of local authority housing management followed in a 1993 memorandum from the DoEHLG to local authorities on the preparation of the statements of policy on housing management which they are obliged to produce under the terms of 1992 Housing (Miscellaneous Provisions) Act (Department of the Environment, 1993). The introductory section of this memorandum sets out what O'Connell has termed (1999: 60) a 'devastating catalogue of weaknesses common in local authority housing management', the most significant of which are: lack of long- and medium-term planning which is compounded by inadequate management information and insufficient monitoring of the information which is available; over-centralised management structures which prioritise administrative issues over communication with tenants; inadequate co-ordination of different housing management functions; prioritisation of cost reduction over value for money and customer service; over- reliance on the Remedial Works Scheme as a solution to the problems of unpopular estates and chronic inefficiencies in the maintenance service.

Central government concern about the quality of local authority housing management inspired the introduction of a range of ameliorative measures during the late 1990s (Norris and O'Connell, 2002). Some of these had an enabling orientation, insofar as they aimed to assist local authorities to improve their housing management performance through the provision of guidance, training and targeted grant aid, while others can be categorised as enforcement tools, which set benchmarks of required performance and established systems to monitor local authority housing management performance. The Housing Management Initiatives Grants Scheme, which was established in 1995, was the first of the enabling measures to be introduced. It provides grant aid towards the cost of practical pilot projects intended to improve housing management and since its establishment it has funded over 130 projects, most of which are concerned with involving local authority tenants in housing management, and decentralising housing management to focus more on the needs of individual estates and communities rather than solely on the administration of the housing stock as a whole (Brooke and Norris, 2002).

Soon afterwards, three further significant enabling measures were initiated by the Department of the Environment – the Housing Management Group which produced two reports setting out the broad framework which the reform of public housing management should follow; the Housing Unit which was set up in order to provide social housing management guidance, information and training; and the Housing (Miscellaneous Provisions) Act, 1997 which gives local authorities additional powers to deal with tenants and squatters in public sector dwellings who are committing anti-social behaviour (Housing Management Group, 1996, 1998; Housing Unit, 2000, 2001a, 2001b, 2001c, 2003a, 2003b, 2004). Examples of the enforcement measures introduced during the past decade include: the Department of the Environment and Local Government (2000e) circular *LG 9/00* which instructs local authorities to monitor their performance in specified aspects of housing management and to publish this information in their annual reports, and a range of reforms to the Remedial Works Scheme which made funding conditional on detailed monitoring and evaluation of projects (Department of the Environment and Local Government, 1999c).

A Plan for Social Housing also highlights '… the need to avoid building large local authority housing estates which have, in the past, reinforced social segregation', and suggests that as an alternative, local authorities should build smaller schemes in mixed tenure areas and consider purchasing dwellings in private estates to add to their rented stock (Department of the Environment, 1991: 11). In more recent years, the Planning and Development Act, 2000 has provided local authorities with additional options for combating social segregation by mixing different housing tenures in new estates. Part V of this Act obliges local authorities to amend their development plans to incorporate housing strategies which should detail out how future housing demand within their operational areas should be met, including the need for social housing to rent, provided by both local authorities and voluntary and co-operative agencies and for affordable housing for sale at below market value to eligible households. Local authorities can require that up to 20 per cent of land zoned for residential development locally is employed to meet the social and affordable housing need identified in this assessment. The 2000 Act requires property developers to transfer the necessary proportion of dwellings, land or sites to local authorities as a condition of planning permission, although the Planning and Development (Amendment) Act, 2002 also allows developers to meet their obligations in this regard by providing monetary compensation and/or dwellings, land or sites in an alternative location.

The DoEHLG guidelines on the implementation of the 2000 Act specify that among these options 'Provision of houses with the agreement of the developer … is the preferred route from the point of view of achieving social integration' and that 'The number and location of these houses should be such as to avoid undue social segregation and foster the development of integrated communities' (Department of the Environment and Local Government, 2000c: 23). As a result of this measure, it is likely that in the future a significant proportion of new social housing output in this country will be located in estates which are mixed tenure, i.e. include owner-occupied dwellings, bought on the open market or by means of the affordable housing scheme, together with dwellings rented from local authorities, from other social housing providers and from private landlords.

Concluding Comments

This sweeping review has sketched the key trends in the development of social housing provision in Ireland since its foundation in the late nineteenth century until the present day. The changes in the institutional structures for providing social housing are among the most significant of these trends. Non-statutory providers were dominant during the early history of the sector, for most of the twentieth century local authorities were the principal providers of social housing but in recent years social housing has been provided through a mixture of both arrangements. In addition the chapter also highlighted the growth of the sector until the 1960s and its steady contraction since then in relative terms and its related residualisation.

The achievements of the social housing sector in Ireland are rarely extolled and it is worth devoting some space to delineating them, because they are impressive in both quantitative and qualitative terms. The data on local authority house building presented in this chapter indicate that between 1887 and 2001 local authorities in Ireland constructed approximately 300,000 social housing units, 102,789 of which remained rented by 2001, while Mullins *et al* (2003) estimate that between 12,000 and 13,000 dwellings were rented from voluntary and co-operative housing providers in 2001 (Department of the Environment, Heritage and Local Government, various years). Social housing rents related to the income of tenants and the Household Budget Survey reveals that the amounts levied are generally extremely low (Central Statistics Office, 2001a). In 1999-2000 local authority tenants devoted only 7.4 per cent of their household expenditure to rent, as compared to 21 per cent in the case of their counterparts in the private rented sector. Consequently, social housing plays a key and largely unacknowledged role in combating income poverty in Ireland.

Despite the acute residualisation of the social rented sector and the problems in relation to the quality of accommodation provided in some run-down and system-built local authority estates examined earlier in the discussion, Fahey's (ed) (1999) study of seven diverse local authority housing estates in different parts of the country reaches largely positive findings about the quality of life enjoyed by the residents of these areas. On this basis he concludes that: '... local authorities have made a fundamental contribution to social progress and social cohesion in Irish society through the expansion of housing provision and the raising of minimum standards of housing among the less well-off' (Fahey, 1999b: 3). In addition, some 200,000 of the dwellings originally constructed by local authorities have been sold to tenants and data from the 2002 census indicate that dwellings make up 20 per cent of the owner-occupied housing stock (Central Statistics Office, 2004a). The local authority rented sector has therefore made a major contribution to expanding the level of owner occupation in Ireland to well above the European Union average and also to distributing home ownership relatively evenly across the income distribution spectrum, in comparison to other types of wealth (Norris and Shiels, 2004; Fahey, Nolan and Maître, 2004a).

Despite these impressive levels of social housing output during the period examined in this chapter, the 2002 census reveals that only 6.9 per cent of the national housing stock was rented from local authorities, and Mullins's *et al* (2003) figures regarding social rented units provided by voluntary and co-operative organisations quoted above indicate that a further 1 per cent of all dwellings were rented from these agencies (Central Statistics Office, 2004b). This level of local authority renting is far smaller than in 1961, when 18.4 per cent of all dwellings were provided by this source. Moreover, it is significantly below the mean level of the social renting in EU member states which stood at 13.4 per cent during the 1990s and much smaller than the norm in other western European nations such as Denmark, the United Kingdom and the Netherlands for instance where 17 per cent, 25 per cent and 38 per cent respectively of all housing is rented from social landlords (Norris and Winston, 2004). The sharp rise in house prices, falling participation of low-income households in the housing market and growing numbers on social housing waiting lists since the mid-1990s, raise the question of whether the social housing sector in Ireland is too small to cater for those in need of housing and the sector now requires expansion. The recent National Economic and Social Council (2004) report *Housing in Ireland: Performance and Policy* recommends that the total social housing stock should be increased to 200,000 units by 2012 – which would require an increase of 40 per cent on stock levels in 2004. Moreover, the report points out that this question in turn raises additional issues such as whether the tenant purchase scheme for local authority housing should be continued and about mechanisms for funding of social house building.

In relation to the former issue it is worth noting that the method of funding the sector in Ireland is unusual in the wider European context. Between 95 and 100 per cent of the construction costs of social housing schemes in Ireland are funded directly by central government, as are all the costs associated with land acquisition in the case of the local authorities. In contrast, among EU member states only the UK provides significant capital grants for social house building, in France and Finland building is funded by interest subsidies towards the cost of state loans, while in Sweden and Denmark most funding is generated from the private sector, mainly by borrowing (Stephens *et al*, 2002). Significant expansion of social housing output in Ireland may require the use of alternative mechanisms of funding such as those employed in these countries. In addition, as Redmond and Norris discuss in Chapter 9, the relative generosity of capital funding for social housing building in Ireland is counterbalanced by shortage of revenue funding, which is also an issue that must be addressed if standards of housing management are to be improved.

Finally, the other key question which faces the social rented sector in Ireland at the present time relates to its institutional structure. As explained in this chapter over the history of the sector the institutions which provide social housing in Ireland have changed but since the mid-1990s both local authorities and voluntary and co-operative housing organisations have been involved in the provision of this housing. This aspect of social housing in Ireland is also unusual in the wider European context. Stephens *et al* (2002) report that in Sweden and Finland 95 per cent and 63 per cent respectively of social housing is provided by municipal housing companies, which are separate from but under the control of local authorities. In Denmark and the Netherlands the voluntary and co-operative sector provides most social housing, while in Germany the private sector is heavily involved in social housing provision. Apart from the United Kingdom and Ireland, local authorities in most European Union member states play only a minor role in the direct provision and management of social housing and in the former country the role of local authorities in this regard has been reduced significantly since the 1980s as a result of a moratorium on new house building by local authorities and the transfer of a significant amount of local authority stock to alternative landlords (Mullins *et al,* 1993). This raises the question of whether local authorities in Ireland will continue to be major providers of social housing in the future or whether the institutional structure of our social housing sector will come to more closely reflect the norm in other European countries.

9

Reforming Local Authority Housing Management: The Case of Tenant Participation in Estate Management

Declan Redmond and Michelle Norris

Introduction

For most of the period since the tenure was founded in the late nineteenth century, the management of local authority housing has been neglected by both central and local government. From the perspective of the former, new house building, rather than management, has traditionally been the overriding concern. This attitude is not surprising in view of Ireland's housing conditions which, until recent years, have compared unfavourably to other European Union (EU) countries both in terms of housing standards and number of dwellings per head (European Union, 2002). Nor is it atypical in the wider European context where central government influence on social housing has traditionally been exercised mainly by means of capital contributions to building costs, which has limited its control over and interest in housing management (Cole and Furbey, 1994). However, Ireland is unusual in the extent to which the main providers of social housing have devoted scant attention to its management. This oversight on the part of local authorities is linked to the introduction of the tenant purchase schemes in the 1930s in rural areas and in the 1960s in urban areas (Fahey, 1998b). The high rate of privatisation required very limited management capacity from housing departments, whose responsibilities have traditionally not stretched far beyond allocating new dwellings and collecting the rent for the couple of years before tenants exercise their right to buy (O'Connell, 1999).

Over the past two decades this situation has changed radically as both local authorities and central government in this country have begun to devote more attention to the management of the housing stock. This development is related to factors that have inspired a similar growth in interest in social housing management among policy makers across Western Europe (Clapham, 1997). As

Norris mentions in Chapter 8 of this book, the end of large-scale social house building in the late 1970s redefined the housing problem as one of making best use of existing stock rather than the production of new dwellings. Furthermore, increased attention has been paid to the 'difficult-to-let estates' where housing management problems are concentrated and as a result of the work of researchers such as Power (1987) and housing management reform projects such as the Priority Estates Project (PEP) in the United Kingdom, a prevailing wisdom has developed which posits that poor management has contributed to the development of these areas and, more crucially, that improved management will help solve their problems.

In the Republic of Ireland the growth of social problems associated with the residualisation of the local authority rented tenure has added impetus to the drive for the reform of housing management (Nolan et al, 1998; Murray and Norris, 2002). In addition, a range of programmes for the reform of the public services more broadly have been instituted since the mid-1990s under the auspices of the Strategic Management Initiative (SMI) and the Better Local Government plan for the reorganisation of the local authorities and management practices within the sector have changed radically (Co-ordinating Group of Secretaries, 1996; Department of the Environment, 1996a). As a result, recent Department of the Environment, Heritage and Local Government policy statements on housing, beginning with A Plan for Social Housing (Department of the Environment, 1991), have repeatedly exhorted local authorities to change their traditional practices so that they can meet the new challenges of housing management and keep in step with this wider reform process.

Like many aspects of housing policy in Ireland, policy developments in the area of local authority housing management have not generally been evidence-based (National Economic and Social Forum, 2000). Although there is an embryonic literature on housing management reform in Ireland (cf. O'Connell 1998, 1999; Norris and O'Connell, 2002; Conway, 2001) there is a dearth of research which attempts to assess the impact that these reforms have had on the ground. This chapter, which presents the results of empirical research on housing management reform in five different urban local authorities, aims to help rectify this situation.

For reasons of space, the chapter does not examine all aspects of housing management, but rather focuses specifically on the issue of involving local authority tenants in the management of their estates. This issue was selected for attention on the grounds that it has been afforded particular priority by policy makers, to the extent that O'Connell (1998: 25) claims that it has been promoted as a 'panacea for policy failure'. Furthermore, the limited amount of empirical evidence which is available indicates that tenant participation is the aspect of housing management that has seen the most significant and widespread reform in recent years. Brooke and Norris (2002) report that 59 of the 154 projects funded by the DoEHLG's scheme of grants for housing management initiatives, since its establishment in 1995, address this issue. The research examined tenant participation in three local authorities in Dublin (Dublin City Council and Dún Laoghaire-Rathdown and South Dublin County Councils) as well as in Limerick and Waterford City Councils. These local authorities are useful case studies because they have been pathfinders in the area of tenant involvement (Norris, 2000; Bain and Watt, 1999; Kenny, 1998). Moreover, this group includes most of the large social landlords in the country – in 2001 they collectively managed 40,381 dwellings, which constitutes 39 per cent of national local authority stock (Department of the Environment, Heritage and Local Government, various years). For each of these local authorities, documentary information on housing management and tenant participation policy was examined, while case studies of the implementation of tenant participation in eight housing estates were also conducted. The latter aspect of the study was operationalised by means of over 60 semi-structured in-depth interviews with local authority housing management and tenant liaison officials, tenant representatives on estate boards and tenant committees and with estate workers who work with, or as advocates for, tenant groups.

The results of this empirical research are described in the middle section of the chapter. In order to contextualise this discussion, it is prefaced by an examination of the theoretical and policy background to the development of tenant participation and of the good practice guidance on the implementation of this policy. The closing section of the chapter draws conclusions regarding the progress which has been make in enabling tenants of the case study areas to participate in housing management and the achievements of this aspect of housing management reform.

Activating Tenants: Theory, Policy, Implementation

The theoretical literature on tenant participation concurs that initiatives of this type serve two related purposes (Cooper and Hawtin, 1997, 1998). The primary purpose of tenant participation is to give tenants an active voice and real influence in the specification and implementation of housing and estate management services, in order to ensure that services are more customer focused and also more efficient and effective. A secondary, though interrelated purpose, is to empower tenants as citizens, thereby enhancing participative democracy (Taylor, 1995, 2000).

Analysis of policy statements on tenant participation produced by the DoEHLG since the early 1990s reveals that its case for promoting increased tenant participation draws mainly on arguments in the former of these categories. As mentioned above, the 1991 policy statement *A Plan for Social*

Housing was the first occasion on which the Department raised concerns regarding the standard of local authority housing management (Department of the Environment, 1991). This document emphasised the level of expenditure on housing provision and asserted:

> It is essential that this money is spent in the most cost effective way possible and the beneficial effects of the investment sustained in the longer term. These aims can only be achieved by local authorities improve their existing management and maintenance procedures ... To this end, the authorities have been requested to develop more localised management systems involving increased tenant responsibility and participation.
>
> (Department of the Environment, 1991: 13)

Subsequently, the Housing (Miscellaneous Provisions) Act, 1992 introduced two new provisions relevant to tenant participation: it enables local authorities to delegate some of their housing management functions to a 'designated body' which can be a tenants' association and also requires them to devise a written statement of policy on housing management. The associated memorandum on the preparation of these policy statements provides a useful insight into the Department of the Environment's (1993) thinking on housing management practice in the local authorities. As is examined in more detail by Norris in the preceding chapter, this memorandum details a large number of weaknesses in local authority housing management, including tenant participation. In this vein, it complains that 'Management is headquarters orientated' and 'remote from tenants', their needs and aspirations are not always sufficiently taken into account and their '... participation in the running of their estates is inadequate and not sufficiently encouraged' (Department of the Environment, 1993: 6). In order to rectify these problems the memorandum requires that the housing management policy statements should include a description of each authority's rented stock and details of its objectives for the management of these dwellings, the general strategies and specific techniques to be employed in the attainment of these objectives and the arrangements for the monitoring and assessment of performance in this regard. The statements must also devote particular attention to tenant participation in housing management – a requirement which is justified on the grounds that:

> Greater involvement of tenants in the running of their estates is essential to ensure the delivery of the type and quality of the housing services which tenants want. The involvement of tenants can lead to improvements in the standard of an estate, can help to prevent the deterioration of an estate into a problem one and can assist in 'turning around' a problem estate ... it is clear that a more effective, responsive and acceptable

housing service can be provided ... where tenants ... are active participants in the running of their estate.

(Department of the Environment, 1993: 6)

On the other hand, the sizeable commentary on tenant participation that has emanated from the community and voluntary sector in Ireland places more emphasis on the potential contribution of such measures to enhancing participative democracy. In this vein, Watt's (1998: 5) contribution to a Community Workers Co-operative publication on this area argues that 'Tenant participation in estate management is a key arena for the development of more participative structures at local level' and advocates the adoption of '... a community development methodology' to enabling tenant participation 'where tenants and community organisations participate at all levels including the development of overall policy' and 'The emphasis is on empowerment, not management'. He suggests that tenant participation initiatives in this genre would concentrate on the following issues:

- addressing issues of social exclusion associated with housing and related issues
- promoting the common good and consensus in decision making
- pursuing equality objectives by ensuring that tenants are not discriminated against on grounds such as ethnicity, marital status, disability and age
- and including marginalised communities in decision making and agreements that impact on them.

The divergent views regarding the overall objective of tenant participation have in turn inspired a range of ideas about what it should mean in practice. Cairncross *et al* (1997) identify three main forms of tenant participation – each underpinned by different and, to some extent, incompatible, political philosophies. First, there is the 'traditional model' where tenant involvement in housing management is minimal and is informed by a belief in the efficacy of professional housing managers and the value of the representative democratic influence of elected councillors. Thus, tenants exert influence through their local elected representatives and this in turn is implemented through the expertise of local authority housing managers. In this model tenants are the passive recipients of a service with a very limited role in management. Second, there is the 'consumerist model', which has emerged in the past twenty years or so, as public services have had to reform their service delivery arrangements and become more customer-focused. At its extreme, this model assumes that tenants are similar to private customers in the market place and the service they receive should reflect their needs and wants on an individual basis. Tenant participation is seen as a means of delivering improvements in services. As receivers of services, the assumption is that tenants are best placed to specify and prioritise what improvements are needed. The ascendancy of this approach is associated with the rise the 'new right', neo-liberal political philosophy during the 1980s (Goodlad, 2001). The third 'citizenship' approach to tenant participation places greater emphasis on the collective influence of tenants and on their involvement in dialogue, consultation and shared decision making. Although the potential for tenant participation to improve service delivery is acknowledged, the collective empowerment of tenants collectively through participation is afforded equal or even greater weigh. It is envisaged that participation will enable them to be active rather than passive citizens, thereby improving the quality and depth of citizenship and mitigating the alleged deficiencies of traditional democratic representative structures (Chapman and Kirk, 2001; Carley, 2002; Somerville and Steele, 1995).

In tandem with the development of theory and policy on tenant participation, there has also emerged a series of good practice guidance from governmental, quasi-governmental and non-governmental agencies on how to implement tenant participation. This literature is particularly extensive in the United Kingdom (cf. United Kingdom Audit Commission, 1999; United Kingdom Department of the Environment, Transport and the Regions, 1998a, 1998b, 1999, 2001). However, in the Irish context, notable contributions to this literature have also been produced by the Housing Management Group (1996, 1998) which was established by the DoEHLG in the late 1990s to examine local authority housing management performance; the Housing Unit (2001a, 2004) which was established on the recommendation of the Housing Management Group to promote good practice in housing management, to conduct housing management research and establish structures for housing management education and training; and the Irish Council for Social Housing (1997) which is the representative body for voluntary housing associations.

Despite the variety of theories and policies regarding the objectives and arrangements appropriate for tenant participation outlined above, there is remarkable consensus in the good practice literature on how initiatives of this type should be implemented. For instance, the requirement that tenants must be treated as equal partners is consistently emphasised (United Kingdom, Department of the Environment, Transport and the Regions, 1999). The literature is replete with the language of partnership and is generally predicated on the assumption that operating in this way is achievable and unproblematic. The need to ensure that participation is not merely a form of tokenism by affording tenants a real influence which produces identifiable outcomes in terms of service improvements on their estates is also regularly identified as critically important. The further element of good practice relates to the provision of full and comprehensive information on the housing management service as an essential prerequisite for tenant participation (Tenant Participation Advisory Service, 1994; Wilcox, 1994).

Table 9.1: Levels, Aims and Implementation Methods of Tenant Participation

Levels of tenant participation	Aims	Typical methods and structures for implementation
Information	Information is provided to tenants on the housing service and the receipt of feedback from them	Newsletters; meetings; leaflets; tenant handbooks.
Consultation and dialogue	The views of tenants are sought and are taken into account in the making of decisions and the provision of services	Open meetings; questionnaires; tenant surveys; estate boards and forums.
Shared decision making or devolution	Tenants have voting rights or specific agreements over service provision which means that local authorities must act on their views	Estate agreements; delegation orders, estate boards; service agreements; estate action plans.
Tenant management	Tenants have full control and are thus autonomous in making decisions on the housing service	Estate management boards; Tenant management.

Source: adapted from Cairncross *et al* (1997)

In addition, most good practice guidance documents also address the level and structure of tenant participation to be implemented. Following Arnstien's (1969) classic 'ladder of citizen participation', they generally identify four levels of tenant participation, denoting different levels of influence by tenants which could potentially be adopted (Housing Unit, 2001a). As is detailed in Table 9.1, these range from information provision at the most basic level, to tenant management at the other. The literature emphasises the need for broad agreement and understanding between tenants and local authorities regarding the level of participation to be implemented. One of the reasons for this is that confusion over what tenant participation means can lead to frustration for both parties. Consultation, for example, may imply completely different things to tenants and local authorities; the former may see it as conferring real power of decision, while the latter may merely see it as obtaining views and information. All of the guidance documents agree on the necessity for local authorities to have a comprehensive written policy on tenant participation which states the foregoing in clear terms (Chapman and Kirk, 2001; Carley, 2002). In general, the structures and methods required to make participation operational will depend on the level of participation which is being pursued. Table 9.1 also illustrates the typical methods associated with the four levels of tenant participation. For example, methods and structures for consultation will usually include: occasional open meetings, tenant satisfaction surveys or regular estate forums, while shared decision making will normally involve devising delegation orders, as is provided for in the Housing (Miscellaneous Provisions) Act, 1998.

A further key element of good practice is concerned with the crucial issue of what is being participated in or negotiated about. As in any negotiations, the agenda for discussion must be as unambiguous as is possible and also be wide enough to be meaningful to tenants (Cole *et al,* 1999). Moreover, the parameters of decision making must also be clarified. In other words, the degree of influence which each party has on each agenda item must be apparent to both tenants and the local authority.

In addition, the issue of resources for tenant participation is identified as crucial in the literature (Chartered Institute of Housing, 1999). This includes: resources directly provided to tenant groups and the manner in which local authorities organise their service. The literature emphasises that local authorities are comparatively resource rich and that tenants generally speaking are resource poor. While tenants have responsibilities with regard to their tenancy agreements they have no legal or moral responsibility to engage in tenant involvement, which is a voluntary activity. Moreover, in a deprived community participation is not necessarily a natural or rational action. A more logical reaction may be for tenants to argue that the local authority should just do its job properly without recourse to new structures for participation (Bengtsson, 1998). Therefore, if local authorities wish to involve tenants as a basis for providing a better housing management service they must properly encourage and resource tenants' groups. The Housing Unit (2001a) recommends that basic resources such as office space and equipment should be provided where an organised tenant group does exist. In addition, there is also a need to provide modest financial resources, for example delegated budgets for training, the running costs of offices and the costs of estate or community workers who act as advocates for tenants and tenant groups.

Finally, the literature emphasises that the implementation of tenant participation policy should mean significant change in the organisation and delivery of housing management, if participation is not to be merely tokenistic. The types of reform highlighted in the literature as appropriate include: internal re-structuring, de-centralisation of housing management services to local estate offices, the creation of dedicated tenant participation posts and the establishment of dedicated estate budgets (Somerville *et al,* 1998). The support of senior management is also regarded as a vital bulwark for successful tenant participation, as is the co-ordination of all the services provided by different local authority departments at estate level, by means of co-ordinated service plans. The *Second Report* of Housing Management Group (1998) also made the point that many of the problems and issues which are of concern to tenants are outside the remit of local authorities in Ireland, which are responsible for a relatively narrow range of services compared to their counterparts in other European countries. Consequently, it recommended the development of estate action plans which are inter-agency in nature.

Developments in Tenant Participation

Extent

The existing research evidence suggests that, whilst tenant participation initiatives are taking place in many parts of the country, this policy is being implemented in a patchy and uneven manner (Redmond, 2001; Brennan *et al,* 2001; Galligan, 2001). This view is confirmed by the studies of five local authorities which were conducted for this chapter.

On the one hand, this research reveals significant levels of tenant participation in the physical renewal and regeneration of estates in each of the local authorities examined. To a certain extent developments in this regard reflect the requirements of funding mechanisms. For example, in 1995 the DoEHLG issued a revised memorandum on the Remedial Works Scheme, which funds the large-scale refurbishment of local authority estates. This document emphasised the importance of consultation with the local community to ensuring the success of Remedial Works projects and also provided a template for a survey of the estate which would underpin this consultation process (Department of the Environment, 1995a; Norris, 2001). In 1999 further Departmental guidelines on this scheme announced that funding would be provided towards the costs of establishing structures for this consultation and associated housing management reform (Department of the Environment, 1999c). In addition to Remedial Works, more large scale and multi-dimensional renewal programmes, such as those in Ballymun and St. Michael's estate in Dublin, have seen significant involvement from tenants in winning funding and influencing renewal plans (Brennan *et al,* 2001; Power, 1997).

Apart from assessing the extent of tenant involvement in estate regeneration the research did not attempt to gauge its impact and efficacy. However, the available evidence indicates that widespread involvement of tenants in estate regeneration does not always mean that this involvement is effective. Some recent work on community participation in urban renewal in Dublin has taken a sceptical view of the achievements of this form of urban governance (Punch,

2001, 2002). The variations between the regeneration plans for Fatima Mansions which have been produced by the landlord and the local community also reveal that partnership working in this area of housing management is not necessarily straightforward (Dublin Corporation, 2001; O'Gorman, 2000).

It is also important to acknowledge that, to a degree, it is to be expected that tenants would be heavily involved in regeneration projects. In a situation where there are significant financial budgets available for renewal and the prospect of, often dramatic, physical and environmental transformation, generating the interest and involvement of tenants is relatively undemanding (Stewart and Taylor, 1995). Less easy, by far, is achieving tenant involvement in the more mundane day-to-day routine of estate management, where there may be no extra financial resources and the outcomes achieved are less visible. It is in this arena that the long-term efficacy of tenant participation will be tested and the available evidence indicates that progress in this regard has been less compelling than in the regeneration field.

At the national level, the DoEHLG's Housing Management Grants Initiative has been the driving force behind many developments. As its name implies, this scheme funds projects in housing management, a majority of which have been related closely to tenant participation. Projects of this type include: the provision of information to tenants in the form of tenant handbooks, the provision of tenant training and the employment of tenant liaison officers (Brooke and Norris, 2001). Research conducted in 2000 found that officials of this type were employed by over 40 per cent of local authorities in the country and a network of Tenant Liaison Officers has recently been organised by the Housing Unit which meets to share information and best practice on how to implement effective tenant participation policies (Norris and Kearns, 2003; Redmond, 2001). However, Norris and O' Connell (2002) argue that these officials are as yet not firmly established in the local authority housing service, because many are employed on short-term contracts and their posts are funded through a variety of insecure mechanisms, rather than mainstream resources.

Research on the case study local authorities revealed a contradictory situation whereby the often significant progress in the development of tenant participation structures on the ground is generally conducted in the absence of a clear and agreed strategy which sets out the level of participation being sought, what is to be negotiated, the methods and structures to be used or specific outcomes sought. At an even more basic level, there was limited evidence of a formal and systematic approach to the provision of information to tenants by local authorities, although increasingly local authorities have published tenants' handbooks. Moreover, there is negligible evidence of the case study local authorities obtaining formal feedback or satisfaction ratings from tenants – clearly important with regard to monitoring the housing and estate management service. More crucially, there is scant evidence of any specific customer care codes in operation, or of specifications of service standards under the terms of which local authorities would specify the service that it provides, set standards and targets for its improvement and measure outcomes. This lack of specifics with respect to targets and outcomes may in part be reflective of a reluctance on the part of local authorities to critically examine their housing service. Inevitably, this lack of clarity means that tenants have little idea of what service to expect which can in turn lead to frustration.

Structures

On a more positive note the research uncovered evidence of more impressive achievements with respect to the establishment of tenant participation structures in the eight estates examined. One example, from an estate in Limerick City Council's operational area, followed the structure illustrated in Figure 9.1. An estate management board was formed which had tenant representatives, local authority housing department representatives, statutory agency representatives (the Gardaí and Health Boards) and a tenant worker. Tenant representatives on the board were part of the local tenant group – albeit one which was not particularly representative of the local tenant population, primarily because of the difficulties of interesting tenants in becoming involved. This reluctance stemmed partly from the usual reasons of disinterest and cynicism, but also from an unwillingness to be seen working with or for the local authority due to a mixture of intimidation from allegedly criminal elements on the estate and a more general concern over collusion with the authorities of the state.

Also representing the tenants was a tenant worker (who was also a tenant of the estate) whose remit was to develop the tenant group and to liaise with the housing department. This worker, who was funded at arms length by the local authority, performed a role as an advocate for the tenants and as a conduit for day-to-day business between the tenant group and the local authority. In this estate, the tenant group had been provided with a local estate office, which was staffed by the tenant worker. The housing department representatives were dedicated tenant participation officers whose sole function was to develop and liaise with local tenant groups (Norris, 2000). The health board representatives tended to be social workers and the Garda representative was usually the local community Garda. Estate board meetings, which were held monthly, tended to be purely consultative, acting more as a forum for airing views than as a decision-making body. Indeed, the estate board had no formal decision-making powers at all. In theory the estate board was a forum where actions to deal with local issues and problems would emerge.

Figure 9.1: Typical Tenant Participation Structure in Limerick City

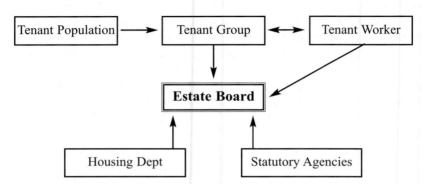

In relation to the effectiveness of this structure, two key problems are worth noting. Firstly, many tenants came to view the tenant group office as being a local authority office, and use it as a first port of call for maintenance complaints and other issues, which should rightly have been directed towards the local authority. This confusion of roles suited the local authority, which was content to have a *de facto* local estate office without having to actually put one in place, but it was not in the interests of the tenant group which was viewed in some respects as synonymous with the local authority. A second more general problem related to the nature of the estate board. The board lacked any powers of decision, even of recommendation, and therefore was not particularly effective from the tenants' viewpoint. Although the tenant representatives were clear that communication with the local authority had improved considerably, they were more cynical regarding the ability of tenant participation to improve the estate. While recognising that the estate board provided a formal mechanism to raise all sorts of estate and neighbourhood issues, there were no mechanisms to ensure that issues raised would actually be dealt with. In other words, there was no necessary connection between the increasingly sophisticated structures of participation and the actual delivery of services.

Outside of the case study estate, there have been significant organisational developments with respect to involving the tenants of Limerick City Council's over 3,000 rented dwellings in housing management (Department of the Environment, Heritage and Local Government, various years). In most large estates in the city, estate boards, similar to the model described above, have been established. Furthermore, the local authority also funds a network of tenant workers, that is a network of tenant advocates or community development type workers, who co-ordinate their activities at a city-wide level by means of a specially established forum. The city council also employs three dedicated tenant participation officers and funds a dedicated budget for estate management, which in turn funds the tenant workers. Thus, there are clear structures in existence and these structures are being steadily developed.

Waterford City Council uses structures similar to those employed by Limerick City Council to manage its rented stock of about 2,200 dwellings (Department of the Environment, Heritage and Local Government, various years). Equivalents of estate boards are in operation on a number of estates in Waterford, the council employs a small team of dedicated tenant participation staff, while the local partnership board funds a tenant worker. Insofar as arrangements for tenant participation in Waterford mirror those in Limerick, the former display many of the strengths and shortcomings which earlier sections of this chapter have highlighted in relation to the latter. Where Waterford differs from Limerick is that tenant participation is organised on a city-wide basis through the medium of a city-wide estate management forum. Membership of the forum is made up of six tenant representatives from estates across the city, a tenant worker, a senior housing officer and two dedicated tenant participation workers from the local authority, health board representatives, Garda representatives as well as a representative from the partnership board. The forum is chaired by a tenant representative. What also distinguishes Waterford is the existence of an Amalgamated Tenants' Group, which encompasses all of the tenants' associations in the city and meets independently of any local or statutory authorities. It seeks to draw from the experience of the various estate-based tenant groups, to formulate common positions and to strengthen the position of tenants through a united voice and common position. While this sounds straightforward in theory, it is also the case that there are differences between some of the tenant groups, although it is also important to acknowledge that the statutory agencies in the city also hold different views in relation to tenant participation.

Dublin City Council had rented stock of over 24,000 units in 2002 and is by far the largest landlord in the local authority housing sector in this country (Department of the Environment, Heritage and Local Government, various years). However, it has taken a different approach to tenant participation from other authorities examined in this research, with few structures similar to the estate boards described above. For the city council the organisation of tenant participation and estate management is firmly about establishing a local presence near or on estates. During the late 1980s and 1990s it re-organised its housing service into a regional structure, with nine regional offices being established.

This type of reform represents one method of improving services to tenants. The establishment of regional offices has led to decentralisation of functions, with tenants able to access housing services at a local level to a much greater degree, and has also led to a certain devolvement of powers to these regional offices. Local authority housing officers in charge of such regional offices have a degree of discretion regarding how they deliver services locally. Some have used this authority to set up local estate offices, with estate management officers taking charge of particular estates and having some limited budgetary discretion. This more hands-on approach certainly gives the local authority greater local information and contacts which are useful for estate management.

Although the housing department does not fund tenant workers as its counterpart in Limerick has done, in most local authority estates in the Dublin City Council area there is a plethora of community workers of various types. The city council's housing and community department has a dedicated staff of estate management officers who work in regional and local estate offices, whose function is to deliver services and to liaise with tenant groups and community development workers whose task it is to form, develop and train local tenant groups. With the exception of Ballymun, there are few examples of separate estate boards within Dublin City Council's operational area where the local authority and the tenants come together in a formal manner. The model of estate management in Dublin City Council is of interaction and consultation between tenants and the local authority primarily through the medium of regional or local offices or directly through meetings with estate management officers. While in some of the estates studied, e.g. Cherry Orchard, there are well-developed local tenants' groups, these often predate the adoption of formal tenant participation policies and also deal with a wider array of issues.

South Dublin County Council also has a distinctive tenant participation structure which was established in 1997 when the council launched a formal estate management policy in relation to its stock of 7,500 dwellings (Department of the Environment, Heritage and Local Government, various years). An estate management section was formed in the housing department as well as a related allocation support unit which deals mainly with anti-social behaviour. There is a dedicated budget for each of these sections totalling approximately €500,000 per annum. This budget is primarily used for various physical and environmental improvements which arise as a result of the tenant participation process. There is also a dedicated estate management staff which consists of five estate officers and eight allocation support officers. Tenant participation in South Dublin is primarily organised through the estate officers; these officers have regular meetings with tenant groups in the estates for which they are responsible. Moreover, regular estate clinics for tenants are held in local offices, which are attended by the estate officer, allocation support staff and oftentimes by the Gardaí. Although long-established and well-developed local community structures exist in many estates, these in many cases predate the formal establishment of an estate management policy. Nonetheless, the estate officers are involved in these local community structures to an extent.

Agendas

Broadly speaking, the agenda of issues to be addressed by means of tenant participation has emerged in an unplanned or organic manner in the various case study areas, primarily in response to the immediate needs of tenants on particular estates, rather than the priorities of the local authority. Nonetheless, despite variations in the location, size and age of the case study estates, certain themes recurred repeatedly on tenants' agendas. These are: housing maintenance and repairs, general estate upkeep, allocations and lettings polices and social order issues.

Among these issues, the latter two were in practice intimately connected and were also repeatedly identified by the tenant representatives interviewed for the research as the key priorities which they hoped would be resolved by means of tenant involvement in housing management. The interviews with tenants revealed social order problems, of varying levels of severity, on all of the case study estates. Their views in this regard confirm the findings of other research such as Fahey's (1999b: 257) landmark ethnographic study of six local authority estates which concluded that 'The prevalence of antisocial behaviour and the absence of a sense that order in the social environment can be taken for granted is the single biggest problem in troubled local authority estates' and argued that 'One of the greatest weaknesses of "traditional" local authority housing management was the unwillingness to address social order problems in their estates'. The tenants of the eight estates examined for the purposes of this study highlighted a variety of types of anti-social behaviour, ranging from neighbour nuisance to a more serious intimidation associated with criminality of various sorts, including vandalism and drug dealing. In a minority of estates there is clearly an atmosphere of intimidation and fear, making daily life difficult and harsh, with very negative consequences for the quality of life of residents. Estates where such problems were particularly prevalent tended to have high rates of vacant dwellings and high turnover of tenancies.

Although the literature identifies a variety of potential responses to the issue of social order problems (cf: Housing Unit, 2003b; Nixon and Hunter, 2001), the organised tenant groups in the eight case study estates were increasingly demanding a role in allocations policies as a means of vetting and policing new tenant households. This demand arises from a belief that influence over allocations and lettings can contribute to a reduction of anti-social behaviour, thereby stabilising estates. Given this high tenant turnover rate, which reached 30 per cent in some estates examined, these concerns regarding the reletting of dwellings are understandable. In addition, tenants' groups are strongly of the opinion that local authorities have contributed to the instability and problems on certain estates through an allocations system which houses unsuitable households or problem households in 'difficult-to-let' areas.

This process is inevitably fraught with conflict, with tenants often desiring strong powers of veto and local authorities attempting to steer a course between stabilising estates and dealing with housing need. The allocation of local authority tenancies is regulated by the Housing Act, 1988 which requires that they should be apportioned strictly on the basis of need. This obviously raises the potential for conflict between local authorities and the tenants' groups interested in influencing this aspect of housing management. Nonetheless, the interviews with local authority officials conducted for this research reveal that many were collaborating with tenant groups in what amounted in some cases to a *de facto* process of vetting applicants for housing. The level and nature of this informal collaboration has varied over the past few years and has ranged from the local authority taking soundings from tenants' groups regarding households on the waiting list to a more pro-active system where tenant groups have had a strong degree of influence, even veto, over housing allocations. However, in all of the estates examined, tenant participation was intimately bound up with issues of social management, social control, indeed social surveillance of estates. It could be argued that the key function of and rationale for tenant participation in the management of these estates was as a mechanism for ameliorating the more extreme aspects of anti-social behaviour.

Whilst acknowledging the dangers inherent in relying on information from tenant groups, as it may be either hearsay or deliberately prejudicial, there was significant agreement among the local-authority officials interviewed that the information supplied by such groups is generally more up to date and reliable than that held by the Gardaí or the local authority itself. Nonetheless, officials were adamant that any information received was always checked and verified and in any case, was only used in a small minority of situations.

It also important to acknowledge that there is some legitimate basis for such negotiations since the Housing Act, 1997 establishes anti-social behaviour as a basis for eviction and also enables local authorities to refuse to let a dwelling to applicants it suspects of involvement in such behaviour. The Department of the Environment (1997a: 8) circular on the implementation of this Act recognises that tenants' associations do request information on applicants for housing in their estate, although it also stipulates that such 'information should only be supplied with the consent of ... the individual concerned and requests and information supplied should be recorded'. In the United Kingdom, the *de facto* situation where local authorities are attempting to balance catering for housing need with building sustainable and stable communities has found formal expression in community lettings schemes which allow local authorities to take account of other factors as well as housing need into decisions regarding allocations and in probationary tenancies which require new tenants to demonstrate satisfactory behaviour for a period prior to being granted a permanent tenancy (Hunter and Dixon, 2001).

The other item which was on the agenda of tenant activists in all of the case study estates related to a range of housing and estate maintenance issues, from the response to requests for individual repairs to the upkeep of estates. Tenant groups were generally heavily critical of the performance of local authorities in this regard and were disparaging about the inability of tenant participation structures to improve matters. While it can certainly be argued that issues of social order are inherently complex and not amenable to easy solutions, the same cannot be said with regard to improving maintenance services. Improvements in this regard may in some cases require additional funding, but the good practice literature is also clear that they are dependent principally on more effective internal practices and procedures (Housing Unit, 2000). The failure to improve such basic technocratic procedures reflects very negatively on the potential of tenant participation to affect any improvement in housing management standards.

Motivation

The research revealed varying levels of interest among tenants in becoming involved in tenant groups, ranging from enthusiasm, disinterest, to cynicism, all depending on the profile and history of the estate as well as the history of tenant participation in housing management locally. Most tenant activists have been driven to take action through the necessity to try and improve the quality of life on estates. Therefore, the motivation to take action was generally stronger on more difficult estates.

However, for many of the tenant representatives interviewed for this study, the process of involvement in tenant participation structures, primarily structures of consultation, was generally a frustrating one. In the context of the severity of social and economic problems on estates, what amounted to small gains and achievements tended to take a disproportionate effort from a small number of tenants. Tenant participation may at first have seemed alluring and promised change but has been slow to deliver. While many of the tenant organisations had formal constitutions and sought to elect tenants on a regular basis, very often the level of interest in joining a tenant group or an estate management board was lacking. Consequently, many tenant groups comprise a small number of dedicated individuals who have been involved for a number of years and which indicates that the underlying strength of such groups is weak.

In the face of these demotivating factors, the provision of funding by local authorities, through arms-length mechanisms, estate or community workers who work with tenants in a form of tenant advocacy, proved to be a vital support for tenants' groups. It is also the case that tenant groups have in recent years been the recipients of other resources from local authorities, which enables them to sustain their activities. The provision of training for tenant representatives has become more common as is the granting of limited finance to run local offices. In some cases tenant organisations are closely linked with the broader community-development infrastructure available in their areas. However, it is also clear that some tenant organisations are also in conflict with other community development organisations over the small scale of resources available and over the agenda for community development locally.

Statutory Response

The most unambiguous finding to emerge from this research is that, no matter what type of formal structure was employed to enable tenant participation in housing management, tenants and local authority officials held very different views of the meaning of tenant participation. To an extent this divergence derives from the very nature of consultation which is elastic and open to various interpretations. The interviews revealed that for tenants, consultation is almost invariably interpreted as meaning that the local authority would not only take their views into account but also act on them. However, for local authorities, consultation generally means just listening to tenants' views but not necessarily acting on them.

On the other hand the research also revealed that one of the most positive steps taken by the various local authorities examined has been the employment of tenant liaison officers or equivalent staff to support the tenant participation process. These officers take an active role in the management of estates, and as a consequence have often developed detailed local knowledge and they also provide tenants with an accessible point of contact with the local authority. The feedback from tenants is generally positive regarding the role of these officials.

Interestingly, these officers, when interviewed, were often critical of the lack of co-operation and co-ordination from other departments in the local authority. As front-line workers they felt that their influence within the local authority was marginal and other housing staff and other departments viewed them as a buffer between the authority and the tenants, but were not necessarily willing to act on their requests. This confirms the view, at least in some cases, that despite seemingly sophisticated forms of tenant participation, the local authority housing service remains largely unreformed. Tenants' groups were certainly of this view, arguing that in some cases the tenant liaison officers created an additional layer of bureaucracy which made it more difficult to get access to the real centres of power in local authorities.

Concluding Comments

The research on tenant participation in five different local authority operational areas which has been described in this chapter indicates that significant progress has been made in the reform of this aspect of housing management over the last decade. Tenants are involved in the design and implementation of estate regeneration initiatives in all of the local authorities examined, and reasonably comprehensive structures to enable tenant participation in the management of their estates by means of tenants' associations and estate management boards have been established. In addition, various arrangements for supporting this participation have been put in place by local authorities, including: the employment of tenant liaison officials and the provision of grant aid and office accommodation to tenants' groups. Although the research raises some concerns about the representativeness of these structures and the extent of the influence they actually afford tenants, there is no doubt that they have made a contribution to enhancing participative democracy which is one of the key objectives of involving tenants in housing management.

The Department of the Environment, Heritage and Local Government has promoted tenant participation as a means of improving the efficiency and effectiveness of housing management. Scott's (ed.) (2001) review of the extensive British literature on tenant participation concludes that it is also replete with claims that tenant participation will improve housing management but notably lacking in evidence in support of these claims. However, the tenants and tenant participation workers in the five local authority operational areas examined in this research were united in the view that, with the exception of combating anti-social behaviour, tenant participation has had a negligible impact on housing management standards. Their opinions in this regard are also supported by the lack of information for tenants on housing services, of systems to ascertain tenant satisfaction and of customer care codes and specifications of service standards in the local authorities examined, and also by the other available research evidence, such as Brooke and Norris's (2001) evaluation of the DoEHLG's scheme of grants for housing management initiatives grants scheme which found that 59 of the 154 projects it has funded since its establishment in 1995 address tenant participation, whereas only a handful focus on the reform of the core housing management services such as rent collection and maintenance.

This emphasis on the establishment of collective structures for participation, coupled with lack of action to address the issues raised by means of this mechanism, indicates that, within Cairncross *et al's* (1997) typology of models of tenant participation, developments in the five local authorities under examination could be categorised as a mixture of the traditional and the citizenship approaches. Therefore tenant participation arrangements in this country do not conform to Cairncross *et al*'s (1997) preferred approach to delivering housing services, which they recommend should combine elements of the consumerist and citizenship approaches. Their justifications for this recommendation are twofold. Firstly they, and many other authors, raise ethical concerns about establishing structures for participation which do not empower tenants to influence service standards. In this vein Somerville (1998: 234) has argued, 'Participation without empowerment is … a confidence trick performed by the controllers of an activity on participants in that activity. To the extent to which the trick works, it must be disempowering rather than empowering.' However, other commentators point out that this 'confidence trick' does have the inherent advantage, from the perspective of the state, of incorporating and therefore diluting potential conflict from grass-roots organisations (Stewart and Taylor, 1995; Cooper and Hawtin, 1997, 1998). Secondly, Cairncross *et al* (1997) point out that participation without action raises questions about the sustainability of tenant participation in the long run. If, as this chapter has demonstrated, tenants' motivations for participation are primarily to achieve change in housing management standards, this raises the question of why they would continue to participate if change is not forthcoming.

The tenants and local authority officials interviewed for the purposes of this research attributed the lack of symbiosis between tenant participation and improved housing management to two factors: varying understandings of the meaning of participation amongst tenants and locals authority staff and an unwillingness on the part of the managers of housing and other local authority departments to act on the issues and problems raised by means of the participation process. The good practice literature recommends that these problems should be addressed by means of training and information for staff and the establishment of senior management implementation teams to support tenant participation (Housing Policy and Practice Unit, 1994). However, in addition to these cultural barriers to change, lack of progress in local authority housing management reform in Ireland is also related to structural factors such as arrangements for funding and staffing the service, and it is likely that these issues may prove more difficult to overcome (Redmond and Walker, 1995).

In relation to the latter issue, Norris and O'Connell (2002) point out that, with the exception of technical staff such as architects, the staffing system in local authorities is generalist. Officials do not possess professional qualifications and since they often advance up the promotional ladder by moving between departments, it is therefore in their interests to maintain a broad knowledge of all the procedures and services within the remit of local government. Although they acknowledge that this system does hold some advantages insofar as it enables officials to '… acquire experience of working in a variety of settings and thus become well rounded, versatile and familiar with a multiplicity of roles', its major disadvantage from the housing management perspective, is that:

... it mitigates against the accumulation of experience and expertise in this complex area and it perpetuates a largely desk bound culture. This leads a strong orientation towards punctilious administration and obedience to rules as opposed to effective management and the pursuit of useful outcomes. While the reasons why this culture has developed are understandable, in light of the critical demands made of the contemporary housing service, it represents a significant impediment to improving management standards.

(Norris and O'Connell, 2002: 252)

Moreover, they also point out that in view of the modest size of the local authority housing stock, coupled with the fact that it is distributed among 88 separate landlords, changing this staffing system would prove difficult, because housing departments are too small to afford professionally qualified staff a viable career path.

In Chapter 8 of this book Norris points out that arrangements for funding the capital costs of local authority housing provision in Ireland are unusual in the wider European context (Stephens *et al*, 2002). Sources of current expenditure for housing management and maintenance of this stock are also atypical. Most current expenditure is funded from rental income (Dollard, 2003). Since 1973 the rents on all local authority dwellings in this country have been linked to the incomes of tenants and not surprisingly in view of their strongly residualised social profile, tenants devote a much smaller proportion of their incomes to housing costs than occupations of any other housing tenure (Central Statistics Office, 2001a). This method of funding curtails the ability of local authorities to raise additional revenue to address issues raised through the tenant participation process and indeed to pay for the supports necessary for tenant participation such as staff and grant aid to tenants' organisations. In addition, as revealed by Figure 9.2 below, it also means that expenditure on housing management and maintenance of local authority housing significantly exceeds income from rents and other charges to tenants – in 2002 the latter covered only 75.3 per cent of the former. In this regard there are marked differences between the different types of local authorities. Town councils' income averaged at 137 per cent of expenditure between 1995 and 2002, but in the five city councils income averaged at only 57 per cent of expenditure during this period. No research has been conducted to explain this discrepancy between urban and rural local authorities in Ireland, although evidence from the United Kingdom indicates that costs of managing housing stock in urban areas is higher because it generally contains more high-density flats complexes and is occupied by more disadvantaged tenants (Walker and Murie, 2004). Whatever the reasons behind this inconsistency, it helps to explain why the five local authorities examined in this chapter have been slow to address the pressures for housing management reform generated by involving tenants in management.

Figure 9.2: Income from Rents and Other Receipts from Tenants as a Percentage of Expenditure on the Management and Maintenance of Local Authority Rented Dwellings, by Local Authority Type, 1995-2002

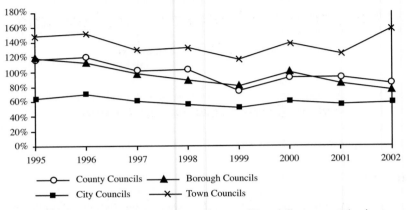

Source: Department of the Environment, Heritage and Local Government (various years). Note: Figures are rounded to the nearest whole number. Town councils also include local authorities designated as town commissioners prior to the Local Government Act, 2001.

10

The Changing Nature of the Housing Association Sector

Simon Brooke and Vanda Clayton

Introduction

The Irish housing association sector has a long history of providing accommodation for people unable to procure suitable private sector housing for themselves. As is examined in more detail in Chapter 8, the modern housing association movement emerged from nineteenth-century philanthropic housing organisations, which pioneered innovative new ways of addressing the severe working-class housing problems of Ireland's towns and cities. Housing associations continued for most of the twentieth century as a small but vibrant sector of the Irish housing market, primarily focusing on the niche of providing housing and other services for people with special needs, particularly older people.

The early 1980s saw the cautious beginnings of state support for housing association activities, with the introduction of the first defined funding scheme for the sector. However, a major change in the focus of Irish housing policy became apparent in 1991, with the introduction of *A Plan for Social Housing* (Department of the Environment, 1991), which envisaged a shift in the role of local authorities away from concentrating principally on the direct provision of social housing, and towards the facilitation of a range of housing options. The plan sought to encourage housing associations to diversify their activities and become major providers of general needs housing for low-income families, a role which had traditionally been the preserve of local authorities. This was reinforced by the *National Development Plan, 2000-2006*, which set the target output for the housing association sector of 4,000 units per year by 2006 (Government of Ireland, 2000a). This very ambitious target represented a huge expected increase in existing housing association output, which varied during the 1990s from less than 500 housing units to just over 1,000 (Department of the Environment and Local Government, various years).

Thus, the housing association sector is changing in response to new funding arrangements and targets, whilst maintaining its traditional role in providing housing for people with needs additional to their housing need.

This chapter begins with a discussion of the development of the housing association sector from the early 1980s; the present funding arrangements are then outlined; characteristics of the Irish housing association sector today are discussed and the chapter concludes with a consideration of the future directions for the housing association sector.

The Development of the Housing Association Sector: 1984-2002

The First Funding Scheme

Until the early 1980s, funding for housing associations had been provided on an ad-hoc discretionary basis from health authorities and local authorities. However, this financial assistance was extremely limited and the sector was heavily dependent on voluntary effort, and in particular the involvement of religious bodies. At this time some 74 housing associations had approval from the Department of the Environment to apply for funding to assist housing provision, while the total housing association stock was estimated at approximately 1,850 flats and houses. Housing associations at this time were predominantly engaged in the provision of special needs housing, that is, housing provided for people who have a particular need in addition to a housing need (Geoghegan, 1983). This includes elderly people, people with disabilities, people who have been homeless, and women who have been victims of domestic violence. The housing may be long-term or short-term, and the provision of this kind of housing includes specific services aimed at meeting the needs of the people being housed. These services might include communal facilities, 24-hour staff cover, health care and counselling.

In the main these housing associations were small and locally-based. Although the valuable contribution being made by housing associations in the field of special-needs housing was attracting increasing recognition, the continued development of the sector was inhibited by the lack of an effective, defined funding scheme.

Up to the 1970s, housing co-operatives, which are a distinct form of housing association in which the members of the co-operative are also the users of the housing services it provides, had played a significant role in providing access to home ownership for low-income groups (Department of the Environment 1991). There are two main forms of co-operative housing: rental housing co-operatives and home-ownership co-operatives. In rental housing co-operatives, tenants share responsibility for the management and upkeep of their homes and communal areas. The homes remain within the ownership of the housing co-operative. Members must be registered on local authority housing waiting lists, and participate in education and training programmes. Home ownership co-operatives are either home ownership building co-operatives in which individual households own their own home, or co-ownership housing co-operatives where ownership lies with the co-operative.

The current legal status of housing associations derives from Section 6 of the Housing (Miscellaneous Provisions) Act, 1992 which gives the Minister for the Environment, Heritage and Local Government the power to grant housing associations 'approved' status or to delegate this power to local authorities. This 'approved' status makes them eligible for assistance including financial assistance by local authorities. Housing associations have four distinct characteristics: they are independent; they are non-profit making; they have a voluntary committee; and they are established for the purpose of providing rented housing for those who cannot secure suitable housing in the private sector. A number of different labels are applied to the housing association sector, which has created considerable confusion. Labels currently in use include 'voluntary housing sector', 'non-profit housing sector', and 'approved housing bodies'. For the purpose of clarity, and in an attempt to promote the consistent use of one label, in this chapter the name 'housing associations' is used.

In 1984, when the government announced that a proper funding scheme would be put in place for housing associations, it was broadly welcomed by the housing association sector. The Capital Assistance Scheme (CAS) was set up to assist housing associations to provide housing for the elderly and other groups such as '... elderly, homeless and handicapped persons, victims of violence or desertion, lone parents, or persons otherwise accepted as qualified for local authority housing' (Department of the Environment, 1991: 18).

The CAS is a capital funding scheme which, whilst it has undergone small changes since its introduction, still retains its original structure. It works like this: a local authority provides the housing association with a grant (technically it is a non-repayable loan but in effect it is a grant) of up to ninety-five per cent of the capital costs of the housing scheme, subject to cost limits which are set by the Department of the Environment, Heritage and Local Government. The local authority has explicit nomination rights to 25 per cent of all lettings; a further 50 per cent have to go to people who 'qualify for local authority housing', that is they are registered on the housing waiting list; and the housing association may let the final 25 per cent to others, so long of course as they are in one of the categories set out in the scheme.

The introduction of the CAS represented '... a significant step in policy development by the Department in the area of encouraging social housing organisations' (Thompson, 1988: 121), and led to an increase in housing association output (see Figure 10.1). However, from the perspective of housing associations, it had and continues to have two weaknesses. The first of these is that the housing association has to provide finance for 5 per cent of the capital cost of most housing schemes, which at present costs is a not inconsiderable sum. This is often done through charitable fund raising, which requires substantial voluntary effort.

The second problem, which is more significant, is that the scheme provides capital funding only, and housing associations are given no assistance with management and maintenance costs once the housing scheme has been let. Setting rents which are affordable to tenants means that there will not be enough rental income to pay for repairs, maintenance, a sinking fund (to pay for regular cyclical maintenance and upgrading), insurance, administration and housing management. This last is crucial since management of special needs housing is more expensive than management of housing for people without special needs. As well as the normal housing management tasks of processing repairs, organising lettings, and dealing with rent problems, there may well be additional costs, depending on the type of housing scheme. These may include twenty-four hour staffing, on-site warden or caretaker, provision of meals and assistance with cleaning etc. The effect of this is that either management has to involve a considerable amount of voluntary effort, or funding has to be sourced elsewhere. Funding from health boards under Section 65 of the Health Act, 1953 has been provided in a number of cases. However, health board grants are awarded on an ad-hoc, discretionary basis and practice varies considerably between health boards (Ruddle *et al*, 1997). The exception to this is projects providing accommodation for homeless people which are eligible for assistance with management costs under Section 10 of the Housing Act, 1988; this funding has recently been put on a more standardised footing (Department of the Environment and Local Government, 2000d).

The Irish Council for Social Housing (ICSH), which is the representative body for housing associations in Ireland, has continually highlighted the difficulties faced by housing associations in planning service provision when funding for running costs and staffing is uncertain from year to year. Throughout the 1980s and 1990s, the ICSH has campaigned for '... an integrated and co-ordinated response to the additional management and staff costs incurred in providing special needs housing for the elderly, for homeless persons and persons with disabilities, in the form of a properly defined scheme of grants' (Irish Council for Social Housing, 1999: i). This need for a defined revenue funding scheme to meet the additional housing management costs arising from the provision of special needs housing has finally been acknowledged. A proposal, initially aimed at housing for the elderly, has been prepared by the Department of the Environment, Heritage and Local Government, and involves a funding scheme established by the Department of Health and Children that will be administered by health boards. At the time of writing it is unclear whether or not this proposal will be acted upon.

General Needs Housing – a New Direction

General needs housing is housing provided for people who have no particular need other than a housing need, that is, for people who before they were housed by the housing association, were living in inadequate housing and could not afford to buy their own home. Although the terms of the CAS specify that the housing provided under its auspices may be let to '... persons otherwise accepted as qualified for local authority housing', the scheme is generally unsuitable for the provision of general needs housing. This is for two reasons.

First, the requirement for housing associations to raise 5 per cent of the capital costs cannot be met if associations are to have a substantial programme of new housing output except by passing this cost on to tenants in the form of increased rents, and then only if a lending body could be persuaded to advance a loan for this purpose. The funding situation was even more difficult for housing associations in the 1980s, during the early years of the operation of the CAS. At that time, a maximum of 80 per cent of the total costs of the housing project could be state-funded so the housing associations had to raise the remaining 20 per cent themselves. Furthermore, uniform grant limits applied then, irrespective of the type of housing being constructed. These factors encouraged voluntary housing associations to concentrate on the niche of constructing and managing smaller, one- or two-person housing units for people with special housing needs. They made it difficult to provide larger, family-type housing for low-income families, which could have led to a wider role for housing associations in the provision of mainstream social housing.

Second, and following on from this, local authorities, which are by far the largest providers of social housing, set their rents according to a differential rent system in which rents are based solely on household income and are not related at all to the size or location or condition of the house or flat being rented. Furthermore, rents under the differential rent system are deliberately set low, to ensure affordability (local authority tenants are not eligible for rent supplement) and, as is examined in more detail by Redmond and Norris in Chapter 9 of this volume, they meet only approximately two-thirds of management and maintenance costs (Dáil Debates, 2000). If housing associations were to provide general needs housing under the CAS they would have to charge substantially higher rents than local authorities in order to meet all of their costs. This could be expected to lead to difficulties in letting properties since prospective tenants would be more likely to choose a low-rent local authority house or flat over a higher-rent housing association property.

As mentioned above, the publication of *A Plan for Social Housing* (Department of the Environment, 1991) marked major changes for social housing. A shift in the role of local authorities was envisaged, which expanded their role beyond the direct provision of housing towards the facilitation and promotion of a range of housing options, not least of which was the housing association sector. The 1991 plan introduced a new funding scheme for housing associations, which aimed to encourage the provision of general needs housing. The Rental Subsidy Scheme would, '… further enhance the opportunities for voluntary housing bodies to respond to social housing needs and widen the housing options available to low-income households' (Department of the Environment, 1991: 19).

At this stage, the housing association sector was still very small and predominantly catered for people with special housing needs, particularly elderly people, people with disabilities and homeless people. The Department of the Environment had granted 'approved status' to 206 housing associations by the end of 1990, enabling them to apply for funding under the voluntary housing schemes. However, many of these organisations were either inactive or very small, as the housing association stock was estimated at approximately 3,514 housing units at the end of 1990, less than half of 1 per cent of the total housing stock (Geoghegan, 1983; Department of the Environment, 1991; Department of the Environment and Local Government, 1995b).

The reasons for the sudden shift in Irish housing policy towards encouraging housing associations to become major providers of mainstream social housing are not entirely clear. It does not appear to have been driven to any great extent by an ideological agenda of welfare state reform and privatisation, as was the case in the UK and other western European countries. Rather, it has been interpreted as a pragmatic response to a combination of factors. These included criticism of local authorities' management and maintenance practices in *A Plan for Social Housing* (Department of the Environment, 1991), and a trenchant critique in *Memorandum on the Preparation of A Statement of Policy on Housing Management*:

> Overall, there are indications that resources are not being put to best use in the management of local authority housing, the stock is not being adequately managed, tenants are often dissatisfied and alienated, dwellings are being allowed to become rundown through poor maintenance, and demands are growing for Exchequer funding for the refurbishment of rundown and problem estates. Tenants, elected representatives and the public generally are frequently critical of the standards of many local authority housing estates and there is a widespread view that action is urgently needed to improve the position. (Department of the Environment, 1993: 7)

Other factors assisting the shift in policy included: increasing social problems in certain 'difficult-to-let' local authority estates; an unprecedented increase in the demand for social housing as a result of the housing affordability crisis of the 1990s; lobbying from the voluntary sector for a greater role in the provision of mainstream social housing and the spiralling cost of managing, maintaining and refurbishing local authority housing (O'Sullivan, 1998a and 1998b; McDonagh, 1993; O'Connell, 1999).

Since its inception, the Rental Subsidy Scheme has undergone a number of metamorphoses and is now called the Capital Loan and Subsidy Scheme (LSS). The scheme currently comprises a non-repayable loan (in effect a 100 per cent grant) for capital works that is provided by the local authority, subject to cost limits set by the Department of the Environment, Heritage and Local Government. The local authority in turn funds this with a loan from the Housing Finance Agency, an independent body operating under the aegis of the DoEHLG that makes loans to local authorities for a number of purposes authorised by the Housing Acts. Repayments on this loan are recouped from the DoEHLG. As can be imagined, these Byzantine financial arrangements frequently result in long delays.

Furthermore, the development process as currently organised requires the involvement of a large number of agencies and considerable indirect communication between housing associations and other bodies. For example, the housing association cannot access funds directly from the Housing Finance Agency, but instead must go through the local authority. Moreover, the local authority role in enabling housing development by housing associations, which was devised when the Rental Subsidy Scheme was piloted in 1991, has not changed significantly since then. This role was specifically designed for small, community-based housing associations without experience, which is why local authorities are expected to have such close involvement with the entire development process. However, this level of scrutiny is inappropriate for experienced larger housing associations with substantial development programmes. The process also involves duplication and indeed triplication of responsibilities; for example both local authorities and the DoEHLG are expected to ensure that schemes are within cost limits and both are expected to regulate governance and the financial affairs of housing associations. This places considerable burdens on already over-stretched local authorities.

As a consequence of these delays in getting financial approval schemes sometimes have to be abandoned because the developer or builder loses patience and seeks another purchaser. So these structural complexities significantly inhibit the ability of housing associations to sustain a substantial development programme (Brooke, 2001).

However, under the Housing (Miscellaneous Provisions) Act, 2002, the Housing Finance Agency is empowered to lend money directly to housing associations, and when this is operational it is expected to lead to a substantial streamlining of the development process.

In addition to the capital grant, the LSS provides for a fixed annual subsidy per unit, which is a contribution to housing maintenance and management costs.

Under the scheme, housing associations have to let three-quarters of the dwellings to people who are registered on the local authority's housing waiting list. Recently arrangements have been agreed for the payment of a development allowance. This is a fixed percentage of the capital loan that housing associations are allowed to retain as a contribution to costs.

Sources of Land

The Subsidised Sites Scheme, which was introduced in its present form in *A Plan for Social Housing* in 1991, enables housing associations (and individuals) to acquire land from local authorities at a very low cost (Department of the Environment, 1991). It has been a substantial source of land opportunities for housing associations. However, of late less land has been available under this scheme, primarily because local authorities are being asked to expand considerably their own house-building programmes. The multi-annual local authority housing programmes established by the Department of the Environment and Local Government in 1999 notified local authorities of their target housing starts for four years, from 2000 to 2003. This has encouraged them to look carefully at their land requirements in years to come. Some religious institutions have provided land and/or buildings to housing associations at no cost or low cost. However, they have only a finite supply of land which is surplus to their requirements and which they can afford to give away or sell at low cost.

Part V of the Planning and Development Act, 2000 enables local authorities to require that up to 20 per cent of land being developed for housing be reserved for the provision of social housing, which may include housing provided by local authorities or housing associations. It is widely recognised that this has the potential to provide substantial opportunities to housing associations. However, at the time of writing, Part V is only beginning to be operational and it is too early to assess its overall likely impact.

Housing Association Output

Housing association output under the two funding schemes from 1984 to 2002 is shown in Figure 10.1. Output under the Capital Assistance Scheme grew steadily until 1993, when it peaked at 749 units. However, subsequently it dropped sharply, due to cost limits failing to keep pace with rising costs, and a fall in the supply of sites, until a trough was reached in 1998 when CAS output was just over one-third of the 1993 figure. The Capital Loan and Subsidy Scheme followed a similar pattern, growing quickly from its inception in 1992 to a peak of around 400 units in 1995-1997 and then dropping sharply to half that in 1998; as with the CAS, this was primarily due to cost limits failing to keep up with rising costs and therefore falling in real terms. Since 1998, output from both schemes has increased as the cost limits have risen, and the total output in 2002 was 1,360 units, made up of 699 built under the CAS, and 661 funded by the LSS.

Figure 10.1: Housing Association Output, 1984-2003

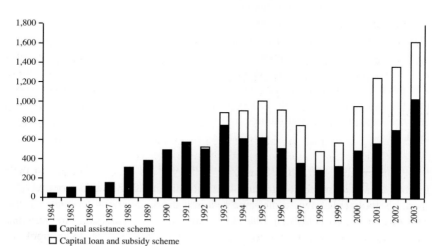

■ Capital assistance scheme
□ Capital loan and subsidy scheme

Sources: Department of the Environment 1991; Department of the Environment and Local Government, 1995b; Department of the Environment, Heritage and Local Government, various years.

The *National Development Plan 2000-2006* (Government of Ireland, 2000a) envisages housing association output rising to a total of 4,000 units per year by 2006: half to come from the CAS and half from the LSS (Dáil Debates, 2000). Interim total targets are 1,250 for 2001, 1,500 for 2002 and 1,750 for 2003 (Dáil Debates, 2000), from which it can be seen that the target for 2002 was not quite achieved. However, reaching 4,000 units per year by 2006 will require the existing high rate of growth to increase still further, and achieving this will present a significant challenge.

An increase in the number of housing associations with active development programmes would significantly increase the likelihood of the targets being achieved. One of the main obstacles facing a new or emerging housing association that is planning to embark on a significant development programme is the lack of income during the early stages of the programme. The effect of the arrangements of both funding schemes is that a housing association will receive no income whatsoever until the first housing scheme is on site (and then only the first tranche of the development allowance), and will not receive any continuous income until the scheme is tenanted. This means that unless it has access to an alternative source of funding a housing association will not, for example, be able to employ development staff. The effect of this will be, at best to delay the development programme, particularly in its important early stages, and at worst to prevent it happening at all.

However, a new funding scheme, comprising a development grant, has been established to target housing associations, whether new or existing, that are planning a development programme. This initiative, which replaces a previous ad-hoc funding system, comprises a grant towards the core funding of a housing association that is embarking for the first time on a development programme. The grant is payable for a maximum of three years, after which it is envisaged that the housing association will be in receipt of the development allowance, and subsequently of rental income and the fixed annual subsidy payable under the LSS.

Relationship Between Housing Associations and Local Authorities

In 2002 local authorities constructed 4,403 housing units; they also acquired 671. As has been stated above, in the same year housing associations completed 1,360 units, just over one-third of total local authority completions, showing that housing associations are making a significant contribution to social housing output (Department of the Environment, Heritage and Local Government, various years). Understandably, perhaps, a number of local authorities initially viewed the growth of housing associations with some alarm. Some believed that housing associations were claiming a superior status; some believed that housing associations should continue to provide special needs housing but leave the provision of general needs housing to local authorities; some were concerned about the ability of housing associations to deliver a quality service; and others wondered whether it signalled the beginnings of a broader policy shift leading eventually to the supplanting of local authorities by housing associations. However, these concerns, whilst remaining perhaps in a few minds, have largely been allayed, and in the vast majority of instances the relationship between local authorities and housing associations is both cordial and productive.

Housing associations are not free agents, building social housing where and when they like. As well as being subject to planning laws, housing association schemes cannot (and indeed should not) proceed without the support of the local authority concerned. There is no point in building social housing in an area where there is insufficient housing need to fill it; and local authorities, through their housing strategies, should be able to ensure that all schemes meet this criterion and others. So in a very real sense, the work of housing associations in the provision of rented social housing can only be successful if it is carried out in partnership with local authorities.

A further example of this partnership is stock transfers. These have to date taken place on only a very limited scale and have been restricted to situations where for a number of reasons a local authority estate, or part of a local authority estate, has deteriorated to such an extent that the local authority concerned has taken the view that a fresh start is needed. In these circumstances one way of achieving this is transferring the estate or part of it to a housing association for renovation and re-letting. This can be a successful way of dealing with specific local problems that may have built up over a number of years.

Profile of the Housing Association Sector in 2000

Relatively little is known about Irish housing associations and their activities. The sector is under-researched, and the Department of the Environment, Heritage and Local Government's data collection appears to focus on accounting for funding disbursed under the voluntary housing schemes, rather than on the collection of information that would be necessary to inform any monitoring or evaluation of housing management performance.

In 2000, a postal questionnaire survey of housing associations in the Republic of Ireland was undertaken (Clayton, forthcoming and Mullins *et al*, 2003). The aim of this survey was to generate some of the basic information necessary to build a profile of the housing association sector, including organisational origins and purpose, board and staff demographics, housing stock and services, tenant demographics and the letting process and, finally, financial indicators. Some of the results of this survey are drawn on in the following discussion of the characteristics of the Irish housing association sector.

Size of the Housing Association Sector

The dearth of information about the housing association sector makes it difficult to determine even basic information, such as the number of active housing associations in Ireland. A surprisingly high total of 474 housing associations were identified in 2000. This figure included 444 associations that had been granted 'approved status' by the DoEHLG, enabling them to apply for funding under the voluntary housing schemes. The remaining thirty housing associations were either newly established or, in some cases, Northern Irish housing associations interested in expanding their operations to the South. However, the DoEHLG's list of 'approved bodies' was out-of-date, several associations were double-listed and it was suspected that many more had either been dissolved or were no longer involved in the housing field.

Clues to the number of active housing associations, with housing units under management or plans to develop in future, were provided by the membership of the representative bodies, the ICSH and NABCo, together with the responses to two recent surveys, the 'ROI Housing Associations Survey' referred to above and the survey of 'Approved Bodies' undertaken by the Department of the Environment and Local Government in August 2000. In the case of the latter, a high response rate may reasonably be assumed as it was stated that non-response '... will be taken as an indication that the body concerned does not want to retain its approved status' (Department of the Environment, Heritage and Local Government, Voluntary and Co-operative Housing Unit, 2000: 1). Based on these sources, it was estimated that there were approximately 330 active housing associations by the end of 2001.

It was similarly difficult to determine the size of the housing association stock. The first survey of Irish housing associations was undertaken by Geoghegan (1983) and it was estimated that the housing association stock comprised approximately 1,850 homes by the early 1980s. A further 11,867 housing units were completed between 1981 and 2002. Thus, the Irish housing association stock comprises approximately 13,717 homes, around 1 per cent of the total Irish housing stock (Department of the Environment, 1991; Department of the Environment and Local Government, 1995b; Department of the Environment, Heritage and Local Government, various years).

Housing Association Size

According to the 'ROI Housing Associations Survey', the average housing stock size for a housing association in the Republic of Ireland was around thirty-eight housing units. However, the housing association sector was characterised by a very skewed distribution of the housing stock and the median housing stock size was only eight housing units. Thus, many small, community-based housing associations existed, managing small numbers of homes, while there were very few medium- and large-sized housing associations, managing much larger housing stocks. Based on a combination of the postal questionnaire survey and interviews with statutory and non-profit organisations involved in the sector, it was possible to estimate the number of housing associations in each housing stock size category, as shown in Figure 10. 2.

'Small' housing associations were defined as those managing fifty or less homes, while the 'medium'-sized category covered housing associations managing between fifty-one and 250 homes. This threshold of fifty housing units between small- and medium-sized housing associations was selected on a fairly arbitrary basis. However, it did prove useful in establishing characteristics that appear to be related to housing stock size, particularly staffing. It appears that the maximum housing stock size that can be managed on a voluntary basis is approximately fifty homes, as all of the housing associations surveyed employed paid staff if their housing stock exceeded this size. Small housing associations were certainly the most numerous, comprising an estimated 93 per cent of all housing associations. 'Medium'-sized housing associations were far less common, comprising an estimated 5 per cent of all housing associations.

'Large' housing associations were defined as those managing in excess of 250 homes. Just seven housing associations, an estimated 2 per cent of the total, were classified in this category. However, these seven organisations accounted for 44 per cent of the total housing association stock. Indeed, the largest housing association alone managed almost 2,000 homes, around 15 per cent of the total housing association stock.

Figure 10.2: Housing Associations by Housing Stock Size, 2001

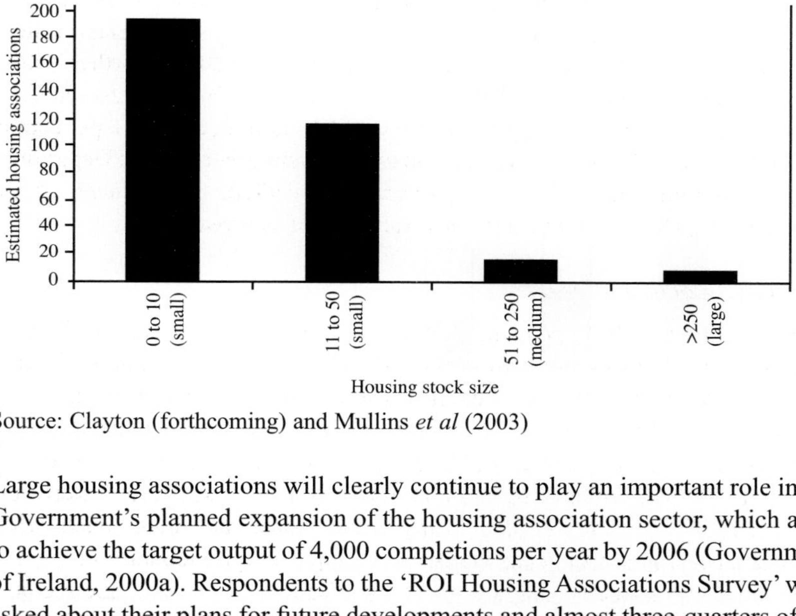

Source: Clayton (forthcoming) and Mullins *et al* (2003)

Large housing associations will clearly continue to play an important role in the Government's planned expansion of the housing association sector, which aims to achieve the target output of 4,000 completions per year by 2006 (Government of Ireland, 2000a). Respondents to the 'ROI Housing Associations Survey' were asked about their plans for future developments and almost three-quarters of the housing units with approved funding that were planned for 2001 and 2002 were being developed by large housing associations.

Furthermore, the large housing associations will also be important in continuing the expansion of the housing association sector's role envisaged by the government – to encompass the provision of general needs social housing for low-income families in addition to the sector's traditional niche of providing housing for special-needs groups (Department of the Environment, 1991). Indeed, 89 per cent of the family-type housing units completed under the LSS between its introduction in 1991 and 1999 were constructed by the seven largest housing associations.

Housing Association Tenants and Services

Irish housing associations have historically focused on the niche of providing housing for special needs groups, particularly for elderly people and people with disabilities. Since the introduction of the LSS in 1991, housing associations have increasingly been encouraged to engage in the provision of general-needs social housing for low-income families, in addition to their traditional remit. However, just 17 per cent of the housing associations that responded to the survey accommodated tenants requiring no additional services or supports.

Figure 10.3: Housing Associations by Category of Tenants Accommodated, 2001

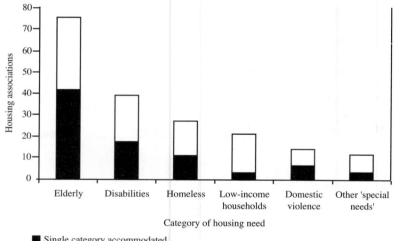

■ Single category accommodated
□ Multiple categories accommodated

Source: Clayton (forthcoming) and Mullins *et al* (2003).

Notes: Of the 185 survey respondents, 121 housing associations provided details of their tenants' support requirements, as shown above. However, the total number of housing associations appears to exceed 121 on the graph because 30% accommodated tenants from multiple categories of need.

The majority of the survey respondents accommodated at least some tenants requiring additional services or supports. A marked tendency for housing associations to focus on one particular category of housing need existed, with 70 per cent of the survey respondents drawing all of their tenants from the same category of housing need, while the remaining 30 per cent housed tenants from a mix of categories. The tenants accommodated fell into the following main categories of housing need: elderly people (62 per cent), people with disabilities

(32 per cent), homeless people (22 per cent), victims of domestic violence (12 per cent) and people requiring support for other reasons (9 per cent), as shown in Figure 10.3. This 'other' category included a diverse range of support needs, including people who are HIV positive, refugees and released prisoners.

The Traveller community was one notable section of the population whose housing needs did not appear to be addressed by the housing association sector. Surprisingly, in the context of the many specialist associations, none of the survey respondents catered solely for Travellers. Furthermore, none of the respondents had provided halting sites nor did any have plans to develop them. Just fifteen (12 per cent) of the survey respondents, primarily providers of women's refuges or hostels for homeless people, accommodated some Travellers among their tenants.

Figure 10.4: Housing Association Projects by Services Provided, 2001

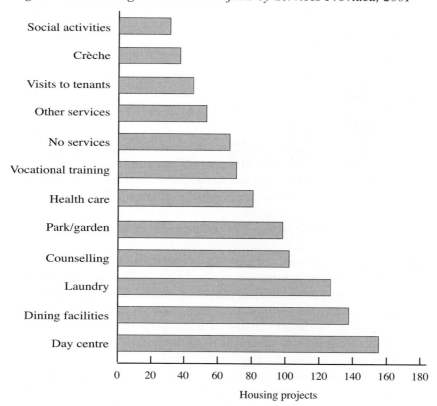

Housing projects

Source: Clayton, (forthcoming) and Mullins *et al.* (2003)

Notes: Of the 185 survey respondents, 137 housing associations, managing 364 completed housing projects, gave details of the services provided at each project, as shown above. However, the total number of housing projects exceeds 364 on the graph because multiple services are provided at many housing projects.

Reflecting the focus of housing associations on the provision of housing for special needs groups, a key characteristic of housing associations in Ireland was the provision of a range of additional services for tenants. At 82 per cent, a high proportion of the housing projects managed by the housing associations that responded to the survey had at least one service available to tenants, and many had several different services, as shown in Figure 10.4. Only 18 per cent of the completed housing projects did not have any services available to their tenants. The most popular services for housing associations to provide appeared to be day centres (43 per cent of housing projects), dining (38 per cent) and laundry facilities (35 per cent). Other services available at some housing projects included park/garden (27 per cent), counselling (28 per cent), health care (22 per cent), vocational training (20 per cent), visitors calling on a regular basis to keep elderly or disabled tenants company and to check on their welfare (12 per cent), crèche (10 per cent) and social activities (9 per cent). A further 15 per cent of housing association projects had 'other services' available to tenants. A wide range of activities were described in this category, including library, chapel, bus, sports equipment, hairdressing, supported employment, therapeutic crafts, home help, cleaning, warden/superintendent/caretaker, respite care, outreach and resettlement services.

Future Directions

Since the publication of *A Plan for Social Housing*, social housing policy has focused on a changing role for local authorities: from direct provision of social housing, to the development of a more strategic role as facilitators of a range of housing options (Department of the Environment, 1991). When it announced the introduction of the rental subsidy scheme (now LSS), it set out a new role for housing associations: providers of general needs housing for low-income families, a role which had traditionally been the preserve of local authorities.

The reasons for this policy change lay not with an ideological agenda of privatisation or welfare state reform, but included significant disenchantment with local authority performance; an increasing demand for social housing that could not be met by local authorities alone; as well as problems in some 'difficult-to-let' local authority estates; and the spiralling costs of managing, maintaining and refurbishing local authority housing.

As the housing association sector has developed, it has become increasingly bipolar. One group contains the great majority of housing associations, and is characterised by small size (nearly 95 per cent of Irish housing associations have less than fifty-one units and nearly 60 per cent have less than eleven units). This group provides mainly special needs housing; mainly for older people and people with disabilities, and very few have a significant development programme.

The other group comprises a very small number of larger housing associations (only seven have more than 250 units), which provide mainly general needs housing, and most of which have significant development programmes.

The future direction of the housing association sector will be greatly influenced by the way it has developed in recent years.

National Development Plan Targets

The *National Development Plan 2000-2006* (Government of Ireland, 2000a) places housing associations as significant providers of social housing. The plan envisages housing associations providing approximately one third of total social housing output by 2006. This is an ambitious target, the achievement of which will require housing association output to increase by over 30 per cent per year until 2006.

A number of significant obstacles stand in the way of the achievement of this objective. Despite the fact that legislation empowering the Housing Finance Agency to lend money directly to housing associations instead of via local authorities has been in place since 2002, at the time of writing this has yet to be implemented. Furthermore, many of the administrative systems established to assist the housing association sector were designed to assist the majority of very small housing associations, and are proving to be increasingly problematic for larger general needs housing associations with sizeable development programmes. The unnecessarily complex arrangements referred to above: too little direct communication between the key players; an inappropriate role for local authorities; duplication of responsibilities; wide variation in local authority practice; and additional administrative burdens placed on already over-stretched local authorities – all combine to curtail very significantly the housing association development programme.

The housing associations most affected by this are, as already stated, those that are planning significant development programmes; in other words the very housing associations that will be making the biggest contribution to housing association output. So whilst on the one hand the Government, through the National Development Plan, is expecting housing association output to increase substantially, on the other, its failure to make relatively modest administrative changes to alleviate these problems imperils the achievement of the plan's targets.

Fears that such changes might result in less scrutiny of housing associations, with consequent risk to public funds, could be allayed by the introduction of a regulatory system targeting those housing associations with significant development programmes.

Special Needs Housing

Housing associations have a long association with the provision of special needs housing, and this is likely to develop in a number of ways. Firstly, it is probable that there will be a continuing increase in the number of small, community-based housing associations building one or two schemes, frequently for elderly people. These housing associations, frequently run entirely by voluntary effort, will continue to play a vital role in responding to local need.

Secondly, there is an increasing trend for housing associations that are primarily providers of general needs housing to include the provision of special needs housing in their housing schemes. This may be in the form of single houses, for example adapted for a person using a wheelchair; or it may comprise a sheltered housing scheme for the elderly, incorporated within a general needs housing scheme.

A third way in which special needs housing may develop is through a partnership between a housing association with experience in development, and another housing association or voluntary sector organisation with experience in managing a particular kind of housing project. The first housing association builds and maintains the house or hostel, and the second organisation, through a management agreement, manages the project. There are a number of different models for this kind of partnership which, by bringing together organisations with complementary areas of expertise, can be an effective way of delivering a very high quality housing service.

However, in the absence of a defined revenue funding scheme referred to above, which will enable housing associations to employ staff to provide the additional housing management necessary in special needs housing, expansion of special needs housing will be limited.

Long-Term Financial Viability

Currently a housing association's only sources of income once a housing scheme has been let to tenants, are rent from tenants, and the management and maintenance allowance, together with funds raised from other government sources and charitable donations. These have to pay for all the housing association's costs including housing management, administration, repairs, and cyclical maintenance. The last of these is a significant amount, requiring the establishment of a sinking fund that will pay for major items such as re-roofing and boiler replacement in the future. Housing associations do not have access to the remedial works scheme that funds local authorities for the upgrading of run-down estates, and so have to make provision for this out of their own resources.

Research currently being carried out is examining the long-term viability of this funding system. It is likely that it will show that the income from rents and the management and maintenance allowance will not be adequate to sustain the long-term financial viability of housing associations. A major challenge for the future then is to tackle this emerging problem, *before* financial viability of the sector is threatened.

Conclusion

Housing associations have been providing housing in Ireland for over a century, but until fairly recently they have played a minor role in the housing system. However, policy changes that aimed to encourage the growth of housing associations, after a shaky start caused by cost limits failing to keep up with rising costs and lack of land opportunities, have begun to bear fruit with a substantial increase in housing association output in recent years.

As housing associations both develop their traditional role as providers of special needs housing, and expand their provision of general needs housing, they will, in partnership with local authorities, make an increasingly significant contribution to the development of social housing provision in Ireland.

11

Housing, Equality and Inequality

Eithne Fitzgerald and Nessa Winston

Introduction

The Introduction to this volume identifies high levels of home ownership as one of the distinguishing characteristics of the Irish housing system in comparison with other EU member states. These home ownership levels are linked to longstanding and numerous state subsidies for home buyers, as outlined by O'Connell in Chapter 2. In the absence of similar incentives in the other housing tenures, owner occupation became the tenure of choice. A persistent theme in the housing literature is that inequalities are exacerbated when market provision is dominant and that this pattern of inequality is heightened during a property boom with rapid house price growth relative to the increase in the average industrial wage (Lee *et al*, 1995; Forrest and Murie (eds), 1995; Thorns, 1989). In the Irish context, house price inflation since the mid-1990s has effected a silent redistribution of wealth in favour of home owners and owners of development land at the expense of those trying to enter the housing market.

In these circumstances, the highly subsidised home owing majority became increasingly privileged compared with people in other tenures. The result is a situation where there are stark inequalities in the Irish housing system. The experiences and outcomes for landowners, financiers, estate agents, landlords and speculators are dramatically different from those outside of this circle, including: the increasing number of homeless people; private tenants paying escalating rents; those on low incomes; those on growing waiting lists for social housing, and others in housing need. Furthermore, residualisation in the local authority sector is such that its tenants are increasingly characterised by low incomes and multiple deprivation compared with tenants in other sectors and owner occupiers.

Interventions by governments over many decades are a key cause of inequalities in the Irish housing system and current housing policy continues to sustain them. For example, schemes such as the Seaside Resorts Scheme facilitate the acquisition of second homes by wealthier people during a period when many first-time buyers cannot afford to enter the private market. This chapter outlines many of the policy instruments used to favour the private housing market, including taxation issues. Many of these schemes are regressive and result in substantial transfers of resources to owners of development land and home owners.

This chapter presents an analysis of some of these inequalities in the Irish housing system, with the main emphasis on comparisons between different tenures, specifically the owner-occupied, private rented and local authority rented sectors. There are significant inequalities between the tenures along a number of dimensions. In terms of access to housing, many first-time buyers on or below the average wage cannot afford to purchase a home. However, those from wealthier backgrounds may have access to parental financial support for purchase. In terms of housing costs, private rent inflation has resulted in problems of affordability for some tenants. In addition, some tenants on rent supplement face problems of discrimination in trying to access private rented accommodation. Applicants for social housing face access problems as the number of households on the waiting list has grown significantly in recent years. Local authority tenants also face some problems with the quality of their accommodation, especially with regard to heating and the dwelling size. Significant geographical inequalities exist in the Irish housing system including variations by region in the affordability of house purchase, levels of new construction, waiting lists for social housing, allocations to social housing and homelessness. Many of these issues are addressed in this chapter. Unfortunately, space does not permit an analysis of inequalities associated with different groups with specific housing needs such as disabled people, older people, and refugees and asylum seekers. However, some of the concerns of these groups are highlighted elsewhere (Commission on the Status of People with Disabilities, 1996; Fahey, 2001; Fanning, 2002; McGettrick, 2003; McKeown and McGrath, 1996; National Council on Ageing and Older People, 2001; Norris and Winston, 2004; Ruddle *et al*, 1997; Weafer, 2001; Woods and Humphries, 2001), while the housing and accommodation problems faced by Travellers and homeless people are examined in Chapters 12 and 13 of this book respectively.

Housing Wealth, Income and Inequality in Ireland

Irish society is marked by significant disparities in income and strong social class gradients in income, education and health (e.g. Cantillon *et al*, 2001; Lynch, K., 1999; Nolan *et al*, 1998, Nolan and Whelan, 1999). Comparative figures show that in the mid-1990s, the distribution of income in Ireland was one of the more unequal in the EU (Nolan *et al*, 1998). During the years of strong economic growth in the second half of the 1990s, inequality in disposable income widened, primarily due to taxation and welfare policies (Fitzgerald, 2001).

While those who are poor are at a higher risk of housing difficulty, there is not a straightforward relationship between low income and housing deprivation (Nolan and Whelan, 1996). On average, there is not a strong correlation between poor physical standards of accommodation and income poverty (Nolan and Whelan, 1996). There are two main reasons for this. First, over 350,000 homes built by local authorities since the foundation of the State have enabled low-income families to secure better accommodation at a much lower rent than if housing had been left entirely to the market. Second, sales to tenants of over two-thirds of local authority dwellings have provided an important route to home and asset ownership for lower-income families.

Tenant purchase policy has contributed significantly to the achievement of virtually universal home ownership in Ireland by older households, as shown in Table 11.1. This table shows that the housing wealth of older people provides some counterbalance to their lower average levels of income.

The high level of life-time owner occupation helps to explain, as shown in Table 11.2 below, why the distribution of housing wealth in terms of the value of one's own home is significantly more equal than the distribution of income.

Table 11.1: Housing Wealth by Age, 2000

Age group	% Owner occupiers	% of total housing wealth	% of total equivalised income
Under 35	56.7	14.1	25.4
35-44	86.9	19.4	20.0
45-54	88.0	23.9	21.7
55-64	88.5	16.8	15.0
65-74	95.0	14.7	10.7
75 +	91.1	11.0	7.3

Source: Fahey and Nolan (2003).

Table 11.2: Housing Wealth by Income Quintile of Households, 2000

Income quintile	% of total equivalised income	% of total housing wealth
Bottom	7.3	15.2
2	11.3	16.1
3	17.0	19.2
4	23.8	24.3
Top	40.7	25.3

Source: Fahey and Nolan (2003).

In addition to housing wealth tied up in one's home, there is also property owned as an investment or holiday home. The latest survey of housing conditions in Ireland shows that 5 per cent of households own another dwelling in Ireland, including approximately 15,000 holiday homes (Watson and Williams, 2003). Furthermore, a significant proportion of newly constructed dwellings between 1997 and 2002 have been purchased as holiday homes (FitzGerald *et al*, 2003).

Residualisation and Local Authority Housing

Residualisation refers to a tendency for the social rented sector to cater for an increasing proportion of deprived people and to cater more exclusively for this group (Lee and Murie, 1997). It is a trend which has been witnessed in many EU member states (Stephens, Burns and McKay, 2002). The sale of local authority housing to sitting tenants in a position to buy has contributed to the residualisation of those who remain as tenants.[1] Another influence was the Surrender Grant scheme of 1984-87 which encouraged council tenants in employment to buy a home in a private estate. Irish research confirms that those remaining as local authority tenants are a group characterised by low incomes, vulnerability to poverty and multiple deprivation (Murray and Norris, 2002; Nolan, Whelan and Williams, 1998; Nolan and Whelan, 1999).

The concentrated deprivation associated with local authority housing is more frequently found among council tenants in urban than rural areas and income poverty increased more rapidly among urban tenants between 1987 and 1994 (Nolan and Whelan, 1999). Nolan and Whelan (1999) contend that this is due to the combined influence of the urban location and living in local authority rented housing. This urban tenure effect is due to the selection in urban local authority housing of those with the multiple disadvantages associated with poverty (long-term unemployment, low levels of educational qualifications, lone parenthood and a large number of children). A recent study of Dublin City Council tenants revealed a very high proportion of tenant households with incomes below 40, 50 and 60 per cent of the national average (Murray and Norris, 2002). The study showed that each type of household accommodated by the Council was poorer than their counterpart in the general population.

Inequality in Access to Housing

Owner Occupation

As outlined by Downey in Chapter 3, house price inflation in the 1990s was not matched by similar increases in earnings. Prices almost trebled over this period while the average industrial wage rose by approximately 50 per cent (Department of the Environment, Heritage and Local Government, various years). One factor driving higher house prices was the fall in interest rates as Ireland joined the Euro zone, making any given mortgage cheaper to service for existing homeowners. However, at national level, house prices are now approximately nine times the annual average industrial wage, while in Dublin, they are twelve times the annual industrial wage (Permanent TSB and the Economic and Social Research Institute, 2004). For first-time buyers with incomes at that level the difference between the amount of the mortgage loan they can access and the price of a house ('the deposit gap') is now substantial. The result is that house purchase is out of reach for many aspiring first-time buyers, especially those on or below average incomes.

Figure 11.1: Mortgage Loan Approvals by Previous Tenure of Borrowers, 1994-2003

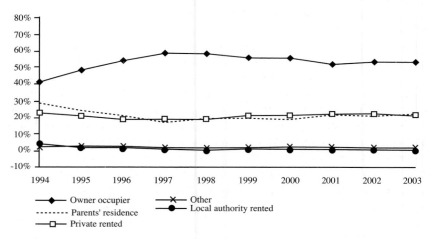

Source: Department of the Environment, Heritage and Local Government (various years). Note: These data include loans issued for the purchase of both new and second-hand dwellings nationwide. Comparable information is not available for the years 1990 to 1994.

Evidence of these trends is revealed in data on the incomes of those obtaining mortgages in the latter half of the 1990s and early years of this decade (Norris and Winston, 2004). The participation in the private housing market of households with lower incomes (under €25,395) sharply contracted, particularly in the Dublin area. Similarly, households with incomes between €25,396 and €31,743 also experienced a significant but less dramatic fall in the level of mortgage borrowing. By contrast, households with incomes in the top three divisions of the income scale increased their participation in the private housing market (Norris and Winston, 2004). However, since about 2001/2003, there has been a slight rise in the proportion of loan approvals to lower income households.

Further evidence of the affordability problem for aspiring first-time buyers is reflected in the decline in the proportion of mortgage loan approvals to people living in their parents' residence, as shown in Figure 11.1. In each year since 1995, over half of mortgage loan approvals were to people who were already owner occupiers. While some first-time buyers may obtain parental contributions towards the cost of house purchase, parents on low incomes, those who are tenants, and those with large families are less likely to be in a position to assist even with the cost of a deposit for a house. Thus, parental contributions to the house purchase of their children counterbalances, to some extent, an intergenerational housing inequality whereby housing wealth in the form of home ownership is greater for those in the older generations than those trying to form their households.

Additional evidence of inequalities in access to home ownership is revealed in data on the occupation of those obtaining mortgages (Department of the Environment and Local Government, various years). The plurality (41 per cent) of those who had mortgages approved in the year 2003 was from a professional/managerial background. About a quarter of loan approvals were to salaried (non-manual) employees, 21 per cent were to skilled/semi-skilled manual workers, while 12 per cent were to unskilled manual workers. It is interesting to note that since about 2001, the share of loan approvals to salaried (non-manual) employees has increased. This trend, together with the recent rise in the proportion of mortgages issued to low-income households which was highlighted above, may be due to the effects of increased expenditure on supports for low-income homeowners such as shared ownership and affordable housing schemes (Department of the Environment, Heritage and Local Government, various years).

Social Housing

The extent of the problem of access to social housing is revealed by examining local authority waiting lists which have risen significantly in recent years, following a sharp decline in the 1980s. As Norris and Redmond reveal in Chapter 1, the number of households on the waiting list rose from 27,247 in 1996 to 48,413 in 2002.

The decade to 2004 saw some resumption in the construction of new public housing after it had sunk to historic lows in the late 1980s. However, taking local authority and non-profit housing together, the combined share of new building is now under 10 per cent, compared with historic shares of up to a third for social housing in the 1970s and early 1980s (Department of the

Environment, Heritage and Local Government, various years). Consequently, the rate of new lettings has been insufficient to cope with the inflow of applicants to the waiting lists, with the result that waiting lists have risen. A recent report estimates that it would take approximately 40 years to eliminate the waiting lists nationally under existing plans for social house building (Hickey *et al*, 2002). Moreover, data from 2002 indicates that two-thirds of households on the housing list have incomes of less than €10,000 a year and 86 per cent have incomes below €15,000 (Department of the Environment, Heritage and Local Government, various years). Consequently their chances of securing affordable alternative accommodation in the private sector are slim.

The Private Rented Sector

Under the Equal Status Act, 2000, it is illegal to discriminate in the provision of goods or services, including access to housing, on any one of nine grounds: age, disability, family status, gender, marital status, membership of the Traveller community, race, sexual orientation and religion. Nevertheless, at the lower end of the rental market, suitable, affordable accommodation can be difficult to find, and discrimination against tenants on rent allowance or tenants with children has been noted in tight rental markets (Guerin, 1999). One study of rent supplement recipients in Cork, Dublin and Limerick showed that two-thirds of respondents had experienced problems in finding a landlord who would accept rent supplement (Guerin, 1999). This study also noted a reluctance among landlords to accept tenants with children as well as the unsuitability of much of the accommodation that is available to them in the sector in terms of poor quality standards, lack of space and insecurity of tenure (Guerin, 1999). Another study reported that in order to secure accommodation, additional payments were required from tenants on rent supplement (Lynch, R., 1999).

Inequalities in Housing Costs

For most goods and services there is little difference in the cost faced by one consumer over another, and paying a higher price usually secures a higher quality or quantity. However, housing is different. Housing tenure and, for owner occupiers, the date of purchase are the main determinants of the weekly or monthly outlay on housing. There may be little relationship between the current level of spending on housing and the quality of housing services consumed. This section probes these issues using data from the Household Budget Survey (see Chapter 4 of this volume for further examination of these data) (Central Statistics Office, 1977, 1984, 1989, 1997, 2001a).

Private Tenants

Private rents are determined by the supply and demand for this type of housing, and rents for individual dwellings usually reflect the size, location and quality of the accommodation. New landlords enter the market only where rent levels can cover the cost of financing the acquisition of the property in addition to maintenance and management costs, and rent levels may closely track the cost of servicing a loan on new build housing.

While there is evidence of a decline in private rent levels since 2002 in some areas, private tenants had the highest expenditure on housing during the period 1973-2000 when compared with people in other tenures. In the latter year they devoted 21 per cent of household expenditure to housing, compared to 9.6 per cent and 7.6 per cent among home owners with a mortgage and local authority tenants. Furthermore, private tenants experienced the highest percentage increase in expenditure (48 per cent) across the tenures since 1973. In return, they receive the least security of tenure and, at the lower end of the market, a relatively poor standard of accommodation.

For those buying their own homes, a rise in income has no impact on housing costs. Low-income households in public or private rented housing may however be penalised when their incomes rise through withdrawal of subsidy or an escalation in rent levels. The scale of this penalty is far higher for private tenants on rent allowance and traps many into unemployment. Publicly subsidised households in the private rented sector and in the public rented sector are treated very differently in this respect.

Welfare recipients in the private rented sector may be eligible for a rent supplement. Over 59,976 households were in receipt of rent supplement in 2003 (Department of Social and Family Affairs, various years), just over half the number of those in subsidised council housing. However, the rules for this rent subsidy may trap low-income families into unemployment.

Additional earnings, after the first €50 of part-time earnings, reduce the rent subsidy payable on a €1 for €1 basis. A tapered withdrawal of rent subsidy for those moving from welfare to work is of very limited value as it only applies to those whose incomes come below €317 a week. The loss of rent allowance is a critical deterrent to employment for those whose rents are high relative to earning capacity (e.g. low-paid workers and one-earner families), or where childcare or transport costs of taking a job would be substantial.

Local authority tenants and their adult children also pay increased rent if their earnings rise. However, unlike publicly subsidised private sector tenants, the rent 'tax' on working never goes higher than 20 per cent, unlike the 100 per cent withdrawal rate for private tenants. The integration of the two schemes by moving the rent supplementation scheme to the local authorities was recommended in principle by a government report on the topic (Inter-

Departmental Committee on Future Rental Arrangements, 1999). The most recent proposals suggest that households on rent supplement for more than 18 months will become the responsibility of local authorities who will be using leasing arrangements with private landlords to provide accommodation to households in this category (Norris and Winston, 2004).

Home Owners

About half of all home owners own their homes outright, so their housing costs are limited to repairs and maintenance. For the others, mortgage repayments are the main housing outlay and their current expenditure tends to relate to the date of purchase more than any other factor such as location, size and quality of the dwelling. That is, the size of the mortgage reflects the historic price paid for the house and the number of years outstanding on the loan. With the high house price inflation of the past decade, families buying identical houses in the same housing estate ten years apart may have paid very different prices for their homes, and one may have a mortgage which is three times that of the earlier buyer.

Despite this, data from the Household Budget Survey reveal that the housing costs of owners with a mortgage are less than half those of private renters. This is because the original mortgage is usually fixed in nominal terms, and repayments vary only with changes in interest rates. Moreover, declining interest rates since Ireland joined the Euro zone have resulted in mortgages being cheaper to service. For example, a €100,000 loan at 8 per cent interest over 25 years would cost €775 a month to service. If interest rates fall to 4 per cent, the same monthly repayments could service a mortgage of €147,000. The real value of repayments also typically declines over time in line with inflation, in contrast to private sector rents which normally increase in nominal terms over time. In a rising market, a home owner a few years into buying a house is likely to be paying less per month than a tenant in comparable accommodation and, unlike the tenant, acquires an asset in the process.

Local Authority Tenants

The differential rent scheme applying to local authority tenants means that rents vary with the income of the tenant and his/her household rather than the quality, size or location of the accommodation provided. Average rents in the sector are low relative to corresponding private sector rents, with an average weekly rent in 2002 of €29.62 (Department of the Environment, Heritage and Local Government, various years). The share of family expenditure going on rent remains fairly stable given the rent formula and remained at 7.6 per cent from 1973 to 2000. Home owners without a mortgage are the only group whose expenditure on housing as a proportion of income is lower than that of public sector tenants.

The rental income of local authorities has covered from 64-73 per cent of the maintenance and management expenditure in recent years (Department of the Environment, Heritage and Local Government, various years). The relatively low rental income undermines the capacity of local authorities to provide an effective management and maintenance service on their estates. The disadvantages of local authority housing are well publicised and include: a concentration of poor families leading to wider concentrations of deprivation; the emergence of some 'problem' estates, characterised by anti-social behaviour; and some physically run-down and poorly maintained neighbourhoods (Fahey (ed), 1999). However, it is important to emphasise that there are significant positive features of this tenure. These include: low rents for a low-income group; security of tenure; in most cases, good building quality; and older estates tend to be very conveniently located (Fahey (ed), 1999). Unfortunately, it is often extremely difficult for estates to shake a poor reputation even after they have experienced substantial regeneration (Dean and Hastings, 2000).

Inequalities in Security of Tenure

Those who own their homes outright have a very high security of tenure. Article 43 of the Irish constitution protects private property as an institution as well as the rights of an individual to own property, although compulsory purchase for essential public purposes, such as road widening, is permitted. While there is a risk that house buyers who default on mortgage payments may face repossession by the lender, the fact that repayments under standard mortgages do not adjust in line with inflation reduces the real burden of repayments over time and thus the default risk. However, if interest rates rise or unemployment worsens the number at risk of default could rise.

While most local authority tenancy agreements stipulate that they can be terminated by 28 days notice by either party, in practice local authority tenants in good standing have *de-facto* lifetime security of tenure. Local authorities may repossess a dwelling on the grounds of serious anti-social behaviour under the 1997 Housing (Miscellaneous Provisions) Act. The Act defines such behaviour as drug dealing or violence and intimidation. This provision of repossessing a dwelling due to criminal acts does not apply to any other housing tenure. Brooke (2001) points out that there is no evidence of arbitrary evictions by local authorities and 'tenants are assured by their landlord that this will not happen so long as they behave themselves'. However, he highlights the point that this 'imbalance of rights between landlord and tenant can only reinforce the tenants' perception that they should be grateful to have a place to live in at all; and that they are entirely dependent on the good-will of their landlord if they want to continue to live in it' (Brooke, 2001: 58).

Private sector tenants have far less security. The typical tenancy is from week to week or month to month and the minimum notice to quit is just 28 days, with no requirement for the landlord to give any reasons. Where the duration of a tenancy is spelt out in a formal lease, the tenancy expires at the end of the fixed term. While six-month tenancies are increasingly evident (McCashin, 2000), leases rarely run for more than a year. If a tenant refuses to vacate at the end of the fixed term or Notice to Quit, the landlord may pursue repossession. Under new legislation, which came into effect in December 2004, private tenants will have security of tenure for up to four years (subject to certain conditions) on completion of a six-month initial tenancy. The legislation gives effect to the recommendations of the Commission on the Private Rented Residential Sector, and will also require landlords to give reasons for Notice to Quit. However, a key factor in the success of this aspect of the legislation will be the compliance of landlords and available evidence indicates that compliance by landlords in the previous system, whereby landlords were required to register with local authorities, was relatively low (Norris and Winston, 2004).

A very small minority of private tenants, those covered by rent control prior to 1982, or those who acquired a long-term tenancy after 20 years' continuous occupation, do enjoy security of tenure. The evidence is that landlords terminate tenancies in advance of the 20-year threshold, ensuring that tenants do not obtain such leases (Working Group on Security of Tenure, 1996). While the Working Group on Security of Tenure recommended voluntary relinquishment of the right to renew a 35-year lease after twenty years' tenancy, the Commission on the Private Rented Sector recommended the abolition of this provision entirely. The Residential Tenancies Act, 2004 has implemented this recommendation.

One study of tenants on rent supplement in Cork, Dublin and Limerick found that two thirds of the sample viewed insecurity of tenure as a problem, especially those with child dependants (Guerin, 1999). Tenants who find it hard to secure alternative accommodation, e.g. tenants on rent supplement, can be at risk of becoming homeless if their tenancy is terminated. This is supported by the findings of a study of homelessness in Cork which showed that the largest share of people becoming homeless (36 per cent) came from the private rented sector, with 20 per cent from local authority housing and 16 per cent from the homes of parents or relatives prior to becoming homeless (Kearns et al, 2000). Only 3 per cent of homeless people came from the owner-occupied sector (Kearns et al, 2000).

Inequalities in Housing Amenities and Neighbourhood Quality

There are significant differences in housing facilities and perceived neighbourhood characteristics by tenure as revealed in data from the Quarterly

National Household Survey. Table 3 shows that, in general, occupants rate the housing stock as of good physical standard and the vast majority are satisfied with their accommodation. However, local authority tenants (14 per cent) and private tenants (9 per cent) are most likely to express dissatisfaction. About one half of local authority tenants have central heating compared to virtually all those buying a private home on a mortgage and three quarters of private renters. In addition, local authority renters are more likely to see their home as too small compared with those living in other tenures. Typical local authority housing was built to higher construction standards but with smaller rooms than corresponding private building. While problems of damp dwellings were limited to a small proportion of respondents, local authority and private tenants were more likely than owner occupiers to identify dampness as a problem.

Differences in the quality of neighbourhoods by tenure are also evident in Table 11.3. Approximately one quarter of those living in local authority neighbourhoods expressed concerns about graffiti, vandalism, public drinking or a drug problem and at feeling unsafe. These concerns were much less likely to be felt by those living in other housing tenures.

Table 11.3: Housing Facilities and Neighbourhood Amenities by Tenure, 1998

	Owned With Mortgage (%)	Private Renting Tenant (%)	Local Authority Tenant (%)
Central heating	96	76	51
Too small	4	9	12
Damp	2	7	11
Noise	9	17	18
Graffiti	5	8	27
Vandalism	7	11	25
Unsafe	12	14	24
Drugs	9	16	29

Source: generated by the Central Statistics Office from the Quarterly National Household Survey, 3rd Quarter, 1998.

Geographical Inequalities

From the mid-1990s, there was a dramatic increase in the number of people who require social housing because they are unable to afford the cost of their accommodation or find suitable alternative accommodation (Department of the

Environment, Heritage and Local Government, various years). By 2002, 21,452 people were in this category, representing 44 per cent of total need. However, as Table 11.4 demonstrates, there are significant geographic variations in the proportion of the population officially assessed as in housing need. The number of approved housing applicants relative to population is almost four times higher in Galway and Waterford cities (at 23 per 1,000 population) compared with County Mayo (6 per 1,000 population).

Table 11.4: Households Assessed as Qualified for Social Housing per 1,000 Population in Selected Local Authority Operational Areas, 2002

Local Authority Operational Area	Households Approved for Social Housing	Households Approved for Social Housing per 1,000 population
Dublin City Council	6,993	14.1
Dún Laoghaire-Rathdown	2,118	11.0
Fingal	1,769	9.0
South Dublin	3,817	16.0
Dublin area total	14,697	13.1
Cork City Council	2,282	18.5
Galway City Council	1,320	23.1
Limerick City Council	581	10.8
Waterford City Council	1,034	23.2
Kildare	1,421	8.7
Donegal County Council	1,565	11.4
Mayo	749	6.4

Source: Department of the Environment, Heritage and Local Government, various years; Central Statistics Office, 2004b

Over the last ten years, the spatial distribution of new social house building broadly matched local demand (Norris and Winston, 2004). However, there are significant differences between local authorities in the proportion of those on the housing list who are offered a tenancy. In 2002, only 7 per cent of those on the housing list in Dún Laoghaire-Rathdown, and 13 per cent in the Dublin area as a whole, were offered a tenancy, in contrast to almost a third of those on the Limerick city council list.

Table 11.5: Households Allocated a Social Rented Dwelling as a % of Households Assessed as Qualified for Social Housing in Selected Local Authority Operational Areas, 2002

Local Authority Operational Area	Households Allocated a Social Rented Dwelling as a % of Households Assessed as Qualified for Social Housing
Dublin City Council	18.1
Dún Laoghaire-Rathdown	7.1
Fingal	11.8
South Dublin	10.2
Dublin area	13.7
Cork City Council	13.7
Galway City Council	11.7
Limerick City Council	31.8
Waterford City Council	23.4
Kildare County Council	14.8
Donegal County Council	28.0
Mayo County Council	14.6

Source: Department of the Environment, Heritage and Local Government, various years.

An important feature of the approach of government to tackling the affordability problem has been to increase the output of new private housing. However, while the construction of new dwellings has expanded, this output of private houses was not evenly distributed across the country (Norris and Winston, 2004). For example, Dublin city and county accounted for 29 per cent of the country's population in 2002, but only 22 per cent of new house building, resulting in a significant overspill of Dublin's population into adjacent counties. Moreover, a significant proportion of new housing has been diverted into holiday homes (FitzGerald *et al*, 2003) rather than to meet primary housing needs. Between 1997 and 2002, second or replacement dwellings accounted for over a third of the total new output and these are predominantly located in the Border, Midland and Western region (FitzGerald *et al*, 2003).

There are also significant regional variations in the level of homelessness, reflecting the drift of homeless people to urban centres where services are located. Table 11.6 shows that the largest homeless population (2,560 households) is in the Dublin area. While Dublin constitutes 29 per cent of the population of the State, 39 per cent of the total homeless population is in Dublin. The next highest homeless populations are in Cork, Galway, Limerick and Waterford cities.

Table 11.6: Homeless Households in Selected Local Authority Operational Areas, 2002

Local Authority Operational Area	% of the National Population	Number of Homeless Households	% of Total Homeless Households
Dublin City and County	29	1,466	39
Cork City Council	3	320	13
Galway City Council	2	144	6
Limerick City Council	1	5	0
Waterford City Council	1	33	1
State	100	3,773	100

Source: Department of the Environment, Heritage and Local Government, various years; Central Statistics Office, 2004b.

Perpetuating Inequality in Irish Housing – the Role of Public Policy

Public policy confers significant benefits on some of the most advantaged people in Irish society, specifically those able to afford to purchase land and property. In this way, policy both created and perpetuates inequalities in Irish society. Rising land and house prices have resulted in substantial gains for this group in terms of the unearned increase in the value of their property. As a consequence of this policy environment, property tends to be viewed as an investment or a commodity rather than as a home, a social good or a crucial aspect of human and community development.

It was noted earlier in this chapter that the relatively high level of home ownership in Ireland is largely a consequence of past and present public policies. As the National Economic and Social Council argues, the dominance of owner occupation is 'the result of the constraint of consumer options through the favouring of home ownership in public policy decisions. ... This steering of households towards owner occupation in turn creates a consumer "preference" which in turn leads to policy to encourage it' (National Economic and Social Council, 2004: 500-501). Current government policy explicitly favours home ownership and the range of instruments to encourage owner occupation in Ireland is extensive. It includes the following:

- Mortgage interest tax relief
- Stamp duty remission for those purchasing new houses less than 125 sq. metres, first-time buyers of low cost second-hand houses (of less than €317,500), and other owner occupiers purchasing property valued under €127,000

- No rates or similar tax on house property, unlike many countries
- Tax exemption of the (implicit) investment return on money invested in owner-occupied housing, unlike returns on alternative investments which are taxed
- Until November 2002, a first-time buyer's grant for purchasers of new homes
- No capital gains tax on the sale of a principal residence
- Capital gains tax on the sale of second homes reduced to 20 per cent in Budget 1997
- Rent a room relief exempts from income tax income derived from renting out a room in a principal private residence, up to a limit of €7,620
- Schemes to facilitate home ownership among lower-income groups, e.g. the shared ownership, affordable housing and local authority tenant purchase schemes
- 'Section 23' tax relief for landlords, and similar tax relief for those buying property to live in or rent out under urban, town and rural renewal tax breaks. Private tenants have also benefited from these schemes as the schemes have increased the total stock of rental accommodation. However, it is difficult to assess their overall impact, as they have not been evaluated since 1995 (KPMG *et al*, 1996
- The Seaside Resorts Tax Scheme which led to the construction of 5,000 holiday homes and apartments between 1995 and 1999, mostly private holiday homes for Irish people. The estimated cost to the exchequer of this scheme during the period was between €320 million and €380 million.

A number of the schemes noted above provide an interesting illustration of policies which create and perpetuate inequalities. For example, tax relief on property purchased under schemes like 'Section 23', the Seaside Resorts Scheme or Rural Renewal is regressive (Drudy and Punch, 2002). Such tax breaks served to substantially reduce the tax liability of the 400 highest earners in the country. An analysis by the Revenue Commissioners (2002) showed that 30 of those in the top 400 earners paid no tax whatever and 64 of the top 400 paid under 10 per cent of their income in tax, largely due to benefiting from tax exemptions. People on incomes too low to be liable for tax, cannot benefit directly from such tax reliefs. Furthermore, MacLaren and Murphy (1997: 35-36) argue that the incentives have been beneficial for the 'fiscally aware public', especially young purchasers of professional or managerial status. They contend that the new residential developments have 'the potential of becoming enclaves of young professional persons in an urban landscape of considerable deprivation' (MacLaren and Murphy, 1997: 35). Moreover, the appreciation of land values caused by the schemes has had a number of deleterious effects for the existing communities. These include the displacement of existing community-relevant employment as well as deterring the creation of new employment opportunities (MacLaren and Murphy, 1997). Tax subsidies for building in specific areas also serve to bid up the price of housing, putting it beyond the reach of low-income locals – 'one of the more damaging inequalities in a booming housing market' (Drudy and Punch, 2002: 669). FitzGerald *et al* (2003) calculate that the increase in vacant dwellings between 2000 and 2003 added between 15 and 20 per cent to house prices over this period. They argue that many of these vacant dwellings were constructed under the various tax relief schemes examined above.

The tax system is generous in its treatment of owner-occupied housing, particularly in comparison with the tax treatment of alternative forms of investment. Capital gains on one's own home are exempt from tax whereas other investments come under the capital gains tax regime. No action was taken on the recommendation from the Commission on Taxation (1983) that imputed income from home ownership be taxed. The following simplified example, which assumes a 10 per cent return on housing and alternative investments, illustrates the favourable tax treatment of this imputed return.

Renter

- A invests €100,000 in a commercial venture
- A rents a home at €10,000 a year
- A earns €10,000 on her investment
- A pays €4,200 tax on her investment earnings

Home owner

- B invests €100,000 in buying a home outright
- B lives rent free
- B's return is to live free of rent
- B pays no tax on the 'imputed rent' from home ownership

Bacon (1998) has quantified the advantage of investing in home ownership over other forms of investment, as outlined in Table 11.7 below.

Table 11.7: Degree of Fiscal Privilege associated with Various Investments (Difference between owner's marginal tax rate and effective tax rate on asset's pre-tax rate of return), 1979-1986 and 1986-1987

Investment	1979-1986	1986-1987
Bank deposits	-145.2	-39.6
Building society deposits	-93.5	-39.6
Hares	-27.7	-21.2
Pension funds	38.7	39.5
Life assurance	-20.5	-10.9
Home ownership	179.2	94.7
Inflation	11.4%	3.4%

Source: Bacon (1998).

If housing has proved a profitable investment for home owners, rising house prices have proved more profitable still for owners of development land. As house prices have risen far more sharply than the cost of building, the margin between building cost and price, representing site values and builders' profits, has risen at a much faster rate still. Assuming that site costs were 20 per cent of the overall house price in 1991, Table 11.8 illustrates how the share of total cost accounted for by the site would has evolved over the decade. From this starting point, while house prices have trebled over the decade, site values would have risen eightfold.

Table 11.8: House Prices, Building Cost and Estimated Increase in Site Values 1991-2002

Year	Price €	Price Index	Building cost Index	Building cost €	Site cost €	Site cost Ratio
1991	67,077	100	100	53,921	13,157	0.20
1992	69,090	103	104	56,078	13,012	0.19
1993	69,761	104	107	57,695	12,065	0.17
1994	73,114	109	111	59,852	13,262	0.18
1995	77,810	116	114	61,470	16,340	0.21
1996	87,201	130	116	62,548	24,652	0.28
1997	102,628	153	120	64,705	37,923	0.37
1998	125,435	187	124	66,862	58,573	0.47
1999	148,912	222	131	70,636	78,276	0.53
2000	169,706	253	140	75,489	94,217	0.56
2001	183,121	273	161	86,813	96,309	0.53
2002	199,220	297	173	93,283	105,937	0.53

Source: Department of the Environment, Heritage and Local Government (various years)
Note: The Central Bank Quarterly Bulletin, October 2003, states that 20 per cent is a typical site value overseas. This has been used as the estimated starting site value in 1993 in calculating the table.

One aspect of this problem is the practice by a number of developers of hoarding serviced land and releasing it slowly, controlling prices and making significant profits. To accelerate the release of development land for building, the first Bacon report (1998) recommended a temporary reduction from 40 per cent to 20 per cent in capital gains tax on development land for a four-year period, with a subsequent increase in the rate to 60 per cent. The reduction was implemented but the government has retained the lower rate (20 per cent) on a permanent basis. Rising land values represents a transfer of resources from house purchasers to the owners of development land and it is an unearned capital gain. The rate of taxation on this unearned capital gain is less than half the top rate of tax on earned income. Sweeney (2003) estimated the scale of the transfer of resources to owners of development land in Meath and Kildare alone at about €7 billion. That transfer, he notes, is greater than the annual expenditure on health and dwarfs the €2.5 billion in Structural Funds from the EU from 2000-2006.

The Kenny report (1973) on building land recommended that local authorities should be enabled to acquire building land at existing use value plus 25 per cent. The proposal was never implemented amid concerns that it was unconstitutional, given the protection afforded in the Constitution to property rights. However, as Drudy and Punch (2002: 668) point out, the rights of property owners must be regulated by 'principles of social justice' and the 'common good' also set out in the Constitution. Moreover, in the context of housing shortages and unmet housing need, there is a particularly strong argument that landowners should not accrue significant unearned gains purely as a result of land re-zoning or planning permission. Such planning permission always carries the responsibility to provide services; yet landowners may make little or no contribution to these.

Public Subsidies to Private Tenants

By contrast with the range of incentives for owner occupation, the only forms of support for private tenants are tax relief on rental costs and Rent Supplement. Following the 1995 budget, all tenants are potentially eligible for tax relief, where previously it had been available only to those over the age of 55. However, the relief is minimal when rent levels are considered and it is unrelated to income. It was estimated that the average income tax rent relief in the tax year 2000/2001 was €5 per week (Commission on the Private Rented Residential Sector, 2000). In addition, tenants on very low incomes who are out of the tax bracket cannot benefit from the relief. This includes most of the people on Rent Supplement, students who are not in employment, as well as those who cannot claim the relief because of difficulties in gaining the Personal Public Service Number of their landlord, i.e. those who reside in accommodation owed by landlords who are not registered.

Unlike mortgage interest tax relief which is universally granted to all mortgagees, stringent rules govern qualification for rent supplement. If the rent being charged exceeds the set limit under the Supplementary Welfare Allowance scheme, the tenant is regarded as 'over-accommodated' and forfeits the supplement in full. In contrast, a purchaser who trades in one luxury home to move upmarket is entitled to claim mortgage interest relief on the new home without any question as to accommodation need.

Conclusion

This chapter has highlighted the fact that sustained policy bias towards owner occupation over other forms of tenure has created significant inequalities in the Irish housing system. It outlined a number of these inequalities, including variations across the tenures in terms of: the cost of accommodation; access to housing; the quality of physical dwellings and the environment; and the security with which people occupy their home. In addition, inequalities between generations, classes and regions of the country were noted.

An intrinsic part of this policy bias has been the provision of substantial incentives for people to purchase homes, and, in the absence of similar incentives in the other tenures, owner occupation has become the preferred tenure. One of the consequences of the policy bias has been the creation of a highly subsidised home owning majority. House price inflation over the past decade has exacerbated these inequalities by means of a silent redistribution of wealth in favour of the subsidised home owning majority and owners of development land – assets which are subject to substantially lesser rates of taxation than earned income. Moreover, a number of tax relief schemes operating during this period have enabled a considerable proportion of this group to purchase second or holiday homes.

The structural inequalities in the Irish housing system tilt influence and political power towards those who own land and property rather than those trying to purchase a home or tenants. Home owners form a much more stable and identifiable voting bloc than transient renters. In 2002, there were fewer full-time farmers (42,000) than households on local authority waiting lists (49,000) but, as is demonstrated by the former group's status as a 'social partner', farmers enjoy incomparably more power and influence. The power of land and property owners lies in the combination of their wealth and number. It helps to explain why Government policy tends to favour a sustained growth in house prices. With the vast majority of households owning their own home, those with a strong vested interest in house price growth far outnumber those who would benefit from lower prices. A rise in house prices means an unearned increase in asset values for home-owners with the pain felt only by the minority who are trying to get started on the housing ladder. Ironically, perhaps, it is those who have most recently surmounted the barriers to entering the housing market, who tend to have the strongest financial interest in sustaining house price inflation. For them, a fall in price may deliver negative equity, whereas a rise in price may multiply their financial stake.

Another aspect of the power of home owners is their influence on housing policy issues. For example, proposals for Traveller accommodation in a neighbourhood often encounter substantial opposition from residents, resulting in delays and, at times, the abandonment of such plans (McKeown and McGrath, 1996). A further example of the power of the housing 'haves' is the opposition by both developer interests and residents to Part V of the Planning and Development Act, 2000 which provides for the reservation of up to 20 per cent of sites or dwellings on new developments for social and affordable housing. As a result of this opposition amendments were introduced in 2002 which provided developers with alternative options to meet these obligations including the provision of dwellings or sites in an alternative location or of cash compensation to the relevant local authority. One explanation for this opposition was the belief that such developments would lower the value of residential property in these areas by the interweaving of low-income families with higher income households, in contrast to the traditional policy of segregation.

12

Homelessness

Eoin O'Sullivan

Introduction

This chapter explores the nature and extent of homelessness in the Republic of Ireland between 1988 and 2003. It starts in 1988, largely because this was the year in which inclusionary strategies to deal with homelessness were first legislated for *via* the Housing Act, 1988, and concludes in 2003 with the publication of the fifth national assessment of the extent of homelessness. Thus, this 'long' decade provides a coherent timeframe in which to review both the nature and extent of homelessness, in addition to the various policy responses that emanated from both the voluntary and statutory sectors. During the period under consideration, homelessness, as officially recorded by local authorities, more than doubled and the number of households assessed as in need of housing by local authorities more than tripled. Thus, a crucial concern of this chapter is to attempt to understand the possible underlying explanations for this apparent increase. In addition, the chapter will examine the first co-ordinated statutory policy response to homelessness, *Homelessness – an Integrated Strategy* (Department of the Environment and Local Government, 2000d) and the follow-on document, the *Homeless Preventative Strategy* (Department of Environment and Local Government *et al*, 2002). (In addition, although not discussed in this chapter, a *Youth Homelessness Strategy* was launched by the Department of Health and Children in 2001).

Homelessness in Ireland prior to the Housing Act, 1988

This section summarises and analyses studies of homelessness in Ireland in the 1970s and 1980s and provides a brief overview of how perceptions of homelessness have changed over time. Much of the literature on homelessness before 1988 was concerned with enumerating homelessness and documenting the inadequacy of existing service provision. Ó Cinnéide and Mooney (1972), for example, aimed to enumerate homeless persons in Dublin on one night in

245

1971. It was the first research of its kind in Ireland since the 1920s (Report of the Commission on the Relief of the Sick and Destitute Poor, Including the Insane Poor, 1928) and aimed to especially count those sleeping rough. There were at the time 14 hostels providing 1,310 bed places in Dublin. On the census night, the researchers encountered 47 persons. However, in the previous two months, fieldworkers had encountered a further 43 persons sleeping rough who were not encountered on the night of the census. In addition to the survey of persons sleeping rough, information was sought on those staying in the hostels. Not all hostels co-operated with the survey, and only limited information was provided by others. In total, between those staying in the co-operating hostels and those sleeping rough, basic information was available for 196 individuals. The majority were male and over 30 years of age. The survey suggested that 61 of the respondents were addicted to drugs or alcohol; 21 were mentally ill and 24 were physically ill or handicapped.

Ian Hart's (1978) research into the Dublin Simon Community and the users of their services remains one of the more detailed studies of homelessness and the agencies working with the homeless in Ireland. The Simon Community was founded in England in 1963 by a probation officer, Anton Wallich-Clifford, and while having strong Christian orientation in England, was always a non-denominational organisation in Ireland (see Wallich-Clifford, 1974, 1976). The research described the origins of the Dublin Community, its difficulties in getting established, public attitudes to Simon and a number of tensions that existed in Simon at that time such as the relationship between full-time workers and other volunteers. The Dublin Simon community was also the locus of a study by O'Brien (1979) of the role of criminal justice agencies in regulating homelessness. O'Brien argued (1979: 7) that

> the principal institutions in the social system on which the homeless depend – and which constrain them – are the hostels, managed by the various voluntary and statutory groups, the general and psychiatric hospitals, and the prisons. Invariably, they are arrested because some of the most common and inevitable aspects of their existence conflicts with our criminal law.

The significance and importance of O'Brien's report is that, for the first time in research into homelessness in Ireland, an attempt is made to understand how 'homelessness' is not simply the result of personal pathology, but that State agencies can deliberately or inadvertently confirm and amplify the condition of homelessness. The role of the State in constructing homelessness was also the subject of Doherty's (1982) research on county homes (formerly workhouses) which were, for most of the twentieth century, the primary form of accommodation offered to homeless people. The 'casuals', as homeless persons were known, were generally accommodated in what were termed casual wards attached to the county homes. His research showed that the majority of county homes still made provision for the casuals but that the trend was towards the reduction of facilities for them. In one of the few 'outsider' accounts of homelessness in Ireland, Kearns (1984), an American geographer, argued that Dublin's homeless habitat, unlike American 'Skid Rows', did not consist of a concentrated core or urban strip, rather it assumed the form of a dispersed network.

Initial research into homelessness in Ireland focused primarily on homeless men, mostly as a consequence of the research methodologies utilised (for further details see O'Sullivan and Higgins, 2001). This focus was to shift with the publication of Kennedy's (1985) research into homeless women in Ireland. Kennedy argued that the primary reasons for women becoming homeless were severe family disruption, often involving violence and incest. She argued that 'Once homeless, the women tend to be trapped in a cycle of homelessness, which is very difficult for them to break. There are many factors militating against their breaking this cycle, the main one being their poverty: they have access to neither adequate income, housing, emergency accommodation, information, advice nor creative activity centres' (Kennedy, 1985: 174-5). Although the relative invisibility of homeless women in both research and policy has been partially addressed, analyses of homelessness remain predominantly focused on urban areas and little knowledge is available on the dynamics of homelessness in rural areas (O'Sullivan, 2006).

In 1984, *The Psychiatric Service – Planning for the Future* (Government of Ireland, 1984) was published and recommended the provision of community-based residential care and a move away from the routine institutionalisation of those suffering from psychiatric illness (Walsh, 1997). One of the only studies evaluating the degree to which such patients could be discharged from psychiatric hospitals was conducted by Crehan *et al* (1987). Based on a case study of one large psychiatric hospital in the West of Ireland, this research argued that, of the 704 patients resident in the hospital for over a year in November 1985, only 4 per cent had a home offering adequate care and support if discharged; 48 per cent were absolutely homeless and 36 per cent would not be accepted back into their former homes. The report concluded that the likelihood for homelessness increased with the amount of time spent in hospital.

The lack of co-ordination amongst service providers, both voluntary and statutory, was highlighted by Farrell (1988) in a case study of services for homeless persons in Galway. His research showed that despite the existence of 26 different agencies (17 voluntary and 9 statutory) working with sub-groups of the homeless population, gaps still existed in service provision. Despite popular perceptions that the homeless were 'dossers', McCarthy (1988) showed that the majority of those homeless men living in Simon Community facilities had worked for considerable periods of their lives; they had worked primarily as manual labourers and, for many, their work skills were obsolete. Emigration had featured strongly in their lives and the research argued that 'there seems to be a correlation between the process of emigration by unskilled people from backgrounds of poverty and the incidence of homelessness among returned emigrants' (1988: 178). What is of significance in this study is that in attempting to understand homelessness, the research argued that greater attention needed to be given to the changing nature of the labour market rather than simply on the individual traits of the homeless.

Thus, by 1988, the date when substantive legislative provision was made specifically for homeless persons, a number of themes had emerged from the relatively limited research conducted on homelessness in Ireland. Although difficult to quantify, most agencies working with the homeless identified an increase in homelessness from the early 1970s. Furthermore, homelessness was not the preserve of middle-aged men. Rather homelessness embraced men, women and children. Although a range of voluntary agencies provided an array of services, there was a lack of co-ordination between voluntary and statutory agencies. More significantly, statutory responsibility for the provision of services for the homeless was allocated to two different state agencies (Health Boards and Local Authorities), neither of whom expressed any great interest in developing and expanding services for the homeless. As Harvey (1995: 76) has argued, '[u]ntil the 1980s, homeless people were at best a marginal concern to the Irish administrative and political system. Homeless people were seen as drop-outs, vagrants, tramps, anti-social people, for the most part unwanted elderly men'.

Traditional forms of accommodation for the homeless, such as casual wards, were in terminal decline and many of the existing hostels for the homeless were highly regimented, providing austere facilities which were permeated by strong moral overtones, reflecting the religiously inspired origins of many of the providers (O'Sullivan, 1998a). The role of the criminal justice system in arresting, prosecuting and imprisoning the homeless was highlighted, as was the potential for those discharged from psychiatric hospitals to become homeless unless adequate discharge plans and support structures were put in place.

The Housing Act, 1988

Although a right to housing does not exist in the Republic of Ireland, the Housing Act, 1988 specified the local authority as the statutory agency with responsibility for the homeless, partly ending earlier confusion over which statutory body had responsibility for providing for the needs of the homeless. However, the Act can be described as permissive legislation in that it permits local housing authorities to assist the homeless, but does not place an obligation on them to house homeless people. The Act also provides a (broad) definition of homelessness, empowers housing authorities to provide assistance to voluntary organisations who are approved by the Department of the Environment for the provision or management of housing accommodation; obliges local authorities to conduct periodic assessments of housing need and homelessness; provides for the type of assistance that homeless people may be provided with from a local authority; and requires housing authorities to develop a scheme of letting priority.

Importantly, the Act formally de-criminalised homelessness by repealing the offence of 'wandering abroad ... not having any visible means of subsistence, and not giving a good account of himself or herself' contained under the vagrancy acts. However, offences such as begging and public drunkenness, offences to which the homeless are more vulnerable due to the nature of their enforced lifestyle, remained on the statute books (O'Donnell, 1998).

Prior to the passing of the Housing Act, 1988, statutory responsibility for the homeless was vested in the Health Act, 1953, which under Section 54 obliged health authorities to provide institutional assistance to those who were unable to provide shelter for themselves (Shannon, 1988). In addition, the Housing Act, 1966 obliged local authorities to introduce a scheme of priorities for the allocation of dwellings. However, its main emphasis was on the provision of accommodation for the elderly and families and the single homeless person remained very much marginalised under such a system (Harvey, 1985). The limits of the statutory obligations towards the homeless were manifest in the ambiguity that existed between the local authorities and the health authorities over where responsibility rested for providing for the homeless. The result was that homeless people were being moved from one authority to the other in the absence of clear-cut legislation defining the role of statutory authorities *vis-à-vis* homeless people.

Impact of the Act on Housing Homeless Households

Within a short number of years of the implementation of the Act, a number of reviews were conducted to ascertain the extent to which homeless persons were being accommodated by the local authorities. Kelleher (1990) provided an initial overview of the services available to homeless people in Dublin in the period after the implementation of the Act. The report rather bleakly argued that minimal changes had taken place which had a direct benefit to the homeless. In particular, the report recommended that greater co-ordination between the State agencies should be developed and that a housing forum comprising members of voluntary and statutory bodies be inaugurated. Two years later, Murphy-Lawless and Dillon (1992) in a national survey of housing authorities, showed that, at the time of the research, only five authorities had staff specifically trained to deal with the needs of homeless clients. None of the larger authorities had appointed specific staff to deal with homelessness and six authorities did not recognise those sleeping rough as homeless as defined by the 1988 Act. Furthermore, young people discharged from care were not accepted as homeless by eight local authorities. The report argued that only 157 people were accommodated directly as a consequence of the passing of the Act. For the majority of those local authorities who responded to the researchers, providing basic shelter was the main response to homelessness, with other forms of support being minimal or non-existent. The report located homelessness as primarily a structural problem, claiming that it could only be addressed by political choices that would ensure a more equitable and balanced society. The researchers concluded that the Act did have some positive impact on local authorities but that it was ultimately disappointing, particularly in light of the expectations of voluntary bodies. This was a consequence, they argued, not alone of the permissive nature of the Act, but of the wider structural changes taking place in Ireland. In a similar vein, Leonard (1992a) argued that despite the promise of consultation in the Act, the experience of the Simon communities showed that, in practice, little formal consultation on local issues was apparent and that local authorities, without any significant input from voluntary agencies, were still directing policy towards the homeless.

The pessimistic tone of these initial reviews of the impact of the Housing Act, 1988 on homelessness was not altogether surprising in light of the dramatic changes in local authority housing in the late 1980s and early 1990s. As examined by Norris in Chapter 8 of this volume, local authority housing output fell by two thirds in the late 1980s, compared with construction levels during the preceding decade. Additionally, the level of sales to tenants rose dramatically as a result of further increases in the subsidies to purchasers introduced in 1988. Consequently, the stock of local authority housing declined by 15 per cent – from 116,270 units to 98,395 – between 1988 and 1996. These developments, coupled with the impact of the surrender grant scheme, which enabled 9,000 mainly employed households to move out of local authority housing, contributed to the residualising and stigmatising of the remaining local authority housing estates, particularly in urban areas (Nolan et al, 1998).

Local authorities were thus faced with a declining stock of housing units, a massively reduced social housing budget, largely welfare-dependent tenants, increasingly difficult estates to manage and virtually no form of estate management (except selling the stock) as well as a growing number of households in need of such housing, increasing from 17,685 in 1988 to 28,624 in 1993. Without widespread net emigration that existed at that time (National Economic and Social Council, 1991), it is likely that the waiting lists would have been even higher. Given the scheme of letting priorities, which prioritised families and the elderly, single homeless persons were unlikely to be offered local authority accommodation. Thus, despite the aspirations of the 1988 Act, the structural constraints faced by local authorities in the period immediately after its enactment made prioritising the single homeless unlikely. If offered accommodation, it generally tended to be in difficult-to-let flat complexes, many of which had been ravaged by the opiate epidemic that had emerged, particularly in Dublin, from the early 1980s (Dean *et al*, 1985).

The Extent of Homelessness in the early 1990s

Although a number of estimates of the extent of homelessness had been produced during the 1970s and 1980s, they were either localised (Bell, 1989; Dillon *et al*, 1990; Farrell, 1988) or 'guesstimates' (Daly, 1990; Harvey and Higgins, 1988; National Economic and Social Council, 1988). The figure of 5,000 homeless persons was the one most commonly cited by voluntary and campaigning agencies by the late 1980s and early 1990s.

In 1991, as a consequence of the Housing Act, 1988, the first statutory national count of homelessness since 1925 took place. It comprised a snapshot of those who were deemed homeless by statutory bodies on the night of 31 March 1991 (as part of the more general assessment of housing need in 1989, 987 homeless persons were recorded by the local authorities, but were only those homeless registered for local authority housing). The 1991 separate assessment of homelessness included those on the waiting list and those who were not. The results of this survey suggested that there were 2,751 homeless persons in Ireland. This exercise was repeated in 1993 and saw a slight decrease in the number of homeless persons to 2,667. These figures were considerably lower than the estimates put forward by the voluntary sector, which was not slow in criticising the methodology and administration of the assessment (Harvey, 1990; Leonard, 1992b, 1994).

In light of these criticisms, and the housing assessment methodology more generally, the Department of the Environment commissioned the Economic and Social Research Institute to explore the meaning and adequacy of these assessments. They concluded that 'some undercount has taken place' (Fahey and Watson, 1995: 104) but that they were not in a position to quantify the degree of undercount. They also highlighted the inconsistency in recording homeless persons by different local authorities. The report highlighted two aspects of the local authority approach to housing that militated against responding effectively to homelessness: the tendency to provide long-term accommodation primarily to families, which resulted in a limited number of short-term accommodation options, and the lack of expertise by the local authorities in dealing with households with psychiatric or addiction problems.

The authors recommended greater co-ordination between the health boards and voluntary agencies in meeting the needs of the homeless, in particular in enhancing the possibility of moving them to permanent housing and that the policy regarding the eligibility of one-person households for local authority housing be clarified.

Collins and McKeown (1992) had raised this issue earlier in their study of Simon Community residents. Their report argued that homeless people could settle and maintain a good quality of life in their own accommodation if the proper support structures were put in place for them at the appropriate junctures. While they noted that the guidelines to the Housing Act, 1988 stipulated that homeless persons should not be at a disadvantage compared to other groups in need of housing, in practice the housing needs of single homeless persons were not being met (Collins and McKeown, 1992: 114).

The limitations of the local authority assessment methodology was also highlighted in a study of the men, women, and children who used twelve emergency hostels in Dublin (Kelleher et al, 1992). The data collected during the research showed that, in a three-week period in March and a second three-week period in June/July 1991, the numbers using hostels varied from 545 on 2 July to 595 on 4 March. The vast majority of hostel users were male. Over the six-week Census period, it was estimated that 1,573 people used the hostels. Based on these figures, the number leaving the hostel system, and the length of time in which people stay in hostels, it was estimated that, over a period of a year, there were between 6,500 and 7,500 separate individuals using hostels. Thus, the numbers encountered in this study of hostels in the Dublin region only suggested a higher prevalence of homelessness than did the official assessments, albeit some of the variance is explained by the differing methodologies used.

With total social housing output low and sluggish, the numbers officially recorded as in need of social housing grew from 23,242 in 1991 to 28,624 in 1993 and to 36,172 in 1996. Somewhat surprisingly, the number of homeless households fell from 2,667 in 1993 to 2,501 in 1996 over the same period. Although *Social Housing – the Way Ahead* (Department of the Environment, 1995b) was published in 1995, extending the number of housing options available to local authorities, and expenditure on social and affordable housing grew, demand for social housing considerably outstripped supply.

The recorded decrease in the numbers of recorded homeless persons was surprising in view of the process of de-institutionalisation from psychiatric hospitals, particularly amongst long-stay patients, with a reduction in the number of patients from over 9,000 in 1988 to just over 5,000 in 1996. Indeed, earlier concerns (Crehan et al, 1987) that such discharges might lead to homelessness became a reality, according to the Simon Community (1992).

They claimed that many ex-patients, and those with a mental illness, had become homeless and were living in emergency hostels for the homeless. However, in a case study of de-institutionalisation from one psychiatric hospital, Finnerty *et al* (1995) argued that of the 163 patients discharged between 1987 and 1994, none was homeless when followed up late in 1994. However, their research did not ascertain whether any of the patients had experienced homelessness at any stage between 1987 and 1994. Keogh *et al* (1999) in a later study found a similar lack of association between de-institutionalisation and subsequent homelessness in a case study in Dublin. However, other studies of the homeless population suggested a higher prevalence of psychiatric problems amongst the homeless than in the general population (Cleary and Prizeman, 1998; McKeown, 1999; Mac Neela, 1999).

Due to the limited supply of social housing and a decrease in the number of beds in emergency hostels relative to demand, coupled with a lack of appropriate hostel facilities for couples with children and single parent households, increased use was made of bed-and-breakfast accommodation in Dublin, particularly for those households with children. In the late 1980s, bed-and-breakfast type accommodation for homeless households was virtually unknown. In 1990, only five homeless households were placed in such accommodation, but by 1999, 1,202 households were so placed (Moore, 1994; Houghton and Hickey, 2000). As the number of households placed in bed-and-breakfast accommodation increased, so did the costs, which rose steeply from €660 in 1990 to €5,967,769 in 1999. The increase in the cost of utilising such accommodation was not only a consequence of the increase in the number of households so placed, but also reflected the increase in the average length of stay, from less than a fortnight in the early 1990s to nearly three months in 1999. The 1,202 households placed in bed-and-breakfast accommodation in 1999 comprised 1,518 adults and 1,262 children, and 71 per cent of the adults were female. A series of studies have examined the consequences of providing such forms of accommodation (Halpenny *et al*, 2002; Smith *et al*, 2001; Halpenny *et al*, 2001) and all conclude that such forms of accommodation are detrimental to the health and well-being of both adults and children.

By 1996, it was becoming increasingly apparent that the legacy of dis-investment in social housing in the late 1980s and early 1990s, coupled with the various sales policies, and both exacerbated by demographic trends – was leading to a housing crisis in Ireland. The numbers on the housing waiting list had more than doubled between 1988 and 1996 but, somewhat surprisingly, as recorded by the local authorities, homelessness had not increased.

The 'Celtic Tiger' and Homelessness

Both the national assessment of the extent of homelessness, and the separate, but parallel, survey in the greater Dublin region, showed increases in the extent of homelessness between 1999 and 2002, albeit that these increases were modest compared to the increases enumerated between 1996 and 1999. Nationally, 5,581 homeless persons were enumerated in March 2002, an increase of 7 per cent on the 1999 figure, but an increase of 123 per cent on the 1996 figure. 87 per cent of those enumerated were located in the five main urban areas (see Table 12.1), with 35 out of a total of 90 authorities recording no homeless persons in their functional areas. Indeed, 12 authorities have never recorded a homeless person in the five assessments that have taken place to date. With the exception of the data for the Dublin region, which is collected by the Homeless Agency/ Economic and Social Research Institute, it is difficult to give too much credence to the data produced by some authorities, particularly in light of the fluctuations in their data from assessment to assessment. For example, in Laois County Council, no homeless persons were recorded in the 1996 assessment, 36 persons were recorded in the 1999 assessment and 3 persons in 2002; Longford County Council recorded 103 homeless persons in 1999, but none in 2002; Offaly County Council recorded 70 homeless persons in 1991, but none in any of the subsequent assessments.

The assessment of homelessness in Dublin in March 2002 showed virtually no increase in the number of *homeless individuals* between 1999 and 2002 (2,920 in 2002 compared to 2,900 in 1999) (Williams and Gorby, 2002; Williams and O'Connor, 1999). However, a decrease in the number of *homeless households* was observed (from 2,690 in 1999 to 2,560 in 2002). This is attributable to the decrease in the number of single person households recorded, from 2,050 in 1999 to 1,780 in 2002 (or 76 per cent of the total enumerated homeless population to 70 per cent). Of the single person households, 81 per cent were male, the average age was 39 and the average duration of their period of homelessness was 28 months. In a detailed analysis of national data on the length of homelessness in the United States of America, Allgood and Warren show that the 'length of a homeless spell increases with age and is longer for males, never married persons, and those who have been incarcerated in the past' (2003: 275). Roughly speaking, single homeless persons were more likely to sleep rough and to use hostels than couples or households with children, who were more likely to be accommodated in bed-and-breakfast type accommodation (See Passaro, 1996 for possible elements of an explanation for this pattern).

Table 12.1: Results of the Assessments of Homelessness, 1991-2002

	1991	1993	1996	1999	2002	% change 1996-2002	% change 1999-2002
County Councils (including borough and town councils)							
Carlow	24	27	13	7	2	-84.6	-71.4
Cavan	2	12	11	1	28	154.5	2700.0
Clare	59	0	1	1	3	200.0	200.0
Cork	47	13	10	26	49	390.0	88.5
Donegal	56	18	15	30	37	146.7	23.3
Dublin	187	31	86	278	n/a	n/a	
Galway	0	3	1	29	6	500.0	-79.3
Kerry	34	32	6	4	55	816.7	1275.0
Kildare	66	102	71	105	97	36.6	-7.6
Kilkenny	63	31	41	39	54	31.7	38.5
Laois	19	1	0	36	3	-	-91.7
Leitrim	2	0	0	4	0	-	-100.0
Limerick	17	47	21	39	14	-33.3	-64.1
Longford	48	32	75	108	5	-93.3	-95.4
Louth	68	72	94	33	55	-41.5	66.7
Mayo	0	2	24	10	25	4.2	150.0
Meath	1	12	11	25	77	600.0	208.0
Monaghan	4	3	0	3	14	-	366.7
Offaly	12	73	0	6	0	-	-100.0
Roscommon	0	0	10	0	0	-100.0	-
Sligo	17	1	19	73	51	168.4	-30.1
Tipperary	23	15	23	7	20	-13.0	185.7
Waterford	6	10	1	9	13	1200.0	44.4
Westmeath	51	0	4	0	31	675.0	-
Wexford	29	24	28	15	31	10.7	106.7
Wicklow	10	17	28	35	51	82.1	45.7
Sub-total	845	578	593	923	721	21.6	-21.9
Percentage of Total	30.7	21.7	23.7	17.6	12.9	-45.5	-26.7

	1991	1993	1996	1999	2002	% change 1996-2002	% change 1999-2002
City Councils							
Cork	303	257	308	335	439	42.5	31.0
Dublin	1,351	1,617	1,447	3,640	4,060	180.6	11.5
Galway	97	126	54	144	181	235.2	25.7
Limerick	80	78	37	123	96	159.5	-22.0
Waterford	75	11	62	69	84	35.5	21.7
Sub-total	1,906	2,089	1,908	4,311	4,860	154.7	12.7
Percentage of Total	69.3	78.3	76.3	82.4	87.1	14.1	5.7
Overall Total	2,751	2,667	2,501	5,234	5,581	123.2	6.6

The data collected in the Dublin assessment disaggregate the total homeless population enumerated into those households on a local authority list, effectively separating those who are accepted and registered as homeless by the local authority from those homeless households who access homeless services, but are not on the local authority list. Only 15 per cent of households were recorded in both categories, with the remaining households equally divided between those on the local authority list only and those who accessed services.

Despite the relative methodological sophistication of the Dublin assessment, a number of difficulties were reported. For example, the total number of homeless adult individuals recorded exceeded the total number of emergency beds available in Dublin and the numbers recorded as sleeping rough does not explain the difference. As the Director of the Homeless Agency – the agency with statutory responsibility for the management and coordination of services to people who are homeless in Dublin – has pointed out, this is largely attributable to the discrepancies in the administrative data maintained by the local authorities on the numbers of individuals recorded as homeless (Higgins, 2002:15). It would appear that a number of individuals and households recorded as homeless by the local authorities moved out of homelessness, but remained on the list and therefore counted as homeless at the time of the assessment. This suggests that the data on those using homeless and other services *only* may be a more accurate reflection of the extent of homelessness. On this basis, the number of homeless households increased by 180 from 1,290 in 1999 to 1,470 in 2002. The difficulties encountered with the administrative data held by local authorities by Homeless Agency/ Economic and Social Research Institute researchers reiterates the point above that the data provided by (other) local authorities on the extent of homelessness needs to be treated with extreme caution. That notwithstanding, it does not necessarily follow that the overall number of homeless persons enumerated by local authorities is exaggerated (although it may well be). Rather, by depending primarily on administrative data to assess the extent of homelessness, bureaucratic procedures and priorities, rather than an accurate enumeration of homelessness, may be reflected.

Recent Policy Responses to Homelessness

With the publication of *Homelessness – An Integrated Strategy* (Department of the Environment and Local Government, 2000d) in 2000, the semblance of a coherent policy approach to the needs of homeless households became apparent for the first time in the history of the Irish State. The terms of reference for the cross-departmental team preparing this strategy were to 'develop an integrated response to the many issues which affect homeless people including emergency, transitional and long-term responses as well as issues relating to health, education, employment and home-making' (Department of the Environment and Local Government, 2000d: 3). As Higgins (2001: 5) has argued, prior to the development of this strategy and related developments, homelessness was

> regarded as something apart – much like homeless people themselves – and responses have tended to be 'special' and 'separate', rather than mainstream, with little focus on developing an understanding of the problem or how to prevent it. Within this policy context local authorities have had difficulty in developing responses which will address the needs of homeless people effectively and the implementation of the 1988 Housing Act and subsequent policies have had only limited impact.

The broad principles enunciated by the strategy document were: a continuum of care from the time someone becomes homeless, with sheltered and supported accommodation, and where appropriate, assistance back into independent living in the community; emergency accommodation to be short-term; settlement in the community to be an overriding priority through independent or supported housing; long-term supported accommodation available for those who need it; support services provided on an outreach basis as needed and preventative strategies for at risk groups to be developed. To achieve these broad objectives, Homeless Forums were to be established in every county and three-year action plans prepared. Both the homeless forums and the action plans were to include input from the statutory and non-profit sectors.

In addition, under the Planning and Development Act, 2000, local authorities must prepare housing strategies. These strategies must ensure that: sufficient land is zoned to meet the housing requirements in the region; there is a mixture of house types and sizes to meet the needs of various households; housing is available for people on different income levels and provide for the need for both social and affordable housing.

In early 2002, a *Homeless Preventative Strategy* was published with the key objective of ensuring that 'no one is released or discharged from state care without the appropriate measures in place to ensure that they have a suitable place to live with the necessary supports, if needed' (Department of the Environment and Local Government *et al*, 2002: 3). Specific proposals included the establishment by the Probation and Welfare Service of a specialist unit to deal with offenders who are homeless; the provision of transitional housing units by the Prison Service as part of their overall strategy of preparing offenders for release; and ensuring that all psychiatric hospitals have a formal and written discharge policy. In addition, the vexed question of which statutory agency had responsibility for the homeless was apparently clarified, with the strategy stating that 'it recognises that both local authorities and health boards have key central roles in meeting the needs of homeless persons. Local authorities have responsibility for the provision of accommodation for homeless adults as part of their overall housing responsibility and health boards are responsible for the health and care needs of homeless adults' (Department of Environment and Local Government *et al*, 2002: 6).

As noted above, a key objective of *Homelessness – an Integrated Strategy*, was that local authorities would produce homeless action plans. Unlike the housing strategies required under the Planning and Development Act, 2000, local authorities were not under any statutory obligation to produce these plans. In a review of these plans (Hickey *et al*, 2002), data deficiencies in relation to the extent of homelessness in local authority functional areas emerged as a fundamental problem in devising the plans. Consequently, quite diverse methodologies were utilised to estimate the extent of homelessness in local authorities' functional areas. In addition, the authors noted that 'the content, both general and specific, in the analysed action plans varies significantly from county to county' and that in terms of strategically addressing homelessness, 'the outcomes of the Plans are in general disappointing' (Hickey *et al*, 2002: 107). A crucial finding of the analysis was that, outside of the major urban areas, there was 'little sense from the ... plans on the process for diminishing the incidence of homelessness in source areas outside of major urban areas' and that '(w)ithout appropriate strategies non-metropolitan local authorities will continue to "export" their homeless constituents to large cities' (Hickey *et al*, 2002: 91).

Explaining Homelessness in Ireland

Much of the research on homelessness over the past two decades or so has been polarised between structural (macro-level) and individual (micro-level) factors (Elliot and Krivo, 1991; Thorns, 1991; Jencks, 1994; Neale, 1997; O'Flaherty, 2002). However, a number of important meso-level studies have been conducted in recent years (Anderson and Tulloch, 2000). O'Flaherty (2002) in his review of city-level and individual level studies of homelessness argues that city-level studies find that the housing market primarily determines the volume of homelessness, with personal characteristics such as mental illness having little or no influence. In contrast, individual level studies suggest that housing variables such as rent levels or vacancy have little or no influence, but personal characteristics have a high significance. His interpretation of these apparently contradictory conclusions is that insufficient attention has been given to the interaction between market and individual variables, with homelessness determined by *both* – the number of at-risk individuals in what he terms 'housing-short' cities.

Homelessness – An Integrated Strategy suggested that while 'the dynamics of homelessness involve a complex interrelationship of social and economic factors' (Department of the Environment and Local Government, 2000d: 7), those leaving institutional care of various kinds were most vulnerable to homelessness. According to the *Homeless Preventative Strategy*, the earlier strategy recognised:

> that a solution to homelessness is not just about the provision of housing or shelter and that there is a need for a comprehensive approach involving health, care and welfare, education, training and support, as well as accommodation, to enable homeless persons to re-integrate into society and to prevent others from becoming homeless (Department of the Environment and Local Government *et al*, 2002: 5).

It then went on to state that '[t]here are many reasons why people become homeless, including behavioural or other problems or social phobias which inhibit them making proper use of existing services. Homeless persons may have mental health, alcohol, drug-related problems or multiple needs which are not met effectively either by homeless or mainstream services' (2002: 8). This document reiterated the belief that those most at risk of homelessness were those leaving institutional care. What is of note in these two official analyses is the relative absence of housing availability as an explanation for homelessness, although *Homelessness – An Integrated Strategy* does fleetingly acknowledge that 'the key difficulty in tackling homelessness is the scarcity of more appropriate accommodation' (Department of the Environment and Local Government, 2000d: 34).

Quigley and Raphael (2001) observe that this form of analysis appears to be justified by the traits of the homeless population. Research, both in Ireland and internationally, describes the homeless population as suffering disproportionately from mental illness, drug and alcohol addiction, extreme social isolation with high proportions of the homeless having been institutionalised at different periods of their lives (Costello, 2000; Costello and Howley, 1999; Collins and McKeown, 1992; Fernandez, 1995; Feeney *et al*, 2000; Hickey, 2002; Kelleher *et al*, 2000; McKeown and Hasse, 1997; Mac Neela, 1999; Holohan, 1997). Homeless women, in particular, in addition to the above characteristics, are often recorded as having histories of domestic violence and/or sexual abuse (Kennedy, 1985, Bell, 1989; Carlson, 1990). In addition, counts of the homeless population suggest that they constitute a small fraction of the population (between 0.1 to 0.2 per cent in the Irish case). Given this confluence of personal problems and the relatively low incidence of homelessness, it is tempting to explain homelessness in terms of personal pathologies and to dismiss explanations of homelessness that focus on structural factors such as housing market conditions.

The limited data on the extent of homelessness suggest a very substantial increase in the number of homeless households in the second half of the 1990s. Some of this increase may reflect changes in the administration and recording of homeless persons during the 1999 assessment of homelessness – this assessment stated that a broader definition of homelessness was used compared to earlier assessments, though it does not specify the nature of this broader definition – but the increasing visibility of street homelessness, particularly in urban areas, appeared to indicate a real increase in homelessness during this period. In a survey jointly carried out by Simon Community, Focus Ireland and Dublin Corporation (now Dublin City Council) in Dublin for the week of the 15-21 October 2000, the total number of rough sleepers recorded in Dublin's city centre was 202, representing a 60 per cent increase on the street count of December 1997 and a 36 per cent increase on the street count of June 1998 (Dublin Simon Community, 1998, 2000). Relatively high numbers of rough sleepers were also identified in Galway in 1998 (Mac Neela, 1999). In three border counties, it was estimated that the number of homeless households was ten times the official figure (Irwin, 1998), although little substantive evidence was offered to support this proposition. The extent of homelessness recorded in the various assessments between 1991 and 1996 may have been underestimates, thus exaggerating the magnitude of the increase suggested by the 1999 and 2002 figures. One the other hand, the latter figures, alongside other sources, does suggest a strong rate of increase in homelessness during the second half of the 1990s. How then can we explain these anomalous trends?

De-institutionalisation and Homelessness

Agencies working with the homeless have long claimed a link between the de-institutionalisation of long-stay patients from psychiatric units and homelessness and that a large proportion of the homeless suffer from psychiatric illnesses (Fernandez, 1995). Indeed, Crowley (2003: 7) has argued that 'homelessness and mental illness are firmly causally linked'. However, de-institutionalisation does not satisfactorily explain the apparent growth of homelessness in the late 1990s, since the bulk of the discharges took place in the late 1980s and early 1990s. More significantly – and taking a broader definition of institutionalisation – while we saw a decrease in the psychiatric hospital population, we saw an increase in the prison population (O'Sullivan and O'Donnell, 2003). Studies of the prison population suggest that a high number of prisoners suffer from various psychiatric illnesses (Carmody and McEvoy, 1996; O'Mahony, 1997). Thus, it seems plausible to suggest that some of those discharged from psychiatric hospitals or who would have ended up in such institutions in the past are being re-institutionalised in prison. There were 3,372 proceedings taken under the Vagrancy Acts and 181,581 proceedings taken under the Public Order Act, 1994 between 1996 and 2001 as Ireland adopted elements of a 'zero-tolerance' policing policy (O'Donnell and O'Sullivan, 2003). Homeless persons, particularly those with a psychiatric illness, are likely to be particularly at risk of conviction for such offences. Given that homelessness increased primarily in the late 1990s after the bulk of patients were de-institutionalised, that some were re-institutionalised in prisons, and that a portion of the de-institutionalised are likely to have stable support networks of family and friends, the trends do not indicate that de-institutionalisation was the driving force behind the observed increases in homelessness. However, it is equally plausible to argue that some people end up in homeless services that would otherwise have been in psychiatric services.

This is the view articulated by Harvey (1998: 7), where he observes that 'In Ireland, the evidence is less that discharged former long-stay patients have become homeless but that rather the reduction of long-stay beds closed off what in effect was a residual social accommodation role performed by long-term psychiatric institutions'. However, successive reports of the Inspector of Mental Hospitals (2002: 9) have highlighted the numbers of 'current psychiatric in-patients who are homeless and are accommodated in acute or long-stay hospital wards'. The reason for this, the inspector argued, was the absence of suitable community-based residential facilities. The evidence of the Inspector of Mental Hospitals, while not directly contradicting the claims of voluntary agencies that the numbers of mentally ill homeless persons have increased, does render the issue more complex. If homeless people are in fact being accommodated, albeit inappropriately, in acute and long-stay psychiatric units, how can we explain the reported increase in the mentally ill homeless encountered by voluntary service providing agencies? We might surmise that voluntary homelessness service provision agencies are basing their analyses of the underlying reasons for homelessness on individual level data, primarily individual case studies and relatively crude quantitative characterisations of their clients. On this basis, similar to the studies described by O'Flaherty (2002), mental illness, amongst other personal characteristics, emerges as the essential explanation for homelessness of their clients. However, most estimates of the number of mentally ill persons, substance abusers, persons living below the poverty line and so on, substantially exceed the number of homeless persons at any point in time or, indeed, the number of persons who have been homeless at any time over, for example, the past five years. On the basis of these arguments, and the empirical evidence, the difficulties in securing long-term, appropriate, suitable and supported accommodation is more significant in explaining homelessness than are personal characteristics.

Drug Use and Homelessness

Another explanation may be increased drug use. However, as Neale (2001: 354) points out, 'while the risk factors for homelessness and addiction are strikingly similar, the relationship between the two problems is extremely complex'. As noted earlier, the opiate epidemic of the 1980s was followed by a period of relative stability in heroin uptake rates (Dean *et al*, 1987). However, by the mid-1990s, suggestions of a 'new' wave of young heroin users had emerged (O'Gorman, 1998) and this coincided with renewed attention to the plight of families, parents and children living in urban neighbourhoods, particularly with high concentrations of drug use. Public awareness of drug use and related criminal activities increased quite dramatically around this time (Butler, 1997), largely as a consequence of extensive media coverage of the apparently lavish lifestyles of key perpetrators of organised crime (O'Donnell and O'Sullivan, 2001). This situation intensified during 1996, when residents in a number of areas of Dublin city marched on the homes of suspected drug dealers, with the intention of 'cleaning' their communities of drug 'pushers'. Media attention to the activities of resident anti-drug and vigilante groups intensified, raising public awareness of drug-related activities as well as the link between drug use and crime (Memery and Kerrins 2000b).

In December 1996, the Government introduced the Housing (Miscellaneous Provision) Bill, which was enacted in July 1997. The aim of the legislation was to enable local authorities to evict individuals believed to be engaged in anti-social behaviour (Rourke, 2001). Kelly (1997) expressed concern about the legislation before it was passed, warning that it was likely to increase homelessness, and was particularly critical of the 'loose' definition applied to 'anti-social behaviour'. The impact of the Housing (Miscellaneous Provision) Act, 1997 has been recently assessed by Memery and Kerrins (2000b) and Rourke (2001). Both reports document an initial increase in evictions related to anti-social behaviour by Dublin Corporation in 1997 and 1998, but a decrease in 1999 and 2000. Memery and Kerrins conclude that '[I]nstead of working to resolve the wider and complex drug issues for these communities and address the needs of drug users directly, a very blunt piece of legislation was put in place with the emphasis on excluding those involved with drugs from local authority housing' (2000b: 29). According to the Merchants' Quay Project, the Housing (Miscellaneous Provisions) Act, 1997 has contributed to an increase in the number of homeless drug users in Dublin (Merchants' Quay Project 2000). However, Rourke's (2001) research indicated that just over one-fifth of those evicted by Dublin City Council in 1997 and 1998 were living in hostels when interviewed in late 2000. Indeed, 15 per cent had been rehoused by Dublin City Council and 11 per cent living in housing provided by voluntary housing associations. The degree to which the Act contributed to the recorded increase in homelessness is therefore questionable.

A recent analysis of Dublin Simon outreach contacts has similarly highlighted drug use as a major presenting difficulty among their total contact group. Their 1999 figures indicate that 25 per cent of male, and 32 per cent of female contacts presented with drug problems (Howley, 2000). Between 1996 and 1999, the number of drug users presenting for treatment in the greater Dublin region increased from 4,283 to 5,380, 'due in part to an increase in service provision, and partly due to an increase in drug use' (Health Research Board, 2002: 2). The total treatment cases also increased in the rest of the country from 498 to 920. Thus, increased drug use, allied to the provisions of the Housing (Miscellaneous Provisions) Act, 1997, and the relative absence of services for drug users who are homeless, may have contributed to the increase in street homelessness observed in urban areas, particularly Dublin. However, the opiate 'epidemic' that hit Dublin in the early 1980s does not appear to have caused the same increase in homelessness recorded in the 1990s. Significantly, services for drug users were virtually non-existent in the 1980s in comparison with the plethora of statutory and non-profit services that existed from the mid-1990s. While some increase in homelessness may be attributable to the increase in drug use, it does not fully explain the apparent growth in homelessness in the late 1990s.

Poverty and Homelessness

Most commentaries on homelessness in Ireland, in addition to de-institutionalisation and problematic drug use, suggest a link between homelessness and poverty. The Economic and Social Research Institute have collected data on the extent of poverty amongst individuals and households on a consistent basis in Ireland since 1987. Recent research on poverty in Ireland has employed two primary means of identifying the poor, one using relative income poverty lines and the other using a combination of relative income lines and deprivation indicators (Nolan *et al*, 2002). On the relative income approach, people are counted as poor if they live in households with incomes (adjusted for household size and composition) which fall below a specified proportion, 40, 50 or 60 per cent of average (adjusted) household income. On this measure, poverty increased in Ireland between 1994 and 2000, except at the 60 per cent cut-off point, where a slight decrease was observed. On the combined approach, a household is only classified as poor if household income is below a specified relative income line *and* the household is deprived in respect of one or more of the items included in an eight-item summary index of basic deprivation. Using this measure, a substantial decrease in poverty was observed between 1994 and 2000, except at the 40 per cent cut-off point where a modest increase was recorded. Thus, while the number of households experiencing relative poverty increased, the numbers experiencing absolute poverty decreased between 1994 and 2000.

These trends do not immediately suggest a direct link between rates of poverty and an increase in homelessness. The primary reason for the increase in relative poverty was that social security payments, while increasing by more than the consumer price index for most of the 1990s, did not keep pace with the national average industrial income. Given that the majority of those below the poverty line are dependent on social welfare for their income, they are also entitled to apply for the various social housing programmes offered by local authorities and the non-profit sector and, more significantly, given the considerable waiting lists for such accommodation, are entitled to a rent supplement under the Supplementary Welfare Allowance (SWA) Scheme. Thus, while rents increased significantly in the private rented sector between 1997 and 2002, unemployed households in the private rented sector were largely shielded from the increase in market rents. Rising rents should, in theory, not adversely affect unemployed households in the private rented sector since the increase in the rate of rent is largely met by the State. However, in November 2002, in an attempt to reduce inflation in the rent supplemented residential property market, the Minister for Social and Family Affairs decided to cap the existing rent supplements and increased the minimum contribution from the tenant to 10 per cent of the minimum personal social welfare rate. However, this change would not have affected the existing data on homelessness. While there now may be cases where the rent increase exceeds the maximum rental limit set under the SWA rent allowance scheme, the fact that the numbers in receipt of a rent supplement increased from 34,700 at the end of 1996 to 54,213 at the end of 2002 (an increase of 56 per cent) (Department of Social and Family Affairs, various years), with a further increase in the number of recipients to nearly 60,000 by the end of 2003, gives little credence to support this displacement theory.

Homelessness and the Housing Market

Recent econometric studies of homelessness suggest that tighter housing markets are positively associated with higher levels of homelessness

(O'Flaherty, 1996; Kemp *et al*, 2001; Quigley and Raphael, 2001). For O'Flaherty, the rental vacancy rate exerts a negative and statistically significant effect on homelessness, while measures of housing costs such as median rents and rent-to-income ratios exert positive and significant effects (see also Lee *et al*, 2003 for a similar analysis). It seems likely that many of those who are currently vulnerable with respect to homelessness would be capable of accessing and retaining secure accommodation if affordable and appropriate dwellings were available. Given this, the key underlying cause of homelessness can be seen to lie in the interaction of the labour and housing markets. In the Kemp *et al* (2001) study, unemployment exerted a more significant force on homelessness than did the housing market, but housing affordability and de-institutionalisation were still important factors. Quigley and Raphael (2001) argue that relatively minor shifts in housing market conditions can have substantial effects upon rates of homelessness and that homelessness can be reduced by attention to the better functioning of housing markets. In particular, Mansur *et al* (2002: 333) argue that 'demand-side subsidies cause larger declines in homelessness than do supply-side subsidies' and, holding the cost of each intervention constant, 'demand-side programs yield the biggest "bang per buck" in reducing homelessness'.

The changes that occurred in the Irish housing market during the second half of the 1990s have already been documented in Downey's and O'Connell's chapters in this volume. From the limited available evidence, it is not clear that the tighter housing market that has existed over the past number of years has contributed to homelessness. As noted above, this is largely because of the safety net role that the SWA Rent Allowance system plays in preventing homelessness and the fact that there was no diminution of the numbers on this scheme during the 1990s and early 2000s. Rather, the number of recipients continuously increased during the 1990s and early 2000s, despite a substantial reduction in unemployment, particularly long-term unemployment. Some of this increase may be partly explained by the approximately 5,000 asylum seekers in receipt of the allowance and the retention of the allowance for those on designated back-to-work schemes, but the key point is that the private rented sector successfully accommodated increasing numbers of rent allowance tenants over the period in question. This suggests that the private rented market became more, rather than less, accessible during the late 1990s and early 2000s for these vulnerable households.

Conclusion

During the late 1990s, a substantial increase in homelessness was recorded by both voluntary and statutory agencies. However, an examination of some of the factors that might have explained this growth – de-institutionalisation, poverty, unemployment, drug use and tighter housing markets – offer inconclusive evidence for this. Two explanations may assist in interpreting these findings. Firstly, the quantification of homelessness as offered by various agencies, both voluntary and statutory, are beset by difficulties of definition and measurement. The increase in homelessness between 1996 and 2002 may not reflect the actuality of the extent of homelessness, but instead may be the consequence of changing methodologies and definitions. The definition of homelessness provided for in the Housing Act, 1988 is vague and open to interpretation, and it may be that a more generous definition of homelessness was used in 1999 compared to earlier years. The inclusion of households residing in bed-and-breakfast accommodation helps to explain the increase in recorded homelessness in Dublin. In that case, it may be that the extent of homelessness recorded in 1999 and 2002 was overstated or that earlier counts understated its extent. Based on the research evidence from the early 1990s, the most probable scenario was that the earlier counts understated the extent of homelessness. Thus, no real increase in homelessness occurred; rather, the numbers remained consistently relatively high, but the composition of this population changed with an increasing number of women and children, homeless families and young people.

The second explanation is that homelessness did increase during the late 1990s, but that broad macro-economic and demographic factors are at too high a level of aggregation to explain the micro-dynamics of homelessness, and the subtle changes that impact upon homelessness may not be captured by this form of analysis. Rather, more detailed ethnographic (although see Madden, 2003, for a critique of such an approach) and other qualitative research methods may be required, in conjunction with more sophisticated interrogations of the existing quantitative data, if the factors, or more importantly, the combination and interaction of factors that appear to trigger homelessness are to be fully understood (see O'Flaherty, 2004 for an econometric analysis of the interaction between the personal and the market in determining levels of homelessness).

There has been a range of positive policy initiatives in relation to homelessness over the past number of years. These include increased funding for both voluntary and statutory service providers; reinvigorating the voluntary sector; innovative service delivery such as 'wet hostels' for people with alcohol problems (Costello, 2000); expansion of social and affordable housing schemes (O'Sullivan, 2004); homeless fora; homeless action plans etc. However, it can be argued that the national level action plans etc. devised to deal with homelessness relate homelessness primarily to administrative defects and the absence of specialised programmes that may re-integrate the homeless. Such a perspective acknowledges to a limited degree that structural factors may contribute to homelessness, but ultimately sees the solutions as involving specialist rather than generic solutions. It may potentially see homeless services evolving away from mainstream public policies on housing etc., and create the perception that homelessness is a matter of individual responsibility to embrace the specialist and rehabilitative schemes that aim to normalise the homeless. While the Homeless Agency has warned against such a development in its strategic plan, arguing that responses to homelessness must be mainstreamed, in the absence of a strategic consensus amongst both service providers and policy initiators, contention will continue to persist in quantifying the extent of homelessness, explaining its underlying determinants and identifying solutions.

13

Accommodating the Traveller Community

David Silke[1]

Introduction

A question relating to membership of the Irish Traveller community was included for the first time in the 2002 Census and 23,681 Travellers (accounting for 0.6 per cent of the total national population) were enumerated (Central Statistics Office, 2004a). This figure is lower than previous ones produced by Traveller organisations, which estimated that there were in the region of 25,000-30,000 Irish Travellers. While acknowledging that there may be some difficulty in fully enumerating a population that is socially marginalised – with some members following a nomadic lifestyle and with low literacy levels – the Census figures are, however, very useful in that they give the most complete picture yet of the distribution and nature of this population and provide a baseline for future years.

In addition to the overall number quoted above, two additional statistics from the Census are worth quoting here by way of introduction. Firstly, it was found that the age profile of the Traveller community contrasted with that of the general population – the former having more young people and fewer older people. While the young population aged fourteen years and under accounted for 21.1 per cent of the general population, the corresponding proportion was 42.2 per cent for Travellers. Older Travellers (i.e. those aged sixty five years and over) accounted for just 3.3 per cent of the total Traveller population compared with 11.1 per cent for the general population. The median age of the average Traveller is eighteen years compared with a national figure of 32. Secondly, the tendency for Travellers to marry young was shown – with one-fifth (19 per cent) of males and one-quarter (24 per cent) of female Travellers in the fifteen to twenty four age group married compared with less than 1 per cent and 2.1 per cent of the general population respectively. Marriage is particularly significant in the context of this chapter as it signifies the beginning of a new family and a new household, with related accommodation implications.

Travellers are widely acknowledged as one of the most marginalised groups in Irish society. A recent study by Collins (2001) found that almost half of those interviewed in the general public (44 per cent) said they would not accept Travellers as members of their community, and almost all (93 per cent) said they would not accept a Traveller as part of their family. They also experience high levels of disadvantage, the principal features of which are outlined below:

- Almost 800 Traveller households live on unauthorised halting sites, including on the roadside, many without access to basic services such as water, sanitation, refuse collection and electricity.
- Infant and adult mortality rates are over twice those of the general population.
- Extremely low education participation rates – nearly two-thirds (63 per cent) of Travellers who indicated the age at which their full-time education ceased left before the age of fifteen years compared with 15 per cent of the general population. Two-thirds (68 per cent) of all Traveller school leavers were educated to at most Primary level compared with 21 per cent for the overall population (Central Statistics Office, 2004a).
- High levels of illiteracy – the recent Traveller Health Strategy (Department of Health and Children, 2003), for example, estimated that up to 80 per cent of adult Travellers are unable to read.
- High levels of unemployment and the disappearance of the traditional economic activities of Travellers – WRC Social and Economic Consultants (2003) estimate that the unemployment rate among Travellers could be in the region of 85-90 per cent.
- Direct and indirect discrimination against Travellers, which is experienced at all levels. For example, in 2001-02 three-quarters (75 per cent) of referrals received by the Equality Tribunal for investigation under the nine grounds of the Equal Status Act, 2000 relating to equal access to goods and services were on the Traveller community ground, the majority of which were taken against pubs, nightclubs and hotels (ODEI – the equality tribunal, 2003). In 2002, 137 decisions were issued by the Tribunal, a little over half (53 per cent) of which found in favour of the complainant. However, a breakdown by ground is not published.

The National Co-ordinating Committee for the European Year Against Racism (1997: 2) summarised this cumulative experience as follows:

Travellers fare badly on every indicator used to measure disadvantage: unemployment, poverty, social exclusion, health status, infant mortality, life expectancy, illiteracy, education and training levels, access to decision making and political representation, gender equality, access to credit, accommodation and living conditions.

The National Economic and Social Forum (2002: 63) also acknowledged that this experience is as a result of a 'prolonged history of socio-cultural exclusion, marginalisation and denigration'.

Beyond these basic points, however, it is difficult to be precise as to exactly who makes up the Traveller community (or indeed Traveller communities), or what it means in modern Ireland to be a Traveller. There is recognition that Traveller culture is distinct and different from the 'Settled' culture, and that Travellers are in some ways different from the 'Settled' community. Culture has many intangible and changing aspects to it, and is often more distinct when compared to other 'cultures'. In the *Report of the Task Force on the Travelling Community*, for example, nomadism, the importance of the extended family, the Traveller language (the Cant) and the organisation of the Traveller economy are identified as visible manifestations of the distinct Traveller culture (Task Force on the Travelling Community, 1995).

Indeed, it would be equally fair to say that there are different types of Traveller culture now present in Ireland. Compare, for example, the traditional Traveller with the New Age Traveller who is more likely to be a first generation nomadic. (The traditional Traveller community is the subject of this chapter, as it has the most defined history in relation to accommodation policy.) Even within the traditional Traveller community, different sub-groups are evident: those with a long nomadic tradition; those who come from a tradition of the fairground, carnival and entertainment people; and those who have a lot of contact and relationships with the settled community, including marriage in some cases (McDonagh, 2000).

Whether Travellers constitute an ethnic group or not has been further debated. Ní Shúinéar (1994) puts forward the case that Travellers are an ethnic group. They have a shared physical distinctiveness, shared fundamental cultural values, social separation, a shared language and experience spontaneous and organised enmity. McLoughlin (1994), while agreeing that Travellers form a distinctive group in Irish society, argues against the idea that they form their own ethnic group, pointing out that, for example, the feelings of social isolation felt by many Travellers is part of a larger class separation, nor are their experiences of harassment unique. Helleiner (2000) has also traced a resistance on the side of politicians to accept that Travellers are an ethnic group. Whyte (2002) points out that definitions of the community in recent legislation, such as the Equal Status Act, 2000, recognise Travellers as a distinct ethnic – as opposed to economically deprived – group in Irish society. However, it is noteworthy that the Act does identify discrimination on the grounds of race (ethnic minority) and membership of the Traveller community as two separate categories.

This appreciation of difference is an important starting point in trying to understand this policy area because it is generally recognised that there is a tendency for the majority culture to be taken as the norm, with a risk that other cultures are viewed as outside that norm. In this situation, minority groups can end up being labelled as 'outsiders' rather than just different, and this has important implications for their relationship with and treatment by others. In the case of the Traveller community, while policy-making has become increasingly informed by the need to respect cultural difference, Crowley (1999) notes that this change in thinking has been slower to alter the nature of policy implementation. Fanning (2002) also concludes that the way in which the needs of the Traveller community have been responded to has implications for emerging responses to new minority communities within Irish society. He writes: 'A past unwillingness to acknowledge or challenge institutional racism is likely to contribute to the marginalisation of new minority communities within Irish society' (Fanning, 2002: 174).

Others have emphasised that appreciation of difference is not all one way. In an addendum to the Task Force on the Traveller Community's report, four members of the group from political/local authority backgrounds argued that negative consequences of the Traveller nomadic lifestyle was a main reason for increasing conflict with the settled community. They commented:

Part of the conflict is also due to the failure of Travellers and Traveller organisations to recognise that today's society finds it difficult to accept a lower standard of conduct from a section of the community who consciously pursue a way of life which sets its members apart from ordinary citizens, appear to expect that their way of life takes precedence over that of settled persons, and which carries no responsibility towards the area in which it resides (Task Force on the Traveller Community, 1995: 290).

This chapter will begin by tracing the trends in government policy in relation to the accommodation of Travellers, with particular emphasis on developments since the publication of the *Report of the Task Force on the Traveller Community* (Task Force on the Travelling Community, 1995). Recent legislative developments are outlined, as well as the inclusion of Traveller accommodation issues in mainstream policy development, such as social partnership agreements and social inclusion strategies. The current accommodation situation of the Traveller community is then outlined and discussed. The chapter concludes by examining policy implementation issues, particularly why progress has been slow in achieving accommodation targets.

The Development of Policy in Relation to Traveller Accommodation

The Traveller community has a long tradition in Ireland. McDonagh (2000) traces the existence of Travellers in Britain and Ireland back to the twelfth century, and possibly earlier. He especially contradicts the theory that Irish

Travellers are the descendants of the people who lost their lands at the time of the Famine, arguing:

> It suits a lot of people to say that Travellers originate from this point in history because then it allows people to believe that prior to this, Travellers would have been settled people. Hence, Travellers appearing in 1840 would mean that they were in some way 'failed settled people' and hence the whole concept of rehabilitation and re-assimilation comes into play (McDonagh, 2000: 22).

Travellers were not a prominent feature of social service developments in the early years of the Irish State. Some were housed in standard housing under the terms of the Housing Act of 1931, but halting sites and group housing were not provided. The first explicit statement of government policy in relation to Travellers was in the *Report of the Commission on Itinerancy*, published in 1963 (Commission on Itinerancy, 1963). The Report identified the 'problem of itinerancy', the solution to which was to be based on a 'positive drive for housing itinerants'. It reported the results of the 1960 census of the community, undertaken by the Garda Síochána, which enumerated 6,591 Travellers in 1,198 family units. The majority of those enumerated were living on the roadside (1,142 families) in horse-drawn caravans and tents (738), tents only (335), motor caravans (60) and no abode (9). An additional 56 families were living in a house or room. Three-quarters (77 per cent) of families reported that they travelled all year, but the majority of husbands and wives (78 per cent in each case) said they would prefer to settle in one place if a means of livelihood was available. Only one in five (20 per cent), however, reported that they had ever applied for a council house or flat.

The clear thrust of the Commission's approach was the absorption and assimilation of the Traveller community into the general community. A carrot and stick approach was put forward which recommended the provision of serviced camping and halting site facilities for Traveller families combined with the prohibition of camping, other than on approved sites. The Commission recommended that local authorities, with financial support from central funds, provide serviced halting sites, with adequate room for animals and the storage of stock-in-trade, close to urban areas and facilities such as schools and churches. Sites should be chosen and designed with the possibility in mind of their use in due course for housing purposes. Camping and parking a caravan within a day's journey of an approved site was to be made an offence. The Commission recommended that a Government Minister be given overall co-ordinating responsibility and an unpaid central body be established to '… promote the rehabilitation and absorption of itinerants and to examine the progress' (Commission on Itinerancy, 1963: 107). The importance of local level activity was also stressed and local level committees were proposed to bridge the gap between the Traveller family and the settled community. The Government gave the lead implementation role to the Minister for Local Government, an advisory body was set-up by that Minister (which lasted until 1970) and the establishment of local Itinerant Settlement Committees was supported. Central funding was also made available to local authorities to provide serviced camping sites.

Almost twenty years later, in January 1981, a Review Body was jointly established by the Ministers for the Environment and for Health and Social Welfare to review policies and services and make recommendations to improve the situation. The composition of this Body, with 23 members, was twice the size of its predecessor and was also more diverse. The Commission had been chaired by a Judge of the High Court and included senior local authority officials, medical officers, a Garda Chief Superintendent, a former Chief Inspector in the Department of Education and a representative from the National Farmers' Association. In addition to Departmental officials, the Review Body included ten nominations from the National Council for Travelling People and a representative from the National Association of Tenants' Organisations. The Review Body took two years to report.

The Review Body noted that significant progress had been made since the publication of the Commission's report in providing dwellings for all Travellers who wished to settle. As noted earlier, in 1960 only 56 families were housed; but by 1980 this had increased to 1,210 Traveller families (957 in houses, 253 in chalets) and a further 131 families were living in trailer caravans on authorised sites (Travelling People Review Body, 1983). Over the period, however, the Traveller population had doubled, leaving virtually the same number living on the roadside as twenty years earlier. The Review Body noted differences in local authorities' responses to the issue: some took care to suit the particular needs in their area while others were tardy in their response. 'In practice, implementation was geared to what was feasible, or politically possible, rather than what was required' (Travelling People Review Body, 1983: 35). The lack of penalties for low performance by local authorities and the absence of surveillance systems to ascertain whether or not Travellers were given their due priority were noted. The Review Body concluded that, in some cases, local opposition to the development of Traveller accommodation had thwarted local authority progress and emphasised the need to balance consultation with the need to take effective action to meet the needs of families in their areas.

The Review Body put forward the following definition of Travellers, which demonstrates an important shift in thinking:

They are an identifiable group of people, identified both by themselves and by other members of the community (referred to for convenience as the 'settled community') as people with their own distinctive lifestyle, traditionally of a nomadic nature but not now habitual wanderers. They have needs, wants and values, which are different in some ways from those of the settled community. (Travelling People Review Body, 1983: 6)

As Crowley (1999, p. 247) notes, however, the Review Body did not develop on the possible implications of this definition, considering Travellers as an ethnic group, but rather considered that the extent to which they integrated with the settled community would be a matter of choice for each individual family. So the emphasis had shifted from absorption and assimilation to integration, a 'long and complex process implying adjustments of attitudes towards one another, both by the traveller and by his neighbour in the settled community' (Travelling People Review Body, 1983: 6).

The Review Body report also emphasised that Travellers had different accommodation preferences and multiple needs. The report favoured standard housing as the best accommodation for Travellers, arguing against caravans as a long-term option on health grounds (Travelling People Review Body, 1983). In addition this was a period of expansion for the social services (both generally and in terms of services specifically targeted to Traveller families) and permanent accommodation was regarded as critical if Travellers were to be able to avail of services such as education, health care and welfare.

The Review Body recommended the establishment of a corporate body under the aegis of the Taoiseach to promote the general welfare of Travellers by working towards the elimination of discrimination against them, ensuring proper co-ordination of government programmes to assist them, advising, assessing and reporting on the implementation of programmes, operating a referral system to the ombudsman and promoting appreciation of the rights and obligations of both Traveller and settled people (Travelling People Review Body, 1983). It was envisaged that responsibility for service provision would remain with the relevant statutory authorities, however. Similar to the experience of the Commission's recommendation to establish a central body to review progress, this recommendation was not accepted by the Government of the day and again an advisory body was established.

By the early 1990s the circumstances of the Traveller community were again the focus of attention and a third group, the Task Force on the Travelling Community, was established by the Minister for Equality and Law Reform to review and make recommendations in relation to relevant Government policy. The Task Force consisted of eighteen members, including nominations from the main political parties, relevant government departments, Traveller organisations and South Dublin County Council. The Task Force produced an initial report in January 1994 and a final report in July 1995. The latter report, which contained 380 recommendations, provides the framework for much of the current policy development in this area.

The Task Force stressed the persistent difficulties experienced by the Traveller community – insufficient accommodation, poor health, low education participation and high levels of illiteracy, unemployment and discrimination. It emphasised the need for an integrated and urgent response in relation to Traveller accommodation, noting that local authority performance had been 'uneven' and that accommodation remained a major issue for the Community (Task Force on the Travelling Community, 1995: 101). Responsibility for Traveller accommodation should stay at local authority level, the Task Force felt, but it recommended that the authorities' role in this regard should be carried out within a framework of a national programme and called for the establishment of a Traveller Accommodation Agency on a statutory basis. The Task Force proposed that the Agency would have a Chairperson and nine Members including elected local representatives, equality experts and nominations from national Traveller organisations. Its central functions would be to draw up, in consultation with local authorities, a National Programme for the provision of Traveller specific accommodation and to monitor and review local authorities' Traveller specific building and refurbishment programmes. It would also be charged to advise the relevant Minister, draw up guidelines for planning authorities, carry out research, undertake intercultural training and liaise with other bodies. The Agency would have a range of powers to direct local authorities in relation to the provision of Traveller accommodation and, if necessary, it would have the power to apply to the High Court to compel compliance. This raises important issues concerning the relationship between central government and local administration, between policy making and policy implementation, to which we will return.

The Task Force proposed that a National Strategy on Accommodation be developed, with a target of the provision of an additional 3,100 units of accommodation by 2000. The Traveller Accommodation Agency, as a statutory body, would draw up, in consultation with local authorities, a National Programme for the provision of Traveller specific accommodation and monitor it. Traveller Accommodation Committees would be established in every local authority area, to include representatives of elected members and officials of the local authority and Travellers to facilitate consultation and to assist in the development and implementation of the local programmes. Planning Acts would be amended to facilitate the provision of accommodation and local authority powers would be improved to deal with anti-social behaviour among tenants and illegal camping (Task Force on the Travelling Community, 1995: 102).

Following publication of the report in July 1995, the Minister for Equality and Law Reform established an Inter-Departmental Working Group of officials to prepare a response. The Inter-Departmental Group was consistent with the Task Force's general approach, but put forward a different implementation approach. This was based on the idea that each local authority would be obliged by law to prepare and have adopted by the elected Council a 5-year plan for the provision of Traveller accommodation in its area. If the elected members failed to adopt a plan within the time allowed, the Manager would then be empowered and required to formally draw up the plan.

The Inter-Departmental Group proposed that the development and implementation of these plans would be supported by a number of new structures. A special unit within the Department of the Environment would be established to oversee the preparation, monitoring, implementation, co-ordination, etc. of the accommodation programme, including the preparation and enactment of the necessary legislation. A National Traveller Accommodation Consultative Group would be established on a statutory basis to monitor the preparation, adequacy and implementation of the local accommodation programmes, and to advise the Minister as necessary. There would also be a statutory requirement that each local authority establish a Traveller Accommodation Committee, to include representatives of the elected members and officials of the local authority and Travellers.

As part of this package of reform, the Group also recommended additional legislative changes. The Planning Acts would be amended to facilitate implementation of the plans. Wider legislative powers were recommended to be given to local authorities to deal with illegal, indiscriminate and unauthorised parking by Travellers. Management and maintenance of Traveller accommodation by local authorities was also identified as in need of improvement and additional funding was proposed to improve standards of upkeep.

The Government agreed a package of measures in line with the Inter-Departmental Group's recommendation in March 1996 and set about putting in place the necessary administrative, legislative and financial frameworks. A dedicated Traveller Accommodation Unit was established in the Department of the Environment and Local Government in May 1996 and in December of that year a National Traveller Accommodation Consultative Group was set up under the aegis of the Department.

Legislative Developments

The Housing (Traveller Accommodation) Act was enacted in July 1998. It provides the legislative backing necessary to further the implementation of the recommendations of the Inter-Departmental Group. It requires local authorities, in consultation with Travellers/Traveller organisations, to prepare and adopt 5-year programmes to meets Traveller accommodation needs and obliges authorities to take the appropriate steps to secure implementation of these programmes. All local authorities defined under the Act adopted 5-year programmes with effect from March 2000. It also established on a statutory basis the National Traveller Accommodation Consultative Committee and required local authorities to establish Traveller accommodation consultative committees. The role assigned to consultative committees under the Act is to facilitate consultation between housing authorities and Travellers and to advise on any aspect of accommodation for Travellers.

Section 32 of the 1998 Act increased local authority powers to move on unauthorised temporary dwellings parked in a public place. This was subsequently amended by Section 24 of the Housing (Miscellaneous Provisions) Act, 2002 by the insertion of a new Part in the Criminal Justice (Public Order) Act, 1994 to prohibit any person entering and occupying land or placing any object on the land without the owner's consent where doing so is likely to substantially damage the land or prejudicially affect an amenity. Both public and private lands are covered, but not public roads (which normally include road margins and lay-bys) or occupation of private land with the owner's consent. The Gardaí have been given additional powers to enforce the new provision, including powers to remove offending items and to arrest without warrant anyone committing such an offence, thereby making it a criminal rather than a civil matter.

This particular piece of legislation was introduced by the Government in response to problems caused by large-scale unauthorised temporary encampments. Such powers were also considered to give reassurances to the settled community about the management of approved accommodation, which would assist in the consultation process in relation to additional accommodation projects (National Traveller Accommodation Consultative Committee, 2004). But concerns have also been raised by groups representing the interests of the Traveller community. They have argued that the measures were introduced without adequate consultation, are counter to the Traveller culture, are unfair in the context of the lack of adequate accommodation facilities and are being applied to families on their own and small groups (see Irish Traveller Movement, 2003).

Traveller issues have also been included as part of mainstream legislation in recent years. One example of this development is the Equal Status Act, 2000, which came into force in April 2000. It deals with discrimination outside of the employment context (which is covered by the Employment Equality Act, 1998), such as accommodation, and covers nine discriminatory grounds including membership of the Traveller community. As outlined above and as already mentioned, about three-quarters of the cases referred by the Equality Tribunal for investigation under this Act relate to the Traveller community, the majority of which were taken against pubs, nightclubs and hotels.

National Strategies

Travellers have also been mainstreamed into policy making. Throughout the 1990s Travellers have been named as a group in successive social partnership national agreements, as outlined in Table 13.1 below. The national agreements show consistent support for the design and implementation of Traveller accommodation plans at a national level over this period. However, as we shall see later on, actual output has not met with original targets.

Traveller accommodation issues have also been mainstreamed as part of the Government's anti-poverty strategy. The Review of the National Anti-Poverty Strategy named the Traveller community as a vulnerable group and set a number of key targets, including: 'All Travellers' families identified in the local authority five-year Traveller accommodation programme process as being in need of accommodation will be appropriately accommodated by end 2004' (Department of Social, Community and Family Affairs, 2002: 16).

Table 13.1: Provisions Relating to Accommodation of the Traveller Community in National Partnership Agreements, 1991-2005

Programme for Economic and Social Progress, 1991-1993
The Government are fully committed to maintain progress on meeting the accommodation needs of Travelling people. The special capital provision of £3m will be maintained in 1991 and following years and local authorities have been and will continue to be urged to push ahead as quickly as possible with specific proposals to accommodate Travelling people in their areas. (paragraph 84)

Programme for Competitiveness and Work, 1994-1996
The housing and halting site requirements of Travellers will form an important element in the overall development of housing programmes. All housing authorities have been advised of the need to include proposals for the provision of fully serviced halting sites for Travellers in their wider housing programmes for 1994. The Government are committed to ensuring that resources will continue to be made available to fund proposals by local authorities for the provision of these sites. The Task Force on the Travelling Community, set up by the Minister for Equality and Law Reform, has published an interim progress report and is now proceeding to develop detailed recommendations. The recommendations that relate to accommodation will be given the fullest consideration in the context of the ongoing programme for the accommodation of Travellers. (paragraph 6.52)

Partnership 2000 for Inclusion, Employment and Competitiveness, 1997-1999
Under the national accommodation strategy announced by the Government, local
programmes will be drawn up and adopted by local authorities to put in place a
national programme to provide 3,100 units of accommodation for Travellers
recommended by the Task Force on the Travelling Community. Implementation of
the national programme will make significant progress during the Partnership.
(paragraph 5.33)

Programme for Prosperity and Fairness, 2000-2002
Local Traveller Accommodation programmes adopted during the lifetime of this
Programme, including the target for Traveller specific accommodation set by each
Local Authority, will be monitored and procedures evaluated in the light of their
effectiveness in meeting the backlog of Traveller accommodation provision.
(paragraph 3.7.11)

Sustaining Progress, 2003-2005
Specific attention will be paid to ensuring greater progress in implementation of the
Traveller Accommodation Programme. The challenges involved seem particularly
appropriate to the spirit of the Social Partnership Agreement. Therefore, there will
be a priority focus within this Special Initiative [Housing and Accommodation] on
identifying and addressing the barriers encountered to-date in the implementation
of the Traveller Accommodation Programme, so as to push forward implementation
within the lifetime of the Agreement. (paragraph 2.3.2)

Source: Government of Ireland (1990, 1993, 1996b, 2000b, 2003b).

The Framework Document 2001, which reported the outcome of the
consultation process around the review of the NAPS, included the following
measure to be undertaken, if necessary, as part of the review of the Housing
(Traveller Accommodation) Act, 1998, then scheduled for end-2002:

> … if 35% of the accommodation needs identified in the local 5-year programmes have
> not been, or will not be, provided before the end of 2002, include an examination of
> mechanisms to ensure that the end 2004 targets are met. (Goodbody Economic
> Consultants, 2001: 62-63)

Local Government has also undergone a programme of modernisation since the
mid-1990s, which is relevant here. *Better Local Government: A Programme for
Change* (Department of the Environment, 1996a) led to a package of reforms of
local government, which put an increased emphasis on enhancing local
democracy, increasing efficiency and serving the customer better. Strategic

Policy Committees were established within each local authority, with responsibility for initiating and developing policy for different policy functions, including housing. Strategic planning approaches were introduced with housing, Traveller accommodation and homelessness strategies drawn up at local level. Furthermore, in January 2004 the Minister for the Environment, Heritage and Local Government introduced forty-two services indicators to measure local government performance, one of which relates to the provision of Traveller accommodation.

So far we have concentrated on outlining policy design and implementation in relation to accommodation for the Traveller community. In the next section, the current situation in relation to accommodation is examined in more depth.

Traveller Accommodation – the Current Situation

Table 13.2 provides details on the findings from the Annual Count of Travellers carried out by local authorities. This focuses mainly on those in local authority and local authority assisted accommodation and those on unauthorised sites. When comparing the figures from different Annual Counts, it is important to keep in mind that the count format has been revised a number of times (National Traveller Consultative Committee, 2002) and so here it is only possible to focus on general trends.

Table 13.2: Results of the Annual Counts of Traveller Families by Accommodation Type, 1996-2003

Accommodation type	1996	1997	1998	1999	2000	2001	2002	2003
Local Authority Housing*	2,135	2,260	2,367	2,483	2,653	2,941	3,208	3,554
Halting Sites+	1,143	1,134	1,148	1,100	1,152	1,192	1,314	1,398
Unauthorised Halting Sites#	1,040	1,127	1,148	1,207	1,093	1,017	939	788
Grand Total	4,318	4,521	4,663	4,790	4,898	5,150	5,461	5,740

Source: Department of the Environment, Heritage and Local Government (various years).
Note: * includes families in local authority standard housing, local authority group housing, private houses assisted by local authorities and housing provided by voluntary bodies assisted by local authorities; + includes permanent, temporary and transient halting sites; # includes on the roadside, private field/garden and other sites.

The figures show a steady increase in the overall number of Traveller families, up by a third between 1996 and 2003. The number of families in local authority housing has steadily increased, up by two-thirds over the period, while the numbers living on halting sites held fairly steady up until 2001, but increased by almost a fifth in the two years 2002-2003. There has been an overall reduction in the number of families living on unauthorised halting sites, which includes those on the roadside. This decrease is both absolute (a reduction of 252 families living in unauthorised halting sites between 1996 and 2003) and relative (a reduction from one-quarter to just over one-eighth of Traveller families living in these conditions during the same period). But the number of families in such conditions is persistent. Using the benchmark of the 1963 Commission on Itinerancy (see above), we see that while in relative terms the proportion of families living on the roadside has reduced considerably, in absolute terms the reduction is much less impressive, with only 354 fewer families living on unauthorised sites in 2003 compared to forty years earlier. Of the 788 families living on unauthorised halting sites in 2003, a little over a half (52 per cent) were on the roadside and the remainder were in private gardens and other sites. Over two-thirds (68 per cent) were without access to basic services; this proportion was higher for those living on the roadside (79 per cent). Over two-thirds (70 per cent) had applied for accommodation from the local authority in whose area they were living.

Not included in Table 13.2 are the Traveller families who provide accommodation from their own resources, live in private rented accommodation or share accommodation (443,293 and 323 respectively in 2003). This brings the total number of Traveller families in 2003 to 6,799. It should be noted that there has been a steady increase in the number of Traveller families living in private accommodation in recent years. Empirical research is lacking to explain this change, or indeed to gauge its impact on Traveller lifestyles. It is reasonable to speculate, however, that both push, e.g. lack of alternative quality accommodation, and pull e.g. personal choice, easier access to public services, factors are at work here, and that these are likely to have different weights for each family.

Expenditure on Traveller specific accommodation has increased steadily since the mid-1990s, but particularly since 2001. As Table 13.3 shows, over the period 1996-2004, €172 million has been spent on providing new accommodation and refurbished Traveller specific accommodation. This figure does not include expenditure on houses provided to Traveller families through the local authority capital programme.

Table 13.3: Traveller Accommodation Expenditure, 1996-2004

Year	Expenditure (€)
1996	
1997	12,062,512
1998	10,354,333
1999	11,266,475
2000	15,120,041
2001	23,699,661
2002	26,642,640
2003	28,950,000
2004	35,691,000
Total	172,039,960

Source: data supplied by the Department of the Environment, Heritage and Local Government.

Figures provided by the Department of the Environment, Heritage and Local Government (Table 13.4 below) indicate that accommodation provision was low in the late 1990s but is now increasing. Since 2000, output has remained above 300 units per year, reversing the trend towards the end of the 1990s of decreasing output. It should be noted, however, that the local authority programmes have identified that in excess of 3,700 units are required in the period 2000-2004, leaving a shortfall of 2,255 units to be built in the last year of that planning period.

Under Section 9 of the Housing Act, 1998 local authorities are required to carry out periodic assessments of accommodation needs in their areas. Authorities must give particular regard to the housing needs of Travellers in these assessments, including the need for sites for caravans. Authorities are also required to consult with the local Traveller Accommodation Consultative Committee and to involve social workers employed by authorities to work with Travellers, where relevant.

Table 13.4: Traveller Accommodation Output, 1996-2003

Units of Accommodation Provided	1996	1997	1998	1999	2000	2001	2002	2003	Total 1996-2003
New Halting Sites and Group Housing	71	63	27	4	18	54	80	76	31
Schemes	24	31	6	26	49	83	39	58	316
Refurbished Halting Sites and Group	91	83	63	34	81	23	73	45	493
Housing Schemes	4	29	26	15	22	22	18	42	178
Standard Housing*	111	76	83	84	143	167	127	225	1,016
Grand Total	301	282	205	163	313	349	337	446	2,396
Traveller accommodation expenditure	€8,253,298								

* includes single instance purchase units, introduced in 1999

Source: Department of the Environment and Local Government, 23 May 2002. Figures for 2002 and 2003 provided by the Department of the Environment, Heritage and Local Government.

The results of the last three assessments are presented in Table 13.5, in relation to the Traveller community. The trend is towards a substantial increase in the numbers of such households assessed by local authorities as in need of accommodation (up almost 46 per cent in the six-year period), with a reduction of over one-fifth (21 per cent) in the numbers assessed as in need of permanent residential caravan parks and a more than doubling (111 per cent) in the numbers assessed as in need of permanent housing. It should be noted, however, that much of this change can be seen to have occurred during the first three years of the period under review, with much less pronounced changes evident between 1999 and 2002.

Table 13.5: Results of the Assessment of Housing Needs – Traveller Households, 1996-2002

	1996	1999	2002	% change 1996-2002
Permanent housing	749	1,406	1,583	+111.3
Permanent residential caravan parks	734	622	578	-21.3
Total	1,483	2,028	2,161	+45.7

Source: Department of the Environment, Heritage and Local Government (various years).

Policy implementation

In 1986 a report by the Economic and Social Research Institute (ESRI) concluded that: 'the circumstances of the Irish Travelling people are intolerable. No decent or humane society once made aware of such circumstances, could permit them to persist' (Rottman *et al*, 1986: 73). The Committee set up to monitor the implementation of the Task Force Report concluded that the ESRI's quotation was still relevant in the year 2000 (Committee to Monitor and Co-Ordinate the Implementation of the Recommendations of the Task Force on the Travelling Community, 2000). We have seen in previous sections that the strategic plans have been drawn up, the legislation has been put in place, but yet about 1,000 Traveller families remain living on the roadside without access to basis facilities. Here we concentrate on why progress has been slow to date and what might be the possible barriers to policy implementation.

Implementation is putting (or trying to put) policy into practice and in so doing achieving (or trying to achieve) the policy objectives. There is a body of literature concerning policy implementation, including theories of implementation, case studies, etc. An early view of implementation regarded it as 'top-down' in nature, beginning with agenda setting and policy formation, underpinned by legislation and organisational structures and then implemented by administrators and evaluated. Policy in relation to the accommodation for Travellers can be seen to fall into this model to a certain extent – the 1963 Commission on Itinerancy setting the agenda, the lack of legal underpinning and organisation development slowing the policy implementation process, the re-defining of the agenda by the 1983 Review Body, again lacking implementation carry-through, and then the 1995 Working Group managing to overcome these barriers with strong enforcement legislation and the development of the organisational structures such as the National Consultative Committee necessary for implementation.

This 'top-down' model of implementation is weak, however, in over-estimating the power of policy makers to influence and control local players. Even with supporting legislation in place and institutional mechanisms such as a special unit within the Department of the Environment, Heritage and Local Government, output of accommodation units for the Traveller community are slow to meet the targets set. The possible reasons for this are explored in greater detail below.

The 'bottom-up' perspective on implementation gives more weight to the influence of the network of actors involved in service delivery at a local level, what are referred to as 'street level bureaucrats' (for example local-level service providers) – in this case local authorities' housing officials, social workers, etc. This model argues that these officials play an important role in policy implementation, viewing it in dynamic rather than rational terms. Again, aspects of this model may be useful in examining the pace of policy implementation in this area and it may also help to explain the unevenness of Traveller accommodation in different local authority areas. The 2001 Annual Count of Traveller Families, for example, shows that in county Clare 44 per cent of Traveller families are on the roadside compared to 20-23 per cent in the neighbouring counties of Limerick, Tipperary and Galway.

These two models of implementation should not be seen as either/or but more in terms of explaining different aspects of the same process. It is important that consideration be given to the organisational context in which policy is acted out and the uneven distribution of power and influence between players. This is particularly relevant in relation to this policy area, where the influences of both residents' groups and Traveller organisations on policy implementation at a local level are important considerations.

Turning now to examine the practice of implementation more closely, the Committee to Monitor and Co-ordinate the Implementation of the 1995 Task Force Report, reporting in 2000, noted these developments in the implementation structure, but concluded that in terms of new accommodation progress was slow:

> Progress in the actual provision of new accommodation has been very slow. Between 1998 and 1999, for example, there was an increase of only 68 in the number of Traveller families in accommodation provided by local authorities, or with local authority assistance. It is particularly unsatisfactory that, over the same period, the numbers of families on the roadside or in other unauthorised sites, rose from 1,148 to 1,207. (Committee to Monitor and Co-ordinate the Implementation of the Recommendations of the Task Force on the Traveller Community, 2000: 13)

Reporting in 2004, the National Traveller Accommodation Consultative Committee (2004) reported that some local authorities have made progress in providing accommodation, but this progress is uneven across authorities. The Consultative Committee had sought submissions from interested parties on what were perceived as barriers to implementation, and the following issues were flagged: difficulties in sourcing affordable land for Traveller specific accommodation, the weaknesses in driving the implementation of the programmes (for example, the lack of a Traveller Accommodation Agency), difficulties arising due to delays in the consultation process, the absence of an absolute statutory requirement on local authorities to implement the programme and planning issues regarding the inter-relationship between the Housing (Traveller Accommodation) Act, 1998 and the Planning and Development Act, 2000.

Public objections to the development of halting sites have often been put forward as a reason why these delays occur. McKeown and McGrath (1996) have tested this hypothesis by asking a representative sample of almost 600 people in the Greater Dublin area what they would do if they heard that a halting site was going to be located in their neighbourhood. Approximately one-third of respondents (36 per cent) said that they would actively oppose the development, through protests to the local authority and demonstrations, for example. Another third (35 per cent) said they would do nothing while another third would get more information or try meeting the Travellers before making up their minds what to do. Only 4 per cent of respondents said that they would support the proposal (McKeown and McGrath, 1996: 178-181). The survey also found that the level of concern settled people would have if a halting site were to be developed in their area seemed to be greater the further away they lived from existing halting sites. The authors believe this suggests that the lack of practical experience of halting sites exacerbates fears about such sites among settled people. This suggestion is supported by one of the case studies they used. It found a reduction in negative attitudes to a site once it was up and running, as one respondent said:

> When they decided to build it, there was a big uproar, we blocked the roads, we just didn't want them. But when we sat down with the Council, they gave us reassurances. Since the site was built we've never had any trouble. The Travellers that's in it are all nice people; they're not rowdy, they don't fight. It's just a nice clean site. The site is fantastic; you can go into the site any day you like. We've got no problem with them. (McKeown and McGrath, 1996: 128)

This research indicates that there is some potential for attitudinal change among the settled community, and that greater public awareness of good practice could play an important role in this regard.

Lack of public confidence in the ability of the local authority to manage halting sites has also been identified as a potential cause of public objections to their development. Under Section 9 of the Housing (Miscellaneous Provisions) Act, 1992, local authorities are required to draw up and adopt a written statement of policy for the effective performance of their function of management of their rented housing stock. A pilot scheme has been in operation for some years now (since 1998), supporting activities such as the employment of liaison/facilitation personnel, tenant participation initiatives, management and maintenance training programmes, the development of resident charters. The National Traveller Consultative Committee (2001) in its 2000 Annual Report commented on the limited impact of the first round of the initiative. A new scheme of pilot initiatives was launched in May 2001, which places a stronger emphasis on a community development approach.

The achievement of outcomes can also be affected by the nature of the underlying strategic framework informing implementation. A critique of the

Local Authority Traveller Accommodation Programmes (Fahy, 2001) drew attention to a number of weaknesses in the plans. The survey reported problems with the assessment process and findings, namely that the plans were based on inaccurate figures leading to under-estimations of need and that there was a lack of consultation with Travellers. The plans were also criticised on the basis that they tended to have settlement overtones, that they lacked implementation details and in some cases did not comply with Departmental Guidelines regarding meeting the distinct needs of Travellers. The exclusion of transient sites as an accommodation option in the plans was also highlighted in the study as particularly problematic.

Commenting on the lack of progress in increasing the supply of Traveller specific accommodation, an Expert Committee established by the Irish Traveller Movement to develop a future strategy for the delivery of Traveller accommodation concluded that three issues in particular were to blame for the lack of outputs:

> The ongoing racism at an institutional and community level, inflexible planning laws and lack of a centrally driven approach has ensured that the delivery of Traveller accommodation is frustrated at every turn. (Irish Traveller Movement, 2002: 30)

The Committee made a number of recommendations to strengthen the current National Traveller Accommodation Strategy, namely: increasing the powers of the local authority manager and the Local and National Traveller Accommodation Consultative Committees, promoting anti-racism and increasing cultural awareness of Traveller issues with local authority staff, communities and local politicians and addressing blockages in the planning system. Alternatively, they felt that a more centralised approach may be needed to overcome the highly politicised nature of Traveller accommodation at a local level. The establishment of a National Traveller Accommodation Agency, as proposed by the Task Force on the Traveller Community (see above) but with direct authority to act in cases of non-compliance (along the lines of the National Roads Authority) was proposed.

A High Level Group, chaired by the Department of Justice, Equality and Law Reform and reporting to the Cabinet Committee on Social Inclusion, has recently been established by Government with a particular focus on the implementation of policy in relation to Traveller issues, including accommodation (National Traveller Accommodation Consultative Committee, 2004: 35).

Conclusion

Accommodation issues are extremely important to members of the Traveller community. At a practical level, good quality accommodation is vital in terms of quality (and length) of life, the ability to access other services and indeed to participate fully in society. At a more philosophical level, it is also important in that the way in which the State treats and addresses Traveller accommodation needs is a reflection of the general population's attitudes to how the needs of minority communities should be met. The Traveller community is a young and growing population, with increasing accommodation needs as new households are formed. It is also a marginalised community; this isolation is partly accommodation-related. At an extreme level, for instance, participation in general social activities cannot be easy for families living on the side of the road with no access to basic amenities.

Expenditure on Traveller specific accommodation has increased in recent years, but progress in reducing the number of Traveller families living in very poor conditions has been slow and uneven. The development of a more positive relationship between the Traveller and settled communities remains a crucial issue in this regard. On a positive note, the legislative and institutional infrastructure necessary to facilitate local level implementation is now in place. Consensus is yet to be reached, however, on the most effective organisational framework to steer this change. The next three-to-four years will be crucial in realising whether sufficient culturally-appropriate accommodation can be provided. It may take considerably longer to realise better quality of life outcomes for the Traveller community.

14

Spatial Planning Frameworks and Housing

Michael Bannon

Introduction

The concept of planning is open to many interpretations and may validly be applied to any action which involves the formulation of a detailed method by which something is to be done – any type of thought-out procedure or action. In this broadest sense there are many types of planning including military planning, company planning, economic planning and what is currently referred to as 'spatial planning'. The term 'spatial planning' has been brought into use by the EU Commission to embrace the different nuances inherent in the concepts of *amenagement du territoire* in France, 'town and country planning' in Britain and *raumordnung* in Germany (European Commission, 1997: 23). As defined, spatial planning loosely corresponds to what is meant by 'physical planning', 'land use planning', the Irish concepts of 'regional and urban planning' or the legal title of 'planning and development', as in the Irish legislation.

The specific title used in a country is often less important than the nature of the *aims* and the *scope* afforded to planning by a society and its government. Thus, physical or aesthetic aims tend to dominate under absolutist or authoritarian regimes. Typically such 'plans were predominantly concerned with form and arrangement and relate to the art of planning as often propagated by some in the architectural profession. Modern town planning emerged as a comprehensive response to the housing, health and atrocious environmental conditions created by the industrial revolution' (Cherry, 1995). Modern town planning embraces a balanced mix of aesthetic, economic, social and public aims, much as the EU's *European Spatial Development Perspective* is constructed on the balancing of economy, society and environment (European Commission, 1999a: 10).

The extent to which an administration can implement such aims depends upon the *scope* afforded to underpin planning. In turn the scope of planning in a given society at a point in time is determined by four key criteria. First, the nature of government, whether dictatorship, oligarchy, totalitarian or democracy, affects the remit given to planning and its duration. Even in the case of an established democracy, such as in Britain, any examination of post-war governments can clearly see definite cycles in the commitment to planning. Second, the extent of the legal powers underpinning the system is significant, whether permissive or mandatory and whether they have been revised, updated or whether they embrace the modifications required by recent case law. Third, importance must be placed on the resources available to administer a planning system and to ensure the implementation of plans, be they financial, technical, land or personnel. Fourth, the nature of the implementing administration also affects the effective scope of planning: Are local administrations up to the tasks? Do they have the expertise? Are they in sympathy with the broad aims of planning and do they have a true understanding of these? (Campbell and Fainstein, 1996). Only when a system is able to meet these criteria can it be meaningfully described as a planning system or framework. In that context, this chapter traces the evolution and development of the Irish planning system, placing particular emphasis on more recent developments since the introduction of the Planning and Development Act, 2000. The chapter highlights the potential for these recent changes in planning to make a positive contribution to achieving sustainable development, but the chapter also points to some of the factors which may inhibit the proper working of the planning system.

The Pre-2000 Irish Planning Context

Prior to 1963, Irish planning operated under the permissive Town and Regional planning acts of 1934 and 1939, with minimal resources, little public interest and even more limited results. The Local Government (Planning and Development) Act, 1963 established planning on a statutory basis across the country; it established local authorities as planning authorities, required the making and implementation of development plans and put in place development control procedures, and an appeals mechanism. The 1963 Act and the eight subsequent amending acts did much to establish a coherent planning framework and to bring a degree of order and management to Irish development in the thirty-five years from 1965 up to 2000 (European Commission 1999b; Government of Ireland, 2000a). Successes were achieved in the face of many obstacles. These obstacles included a serious under-funding of the planning system and insufficient guidance by the lead Department (which is currently the Department of the Environment, Heritage and Local Government). In turn, these were compounded by the failure to establish regional planning frameworks (Buchanan and Partners, 1969). There was also a significant lack of qualified staff and an almost complete absence of any concept of land management, often bordering on outright hostility. In addition, Ireland had to grapple with the almost unique problem, by European standards, of endeavouring to implement a land management policy in a post-colonial society where the freehold titles to land had been widely vested in a small farming class (Bannon, 1983).

There were also issues relating to planning administration, including the absence of a national framework of guidelines and the neglect of the regional dimension. Within the various planning authorities, the planning function was almost always based in the engineering domain and the 'planner' was to report to the senior engineer! (Stringer, 1971). This problem was further compounded by the reality that the City or County Managers who took the decisions on most planning issues usually had no training or education as to what planning was really about. It was hardly surprising that in such circumstances planning was seen as being largely concerned with infrastructure and physical matters. In this context, the implementation of the EU-funded Operational Programme for Local Urban and Rural Development 1994-1999 (ESDP) and the establishment of the Partnerships and other community groups was to have a considerable impact on how local authorities operated and the role of planning therein (Goodbody *et al*, 1997).

The Irish planning experience from 1963 up to the late 1990s was one of limited achievement, deriving from the inadequate scope given to the role of planning by government and most local authorities. In this they reflected many of the values of Irish society and the primacy given to the individual and the immediate over the strategic needs of society. Moreover, the fledgling infrastructure of planning research had been dismantled in 1986 and, in the face of scarce resources, development control processes took precedence over investment in development plan making. The hierarchical nature of Irish administration and the virtual lack of horizontal integrating mechanisms at almost every level made it difficult to demonstrate the true potential of a planning system. This was especially the case in many local authorities which, being devoid of most social and economic functions, saw planning as merely an adjunct to the engineering functions of the authority.

The Genesis of a New Planning Framework

By the late 1990s a variety of complex issues created the need for a substantially revised planning system for Ireland. One of the factors driving this change was the accelerated growth of the economy, especially around Dublin, where foreign direct investment generated rapid growth and expansion (Organisation for Economic Co-operation and Development, 1999). It quickly became evident that Dublin could not continue to be planned by four separate local authorities alone. Rapid economic growth, immigration, land speculation and house price inflation all contributed to serious housing and transportation crises, given the long record of minimal strategic planning or investment. Some form of regional approach was required. Irish officials had been actively involved in the work of the EU Committee on

Spatial Planning, were cognisant of the leading approaches to planning in other member states and of the recommendation in the ESDP Potsdam report that 'Member States regularly prepare standardised information on important aspects of national spatial development policy, and its implementation in national spatial development reports, basing this on the structure of the ESDP' (European Commission, 1999b: 38). The Potsdam report also outlined the themes for such national reports, which were also to be the subject of further EU-wide studies (Study Programme on European Spatial Planning, 2000).

These positive and negative factors combined to create an urgency for change and reform in the Irish administration. A review of the planning legislation was initiated and this resulted in the comprehensive Planning and Development Act, 2000, the establishment of 'regional planning guideline' procedures for the Greater Dublin Area and other regions, and a commitment to produce a national spatial strategy for the State. In short, a new Spatial Planning Framework was to be put in place. The remainder of this chapter is devoted to an outline of each of these initiatives and their implications for development, and for the housing sector in particular.

The National Spatial Strategy 2002-2020

As stated above, the ESDP programme had called for member states to produce 'national spatial development reports', and, in Dublin, the ESRI in its early 1999 review of national investment priorities called for the implementation of a 'nodal strategy which will have the best chance of promoting balanced and sustainable regional development' (Economic and Social Research Institute, 1999). This call was also taken up in the Government's National Development Plan, 2000-2006 (NDP) in which it argued for the 'promotion over the period of the Plan of a small number of additional regional Gateways (urban growth centres) to complement the existing Gateways and to drive development throughout both Regions' (Government of Ireland, 2000a: 9). The NDP further confirmed that 'A National Spatial Strategy is to be completed within two years, which will include identification of a small number of additional regional Gateways (urban growth centres) to be promoted over the period of the Plan' (Government of Ireland, 2000a: 9-10).

In November 1999 the government mandated the Department of the Environment, Heritage and Local Government to prepare a National Spatial Strategy, having regard to the context set out in the National Development Plan, 2000-2006. A Spatial Planning Unit was established within the Department to undertake the work, assisted by a Technical Working Group and an Expert Advisory Group. Cross-departmental involvement was secured 'through a Steering Group representative of the relevant government departments' and the use of a consultative process 'across a wide spectrum involving the social partners, local and regional authorities and many different interest groups both North and South' (Department of the Environment and Local Government, 2000f: 29). In addition, a team of consultants was appointed to assist with a total of approximately 30 research tasks and covering topics such as population, household formation and the Irish urban and rural systems.

Figure 14.1: The National Spatial Strategy: Gateways and Hubs

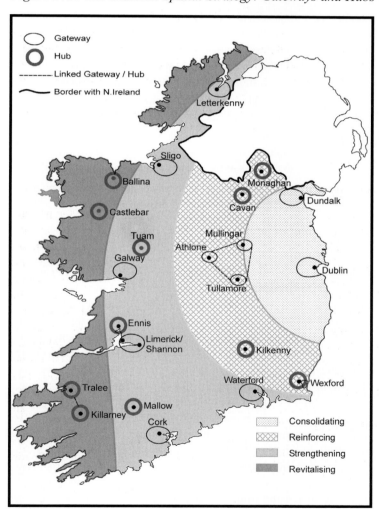

Source: Drawing by Stephen Hannon, Geography Department, University College Dublin based on Department of the Environment and Local Government, 2002.

Table 14.1: The Five Spatial Elements of the National Spatial Strategy and their Future Roles

Spatial Element	Future Roles
A more efficient Greater Dublin Area	The vital national role of the Greater Dublin Area is secured in terms of improved mobility, urban design quality, social mix, international and regional connections.
Strong Gateways in other Regions	Balanced national growth and development are secured with the support of a small number of nationally significant centres, whose location and scale support the achievement of the type of critical mass necessary to sustain strong levels of job growth in the regions.
Hubs	Balanced patterns of growth are supported by towns that link the capabilities of the gateways to other areas.
County and other town structures	Balanced patterns of growth are supported by towns that capitalise on local and regional roles and are also linked to the roles of the gateways and development hubs.
Vibrant and diversified rural areas	Rural areas benefit from enhanced employment options and from development of their local resource potential.

Source: Department of the Environment and Local Government, 2002.

The National Spatial Strategy 2002-2020 (henceforth the NSS), was released on 28 November 2002 (Department of the Environment and Local Government, 2002). Having reviewed the key development trends within Ireland and their spatial consequences, the NSS report addressed the likely future trends under a number of alternative scenarios. Thus, the population of the state could increase from 3,787,000 in 2000 to between 4,391,000 and 5,013,000 in 2020. On the basis of recent trends, 'up to four-fifths of the population growth in the State could take place in or in areas adjoining the Greater Dublin Area over the next twenty years' (Department of the Environment and Local Government, 2002: 24). The number of cars on the Irish roads could double between 1996 and 2016. Of more significance in terms of this chapter, the number of households could increase from a 1996 baseline of 1.123 million to a 2020 estimate of 1.889 to 2.083 million. This would represent an increase of between 68.2 and 85.5 per cent over the period, with the share of the national housing stock located in the Greater Dublin Area increasing from 38.8 per cent in 1996 up to 44.4 per cent of total in 2020, were current trends to continue. Having regard to the need for balanced regional development in the interests of economic efficiency, improved quality of life, a more coherent pattern of settlement and securing proper planning, the NSS proposed the development of a major modification of current trends to secure a better and more rational future spatial pattern based on the following five elements of spatial structure and their policy roles.

The spatial pattern of gateways and hubs is set out in Figure 14.1. Table 14.2 sets out the possible populations for the 'existing gateways'.

The figures set out in Table 14.2 are indicative of the scale of change envisaged in the NSS – a scale necessary if the current patterns of population, housing and employment are to be significantly changed in the years ahead.

Table 14.2: Possible Population Growth of 'Existing Gateways' (millions)

Gateways and Catchments	Population 2002	2020 Population Current Trends	2020 Population Economic Growth
Greater Dublin Area	1.535	1.938	2.200
Cork	0.350	0.360	0.454
Limerick	0.236	0.260	0.284
Galway	0.146	0.181	0.192
Waterford	0.119	0.138	0.164
Total:	2.386	2.877	3.294

Source: Department of the Environment and Local Government (2002: 49).
Note: data refer to the Gateways and their surrounding catchment areas.

While the NSS does not provide precise future populations for the 'new gateways' or for the proposed hubs, the given characteristics of gateways include populations of the order of 100,000, wide ranges of primary and secondary education as well as a third level facility, large clusters of modern industry, a regional hospital, theatres and a focal point for transport and communications, etc. Hubs are described as having a population within the range of 20-40,000, a good mix of medium and larger businesses, a local and/or regional hospital, good amenities and an effective transportation system.

Such a scale of possible future growth and its redistribution could bring about a very different future geography of the country. In launching the strategy, the Taoiseach stated that 'the strategy marks a new stage in our maturity and development as a nation, as we plan for the future development of our country … The Strategy will act in three ways: It will bring a better spread of job opportunities … It will bring a better quality of life … It will bring better places to live in.' One thing is certain. The projections point to a continuing and significant growth of households for the foreseeable future, whatever strategy is pursued. As for the NSS, much depends on the continued commitment to implementation and the effectiveness of the policies to deliver it over the period up to 2020.

Implementation of the National Spatial Strategy?

Chapter Six of the NSS report was devoted to the question of implementation and the integration of the policies of a network of agencies if the strategy were to be delivered. The implementation of the National Development Plan, 2000-2006 is considered as a first step as is the implementation of land-use/transportation frameworks for the gateways. The report places an emphasis on various forms of partnership, on cooperation, both public and private, and on central/regional/local coordination and collaboration. According to the report, 'relevant public sector policies and programmes will have to be consistent with the NSS and will be required to demonstrate that consistency' (Department of the Environment and Local Government, 2002: 119). The Cabinet Sub-Committee on Housing, Infrastructure and Public Private Partnerships was earmarked to monitor the implementation of the strategy and Government departments and agencies were 'to put structures and mechanisms in place to support the NSS and ensure that it is embedded in their policies and programmes' (Department of the Environment and Local Government, 2002: 119).

Since the report's publication, much of the media attention and commentary has focused on the question of the gateways and hubs. Were too many nominated? Can they be delivered? What policies will be enacted to support designation and, in particular, will future 'decentralisation' initiatives be focused on the Gateways? Comparatively little attention has been devoted to the strategy as a 'process' or to the importance of getting all agencies to think spatially and in terms of the consequences of their actions for planning. For its part, the Spatial Policy Section of the DoEHLG (established in January 2003 and embracing, *inter alia,* the functions of the former Spatial Planning Unit), places particular importance on maintaining continued interdepartmental and inter-agency support for the strategy. The matter of 'regional planning guidelines' is discussed below but in the view of the DoEHLG 'Regional Planning Guidelines are a key part of the process of giving effect to the adopted and published National Spatial Strategy at regional level' (Department of the Environment and Local Government, 2003: 118).

The situation regarding the implementation of the NSS has become even more complicated and controversial since the budget of December 2003. In that budget, the then Minister for Finance outlined a proposal to 'decentralise' or relocate approximately 10,000 civil and public service jobs out of Dublin to 53 centres across the country. While any such relocation undertaking is inherently controversial, the fact that only 24 per cent of the proposed job transfers were to areas identified as Gateways or Hubs in the NSS, has largely removed one of the key potential drivers of the implementation of the NSS. Political considerations rather than strategy appear to have informed the Minister's announcement. Another criticism relates to the potential impact on government and governance. With the proposal to fully move up to eight Departments of government to areas outside of Dublin, it has been argued that this will have deleterious consequences for policy-making and implementation. While the relocation proposals are the subject of examination by the Oireachtas Joint Committee on Finance and the Public Service, politically, at least, the government seems determined to implement the decentralisation programme, although the initial timetable envisaged has been eased somewhat and the costs of providing accommodation in the dispersed locations has been stated officially to 'be close to €1billion'. After a careful examination, Bannon has concluded that if the relocation proposals are implemented without a radical rethink then one of the major impacts is likely to be the further expansion of the Greater Dublin Area (Bannon, 2004b). In his view, the government's proposals appear ill considered, lacking as they do any evidential base for such a complex set of decisions. Above all, the current relocation proposals fly in the face of the National Spatial Strategy, and they are likely to sound the death knell for regional policy within Ireland, at least for decades to come (Bannon, 2004b).

Regional Planning Guidelines: The Greater Dublin Area

Unlike much of Europe, where statutory regional planning is the norm, the British government has a tradition of reliance on 'planning guidelines' as a mechanism to secure consistency and order in planning throughout England/Wales and Scotland. These include 'regional planning guidelines' for many of their regional areas and the conurbations. To deal with the crisis created by the unforeseen rapid growth of the Dublin region in the period after 1995, it was decided to follow this approach and to prepare a set of advisory regional planning guidelines for the 'Greater Dublin Area' (henceforth GDA). The report was prepared by consultants for the local authorities in the GDA and the DoEHLG in conjunction with the Regional Authorities. The report, which was published in 1999, was to 'provide a coherent strategic planning framework for Development Plans and for the provision of major transportation, sanitary services and other infrastructure' (Brady Shipman Martin *et al*, 1999: i). The study adopted a twelve-year time horizon to 2011. The consultants operated under the direction of a Steering Committee, a Technical Working Group and a Local and Regional Authority Members Committee. For the purposes of the guidelines, the two NUTS III (which refer to regions designated for the purposes of planning and statistical purposes at EU level) planning regions of Dublin and the Mid East were combined into the GDA.

The GDA had a population of 1.4 million persons in 1996 which was projected to grow to between 1.54 and 1.65 million by the year 2011. More importantly, household size is projected to continue to decline while the number of households was projected to increase from 450,000 in 1996 to up to 665,000 in 2011 – see Table 14.3. The study team examined a total of eight 'strategic models' for the development of the GDA; in turn these were appraised against a range of operational criteria and thereby reduced to three strategic options. These were:

- containment
- Dublin and the north-east and,
- Western satellite towns.

In terms of the planning strategy for the region, the consultants subdivided the region into metropolitan area and hinterland area. The major growth of the region would take place within the metropolitan area (some 56.8 per cent of the expected total population increase and 70.5 per cent of all household growth), while growth throughout the hinterland area would be channelled into a network of primary and secondary development centres. Otherwise the hinterland would function as a 'strategic green belt' area. The development strategy placed special emphasis on transport corridors, the development of public transport corridors and a sustainable approach to the future development of the GDA. From 1999 up to 2004 the Strategic Planning Guidelines acted as the framework within which constituent local authorities were expected to prepare and implement their development plans. The advisory guidelines for the GDA were deemed to have been a successful and effective means of formulating a long-term framework to ensure the coordination of the development and investment policies of local authorities. Accordingly, Chapter III of the Planning and Development Act, 2000 provided a statutory basis for Regional Planning Guidelines (see following section). In 2003 the Department of the Environment, Heritage and Local Government instructed all Regional Authorities, including those in the GDA, to prepare regional planning guidelines for their operational areas.

The consultancy firm of Atkins in association with a number of other bodies were appointed to prepare Regional Planning Guidelines for the GDA – effectively a review of the earlier Strategic Planning Guidelines in the light of post-1999 development and having regard to the implementation of the National Spatial Strategy. The guidelines for the GDA envisage a population of up to 1.83 million living in the Greater Dublin Area by 2020. In terms of household growth the analysis pointed to an increase of 26.3 per cent in the region between 2002 and 2010 (from 508,096 households in 2002 to 641,600 in 2010) and requiring the provision of an additional 39,000 housing units over the 2002-2010 period.

The Guidelines retain the subdivision of the region into metropolitan and hinterland areas but did modify the boundaries of these areas in a number of significant cases. Table 14.3 sets out the Guidelines' new six-fold typology for the region's nucleated settlement, and provides details of the scale and functions appropriate to each type of settlement.

Table 14.3: Classification and Characteristics of Urban Centres within the Greater Dublin Area

Settlement Type	Population Range	Accessibility	Typical Distance from Higher Level Settlement	Service Function		
				Economic Function	Retail	Public
Metropolitan Consolidation Towns	40,000 to 100,000	Quality Bus Corridors/ Rail/Major radial routes	Close to City Centre	Main attractor for major investment. Strong international marketing	Regional/ Major Town Centre	Hospital. Secondary education Possible Third Level facility
Large Growth Town I ('Satellite town')	25,000 to 40,000	At junction of major radial and orbital multi-modal transport corridors. Commuter rail	Within 40 km from Dublin	Main attractor for major investment. Strong international marketing	Substantial comparison retail (mall) Retail park Leisure centre etc.	Hospital. Secondary education Possible Third Level facility
Large Growth Town II	15,000 to 25,000	On major radial multi-modal transport corridor. Commuter rail	15 km from satellite or Dublin	Subsidiary attractor for investment	Comparison retail etc. education	Clinic or small hospital. Secondary education
Moderate Growth Town	5,000 to 15,000	On or near multi modal transport corridor. Rail if possible	10 km from Large Town	Attractor for substantial investment	Limited comparison retail. Good convenience. Medium supermarket(s)	Secondary education. Clinic

Settlement Type	Population Range	Accessibility	Typical Distance from Higher Level Settlement	Service Function		
				Economic Function	Retail	Public
Small Growth Town	1,000 to 5,000	On national primary or secondary road. Good bus links to railway and major settlements	10 km from Large Town	Attractor for investment	Small and medium convenience. Some local retail centres Specialty retail	Primary schools (and secondary in more peripheral areas). Post Office. Clinic
Village	Up to 1,000	Improved Rural road. Bus links to railway and larger settlements	10 km from Small Town (or other town)	Small rural-based enterprises	Small convenience units and a neighbourhood centre	Primary School. Surgery Sub-Post Office

Source: Atkins and Associates, 2004.

The recommended spatial configuration of the GDA is shown in Figure 14.2.

While the planning guidelines for the Greater Dublin Area have provided broad guidance for the development and planning of the region at a time of unprecedented growth and expansion, some difficulties have arisen in relation to the level of adherence by some local authorities to the guidelines and what is the reality of the requirement 'to have regard to'. There is no single effective authority with overall ownership of guidelines or having the necessary teeth to drive such a long-term regional strategy. Guidelines prepared under the direction of a steering committee comprising the managers of seven competing authorities may not arrive at decisions or policies which are the best for the region as a whole. Likewise, neither the local managers nor the consultants had a brief to have regard to developments which were taking place outside the GDA or which might have been encouraged in the interests of the country as a whole, including Dublin.

Proposals for an effective management and planning authority embracing the entire built-up area of Dublin and its commuting hinterland have been made repeatedly throughout the last century (Horner, 1995). A 2001 consultation paper proposed new institutional arrangements for land use and transportation in the Greater Dublin Area, but this has had little impact to date (Department of Public Enterprise, 2001). Such a proposal has most recently been re-echoed in

Agenda for Dublin which calls for the creation of 'a greater Dublin authority to tackle transport, housing and planning issues in the region' and linking together 'the representatives of the Dublin and Mid-East Regional Authorities' (Dublin Regional Authority, 2004b: 30).

Figure 14.2: Overall Strategic Development Strategy for the Greater Dublin Area (2004)

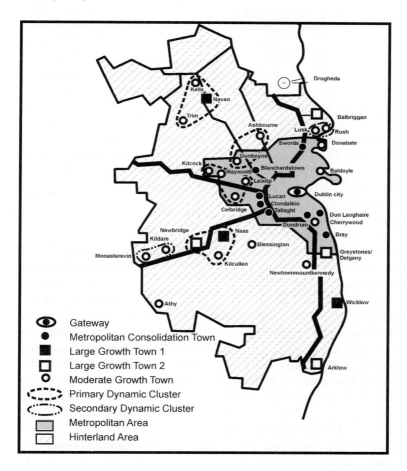

Source: Drawing by Stephen Hannon, Geography Department, University College Dublin, based on Strategic Planning Guidelines for the Greater Dublin Area.

Regional Planning Guidelines for all Regions

Reference has already been made to the statutory basis provided for Regional Planning Guidelines in the Planning and Development Act, 2000. Chapter III,

Sections 21-27 of the Act are devoted to the making and implementation of such guidelines. Section 21.(1) states that 'a regional authority may, after consultation with the planning authorities within its region, or shall at the direction of the Minister, make regional planning guidelines.' Guidelines can be prepared for all or part of a region and section 21(4) provides retrospective statutory effect for the Greater Dublin Guidelines discussed in the previous section. Under the act, Regional Planning Guidelines shall address in accordance with the principles of proper planning and development a wide range of specified matters, including 'projected population trends and settlement and housing strategies'. The act places a heavy emphasis on consultation procedures, but enables both the Regional Authority or the Minister to act where agreement is not forthcoming or is considered necessary. The time span for regional guidelines is between 12 and 20 years, there is a requirement for review and the Minister is enabled to make the necessary regulations. Finally, the Act stipulates that a 'planning authority shall have regard to any regional planning guidelines in force for its area when making and adopting a development plan' and there is provision for the Minister to order a planning authority to comply with any guidelines in force in the area.

In January 2003 the Department wrote to Regional Authorities asking them 'to ensure that the process of preparing and making regional planning guidelines is conducted as expeditiously as possible and that the necessary resources and structures to achieve this are mobilised and put in place' (Department of the Environment and Local Government, 2003: 1). Guidance notes were attached with the circular. In May 2003 a statutory instrument was issued setting out procedural requirements in relation to the preparation of regional planning guidelines by regional authorities. One of the issues covered in both the Department circular and in the Regulations is the role envisaged for regional guidelines in relation to the NSS. Thus 'Regional Planning Guidelines are a key part of the process of giving effect to the adopted and published National Spatial Strategy at regional level' (Department of the Environment and Local Government, 2003: 1). Regional Planning Guidelines have now been completed for all the Regional Authority (NUTS II) regions, including the two such regions within the Greater Dublin Area. While the Guidelines do for the most part reflect the local needs of the widely dispersed representation on each of the Regional Authorities, they do have regard to the need to ensure the implementation of the National Spatial Strategy and they provide a medium-term context and framework for local plan preparation and implementation. In terms of housing, these Guidelines provide a meaningful basis for forecasting and they should provide a framework within which it will be possible to deliver a better quality of life and local environment for citizens.

The Planning and Development Act, 2000

The Planning and Development Act, 2000 is the cornerstone of the Irish Planning system. The 2000 Act represents both a consolidation of the previous acts from 1963 onwards as well as a modernisation of the approach, bringing Irish planning more into line with European principles as enunciated in the *European Spatial Development Perspective* (European Commission, 1999a). Like its predecessor, the Local Government (Planning and Development) Act, 1963, the 2000 act is especially important for the housing sector since housing is the largest component of all development and since it has been estimated that 'housing accounts for approximately half of all urban land' (Bannon, 1979). While the act in general applies to housing, as well as to all other development, in relation to matters such as zoning, density and standards, application procedures and development levies, the remainder of this section will focus on three aspects of the legislation which have special implications for housing and for residential development. These are the issues of Local Area Plans, Part V of the act relating to Housing Supply and the use of the Strategic Development Zones procedure as a mechanism for plan-led housing and other developments.

The 2000 Act: Local Area Plans

Prior to the enactment of the 2000 planning act it had been possible to prepare 'local' or 'area' or 'framework' plans and, while these could be useful, procedures to give statutory effect to such plans were cumbersome and were seldom used. Chapter II of the Planning and Development Act, 2000, sections 18 to 20 inclusive, specifies that a 'planning authority may at any time, and for any particular area within its functional area, prepare a local area plan in respect of that area'. Local area plans may be prepared by one or more planning authorities and there are provisions to involve 'any suitably qualified person or local community group' in the process of preparing such plans.

The Act requires that local area plans be made in respect of designated towns with populations in excess of 2000, excluding designated suburbs. Under the terms of Section 19 (1) (a) of the Act, local area plans may 'be prepared in respect of any area, including a Gaeltacht area, or an existing suburb of an urban area, which the planning authority considers suitable and, in particular, for those areas which require economic, physical and social renewal and from areas likely to be subject to large scale development within the lifetime of the plan'. The act lays down procedures for the making, reviewing and revoking of such plans, as well as the procedures to be followed in respect of consultation. Both the Planning Authority and An Bord Pleanála 'shall have regard to the provisions of any local area plan' prepared for an area to which an application relates.

Local area plans are especially important in relation to housing and community development. Local area plans provide a framework within which an area or neighbourhood can be thought of, planned, laid out and developed as a unit with an appropriate mix of housing types and occupiers and allowing for an adequate and convenient arrangement of services within an area, be they shopping, work areas or schools, community facilities and recreation. Local area plans provide a context within which different developers can be induced to provide a more coherent and logical lay-out of space and uses with a meaningful input by the community and informed public opinion.

The 2000 Act: Part V – Housing Supply and Housing Strategies

One of the major innovations of the Planning and Development Act, 2000 was the introduction of a specific section devoted to the issue of housing supply and the use of the planning code to assist in dealing with the rapidly growing crisis in the availability of social or affordable housing – sections 93 to 101. Section 94 of the act placed an onus on planning authorities to ensure 'that the proper planning and sustainable development of the area of the development provides for the housing of the existing and future population of the area in the manner set out in the strategy'. The act required that 'a planning authority shall take such actions as are necessary to ensure that ... a housing strategy is prepared in respect of the area of the development plan...'. Each planning authority was required to make the necessary arrangements for the insertion of the housing strategy into their development plan.

Housing strategies were to take into account the existing and likely future need for housing within their area, to ensure that housing was made available for persons who have different levels of income and that housing supply was tailored to meet the needs of the population of the area as specified in the strategy. Under the terms of the 2000 Act, the housing strategy must also take into account 'the need to counteract undue segregation in housing between persons of different social backgrounds'. In dealing with housing need, the planning authority was required to have regard to matters such as housing supply and demand, house prices, personal and household income, interest rates and such other matters considered appropriate by the authority. Planning authorities were required to expedite the preparation and adoption of their housing strategies and the strategy was to relate to the period or the remaining period of the development plan.

The housing strategies were prepared by mid-2001 and adopted in accordance with the requirements of the act and the enabling regulations. For the purposes of this chapter, this author has randomly selected the housing strategies of three planning authorities – Monaghan, Sligo and Tipperary SR. The strategies were prepared in the early part of 2001 by consultants appointed by the local authorities and in general they appear to have followed a standard format. It appears that planning authorities closely followed the DoEHLG's *Model*

Housing Strategy and Step-by-Step Guide (Department of the Environment and Local Government, 2000b).

Each strategy dealt with housing demand, housing supply, social and affordable housing and the implications of the analysis for the county's future development of housing. Given that the strategies prepared in 2001 were a first attempt, the approach was inevitably subject to limitations. The latest available data were five years old, the dis-aggregation of national income to local level is a crude and questionable exercise and labour market analysis cannot be meaningfully undertaken at the level of a local authority. Each of the three authorities proposed that in accordance with Part V of the 2000 Act, and in the light of their estimates of need (see Table 14.4), 20 per cent of lands zoned for residential or mixed use development should be reserved for social and affordable housing. Other recommendations in the selected strategies related to the integration of social and affordable housing within housing estates and the limiting of the size of housing developments, with Monaghan recommending clusters of maximum size of 12 housing units. There was some attempt to estimate housing demand by house size, to cater for people with disabilities and the elderly. Estimates of the needs of other special groups including Travellers and refugees are also assessed and included in the strategies.

Table 14.4: Housing Demand and Anticipated Need for Social and Affordable Housing, Selected Counties, 2001-2006

County	Total Household Formations	No of Households Meeting Affordability Criteria	Affordability Percentage
Monaghan	3,454	897	26.0
Sligo	4,832	1,477	30.6
Tipperary SR	3,673	925	25.2

Source: County Housing Strategies inclusive of urban areas in each. Information supplied by the Planning Department, Monaghan Co. Co., the County Manager's office, Sligo Co. Co and Housing Analyst, Tipperary SR Co. Co.

The provision of housing strategies under the planning act represents an important innovation for Ireland. While the strategies have a number of limitations, they represent a start and will be subject to review in 2003 when some improved data and changed economic circumstances may give rise to interesting modifications.

The 2000 Act: Provision for Social and Affordable Housing

In an attempt to deal with the problems of housing affordability, given the reliance of housing policy on a free-market, supply-led approach, and in an effort to reduce the visibility of social class in Irish developments, the Planning and Development Act, 2000 empowered planning authorities, in accordance with the objectives of the development plan, to require housing developers to set aside part of their development area for the accommodation of social and affordable housing. Thus Section 96 (2) stated that 'a planning authority, or the Board on appeal, may require as a condition of a grant of permission that the applicant, or any other person with an interest in the land to which the application relates, enter into an agreement with the planning authority, concerning the development for housing of land to which a specific objective applies in accordance with Section 95 (1)(b)', i.e. to meet the needs of the area for social and affordable housing. Such an agreement could involve the transfer of the ownership of land or the building and the transfer of the ownership of houses or the transfer of sites as specified in the agreements in accordance with the provisions of the act. Generally, the requirement was for the transfer of some 20 per cent of development sites or the equivalent with the allocation between social and affordable being determined by each planning authority on the basis of their housing strategy and the amendments to the development plan.

These provisions were robustly resisted by developers and by house builders, with arguments against them on cost grounds and also on the grounds that the element of social mix would discourage sales. Since early 2002 newspapers have contained many examples of developments advertised and promoted because the social and affordable provisions did not apply! Resistance to these provisions became another barometer of Ireland's 'divided society' and were regarded by some as an unacceptable infringement of the 'market'. More significantly, the controversy over the social provision and affordability became politicised and was an issue in the 2002 general election. In turn, this led to the modification of the procedures and part of the amendments as enacted in the Planning and Development (Amendment) Act, 2002. This act introduced amendments to twelve sections of the 2002 planning act, and some five amendments to the housing legislation. Of most concern in relation to this chapter is the amendment to section 96 of the principal act which set out certain additional ways in which an applicant for permission for development could comply with the requirements of Part V in relation to the provision of social and affordable housing. In addition to the arrangements set out in the principal act, the 2002 amendment allows for agreements to be made 'to reserve land or to provide houses or sites at another location, or to make a payment to the local authority which will be used for the provision of social and affordable housing, or to agree to a combination of any of these options'. Two other modifications of the principal act in relation to housing related to a 'withering clause' in respect of some 1999-2000 permissions and the payment of certain levies.

The 2002 amending act may have freed up the housing market and in that respect it has taken pressure off government without forcing a repeal of the Part V provisions of the 2000 Act. But the amendment has served to weaken the inclusion and social integration thrust of the principal act. Ireland remains a divided society and those divisions will continue to be manifestly evident through the housing market for years to come. Once again, Irish society had effectively rejected any significant attempt to broaden the scope of planning to embrace a socially inclusive dimension.

The 2000 Act: Strategic Development Zones and Housing Provision

There has been a long history of pressure to bring forward some form of 'accelerated, fast-track' planning system to speed up and ease the process of facilitating major projects, usually of an industrial or high employment nature. Such proposals were in circulation during the enactment of the 2000 Act. In the event, the government brought forward and enacted the concept of Strategic Development Zones. 'Where, in the opinion of the Government, specified development is of economic or social importance to the State, the Government may by order ... designate one or more sites for the establishment, in accordance with the provisions of this Part, of a strategic development zone to facilitate such development'. A site having been designated, the relevant development agency is then required to prepare a draft 'planning scheme' for all or part of the area designated. An Bord Pleanála (the planning appeals board) ultimately makes the decision to approve or to refuse approval for the planning scheme. Once a scheme has been approved for a designated area, development applications consistent with the provisions of the scheme shall be granted by the planning authority, subject to conditions as appropriate.

The novel aspect of the SDZ procedure for Ireland is that it gives statutory effect to a 'plan-led' procedure which, though widespread in much of Europe, is uncommon in Britain or Ireland. While promoted by industrial and development lobbies, the SDZ concept can and has been applied in respect of housing developments. Where an SDZ arrangement for a housing development is considered, the scheme must provide for amenities and social facilities and the scheme must be consistent with the housing strategy for the area and embrace all the provisions of Part V of the principal act. In practice, the SDZ procedure has been used principally for major housing schemes, including Clonmagadden in the Navan area and an oral hearing in respect of the draft scheme for an SDZ for the Adamstown scheme in South Dublin took place in mid-2003. The Adamstown scheme has now been approved and construction is underway.

Conclusion

This chapter has outlined the broad spatial planning frameworks now in place within the Republic of Ireland and the principal planning provisions in relation to residential development and housing provision. This chapter has shown that since the late 1990s Ireland has put in place an enhanced set of planning legislation and structures which go a long way towards bringing the Irish spatial frameworks into line with those in many of the countries of northern Europe. These were countries whose traditions of spatial planning had been more developed than that in Ireland prior to 1999. The Irish spatial planning frameworks are now closely in line with the approach adopted in the 1999 report of the Potsdam meeting of the EU ministers responsible for spatial planning (European Commission, 1999a). These frameworks provide a basis within which planning could operate more coherently and more effectively, if this is so wished, by Irish society and the Irish Government on their behalf.

But to be fully effective, there is a need to continue the process of change and modernisation. The planning system requires to be adequately resourced and properly staffed, with attractive career structures for professional planners. At every level there is a need to recognise the economic and social potential of proper planning. The goals set for planning and the scope given to planners by society needs to extend away beyond the mere physical and aesthetic. Now that frameworks have been modernised, there is a need to review the scope of practice and to enable planners to function as the broad horizontal integrators of a deeper and more sustainable form of planning service at every level.

Planning is about the common good within society. In the Ireland of today the commitment to both concepts has weakened in the face of rapid economic advance and personal acquisition. The decline of commitment to, or interest in, either the needs of society or the common good is at the heart of the debate on whether 'Boston or Berlin' should be an Irish role model. In many respects, some planners in Ireland today are expected to play a role rather similar to that of planners in Britain under 'Thatcherism' in the early 1980s. Since there was no longer such a thing as society, the role of the planner was reduced to being the enhancer of the value of land and other private property (Thornley, 1993). As in many market economies, the role of the planner is ambivalent; there exists a forceful 'property contradiction' between the social character of land and its private ownership and control (Campbell and Fainstein,1996: 147).

The debates in Ireland on the public ownership and the price of building land which exercised the Oireachtas Committee on the Constitution go to the very heart of these issues in an Irish context (Government of Ireland, 2004). The successful campaign waged by the construction industry interests against the social and affordable housing provisions of the Planning and Development Act, 2000 clearly illustrate that Ireland remains a deeply divided society, a society that is not ashamed to display such divisions as seen in the exclusion of social housing and minority and Traveller accommodation to the margins, both socially and physically. Work by Nolan sets Irish inequality in its wider EU context (Nolan, 2004). Planning on its own cannot remedy such deep-rooted social divisions but it can show the way forward if the values of society are prepared to take heed and to act accordingly. Social divisions are most clear and visible through the housing market. As the social reformer and planner Patrick Geddes pointed out to the Dublin housing inquiry of 1913, 'the house is the central and fundamental fact of real wages' (Geddes, 1913). Concern with housing, housing provision and affordability must remain a core issue if planning is to build on the frameworks now in place. Good planning and effective implementation should be viewed as part of 'preventive medicine', investing generously and wisely and thus avoid in the future the social and environmental problems so evident in too many of today's housing estates and help redress the social divide within Irish society.

15

Planning and Sustainability: Metropolitan Planning, Housing and Land Policy

Declan Redmond, Brendan Williams and Michael Punch

Introduction

There are now ample policy pronouncements subscribing to the principles of sustainable development. From national policy on sustainable development to all manner of spatial planning policies, there is a commitment to sustainable development principles and practice (Government of Ireland, 1997b). However, as is becoming more evident over time, the gap between policy aims and actual achievements and outcomes is widening. While it would be naïve to expect a simple correspondence between policy objectives and achievements, it does seem that in Ireland the disconnect between policy and reality is wider than in many other EU countries. For example, as Bannon discusses in Chapter 14, the National Spatial Strategy seeks to achieve balanced regional development and, in particular, to restrain the development of the Greater Dublin Region. However, the available evidence suggests strongly that the patterns of development being produced are not coherent with the strategy. Indeed, government policy on decentralisation would seem to put the strategy at further risk. While some analysts take refuge in the ill-defined concept of polycentric development, it could be argued that the National Spatial Strategy exists only as a policy with no concomitant support for policy implementation. Likewise, the development of metropolitan planning policy in Ireland may be subject to similar criticisms. The evidence for the development of the Greater Dublin Area suggests only limited adherence to regional planning guidelines, with the development patterns producing an unsustainable metropolitan area with all manner of transport and housing problems (Williams and Shiels, 2000, 2002). On the economic and social front, there is a commitment to providing adequate and affordable housing for all. This clearly is not happening to its fullest extent, with problems of affordability and access evident for many social groups (National Economic and Social Council, 2004).

What all of this suggests is that, far from moving towards achieving sustainable development objectives, we may be pursuing a path which is leading to unsustainable urban and regional development. How should these patterns be examined? Analytically, we can examine policy at three levels. First, we can ask whether the policy aims themselves are well developed and coherent. Second, and crucially, we can ask whether there are policy instruments available to achieve the policy aims and assess whether they are adequate to the task. Third, we can examine empirically the actual implementation or non-implementation of policy aims and ascertain where the problems lie. In order to illustrate some of these issues this chapter focuses on two interlinked areas of critical concern with regard to sustainable development, first the relationship between metropolitan planning policy and spatial patterns of development and second, the relationship between the provision of affordable housing and land policy.

Unsustainability: Metropolitan Planning and Policy in Greater Dublin

In the past decade the pace, scale and location of development in the Greater Dublin Area (GDA) and beyond have created dispersed and complex patterns of land use with even more complex ramifications with respect to transportation and commuting (Williams and Shiels, 2000, 2002; MacLaran and Killen, 2002). For example, around the M50 motorway there has developed large-scale commercial, industrial and residential development, creating in effect an 'edge city' with its own issues and problems. As a consequence of the massive escalation of house prices and the attendant problem of access and affordability, a dispersed pattern of housing development has occurred not only in what is termed the hinterland of the GDA, but also well beyond into what have been termed the outer Leinster counties. Comparatively low levels of housing supply in the Dublin local authorities have resulted in residential development leapfrogging to towns and villages up to 90km around Dublin, resulting in what can only be described as unsustainable spatial development and commuting patterns (Williams *et al,* 2002). The economic costs, still less the social and environmental costs, of this *de facto laissez faire* approach to development have not been calculated.

Apart from the obvious costs with respect to commuting, there are clear costs associated with providing new transport and social infrastructure in the many towns and villages where new residential estates have mushroomed over the past decade. Ironically, these costs are being incurred at the same time as there has been significant population loss, and potential under-utilisation of services, in many of the mature areas of Dublin city. Research by Williams and Shiels (2002) on the Greater Dublin Area demonstrates the emergence of a *laissez faire* pattern of development, with little linkage to the regional planning policies or the transportation plans of the Dublin Transportation Office. In a related manner, with respect to the delivery of infrastructure, the experience of the past few years has been negative, with significant delays and cost overruns being common.

Metropolitan Planning and the Greater Dublin Area

The long-term success of any kind of regional or metropolitan planning framework is predicated on development patterns complying with the parameters of the spatial plan. However, the evidence summarised above begs serious questions as to the efficacy of regional planning policy as implemented. If a regional planning framework is to have any hope of success, then uncoordinated and unregulated development patterns cannot be allowed to pertain and persist. Dealing with the spatial planning frameworks for the Dublin region, and in particular for development at the edge of the city and beyond, spatial planning policy is relatively well developed at the regional and national scale. Core principles in these spatial plans include adherence to a hierarchy of settlement and development patterns with an emphasis on the need for the integration of land use and transportation.

With respect to the planning of the edge city, the Strategic Planning Guidelines for the Greater Dublin Area (SPGGDA) call for a policy of urban consolidation in the metropolitan area (extent of the built-up area) of Dublin, with development to be focused as far as possible on public transport routes. Outside of the metropolitan area, in what is termed the hinterland, development is to be focused on a series of primary and secondary development centres (Brady Shipman Martin *et al*, 1999). The National Spatial Strategy (NSS) essentially reiterates the policies outlined in the SPGGDA and calls for the consolidation of the Greater Dublin Region (Department of the Environment and Local Government, 2002). The revised Regional Planning Guidelines for the region, published in late 2004, also restate these broad points (Dublin Regional Authority, 2004b).

As shown in Table 15.1, the NSS sets out a series of tests which should in future be used in determining the location of housing in urban areas. While these tests are inevitably general, the emphasis is very much on sustainability, integration and the maximisation of existing urban land and associated services. The core question is whether development decisions will in fact be based on these criteria.

Table 15.1: Housing Location Tests for Urban Areas

Tests	Evaluation Considerations
The Asset Test	Are there existing community resources, such as schools etc. with spare capacity?
The Carrying Capacity Test	Is the environmental setting capable of absorbing development in terms of drainage etc?
The Transport Test	Is there potential for reinforcing usage of public transport, walking, cycling etc?
The Economic Development Test	Is there potential to ensure integration between the location of housing and employment?
The Character Test	Will the proposal reinforce a sense of place and character?
The Community Test	Will the proposal reinforce the integrity and vitality of the local community and services that can be provided?
The Integration Test	Will the proposal aid an integrated approach to catering for the housing needs of all sections of society?

Source: Department of the Environment and Local Government, 2002:103.

Table 15.2: Urban Consolidation Priorities

1	Identify opportunities for re-use	Through the development plan process, identify under-utilised or underdeveloped lands within town and villages
2	Realise options for re-use	Realise identified opportunities using, for example, the Derelict Sites Act and acquisition of key sites
3	Identify extension options	Where sufficient development opportunities within the urban area are not available, consider appropriate extension options to the village or town
4	Realise extension options	Follow up on options for extensions to the built up are using the location tests

Source: Department of the Environment and Local Government, 2002: 104.

Table 15.2, again taken from the NSS, emphasises the need to develop and consolidate existing urban areas before deciding to develop greenfield sites. This sequential approach to development, if actually implemented, would have profound consequences for the planning and development of Dublin, as it would in theory seek to locate most new development within the metropolitan area and within the primary and secondary development centres.

In practical terms, in order to achieve the consolidation of the GDA, one action that is specified in the NSS is the undertaking of 'a comprehensive and systematic audit of all vacant, derelict and underused land to establish its capacity to accommodate housing and other suitable uses. Such an audit should be focused in particular on areas in or close to public transport corridors and areas with under-utilised physical and social infrastructure' (Department of the Environment and Local Government, 2002: 42). While all local authorities have produced Housing Strategies as required under Part V of the Planning and Development Act, 2000, these strategies have only very general estimations of housing capacity. It seems that the NSS envisage something more akin to comprehensive urban capacity studies as produced in the UK. These capacity studies have yet to be undertaken and presumably are meant to be distinct from the general calculations of capacity in the Regional Planning Guidelines. Thus, while we can see that policy is fairly well developed, it is also obvious that spatial planning frameworks seem to be more often honoured in their breach than their compliance and development proposals continue to emerge which contravene the guidelines. In theory, local development plans and development control decisions are meant to 'have regard' to the strategic guidelines for Dublin. However, as Bannon makes clear in the previous chapter, as a result of a recent court case testing the guidelines, it seems that having regard to the guidelines can mean as little as being familiar with the front cover of the report, thus opening up the possibility, maybe even probability, that the guidelines can be breached with ease.

Perspectives on Planning Policy and Implementation in Greater Dublin

Research by Williams, Shiels and Hughes (2002), which interviewed many of the stakeholders involved in planning and development in the region, suggest that there was a recognition across all interests interviewed that traditional approaches to blueprint planning on a 'predict, zone and provide' basis were outdated and that integrated approaches were the only possible future option. This point is made forcibly in the new report on housing by the National Economic and Social Council (2004). The absence of co-ordination between various local authorities in the Greater Dublin Area was evident in the interviews. The inconsistent objectives of the housing strategies of each local authority reflect the absence of a regional framework within which the strategies could operate. The inconsistent implementation of development policies may result in the spatial distortion of development favouring local authority areas with the greatest quantity of serviced development land and which apply relatively less rigorous social and affordable housing criteria.

Local authority interests pointed out that delays were inherent in the planning system, often resulting from the actions of developer applicants. Local authorities are often dealing with normal applications, applications for extension of time and enhanced planning permission, all on the same land. They also pointed out that major delays in servicing rezoned lands can occur if such lands were rezoned against the advice of the professional within the local authority, due to the extent of engineering and other infrastructure involved (MacCabe, 2003). In addition, the nature of consultative processes now expected with local communities and local interests was often deliberative, systematic and relatively lengthy. Development interests found the planning process complex and unworkable. The adversarial nature of the system promotes an often-negative 'cat and mouse' approach within a complex legal negotiating framework. Such interests pointed to the multiple layers of the system, involving development zones, planning guidelines and strategies.

When a system has developed a large degree of complexity, the availability of planning staff with whom development interests can engage is critical. Both planning policy and development interests concurred on the lack of suitable experienced planning staff and the difficulties this presented in terms of achieving decisions within the planning process. Of particular concern to all development interests are time delays inherent within the system, particularly where appeals to An Bord Pleanála result. A broad consensus accepting the new higher densities in residential development was clear across all interests interviewed. Developers and local authority interests pointed out that issues beyond the control of the planning system often complicate development land acquisition. Such issues include title, problems and complexities, fragmented land-holdings and tenures, problems with adjacent owners and interests, fiscal incentives and financial issues. Views regarding the role of government intervention often diverged. A consensus existed that a core problem for the planning and development system was the previous lack of investment in infrastructure and services; such agreement regarding recent specific fiscal charges did not exist.

Supply-side initiatives that could calm the Dublin housing market have, by comparison with demand-side interventions, been lacking in urgency with regard to implementation. Proposals for transportation and utility infrastructure have now been discussed over a twenty-year period. The examples of proposals of increasing capacity on the existing transportation corridors and major enlargement of the urban rail system, without specific guaranteed funding commitments and target completion dates, bring planning policies into question. While the aspiration has now been adopted of dealing with urban development issues in an integrated manner, linking transportation, land use and associated services, the reality of actual development taking place has been that a fragmented approach has continued. By international standards, the Greater Dublin Area has a low level of population, an adequate land supply, a strong economy and adequate levels of public finance available. With good urban governance and management in place and a coordinated response, effective development solutions are possible. The political commitment to reforms and resource delivery has now become critical to the region's future development. However, if the proposal to create an integrated planning, land use and transportation body for the GDA is evidence of intentions, then the future looks bleak (Department of the Environment and Local Government, 2001). This proposal has effectively been abandoned by government, most probably in the face of opposition from local authorities and from other official organisations.

The significant amount of land in the existing urban area in various forms of public ownership represents the most obvious potential to solving the housing problem. Studies have shown that the planned release of a significant portion of such land onto the development market could play a significant role in first stabilising the Dublin market and then contributing to the supply response required. While this process has already commenced in Central Dublin, many of the same factors apply in areas of suburban Dublin, where a previous generation of low-density housing now has an ageing population profile, falling school numbers and infrastructure in place. Such districts are often in need of development in a general sense as they have been neglected and not well provided for in the past. In areas such as the North Fringe of Dublin City, the opportunities for improving peripheral disadvantaged areas through redevelopment are evidenced by projects such as the Ballymun Urban Regeneration Project. A reduced emphasis on outdated, single-use land zonings can allow development to occur in an integrated manner. The potential for increased population density with commercial redevelopment complementing a mix of housing types, while re-using disused or vandalised open space, is clear (Williams and Shiels, 2001).

If a serious response to the current housing shortage is intended, the densification and regeneration of the existing urban fabric provides a way forward, although it is likely to be subject to considerable opposition at local level. An approach based upon this option has the additional twin merits of utilising existing infrastructure and facilities and a capacity to be implemented over a shorter time period than continued expansion at green-field locations. An essential element to the success of such policies would be a new approach to urban planning and development based upon integrated policy objectives and an acceptance of the necessity for explicit community planning gain arrangements. This would involve additional resources or infrastructure necessitated by new development.

Unsustainable Development: Housing Provision and Land Policy

Affordability and Access to Housing

Developments in the housing system have been considerably uneven both geographically and socially, as expressed by, on the one hand, extraordinary 'booms' in the private housing market and concomitant gains to landowners and developers and, on the other hand, by problems of access to accommodation for less powerful social groups (Fahey, 2004; Fahey, Nolan and Maître, 2004a; Hickey *et al*, 2002; Drudy and Punch, 2002). In recent years direct output of social housing has lagged significantly behind social need, and there has been in general considerable under-development of this sector compared to earlier periods of significant public investment. This is now acknowledged by the National Economic and Social Council (2004) who recommend a major investment in social and affordable housing. At the same time, rapid economic growth, resulting in large-scale increases in employment, alongside significant increases in population and household formation, have resulted in a boom in the private housing market. The past decade of housing market growth has occurred in a highly conducive economic environment, where interest rates have been historically low, financial institutions have ratcheted up their mortgage lending in response and the Fianna Fáil-Progressive Democrat government has pursued policies of low income taxation and control of inflation. The combination of underlying demand for housing and the favourable economic and financial context has driven a sustained boom in the private market.

As is discussed in more depth in several other Chapters of this volume (specifically chapters 1, 2, 3, 4 and 8), nationally, total housing supply has trebled since the early 1990s, but more than 90 per cent of all new housing has been produced for the private market, with social housing accounting for on average 6 per cent of all new building (Department of the Environment, Heritage and Local Government, various years). Moreover, this sustained increase in supply has not resulted in market equilibrium, but rather in one of the most extraordinary rises in house prices seen not only in Ireland but also in Europe (Bacon and Associates, 1998, 1999, 2000). Nationally, second-hand house prices increased by 213 per cent between 1996 and 2004, but prices in Dublin rose much faster – by over 250 per cent in this period, resulting in average house prices in Dublin being over 30 per cent more expensive than in other urban areas (Department of the Environment, Heritage and Local Government, various years). These astronomical increases have had a profound impact on not only the private housing market, but also on the housing system more generally. As Downey discusses in Chapter 3, with incomes increasing at a more moderate pace over this period, the rises in house prices have led to affordability problems for aspiring house purchasers, and in particular aspirant first-time buyers. Norris and O'Sullivan reveal in Chapters 8 and 12 respectively, that over the same period, social housing need and homelessness have also increased dramatically. Thus, while housing supply has increased and house prices have risen, so too have social housing waiting lists.

Despite the evident social access difficulties, the problem has been mainly expressed, politically at any rate, as a problem of access to home ownership. Consequently, the government has initiated a host of policies aimed in some form at ameliorating the problem of affordability. In broad terms, the central thrust of policy has been to assist in increasing supply, with the hope that prices would either stabilise or reduce as demand was met. However, in contrast to the theoretical postulates of neo-classical economics, rising supply has in fact been met with even sharper rises in prices. In addition to policies to increase supply, a number of specific schemes have been aimed at the first-time buyer. Three affordable housing schemes have been instigated since 1999, where central government subsidise the land cost element of house prices, this being in effect state-subsidised private housing. To date, these schemes have had only a limited impact.

However, the subsidisation of the land cost element points to one of the more dramatic and profound consequences of the boom. Some sources have estimated that land cost has increased from 20 per cent to almost 50 per cent of the average house price between 1995 and 2003 (Central Bank of Ireland, 2003). This exorbitant increase in land costs has clearly benefited landowners and developers but has had mainly deleterious effects on house purchasers and those in housing need, to the point where central government instituted a constitutional review of potential ways in which land costs might be controlled by the state.

Responding to Affordability Problems: Part V of the Planning and Development Act, 2000

However, one effort to influence land costs has already been attempted in recent planning legislation. In 2000 the government introduced what has turned out to be a controversial and complex piece of planning legislation, seeking to impose on private sector developers an obligation to subsidise social and affordable housing on sites they wish to develop (Department of the Environment and Local Government, 2000b). As Bannon discusses in Chapter 14, developers are now required, as a condition of planning permission, to transfer up to 20 per cent of their sites for use as social and/or affordable housing and, crucially, to transfer the site to the state at what is termed use value, which is a fraction of the market value. The rationale for this legislation is twofold. First, it was aimed at allowing local authorities to access development land cheaply, thereby enabling them to build social and/or affordable housing at below market cost. Local authorities and other social housing providers have had serious problems accessing land in urban areas, especially in competition with private developers. While developers have the option to pay the local authority the financial equivalent of the land cost, many local authorities, especially in urban areas, are seeking to obtain completed and subsidised dwellings from developers. This is entirely understandable as in recent years direct output of social housing has lagged significantly behind social need, and there has been in general considerable under-development of this sector compared to earlier periods of significant public investment. The new planning legislation has another more social aim, in that by seeking to have social housing built alongside or integrated with private market housing, levels of what were termed 'undue segregation' would be diminished and social mix and social interaction would be encouraged.

From a political viewpoint, the passing of this legislation throws up some interesting lessons in the politics of decision-making in housing and suggests a gulf in power and influence between different social groups. Given the history of market dominance in housing provision in Ireland, and the extraordinary spatial segregation of housing tenure in Ireland, this legislation represented a potentially radical intervention as it opened up the possibility of the creation of long-term imaginative solutions to integrated housing schemes. However, the legislation was subject to all manner of criticism and after persistent lobbying and pressure by property and development interests, the government amended it in December of 2002 (Tribal HCH, 2004). The change allowed developers to offer the local authority land elsewhere (off site) or the financial equivalent of the value of the land transfer, options not available in the original legislation. It seems likely that most developers will seek to exercise these options whenever possible, thereby reducing the potential of the legislation to produce integrated housing. Importantly, this provision survived a constitutional challenge on the grounds that it was in the interest of the common good, an important and encouraging judgement. However, the other lesson was that it was attacked through a very successfully lobby. It is clear from this experience that, in doing anything about land, there will be a considerable political battle, and there will be a lot of resistance to change. It may also be difficult to popularise the idea of the common good.

Nonetheless, the debate on the effectiveness of Part V is in its early stages and, as the work of Williams and Shiels (2002) shows, the complexities involved in the successful implementation of Part V provisions in particular are becoming evident. Applying Part V to every individual site can be difficult for both the local authority and the developer. Complying with legislation on a large green-field development site is easier to achieve than, for example, within a small development in an existing residential area. The engagement of developers and local authorities in individual negotiations on each single site can be viewed as an innovative process to fulfil the needs of proper housing provision or as an additional, complex bureaucratic hurdle presenting further difficulties and delays. Essentially development interests believe that planners are not aware of the difficulty of the market process while some local authority interests find developers unwilling to consider the social and economic context of their individual developments. Critics of Part V deem it unworkable because of problems relating to clarity, consistency and equity in the submission and determination of planning applications. Others, in defence of the process, recognise deficiencies in the legislation and the need for improvement and flexibility but point to the need for any clear alternative to avoid under-provision of affordable housing and social segregation. The early operation of the scheme has witnessed different decision-making processes being employed by various local authorities with the potential for dispute and legal challenge evident within the negotiations process. Development interests in particular pointed to the following difficulties:

- Uncertainty in decision making, delays and disputes
- Greater involvement of An Bord Pleanála
- Confusion as to valuation of land and compensation procedures
- Difficulties of future management of social housing
- Administration and resource capabilities
- Adverse impact on the potential for sustainable in-fill development
- Specific site difficulties not being recognised

Despite opposition, there is an expectation by policy interests that developers will eventually absorb the measures and supply the required housing as they can do so very profitably, particularly in the light of the availability of increased densities. Various local authorities have differed in their approaches to achieving the required social and affordable housing component in a new residential development, with some authorities seeking an equal split between social and affordable, while others lean towards more affordable than social. Integration is also viewed differently by the various local authorities whether fully on site, between sites or, in one example, on a site divided by a road with the social and affordable housing effectively divided from the main development. Such differing views on integration, whether narrowly or more widely defined, are mirrored in other aspects of negotiations such as whether the percentage applied to floor-space or units within the development and a variety of agreement models are being negotiated at present. Such flexibility is viewed favourably by local authority interests, as it enables them to negotiate in regard to varying local housing needs across their areas. Such complex individual negotiations are difficult for many developers to deal with as they are often willing to deal with known or measured risks, but not unclear policy requirements which are difficult to assess and make the development appraisal and financing process more complex and difficult.

Housing associations are exempt bodies from the legislation as their purpose is already to provide social and affordable housing. These bodies are often approached by developers to undertake the social component of some housing schemes or, alternatively, they also act as agents for some local authorities to develop and manage social housing schemes. The management focus of such associations makes them more acceptable to developers than to the local authority whose commitments are less specific. The widespread perception of the absence of long-term management of local authority estates has created the fear of problems of integration by the private market and this perception may only gradually change with improved social housing management systems and community development initiatives. For management purposes, the social and affordable housing units may often be located in one independent block as the difficulties of alternatives such as the full integration of social housing throughout the development are significant. Norris (2004) points to some of the complexities involved in the development and management of such mixed-tenure developments.

The Political Economy of Land

The experience of Part V to date shows that the land issue is both a complex and controversial one. This led to the formation, by the Taoiseach, of an All-Party Committee to examine the need for constitutional change with respect to property rights. The remit of the committee covered the following issues: the right to private property; private property and the common good; compulsory purchase; the zoning of land; the price of development land; the right to shelter; infrastructural development; house prices and access to the countryside. The remit of the Committee was to ascertain whether there is a need to change the provisions in the Constitution which pertain to property rights. There are crucial issues at stake here with regard to social equity and housing provision, the implementation of spatial plans and the efficient and economic delivery of infrastructure. As part of the deliberations of the Committee, views were sought from property and development interests, groups concerned with the delivery of infrastructure and those concerned with issues of social justice and equality. Prior to analysing some of the key conclusions of the Committee we examine some of the core views of these differing interests.

Development and Property Perspectives

Not surprisingly, many of the groups representing development and property interests extol the contribution made by the private sector to the provision of infrastructure and to the provision of housing over the past decade. They argue that the private sector has delivered and that there is no need for fundamental reform of the constitution or for further government intervention in the land market. The arguments of the property interests centre on the barriers imposed by the planning system with regard to supposedly inadequate zoning of residential lands, delays in servicing such zoned lands and delays in obtaining permissions. There is clearly some merit in the argument that the private sector has delivered with regard to the provision of private housing. However, this is a rather limited argument. There clearly still remain severe problems of affordability for aspiring house purchasers and severe problems of access to decent quality housing for those who cannot afford to purchase.

Moreover, as the National Economic and Social Council (2004) point out, between 1991 and 2002, 405,00 new dwellings were built but only 259,000 new households formed, implying that 146,000 dwellings did not lead to the creation of a new permanent household. Thus, the private market system has been good at producing dwellings but not necessarily for the right households, producing many second homes but few for those on lower incomes. Some of the property groups, such as the Irish Auctioneers and Valuers Institute, are prepared to admit that the costs of infrastructure provision by the state might be recouped by increased development levies or charges. However, along with groups such as the Irish Home Builders Association, they are very much against any implementation of proposals such as those contained in the Kenny report of 1973 (Kenny, 1973).

The main proposal in the report was that the state could purchase designated land at use value plus 25 per cent compensation to the landowner. The opposition to this, which is stated quite trenchantly, argues that the state should only purchase land at open market value whether for housing or for infrastructure projects. Undoubtedly there are complex issues at work here. However, to imply that the market in land is operating in some effective and efficient manner clearly contradicts the empirical evidence. The planning system may indeed have an impact here, but so also has the pattern of land ownership.

Infrastructure Delivery Perspectives

With regard to infrastructure delivery, the National Roads Authority and the Rail Procurement Agency, in their submission to the All-Party Committee, estimate that the cost of land acquisition in 2002 for national roads was €150 million and that such costs represent between 12 per cent and 50 per cent of individual road projects. The cost of lands for Luas between the city centre and Tallaght and Sandyford will be €100m approximately (Government of Ireland, 2004). Apart from what are seen as the excessive costs of land acquisition, many of the planning and compulsory purchase procedures are seen as leading to inordinate delays in the delivery of projects. A number of organisations who either directly deliver infrastructure projects or are indirectly involved, such as the Dublin Transportation Office, the Rail Procurement Agency, Forfás and Enterprise Ireland, made submissions to the committee. In short, they argue that compensation should be at less than open market value, that the sections of the constitution on property rights be specifically strengthened by making reference to the need to deliver vital infrastructure as part of the common good and that the regulatory system be streamlined in radical ways. The Dublin Transportation Office, for example, argues that the judgment of the Supreme Court with respect to Part V of the Planning and Development Act, 2000, which concluded that Part V was allowable in the common good, be translated explicitly into the constitution. With regard to planning, they argue as follows:

> The implementation of sustainable planning strategies seeks to enhance the socio-economic well being of the population at large. Such goals and objectives are of sufficient importance to warrant specific acknowledgement in the text of the Constitution in order to allay concerns that are regarded as pressing and substantial.
>
> (Government of Ireland, 2004: A52)

More specifically, they argue that:

> ... in the preparation of development plans it is necessary to 'have regard' to the strategic planning guidelines. Recent case law has demonstrated that the term 'have regard' in this context sets an extremely low compliance threshold and effectively allows a development plan which pays scant attention to the overarching principles contained in the Strategic Planning Guidelines to be legitimately adopted.
>
> (Government of Ireland, 2004: A53)

Many submissions from these groups call for one-stop shops for the assessment of major infrastructural projects, that assessment timeframes be mandatory and that judicial challenges be dealt with expeditiously. While there is much here that property groups would agree with, there is a fundamental conflict over the attitude to the acquisition of land, and philosophical and ideological disagreements centre on this controversial issue.

Social Equality Perspectives

What is termed the social equality perspective comprises views from a diverse range of groups such as the Irish Council for Social Housing, Threshold, Simon Communities of Ireland as well as Feasta (Foundation for the Economics of Sustainability). Many of the social housing groups in particular argue explicitly for a rights-based approach to housing and for the insertion into the constitution of a right to decent and affordable housing for all citizens. The argument by social equality groups is that access to decent-quality, affordable housing should in its essence be a human right. However, in general terms such rights-based approaches are opposed by those on the right of the political spectrum who see the potential proliferation of appeals and campaigns for a right to all manner of service and commodity. Here there is a conflict between those who view housing as a human need and use value and those who emphasise the market nature and exchange value of housing as a commodity. Apart from these opposing views, however, a number of interesting submissions are made. The Irish Planning Institute, for instance, propose the separation of property ownership rights from property development rights, with the development of a potential market in development rights or development permits, as in some US states. This idea clearly has some merit and deserves detailed attention, although it is not elaborated on in the submission. Feasta has a relatively detailed proposal which suggests the introduction of an annual site tax as part of a broader reform of income taxation. A number of organisations argue for the introduction of the Kenny report proposals whereby the state could compulsorily purchase land at use value plus compensation of 25 per cent to the landowner. What all these positions agree on, however, is that there is a need to institute some radical measures to control the price of land. There are mixed views on whether the constitution needs to be amended in order to allow radical intervention.

Analysing Land Values

The report of the Constitutional review committee deals with many aspects of property. However, the analysis presented here focuses in particular on how the issue of land prices is conceptualised. The analysis takes the fairly standard view that the market price of housing is a function of the interaction of supply and demand. In that equation market prices are ultimately determined by the overall level of demand and, crucially, that inputs into the process such as land costs and construction costs are not key determinants of the market value of housing. In simple terms, the argument is that the market value of housing is at the level at which the market will bear, something of a tautology it must be added. The report argues that 'In the housing market builders are price takers and will sell their product at a price determined by the market and not by the value of land and the cost of construction' (Government of Ireland, 2004: 77). The full implications of this are then drawn out as follows:

> When analysing problems in housing markets or in other property markets, urban economic theory points to two important principles. First, the price of landed property, including housing, is not determined by the cost of production. Second, the value of

development land is the result of high property prices, not the cause. These are important insights, which allow a better understanding of the problems of urban development ... It follows from the above that, far from pushing up the price of houses, the price of development land is pulled up by high house prices: the price of the land is a result, not a cause.

(Government of Ireland, 2004: 78-79)

One of the implications of this is that even in a situation where the land cost is minimal the developer will still sell the property at the price the market will bear. This clearly happens on a regular basis, for developers will be using land which has been bought many years previously or will use land which they bought at agricultural value only for it to be rezoned in time. Unlike other markets, the developer will not attempt to compete with other developers by taking advantage of the lower cost of their land, but will sell at current market prices. This is in keeping with the residual view of land prices outlined by the Committee and by Dunne (2003). However, while conforming to the concept, it shows that the housing market is unlike other markets and that the laws of competition do not seem to work as in other sectors.

Consequently, the report is heavily critical of what it terms the 'building-block' approach to house prices. It states that 'The popular perception is that the price of a house is determined by adding the cost of construction to the cost of the site. This is based on what may be called a building-block approach to price determination. It sees the price of houses being driven by the price of land and the costs associated with labour, materials and levies imposed by local authorities' (Government of Ireland, 2004: 79). However, we argue that this dismissal is incorrect. While there may be some degree of truth in the derived or residual approach, it is not the full story. If we take the building-block approach and alter the argument somewhat we get a different picture. Where there exists some form of control not only on the costs of land but also on the selling cost of housing then it is possible to produce houses much cheaper. The evidence already exists in the form of the affordable housing schemes. Here, the land cost is controlled as is the selling prices of the house, thus enabling local authorities to develop houses at an affordable price. The competition here is between different building contractors to deliver the houses to the local authority via a competitive tender. The remarkable thing about this model is that it clearly works but yet only operates at a small scale. If this model were to operate at a bigger scale then it would have major implications for the land market and for the housing market more generally.

The National Economic and Social Council (2004) also examine the issue of land and take a fairly similar conceptual position regarding the relationship between house prices and land prices. However, to their credit, and using some of the work of Evans (2004a and 2004b), they argue that the supply of land for development is not a simple process but is complicated by the behaviour of landowners and by the planning and public investment system which allows land to be used for housing development. Their general argument for improvement in the supply of land revolves around developing a more comprehensive and sophisticated land management system and it is difficult to disagree on this point. More generally, the point that Dunne (2003) makes about the absence of detailed information and research on property markets can be amplified by pointing out that in all the discussion about land there are scarcely any data available on land transactions in Ireland and further, that there are hardly any available data on the economics of housing development. Thus, whatever conceptual position is taken, it is being argued in an information vacuum, one that needs to be urgently redressed.

It is worth pointing out that the debate about house prices and land has adduced some rather curious positions from economists and market analysts. In general, competition, lower prices and efficiency are lauded when it comes to most industries and services. Government policy will, in many cases, seek to enhance competitiveness. However, when it comes to house prices and the housing market, it seems that astronomic increases in house prices are not necessarily all that bad. It seems that many market commentators seek to make the housing market an exceptional case where the rigours of competition should not apply. The consumer, in this case, is not king. There is a standard economic argument for intervention on the grounds of market failure. Many mainstream economists will agree that there is a problem with land even within the context of the market paradigm (Dunne, 2003). The trouble is that land is a peculiar commodity – every parcel of land is unique. Producers cannot, in response to the demand signals in the market, increase the output or generate more parcels of land, unlike the market for DVDs, where producers will compete and innovate in order to meet demand and capture a greater market share (often by reducing prices). In other words, the land 'market' is highly inefficient. Many of the features of a functioning market system – competition, free entry, the mechanisms of supply and demand, equilibrium – are arguably absent from the land market.

Moreover, because every site is unique, there is an immediate problem of monopoly. Under private ownership a monopoly element is introduced within the market situation. And that private ownership can give an individual an enormous amount of economic power in certain circumstances. For instance where the land is rezoned for development, reflecting the community's willingness to accept the negativities of development, or where services are supplied publicly, there is an immediate private windfall gain for the owner, as its value escalates almost overnight. This possibility for windfall gain creates a hope value, and this creates, in turn, considerable speculative interest, in that people will gamble that, at some future time, land will be rezoned or may be serviced and when this happens you have a situation where non-productive speculative activity is rewarded and sometimes spectacularly rewarded. Although the recent report by Goodbody Economic Consultants (2003) claims that there is little evidence of land hoarding and control of the land market in Dublin, the report suffers from the difficulty of obtaining decent evidence on patterns of land ownership and land transactions.

A further important consideration is whether changing development land policies can in turn help to facilitate other types of changes in the housing system such as, for instance, increased non-profit housing systems, which would be a means of increasing housing choice. In a way, many of the people arguing against interfering in the market are, ironically, arguing for monopoly and against free choice and competition. One way of increasing housing options and competition is by facilitating a broader non-profit sector that produces rental and other housing not just for the most marginalised but for the general needs of the population. This is a routing that might help to ameliorate the urban housing crisis, unsustainable commuting patterns, segregation and stigmatisation, as well as making the non-profit sector generally more viable (through the mechanisms of general-needs provision and rent pooling). Dealing with the blockages and limits of the land market as it is currently configured would be a vital first step to making these aims feasible.

Considerations and Conclusions

This brings us back to some of the points made in the introduction. The development of policy formulation in planning and housing has improved strongly over recent years and we are moving towards a plan-led system. There are now a raft of various plans, from national to local, available on many aspects of the planning and development process, and although they are not necessarily integrated to the best possible level, they are a substantial improvement on the situation that pertained a decade ago. However, it is also evident that these policies are unlikely to be delivered on, due to the paucity of available policy instruments. With regard to spatial planning, for example, it is abundantly clear that in the absence of a strong regulatory framework which insists on planning decisions cohering with policy, it will be easy to breach most spatial planning policies. Reliance on general exhortations and aspirations has proven to be of limited value in the face of massive development pressure and political influence. It is also evident that there is a general paucity of policy instruments other than the fairly weak regulatory ones. The NESC (2004) report points to an underdeveloped system of land and infrastructure management.

With regard to implementation, the politics of these debates are also important as ultimately the question is whether Government will agree with some of the various diagnoses and then take remedial policy action. For example, although the All-Party Committee on property was instituted by the Taoiseach, there were dissenting views within government. In what might be termed a pre-emptive strike, Mr Tom Parlon, a Minister for State and member of the Progressive Democrats, made a startling intervention in the debate, claiming that proposals for interventions in private property and in the land market were emanating from political positions to the left of Stalin. Forfás and Enterprise Ireland may have been surprised to learn that their stance on compulsory purchase is a Stalinist one. Leaving aside this rather fanciful claim by the Minister, it is worth reminding ourselves that although the common good may be difficult to define with precision, the current system with regard to the provision of housing and infrastructure very often benefits the few rather than the many. Both the Constitutional review committee on property and the National Economic and Social Council make recommendations on land, with the former specifically endorsing the introduction of a Kenny-type betterment system for land acquisition. Whether these recommendations will come to anything over the coming years is difficult to tell. What we can say, however, from historical experience, is that without a robust planning framework that can be actually implemented, and without change in land policy, spatial planning aims and social aims on housing are going to be difficult to achieve.

16

Urban Design and Residential Environments

Derry O'Connell

Introduction

Circumstances are right for positive development in housing design. Internationally and nationally, the core aim of planning policies is to achieve sustainable development. While this is sometimes seen as a fairly loose and vague concept, with respect to planning it is clear that at the very least it means that planners should attempt to use land efficiently and create places which are liveable. In Ireland, through the national policy on Sustainable Development and the National Spatial Strategy, planning policy seeks to achieve environmental sustainability and to produce a spatial settlement pattern which is likewise sustainable (Government of Ireland, 1997b; Department of the Environment and Local Government, 2002). In terms of urban and regional planning, for example, one of the key aims is to generate a more compact urban form, which in turn means building housing at higher densities than we have done historically. This turnabout in policy presents many challenges to planners, developers and consumers alike, both at the macro level of city planning but also at the micro level of urban design. This chapter reviews and assesses the changes in the design of residential areas arising from these policy changes.

Increasing Residential Density

The need for higher residential densities has now been clearly outlined in Government policy (Department of the Environment and Local Government, 1998b, 1999d). While this will facilitate more sustainable urban infrastructure and support higher populations, it will also favour the design of quality environments. It is easier to create good urban place at higher densities (Carmona, 2001; Gehl, 1996). With a greater quantity of building mass it is easier to enclose external space with buildings, and also easier to sub-divide space using buildings. With more covered floor space per area of land, buildings can be taller and therefore more easily address space. In the twenty years up to 1998 most urban expansion in Ireland yielded densities of six to ten houses per acre (Bacon and Associates, 1998). As an increase on this, many local authorities are now prescribing thirteen units per acre, with much higher in areas like Dublin. Such densities are, however, still well below those sought elsewhere in urban Europe. A recent study in the UK recommended that densities there should be increased from the current average of twenty to twenty-five dwellings per hectare to thirty-five to forty dwellings per hectare in order to secure basic levels of infrastructural sustainability (Llewelyn-Davies, 1998, 2000). Indeed, many of the most sought-after quarters of European cities have densities of 100-200 dwellings per hectare – density levels that current development controls would not permit (Urban Task Force, 1999). Measurement of density by number of units per area of ground can, however, be an imprecise measurement of urban form. In urban design terms it is more appropriate for proposed density to be decided case by case by an assessment of surrounding circumstances (United Kingdom, Department of the Environment, Transport and the Regions and Commission for Architecture and the Built Environment, 2000). Many UK local authorities are now either prescribing minimum density levels or abandoning prescribed density control altogether (United Kingdom, Department of the Environment, Transport and the Regions, 1998b).

It is important to dispel the misplaced association between high-density and high-rise. Schemes that contain tower blocks in an open setting, such as did Ballymun in Dublin or Rahoon in Galway, actually represent quite a low density when one calculates the open space between the blocks in addition to the enclosed floor space. Areas such as Portobello in Dublin or Shandon in Cork would contain a much higher density with streets of two and three-storey houses. Densities here are of 30 units per acre (McCabe et al, 1999). One has to concede, however, that at any building height, high density with poor design has produced poor living environments. In low-density housing, privacy can be achieved by distance between dwellings but when density increases, households are brought closer together and the position of each relative to others demands more careful assembly. The creation of good high-density neighbourhoods requires sensitive design, in which space is maximised and the influence and orientation of each element of a house, internal and external, is calculated to protect privacy and security while at the same time developing domestic amenity.

Design Innovation

New demands have emerged which encourage better residential environments. Household types have expanded in range, calling for a corresponding diversity in housing form. In social housing, the expanded variety of tenure types further facilitates greater household mix. These developments bring an exciting challenge to the designer as the range and variety of design options becomes broader. With the ratification in 1998 of government policy encouraging higher densities, the planner and the developer now have conforming objectives, albeit for different reasons, the planner seeking a more intense urbanism, the developer seeking more units per area of investment, both together supporting a more attractive and sustainable urban environment (Department of the Environment and Local Government, 1999d). All of this should facilitate better housing design, with house types tailored to household needs in a better spatial environment. Yet, although dwellers and providers are becoming increasingly aware of the difference between good design and bad, still only a small proportion of housing in Ireland is professionally designed (Reddy, 2002). With so much national investment in residential construction, this must represent an enormous loss of opportunity.

Up to 1990, experiment and innovation in housing design had largely been associated with social and local authority housing. In private housing, developers had been more reluctant to deviate from the certainty of established styles. Either as the reason for this or as the result of it, private housing design has been largely carried out without architects (Ó Cofaigh, 1998), while public agencies have generally employed qualified designers, for reasons associated with legal liability. Although public housing has generally been of a higher construction specification than speculative private housing, new ideas both succeed and fail, and when they fail in public housing, their failure tends to take a high public profile. Invariably, although the failure may have social origins, it tends to be associated with the failed physical environment (Norris, 1999). Design innovation can often therefore be dismissed at a stage that might have been relatively early in its process of development. High-rise dwellings have, for example, suffered in this regard, although high-rise residence has, by the year 2004, been home to over two generations of some Irish households. High-rise has been essentially dismissed for public sector family residence, though showing positive advance in sectors of private housing.

Although in family housing the private market is still largely reluctant to accept innovation in design, this is changing slowly. The sceptics argue that the growing use of qualified designers by developers is merely due to the fact that, with recent legislation, it requires qualified professionals to confront planning and building regulations. More optimistically, however, there is evidence of a growing realisation by developers of the marketability of good design. Promotional material now frequently quotes the term 'architect designed', indicating an expectation of buyer response. Perhaps still the private buyer seeking a safe investment will generally reject innovative design. He or she seeks a secure once-in-a-lifetime place of living that will be commonly recognisable as attractive, facilitating a lifestyle that will be similarly recognisable, albeit with a growing requirement to express wealth and taste (Treacy, 2002). As a result, the developer is reluctant to depart too far too quickly from design that is traditional and understandable. Many local authorities have, since 1991, attempted to provide social housing that is perceived to be similar in appearance to private housing, reducing the image of social provision and also perhaps increasing the reality of the sell-on option (Department of the Environment, 1991). Other social housing organisations have also attempted to create house types that are similar in form to those in the private market. This has led to a continued use of common semi-detached houses where more innovative design might have developed alternative forms.

While change in the design of private family residence may be slow and cautious, however, innovation is evident in the design of new dwelling types, such as the urban apartment. Perhaps this is because buyers here are often single, young urban people who represent probably the most adventurous category in the appreciation of good modern design. As new forms are accepted by the market, a greater security develops for the risk-takers, and as a result, the climate of innovation expands. The first purpose-built apartments in smaller urban centres only appeared with the tax incentives of 1986, so outside the major cities the purpose-built apartment is quite new (National Building Agency, 1989). The development of its form, however, has been quite successful in remaking the fabric of the Irish town and city. Although apartment blocks have in some instances followed traditional building forms, the apartment is a new element, and there is therefore less limitation in the expectation of traditional forms by the user. For this reason, good modern residential environments are developing particularly well in the field of apartment design.

New Urban Forms and the City

The dominance of the suburb by either two-storey or semi-detached building form may well be changing (Rudlin and Falk, 1998). The emergence of multi-storey residential buildings in outer suburbs, facilitated by the mix of various smaller household units, signals a new urban architecture that is unlike anything previously common in Ireland. Significantly, much of this has been created by private developers. Many recent masterplans, such as those for Pelletstown and Adamstown in Dublin or the Dublin North Fringe Action Plan, propose nodes of higher density, calling for appropriately denser building form (South Dublin County Council, 2003). They suggest identifiable statements of place collecting many housing units into single incidents of form such as terraced crescents, formal planted boulevards, squares and streets of differing character and dedicated areas of large-scale passive landscape. This reflects the concept of strong legible places in the manner of Merrion Square, Dublin or as the traditional central spaces of Irish towns.

Although many new schemes will include in their mix a quantity of two-storey dwellings with gardens, in response to market demand, the potential monotony of these will be broken by the use of much taller buildings, particularly to define the corners, edges and foci of significant spaces. Indeed much of the sense of place achieved in the non-adventurous public housing developments of the immediate post-war period in Ireland has resurfaced in the principles underlying the layout of these new suburbs. Applewood village in Swords, a recent development, creates symmetrically balanced formal spaces, using a building form that is generally three-storey, all in an outer suburb. Although therefore streets may be broad to facilitate regulated circulation, the taller building height attempts to provide an enclosing relationship that is appropriate. Such places may use repetitive elements as does a terrace or crescent of identical houses, but the regularity is of distinct relationships and is not reproduced in a featureless system as in the suburbs of the 1970s.

The Family Dwelling in the City

The challenge to the designer, however, of relating the family dwelling to a more intense urban environment cannot be underestimated. In the inner cities the task of creating tall, urban-scale building mass with family dwelling houses alone has preoccupied housing design throughout the 1980s and 1990s. The Irish family likes to control its property from ground to sky and generally likes its privacy to be achieved by a front and back garden as zones of separation from others. The small housing schemes that rebuilt much of the fabric of Dublin in the 1970s were all of relatively low density. Some included three-bedroomed houses with front and back gardens within 300m of O'Connell Street.

When some urban environments require at least three storeys to define and address strong outdoor spaces in residential areas, designers have found it difficult to spread the floor area of an average 3-bedroomed house over more than two floors without having to allocate a disproportionate area to stairs. A vertically stretched house on three floors develops quite a small footprint so that the living floor, on whichever level it occurs, has difficulty accommodating together all of its supporting spaces such as for sitting, dining and kitchen. The natural subdivisions of household activities such as living, sleeping and others do not distribute themselves easily over three equal subdivisions of the total house area. Three-storey houses with this small footprint or tall, thin characteristic are typified in some infill schemes in Dublin from the early 1980s, such as at Dorset Street or Hollyfield, Rathmines. A response to this condition was to introduce a further single-aspect dwelling on the same footprint by placing, for example, a single-bedroomed senior citizens dwelling on the ground floor, with a two-floor or duplex dwelling above, the upper dwelling accessible by steps from the street. A typical scheme illustrating this response is the City Quay housing in Dublin from the late 1980s.

From these beginnings, considerable progress has been made. With the now broader range of different household types from family residence to single apartments, far greater flexibility is available to the designer in the development of urban typologies. Taller urban form is now easily possible, with significant development of multiple own-door access on single frontages, relating to single external spaces. In public housing, Dublin City Council have developed family dwellings to four floors in two-floor over two-floor schemes at Bride Street and North King Street, with external access from the street to the upper units. This creates intense urban incident between dwelling and street, at a density of 60 dwellings per acre. Variations on this concept have also been developed particularly well in the regeneration of Ballymun. In a four-storey block at Cherry Orchard in Dublin, residential layering has been brought to an advanced level, providing family units in two-floor over two-floor stacking, but in combination with apartments and smaller units at corners and more constricted positions. This develops a block load which borrows certain qualities from the deck access model of the 1960s, but with separate units having own door access from ground level in close proximity to each other. This, part of a scheme that achieves 38 dwellings per hectare, represents an advanced stage of multiple-level dwelling in Ireland.

The Urban Block

The use of high residential buildings around the perimeter of the urban block to enclose and define private spaces within the block core could be identified as a particularly dominant progression in the typologies of urban residence since 1990. Passive space in the form of semi-private internal courtyards has developed at both ground level and internal deck or roof levels. There has been some criticism of this typology, suggesting that the perimeter block scheme tends to become an urban fortress with little opening connections between enclosed centre-block spaces and the spaces of the street or the city. In such edge blocks, the relationship between household and city or between the house and the surrounding external environment is much richer if the residence can relate to both the block interior and the street. Early private apartment schemes had used the principle of a spinal corridor giving access to single aspect apartments to courtyard or to street, with a minimal number of staircases. The tendency in more recent developments is to use more vertical access positions serving fewer apartments per stair but allowing the apartments to be dual aspect. The diseconomy of having more vertical circulation positions reaches a point where it may be balanced against the higher return on apartments of greater amenity in a stronger market. Recent developments include a greater use of double height internal and semi-internal spaces in both living and circulation, as at Clarion Quay in Dublin. Apartments here are no longer separated by standard floordecks. Instead the concept of double-height space is explored, as is the amenity of larger floor areas.

Living-Retail Mix

The idea of creating living-retail combinations in urban blocks has been developed quite successfully in many locations since 1988. This is a worthy return to the concept of urban diversity. Because land use policies had tended until recently to segregate housing from other activities, the traditional mix of uses common in urban Ireland as elsewhere had been extinguished. There is nothing modern about such segregation, as outlined by the EU green paper on the urban environment (European Union, 1990), and modern architecture in towns and cities can be much more intense if it houses a range of uses together in urban form. While the living-over-the-shop scheme in existing urban fabric enjoyed very moderate success with some exceptions, a number of urban reconstruction schemes have, since 1988, facilitated interesting typologies in the residential-retail mix. The concept of perimeter housing at upper level around the edge of an urban block, above a retail ground floor, with dwellings having own-door access from the block interior at an upper level, has become popular as a block typology. This has been developed with success in Galway and Sligo with a particularly well-developed example at Wolfe Tone Close in Jervis Street, Dublin which achieves a density of 80 dwellings per acre, addressing a central courtyard over a totally retail ground floor. This typology, which has been popular in the UK and Scandinavia, has now enjoyed success in both private and public housing schemes in Ireland.

Densification of the Suburbs

While it makes good planning sense to create a more dense urban fabric in the future, it may be that in Ireland, with falling birth rates, most of our suburbs are already built. We may no longer have the momentum to extend our cities significantly beyond their present size, nor would we want to, even at higher densities. Instead, in order to support a better infrastructure, it is the view of some local authorities that the density of existing suburbs requires strengthening (Brennan, 2002). The process of increasing density in existing low-density environments however is a delicate one. Inappropriate densification has destroyed suburbs in some cities and many bad examples can be seen in some of the older suburbs of Irish cities, with back and side gardens being used for new housing (Llewelyn-Davies, 1998; Llewelyn-Davies and the Bartlett School of Planning, 2000). In Ireland we do have some successful low-density suburbs, which at this stage have an established heritage. Upsetting this heritage in order to make it more accessible to public transport may not represent progress. One proposed solution is to build specific suburban segments to much higher densities in order to strengthen the population base, whilst controlling the established environment of the surrounding suburb where dwellers remain as they are (Brennan, 2002). In this concept the density of one suburban section compensates for another. As building fabric reproduces itself over time of course densities can increase, with appropriate development control.

Because the average number of persons in a household is now falling from 3.4 towards the European average of two, the family-based three-bedroomed house with front and rear garden can no longer be the standard building unit of residential areas (Conroy, 1997). In the 1970s the systematic reproduction of economic family housing units did make sense against which it was difficult to argue other than on environmental and planning grounds, arguments which were respected by neither local authorities nor developers at the time. Such systems reproduced suburbs that were repetitive and dull because they were without incident, such as one finds in the variety of more slowly assembled places. There were no reference points or hierarchical spaces to support urban legibility or sense of place. These suburbs were dominated by the semi-detached house.

Although there may be certain opportunities with the two-storey, semi-detached house for creating space and place for the needs of a three-bedroomed household, these are limited. Plan forms may be varied slightly, with further variety in the position of outdoor elements such as garage, fuel store and screen walls to develop focused spaces of some quality, but at the scale of the broader environment the two-storey semi-detached house offers little opportunity for spatial definition. It has an open space requirement on three sides, encouraging it to be used in a single standard relationship with its neighbours, which does not facilitate spatial definition or enclosure. Attempts to marshal groups of semi-detached houses in order to define quality streets or places can be a hopelessly frustrating experience for the architect. When one adds expansive road layout standards to this, the resulting environment leaves little opportunity to create public spaces with any sense of enclosure or definition. In the traditional urban spaces of Irish towns and cities as elsewhere in Europe, the enclosure ratio between space width and building height is seldom greater than 2 to 1 (Moughton, 1992). Yet the closest ratio achievable with two-storey buildings under the roads standards of most local authorities in Ireland has up to recently been 4:1, the more typical ratio being 9:1.

In the lower density environment of the suburb, there have been a number of changes in layout principles, and in basic typology (Patricios, 2002). The cul-de-sac has come and gone, having developed in both local authority and private housing from the late 1960s. The cul-de-sac was expected to secure social cohesion among resident groups by creating supervised semi-private streets, quietly removed from the noise and intensity of primary routes. For twenty-five years the cul-de-sac dominated housing layout, until a revised social thinking concluded that the contact and intensity that the cul-de-sac sheltered from, was actually a positive feature of urban life. Dead-end streets are thus no longer fashionable. Housing layout now attempts to avoid cul-de-sacs.

The rear access laneway has also been withdrawn from most local authority housing layouts since 1990, after almost a century of use (Department of the Environment and Local Government, 1999e). Residents of terraced housing no longer demand that they have alternative access to rear gardens without going through the house, or at least they regard it as less important than the security risk created by the laneway. Of significance here is the acceptance of compromise between provider and tenant in the resolution of a design problem. One of the most significant effects on space around the dwelling will be felt when the incoming requirements of waste management legislation are applied fully. The need to sort and store separated quantities of waste for recycling will change fundamentally the amenity of the domestic garden. Already the presence of multiple quantities of wheelie-bins, in front gardens and external spaces, is making a noticeable impression on carefully tended streets.

Road Space and Regulation

Among the main culprits of excessive space and low densities in urban areas, particularly in the suburb, are the expansive road design standards that have governed suburban layout in Ireland for many years (Dublin Transportation Office, 1998). In many cases these standards continue to reduce the capability for environments of any spatial quality to be created. In the compensation-rich climate of Ireland, local authorities seek shelter in standards of maximum safety. One of the most unimaginative ways to secure safety is to separate activities by space or distance. Invariably the roads that serve residential areas, where there are children and elderly people about, have not-surprisingly been associated with what might be described as excessive safety space. These include setback space for junction sightlines, broad corner radii and the spatial satisfaction of any hazard-inducing eventuality. Most local authorities also reserve additional access space on roadside margins for machinery to reach buried underground services should they ever require repair or replacement. A study of new suburban layouts in 1988 found that when road space and statutory open space had been factored into residential densities, gross density was in some areas coming down to four units per acre (Gribbin, 1998).

In traditional towns and cities the quality spaces of the urban environment were created out of a hierarchy of functionally formulated spaces, in the shape of squares and streets, where the width of the space related to the nature of its human activity as did the height of the forms that enclosed it. The relationship of spaces to each other was a reflection of the relative function of these spaces, and circulation served those functions without dominating them. Here the function of each space was understood intuitively by the user. It was legible. Instead, the public space of the modern housing environment tends to be governed by safe vehicular access, through the road and its tributaries, at sufficient widths to accommodate safely all eventualities, supported by setback distances from buildings and boundary walls. The design of the residential environment then follows. Maintenance of sightlines often prohibits even the planting of trees. In many cases, the emergence of gated communities in urban areas is a reaction against the demands of public road standards. Private developers will often forfeit the requirement to have their roads taken in charge as public road space by local authorities, so that by remaining gated under their own residents' management, they can avoid public road dimensions and therefore create a more attractive environment.

The effects of such standards in a residential environment are not confined to road layouts. The façades of domestic buildings can now be significantly affected in appearance by regulations. For example, the minimum cill height above floor level for upper-floor windows reduces flexibility in façade design, as do the specified separation distances across façades between the windows of adjacent houses. As a result of these regulations, more onerous now than in most European countries, we can in some cases neither create good modern façades, nor reproduce the qualities of proportion enjoyed in our traditional architecture. It is no longer possible for example to build to the standard cross-section of the typical Irish street with glass-fronted shopfronts at street level and two-storey residence above. Regulations governing the proximity of adjacent structures have now extinguished that heritage.

There has been some revision of thought regarding the effect of over-cautious roads standards, and some recent relaxation has been encouraged by a number of local authorities. The realisation, for example, that narrower road spaces cause users to be more careful is one that has had a recent effect on design. Once a safety regulation has been established, however, retreat from it is almost impossible as those responsible for the retreat can become liable for a range of future eventualities, which might have been prevented by the established safety of the intermediate stage. While we have, to our certain credit, established a framework of regulations that give us super safety, we may now have to accept the limitations of the environment that that calls upon us.

Urban Housing in the Countryside

Whatever we do in cities and towns, it could be suggested that nothing threatens the urban residential environment as much as the now rampant migration of residence back to the countryside, which from a planning point of view might well be defined as out of control (Department of the Environment, Heritage and Local Government, 2004b). Irish towns and cities are now showing significant diffusion of residence by a community who prefer to live in the countryside, commuting to the town for work and services. The rural hinterlands of many towns show much greater increases in population than do the towns (James,

2003). In some major towns residence has ceased to be the dominant land use (National Building Agency, 2003), indicating a very poor future for towns as settlements. As residents migrate outwards, the town becomes less attractive for those who remain. While every county development plan recites its intention to reduce this migration and while there are many established opinions on it, there is relatively little reliable research on its true causes and effects.

Single Rural Dwelling Design

There are two discussions that become consistently confused in Ireland regarding one-off housing in the countryside. One concerns whether or not we should build single houses individually in the countryside, and the other concerns how such houses should be sited and designed, if we have decided that they may be built in the countryside. The first discussion is governed by such issues as long-term sustainability for the servicing of a scattered community, the diffusion of towns where residents are urban-generated having no occupational association with the landscape, and the environmental degradation of the rural environment through suburbanisation. It also addresses the circumstances of households associated with the countryside such as with agriculture and rural services, which need to build new and modern houses in the landscape (Department of the Environment, Heritage and Local Government, 2004b). The second discussion is governed by such issues as the location and design of individual buildings, once it has been concluded that they should be built in the countryside (Corbett and Corbett, 2000). Since the first discussion is one not primarily concerned with design, we do not open it here but concentrate instead on some of the factors in the second or the design discussion.

It has been suggested that one of the attractions in moving from town to countryside is the opportunity to design one's own house on one's own land, without obligations to surrounding uses. Recent research in the midlands would suggest, however, that few new residents actually have a significant input into the design of their houses (James, 2003). In most cases they are designed by the builder using a design from one of the many pattern books, adjusted in discussion with the resident (James, 2003; McDonald 1997). Similar circumstances apply where rural inhabitants build new homes (James, 2003). Placing a house or placing a built form in the Irish landscape is a complex operation full of enormous potential for both building and landscape when correctly executed, but prone to conspicuous and often spectacular failure when poorly executed. Traditional buildings were placed with a calculated and practised relationship to landslope, orientation, field boundaries and microclimate. This placing created environments and spaces of quality, both around the house and in the relationships between internal space and surrounding aspect. When the new house does not have the sensitivity of a designer who might have taken orientation or site factors into account, its design will tend to be governed instead by a pattern of common elements that act against quality of place. Its biggest and best rooms will be presented towards the road, whatever the orientation. It will be placed high in the landscape, presumably in order to be seen and to avail of views. It will tend to stand alone, unlinked to field boundaries or areas of structural tree planting.

Attempts by the planner, with limited resources, to develop a standardised controlling mechanism for rural housing design have in some cases created more problems than they solve. The creation of a building setback line at a standard distance from the road, which is essentially a suburban rule, fails to allow building designs to explore traditional relationships with either the landscape or the road (Ní Nualláin, 2003). The creation of parking and setback space for site entrances leads to large unused margin space outside the front boundary walls of houses, destroying the existing character of the road and its boundaries (Ní Nualláin, 2003). It also wastes space. Design guidance for the form and material of houses is often laid out to give a safe vocabulary that accommodates a situation where the planning application is not prepared by a qualified designer nor is it assessed by a qualified designer from the local authority. Thus all of the opportunity that might exist in a particular design on a particular site is lost, and the elements of each rural house begin to reproduce standardised design characteristics, many belonging to safe suburban solutions.

Conflicts of Image

If good modern house design interprets accurately its relationship with the landscape and with the indigenous forms of earlier buildings, it will be simple. In Ireland it might be suggested, however, that many people see an established association between simplicity and poverty. A conflict therefore emerges when the new house owner in the countryside wants to display wealth as evidence of status. The house will be measured by degree of ornament or of complexity, or of course by size. References from established schools of wealth-related aesthetic will be popular, as these are universally understood. For example, the classical language of pediments, porticoes and columns has been popular, as has the exotic language of arches. On the other hand entirely, the properly designed house attempting to sit less obtrusively in the landscape, having simple walls with simple unlatticed openings, attempting to reduce the impact of its volume in a series of less-heavy shapes, would tend to defeat totally the objectives of the owner.

Design Reference

A fundamental problem for the form of the modern family house in the Irish countryside is that it has few sources of reference in history. In traditional rural house types, as they emerged over three centuries, the large house of the landlord and the small cabin of the peasant formed between them the dominant quantity at the extremities of an otherwise empty range. Neither of these provides appropriate models for the current family dwelling. Although in the traditional settlement system there were houses in between, such as the dwellings of estate personnel or farmhouses of the middle size, these were limited building forms that do not sufficiently inspire the form of a modern house. In towns a much greater range of dwellings did exist for the greater range of households in traditional urban society, but these forms are not comfortably transferable to the landscape. As a result, the large family house as a simple building in the landscape tends to look incongruous, dragging its suburban references with it. Front gardens with suburban lawns and showy shrubs (McDonald, 1997) are still uncertain of their place within the more robust elements of the surrounding landscape. However, there have been some recent attempts, at least, to provide some detailed design guidance on the building of new dwellings in the countryside, although it remains to be seen whether the regulatory framework will support these guidelines in their implementation (Cork County Council, 2003).

Clusters

Since urban diffusion began in the 1960s, local authorities have been attempting to encourage the clustering of dwellings in the landscape in order to reduce impact on the rural environment. Clustering even two dwellings together can reduce the overall impact on the environment by half, over a whole range of factors (Suffren, 1974). In the traditional Irish *clachan*, farm dwellings were clustered in a village format and there have been some successful modern clusters based on that concept. Castle Park Village near Kinsale, built in the 1970s, continues to be one of the best examples where a number of dwellings, albeit holiday homes, are clustered in a *clachan*-like relationship. There have been many studies on the capability of cluster to satisfy the needs of those who build single houses in the countryside (Suffran, 1974; Frehill, 2003). Some reveal an unwillingness to consider the option, as the advantages of spatial freedom in the single house are reduced (Frehill, 2003). If it became government policy to levy single house dwellers with the true cost of supplying services to their homes, as elsewhere in Europe, the spatial qualities of cluster might become more evident (Ó Gráda, 2004).

Privacy and Flexibility in Urban Residence

The desire by so many households to live in an open rural site unrestricted by or unobliged to other households around them may reflect certain needs regarding privacy and flexibility, which the design of residential areas has not properly addressed. If housing in denser settlements appears to be the objective to which we are aspiring, the relationship between those needs and this objective cannot be ignored. As settlements become denser, flexibility and security for dwellers as participants are aspects that require greater design effort to achieve. There have been many attempts in recent years to address the specific concept of the flexible house or the extendable house as it might relate to the changing needs of households. In the marketplace, however, the concept is not widespread in built form. The private developers brochure still offers the ubiquitous garage conversion as the extent of structural flexibility. In a recent apartment block, however, for affordable housing at Holles Street in Dublin, internal walls within floors are structurally flexible to allow adaptation over time to changing household needs. This represents a particularly significant development, as with the vertical subdivision of ownership now emerging in urban areas, freedom to adjust the layout of one level without structural obligation to levels above becomes an important bonus.

Just as important as the necessity to be flexible of course is the necessity to protect each household against the flexibility of others, with particular attention to security and privacy. Recent relaxations in planning law, contained in the Planning and Development Act, 2000, have increased the range of development deemed exempt from the requirement to have planning permission. While this increase may reduce development control workloads for local authorities and give greater freedom to the individual to modify and adjust the place of residence, it does create a less controllable environment for adjacent households, in high-density urban environments. One can now build a five-storey extension to the back of an unlisted Georgian residence, without planning permission, with considerable effect on the amenity of a neighbour, who has no redress through the planning system. Buyers are therefore less encouraged to take the risk of investing in the more volatile urban environment. If they build their bungalows far from the town, such uncertainties would not be as significant. If we begin to create higher density urban environments, we must accept that detail is critical and that ongoing planning controls will be necessary to protect that detail for all participants in a more sensitive context.

Conclusion: The Suburb as Solution?

The urban environment is regarded quite rightly by designers as a place where great spatial character is achievable with good design. There is a similar regard for the spatial characteristics of the rural environment, for different reasons. It has been fashionable to regard the suburb, however, as something less than the city or countryside. The suburb is seen as a hybrid invention carrying some structural failures as a poor record. Yet in Ireland most of us live in a suburban environment (Gribbin, 1998; Reddy, 2002). It may well be that we do not yet have sufficient research to confirm to what degree various residential environments satisfy quality of life for dwellers. Urban apartment living may satisfy parents but severely deprive their children of a full life, just as living in an isolated rural bungalow may do, for opposite reasons. It is possible, however, that in a suburb no such extremities of deprivation would be suffered and the balanced needs of all might be more accessible. Many of the smaller towns of Ireland, as elsewhere in Europe, contain successful suburbs from where children may walk or cycle to their friends.

Recent research in some towns among suburban residents (James, 2003) revealed, however, an ambition of almost all respondents to build at some stage in their lives a single house in the countryside. Most cited an absence of individuality in their house and the sameness of the surrounding houses as their reason for rejecting the suburb. Yet the level of convenience in their present lifestyle was possibly much higher than that in the lifestyle to which they aspired. Since the 1950s, private housing in Irish suburbs has been largely provided in housing estates built by the middle-market developer, reducing the potential for an environment that might have facilitated individual input into residential place. To facilitate this individuality, a number of local authorities did create estates of serviced sites in which single dwellings have been separately built. This concept has been very successful where attempted but it is not common, and is seldom attempted by private developers, as it is not economically lucrative. The idea is, however, very popular in many European countries and in the United States. There are good reasons for condemning the suburban environment, as we know it, from our experience of some suburban environments in Ireland. But if the suburb is correctly designed and managed, it can provide a lifestyle incorporating the best of the garden city vision, which creates a rich relationship with the city or town, for family living (Whitehand and Carr, 2001).

Many smaller settlements in particular have spare capacity to create walk-to-work suburbs where an ideal lifestyle is achievable. In the larger cities we have set up the framework for good suburban places but perhaps failed in the detail of making them. The problem of collecting the housing of the suburb to support the town centre is probably less urgent than is the problem of collecting the scattered one-off housing in the countryside to support the town. Retaining the latter in successful suburbs may be our most workable solution. Although we despise the suburb because we have created poor examples of it in Ireland, it may represent for us our only chance to prevent the residents of our towns from diffusing totally to the countryside.

17

Rural Housing: Politics, Public Policy and Planning[1]

Mark Scott

Introduction

In recent years, sustainable management of rural housing has emerged as one of the most controversial and contentious issues in Irish public policy. Dispersed rural dwellings have been a long-standing feature of Irish settlement patterns. However, rural housing has increasingly been in the public spotlight, particularly with background analysis undertaken during the preparation of the National Spatial Strategy (NSS) (Department of the Environment and Local Government, 2002), which suggested that between 1996-1999, over one in three houses built in the Republic of Ireland were built as single dwellings in the open countryside (Department of the Environment and Local Government, Spatial Planning Unit, 2001). The subsequent debate surrounding housing in rural areas has become increasingly polarised between rural community and conservation interests due, in part, to the increased pace of development, the changing population dynamics of rural areas, and the increased pressure to include environmental considerations in the land-use planning process. The key question here is how much development should be accommodated for in rural areas in an equation which attempts to balance the need for homes and jobs and their related developments with the case for conserving the countryside (Gilg, 1996).

This chapter evaluates policy and planning processes applied to managing housing in the Irish countryside and identifies a number of challenges to developing holistic approaches to rural planning practice. The first part of the chapter briefly reviews key issues surrounding rural housing growth, including an assessment of the wider rural development context. Secondly, the chapter examines the contested debate surrounding rural housing, and highlights various selective interpretations of rural sustainable development. The chapter then considers the contemporary policy framework for rural housing at a national level, in particular focusing on the National Spatial Strategy and the recently published *Planning Guidelines for Sustainable Rural Housing* (Department of the Environment, Heritage and Local Government, 2005). The final part of the chapter identifies a series of local planning responses to managing rural housing and reflects on the effectiveness of planning policy to integrate housing policies with wider concerns of sustainable rural communities.

Rural Housing Growth in Ireland

Fundamental transformations have taken place in Europe's rural economy and society, and new patterns of diversity and differentiation are emerging within the contemporary countryside. These may be summarised as (drawing on Marsden, 1999):

- the decline in agricultural employment, and in the relative economic importance of food production, accompanied by structural changes in the farming industry and food chain
- the emergence of environmentalism as a powerful ethic and political force
- the related emergence of new uses for rural space, and new societal demands in relation to land and landscape and the treatment of animals and nature
- increased personal mobility, including commuting, migration, tourism and recreation
- the emergence of new winners and losers from change processes, and especially recognition of 'excluded groups' suffering from poverty and economic and social vulnerability.

Given the depth and prolonged character of crisis in the agricultural sector, some commentators have suggested that rural areas are experiencing a shift from a 'productivist' to a 'post-productivist' era in the countryside (Halfacree, 1997; Hadjimichalis, 2003). In this post-productivist phase, rural localities are now places that people from outside come into in order to consume the diversity of things that now make and constitute rural space (Gray, 2000), and as Marsden (1999: 506) notes:

> This is a general process of externalisation of the consumption countryside, one which exhibits a wide range of external relationships and is subject to wide-ranging demands (not least from new residents, developers, tourists, food consumers).

In this sense, Halfacree (1997) suggests that post-productivism may signal a search for a new way of understanding and structuring the countryside, as non-agricultural interests move central in processes shaping rural space.

Few places in Europe are so closely identified with the 'rural' as Ireland (McDonagh, 2001). Despite growing industrialisation and urbanisation throughout the country, few places outside of Dublin, Cork, Limerick, Galway and Waterford are referred to in any other context. In the most recent census in 2002, 40 per cent of the State's population lived in settlements smaller than 1,500 people or in the open countryside. However, Ireland's rural communities are undergoing rapid and fundamental changes: the agricultural sector continues to restructure; the economic base of rural areas is diversifying; new consumer demands and practices have emerged; there is a growing concern for the environment and increased pressure to include the environmental dimension in decision-making; and some rural communities are under intense pressure from urbanisation, while other areas continue to experience population decline. Within this context of change and new demands on rural space, rural sustainable development has become a highly contested and divisive concept. For example, housing in the countryside, environmental directives for landscape protection, potential wind-farm development, access to farmland for recreation, and the Government's decentralisation programme for civil service departments, have all been marked by high-profile and polarised debates in the popular media. As McDonagh (1998) argues, in this era of what is increasingly being referred to as a 'post-agricultural' society, there is an urgent need to question the understandings of the term 'rural' in Ireland and whether there is a coordinated policy direction for the changing future of rural areas.

 Within this wider rural development context, rural housing has emerged as a contested issue among competing stakeholders, particularly as building projects involve often highly visible indicators of rural structural change. Dispersed rural settlement growth over the past thirty years is a distinctive feature of many rural areas of Ireland (McGrath, 1998), with contemporary rural settlement patterns predominantly comprised of single dwellings in the open countryside. Analysis undertaken during the preparation of the National Spatial Strategy suggests that between 1996-1999 over one in three houses built in the Republic of Ireland have been one-off housing in the open countryside, and highlights that the issue of single applications for housing in rural areas has become a major concern for most local planning authorities (Department of the Environment and Local Government, Spatial Planning Unit, 2001). This increased scale and pace of development has resulted from both demand-side and supply-side factors.

On the demand side, Duffy (2000) suggests that factors driving rural housing trends include the wider demographic recovery of many rural areas and a cultural predisposition among Irish people to living in the countryside (rather than villages). Other factors include the relative lower costs associated with developing a single dwelling (Clinch *et al*, 2002), the desire for living in a rural environment, in particular with good accessibility to urban areas (Department of the Environment and Local Government, Spatial Planning Unit, 2001), increased personal mobility, the lowering of average household size in rural areas and the growth of second-home ownership. On the supply side, the increased availability of sites has been a major driver of rural settlement change, as farmers (in the context of agricultural decline) are more willing to sell half-acre parcels of farmland for housing development, which in many cases has been facilitated by relaxed local planning policies.

These factors are not exclusive to the Republic of Ireland. With a comparative rural culture, but with a contrasting centralised planning regime with less political control, Northern Ireland has experienced similar rural housing trends, with approximately 27 per cent of private house-building completions comprised of single houses in the open countryside (Sterrett, 2003). Similarly, both North American and European countries are experiencing increased demand for housing in rural locations. For example, around 80 per cent of new housing development in the United States between 1994 and 1997 was located outside urban areas (Woods, 2005), and even highly urbanised EU countries such as the Netherlands have experienced increased demands for living in rural environments (see van Dam *et al*, 2002). These trends are driven by consumer preferences for low-density housing and a perception of an increased quality of life associated with rural living (Gkartzios and Scott, 2005; Woods, 2005).

In Ireland, rural housing change and growth is distributed unevenly across space, and in this regard the media portrayal of a 'one-off housing' debate is perhaps misleading. Rather than a singular rural housing debate, in reality the generators of rural housing, development pressures, environmental and community contexts vary widely across space – in other words, housing in rural North Mayo, with a declining population, is a different issue than housing in Fingal's countryside, where urban sprawl is a real threat. In addition, the key issues surrounding managing rural housing growth are complex and multidimensional, including how many and what type of rural houses should be constructed, and whether there should be any attempt to favour local people or local building styles in these decisions. Other issues have focused on ideal rural settlement patterns based on economies of scale both internally and externally in terms of service provision, and attempts to provide for balanced and sustainable communities. The key issues may be summarised as follows:

- Distribution and intensity of rural housing: Where are new rural houses to be accommodated? Is this leading to a suburbanisation of rural areas and urban sprawl? What is the spatial and aesthetic relationship between town and country, urban and rural?
- Environmental costs of rural housing: Does an increase in rural housing lead to a rise in car dependency compared to other settlement forms? What are the positive

and negative impacts of housing on the rural landscape? What is the capacity of the environment to accommodate new development without damage?

- Public health and safety: To what extent does an increase in rural housing contribute to groundwater pollution? How effective are current on-site water treatment systems? What is the impact on road safety of increased housing access directly to major roads?
- Siting and design issues: Do contemporary rural houses reflect local building traditions with local building materials? Are rural houses designed to reduce environmental impact?
- Infrastructural implications: What are the costs of service provision for dispersed rural housing and other forms of rural settlement? Does an increase in rural housing supply assist in maintaining existing rural services?
- Settlement patterns and community vitality: What is the relationship between housing development and viable and vibrant rural communities? Do single dwellings in rural areas contribute to the provision of affordable housing?

Scant attention has been given, thus far, to addressing these issues through empirical investigation, and instead policy formulation has developed largely through a political process characterised by contestation and conflict among competing interests in the rural arena.

The Politics of Rural Planning

Historically, the fate of smaller settlements and rural areas in Ireland has received less than significant attention from economic and physical planners. Rural areas have often been 'perceived largely as scenic backdrops to the drama of urban based investment in infrastructure, industry and services' (Greer and Murray, 1993: 3). This perspective was reinforced with the view of the rural arena equating solely with agriculture as a productivist space with a lack of development pressures on the countryside. The result of this policy standpoint has led to two contradictory trends. Firstly, a professional planning ethos has developed which has favoured urban concentration and its perceived virtues, such as promoting a greater efficiency and economy in the provision of services and the role of urban industrial growth in regional development (Murray, 1993). The second trend has been the operation of a liberal planning system in rural Ireland, described as one of the more lax rural planning regimes in Europe (Duffy, 2000), facilitating the proliferation of dispersed, one-off dwellings in rural areas and incremental change in the Irish landscape (Johnson, 1994). Indeed, commentators such as Aalen (1997) and McGrath (1998) have argued that the planning system is unable to respond effectively to rural settlement growth. In a critique of rural planning, both commentators suggest policy is driven by the priorities of a few individuals, an intense localism, and the predominance of incremental decision-making. Similarly, Gallent *et al* (2003: 90) classify rural planning in Ireland as a *laissez-faire* regime, suggesting that: 'the tradition of a more relaxed approach to regulation, and what many see as the underperformance in planning is merely an expression of Irish attitudes towards government intervention'.

In essence, the rural housing debate is characterised by contestation and the development of two bodies of opinion (Lynch, 2002). One that represents conservation interests, the planning profession and local authority management, proposes severe restrictions on dispersed rural housing as a means to protecting landscapes, achieving economies of scale in infrastructure provision through clustering development, and reducing car dependency. The second body of opinion represents rural communities, local political representatives and agricultural interests, who favour more liberal policies to enable greater social vitality and to protect the further loss of rural services. Indeed, the issue of granting planning permission for housing in the countryside raises fundamental questions surrounding the politics of planning in rural Ireland, including the relationship between national and local planning policies and spatial strategies; the relationship between planning policy and development control decisions; and the noticeable worsening in relations between local authority planning officials and elected representatives evident in recent years.

Although the percentage of the State's population living in rural areas has declined in recent years, the rural remains a large and politically important constituency (Scott, forthcoming). In many rural areas, particularly those not immediately under urban influence, local decision-making works in line with a localistic and communal set of considerations in which development to meet local needs is routinely seen as an intrinsic part of rural life. As identified by Marsden *et al* (1993), at a micro-level, a number of actors interact to make decisions about rural land-use change, for example farmers, financial institutions, builders, planners and other local authority officials, councillors, and local residents. In this context, environmental groups are often perceived as 'external' actors, while development interests purport to reflect the interests of the locality and its traditional rural residents (Murdoch *et al*, 2003). Although rural housing conflicts tend to emerge first on a local scale – the level at which everyday life is most directly impinged upon – recent years have been marked by an 'up-scaling' (as termed by Woods, 2005) of rural housing conflicts, as campaigners have been forced to engage in local, regional and national politics in attempts to change policy decisions. This was clearly evident during the formulation of the National Spatial Strategy (Department of the Environment and Local Government, 2002) and the subsequent publication of the *Planning Guidelines for Sustainable Rural Housing* (Department of the Environment, Heritage and Local Government, 2005).

Given that the national tier of policy making is an increasingly important node in establishing rural planning agendas, it is perhaps unsurprising that local actors should come to realise that political decisions taken at higher spatial scales are important in determining the outcomes of their own struggles (Murdoch *et al*, 2003). In this context, local pro-development interests have begun to build alliances further up the scales of governance. For example, the Irish Rural Dwellers Association (IRDA) has recently emerged as a broad coalition of pro-housing development interests (including farmers, councillors, community development stakeholders), which has successfully adopted a multi-scaler approach to influence policy outcomes, based on lobbying of elected representatives (both local and national), civil servants and local government officials, as well as forming new alliances with other stakeholders, such as the Royal Institute of Architects Ireland (RIAI). This up-scaling of rural conflicts, identified in other advanced capitalist societies undergoing rural restructuring processes as 'rural politics', has been replaced by a new 'politics of the rural' in which the very meaning and regulation of rural space is the defining issue (Woods, 2003, 2005).

To illustrate this issue, this section will assess the viewpoints of a number of stakeholders involved in the rural housing debate. Analysis was undertaken of submissions made to the Department of the Environment, Heritage and Local Government following publication of their *Draft Rural Housing Guidelines* for public consultation in 2004. Both the formulation of the draft rural housing guidelines and the public debate surrounding the consultation exercise have been characterised by a lack of reliable data and an absence of an evidence-based approach to policy development. At present there is a dearth of research relating to, for example, house completions in the open countryside; occupancy; balance between first and second homes; consumer decision-making and housing preferences; and costs and benefits of dispersed rural housing and alternative options. In the absence of research to inform the debate, a number of 'storylines' have emerged that all emphasise rural sustainable development, characterised, however, by selective interpretations. The submissions from the following organisations were assessed for this chapter:[2]

- An Taisce, the National Trust of Ireland (2001; 2004)
- Irish Environment
- Feasta (Foundation for the Economics of Sustainability) (2004)
- The Irish Planning Institute (IPI) (2003)
- The Royal Institute of Architects in Ireland (RIAI) (2004)
- The Irish Auctioneers and Valuers Institute (IAVA) (2003b)
- The Irish Rural Dwellers Association (IRDA) (2004).

This chapter will focus on two key themes that emerged in this assessment: firstly, it will consider selective interpretations of sustainable development applied to rural housing; and secondly, conflicting narratives of rurality underpinning the housing debate will be outlined.

Rural Housing and Sustainable Development

In many respects, sustainable development has become a flag of convenience for actors and interests in the rural housing debate. Dispersed rural housing has been described as both 'inherently unsustainable' by the Irish Planning Institute and as 'enhancing sustainability' by the Irish Auctioneers and Valuers' Institute (2003b). Figure 17.1 summarises the most common reasons cited to impose restrictions on the growth of dispersed settlements (includes submissions from An Taisce, Irish Environment, Feasta, the IPI and the RIAI).

Table 17.1: Summary of Reasons Cited to Limit Dispersed Rural Housing

- Impact on landscapes
- Proliferation of septic tanks (and groundwater pollution)
- Reliance on the car for all journeys
- Ribbon development and urban sprawl
- Decline of smaller towns and villages
- Increased difficulty in the provision of infrastructure
- Increased costs of service delivery.

These arguments against continued dispersed settlement patterns, in general, focus on environmental issues (landscape impacts, car dependency, septic tanks and groundwater pollution) and economic costs (provision of infrastructure, costs of service delivery). Indeed, the use of the term 'sustainable development' in the rural housing guidelines is criticised for 'getting the wrong balance' between economic, social and environmental criteria:

> To strike a balance does not mean that social or economic pressures can override environmental constraints where these are already overstretched. The cumulative effects of many small scale changes does not appear to be recognised. (Feasta, 2004: 5)

Furthermore, the social and community benefits of rural housing are also questioned:

> In its approach to new development in the countryside An Taisce is animated by sustainability. This embraces social, economic and environmental criteria. One-off housing generally fails under each of these headings. (An Taisce, 2001: 6)

> Communities are more sustainable than one-off developments in the countryside. Furthermore for example, as people grow old it is undesirable that they should be far from local services like doctors, social services, meals on wheals as well as shops, pubs, bingo, libraries etc. (An Taisce, 2001: 12)

Interestingly, from An Taisce's perspective, residents in dispersed rural housing are viewed as isolated and dislocated from 'community' and social space.

In contrast, the community and cultural sustainability benefits are emphasised by the Irish Rural Dwellers Association as key arguments for relaxing rural housing restrictions. The following extracts illustrate the importance attached to maintaining population levels, cultural traditions, and community and individual attachment to place:

> Single rural houses are an inherent part of the Irish landscape and a traditional means of housing in rural Ireland for at least five thousand years. Continuing this tradition is protecting our heritage. (Ó Domhnaill, in Irish Rural Dwellers Association, 2004: 73)

> Sustainable development is development that meets the needs of the present generation without compromising the ability of future generations to meet their needs. Rural housing policies that do not meet the needs of those of the present or future generations, who wish to live in the countryside, are therefore unsustainable. Existing rural communities without additional houses are unsustainable, as development requires young vibrant people, who cannot exist in rural areas, without additional housing. There will be no rural communities for future generations if current planning policies continue. (Ó Domhnaill, in Irish Rural Dwellers Association, 2004: 71)

Due to varying interpretations and use of the term sustainable development, different groups of actors adopt contrasting approaches to defining rural housing need. For example, conservation interests suggest that planning permission should only be granted for people who are integral to the rural community or for people who are working in the agricultural or natural resources sector. In contrast, pro-development groups view the right to build and the rights of the individual as paramount:

> Basic civil rights to housing, to freedom of movement within our country, to choosing a personal quality of life, to designing our own houses, to developing our own property and many other fundamental rights have been eroded and are now fully controlled by an authoritarian, sanctimonious and holier than thou planning regime. (Irish Rural Dwellers Association, 2004: 104)

Furthermore, the IRDA contend that limiting planning permission for rural houses to those with a connection to the land and agriculture is 'the most philosophically barren, culturally impoverished, anti-rural community, racist and basically unconstitutional policy that has been attempted in Ireland'. (Irish Rural Dwellers Association, 2004: 8)

Narratives of Rurality

Underpinning the various interpretations of sustainable development outlined above are often conflicting constructions of rurality and perceptions of the urban environment among the stakeholders, summarised in Figure 17.2. Conservation interests and the professional planning institute construct an image of the countryside under widespread pressure from new and inappropriate dwellings. Although the IPI outline the countryside as a place of consumption (for tourists), in general the rural is viewed as primarily a productivist space, which perhaps fails to recognise the changing realities of rural Europe and Ireland:

> Rural land is a finite resource to be respected. It should be used primarily for agriculture or other land-dependent economic activity rather than new housing. (An Taisce, 2001: 2)

> The very uncertainty of the food and farming future should have called the Precautionary Principle into play. The accelerating loss of good agricultural land to housing ... cannot be justified in these times. (Feasta, 2004: 6)

Table 17.2: Construction of Rurality – A Summary

Pro Conservation	Pro Development
Productivist space	Post productivist space
Place of consumption – tourists	Place of consumption – residents
Landscape	Social space
Vernacular house design	'Modern' house design
Landscape and heritage	Rural living and national identity
Positive urban imagery	Negative urban imagery

Instead, pro-development interests appear to recognise the more limited contemporary role of agriculture and the public policy commitment to diversifying the rural economy. Within this context, limiting planning permission to those connected with agriculture would exclude large sections of the rural community in a post-agricultural countryside. Similar to the IPI, the countryside is seen as a place of consumption. However, in this case a key tension can be identified in relation to new uses for rural space between residents and tourists. The IPI argue that the landscape is a key asset in both place-marketing and tourism, providing an important rationale for landscape protection and policies. This perspective is challenged by the IRDA:

> ... [T]he claim of the importance of tourism to the local economy of individual areas must be examined and weighed against the detrimental affect of depopulation caused in large part by planning refusals. (Irish Rural Dwellers Association, 2004: 59)

In addition, a number of other interesting differences in the stakeholders' assessment of rurality can be identified. Firstly, pro-development interests emphasise the importance of the rural as a social space, with a vibrant network of family ties, sporting organisations, the importance of the parish, and a strong community attachment to place, whereas pro-conservation interests often describe rural Ireland in terms of landscape and as a collection of assets. This leads to a position of conservation interests making the case for preservation policies, but with the pro-development lobby arguing that houses can enhance the landscape and outlining the importance of a living rather than 'fossilised' landscape. Secondly (and related), the landscape is closely identified with national heritage among pro-conservation groups. However, for pro-development interests, a (rather idealised) rural community life is associated with nationalistic imagery and 'Irishness': 'our culture, traditions and history are largely rural (not necessarily agriculture) and the urban/rural mix is the key to our national identity' (Irish Rural Dwellers Association, 2004: 12). Thirdly, there are also conflicting approaches to rural house designs. On the one hand, there are those which favour vernacular rural aesthetics, and therefore policies which either assist in restoration or introduce design guidelines. On the other hand, this traditional rural aesthetic is often rejected by rural residents:

> ... [I]t is important to note that the house sizes and styles of bygone days, which in general reflected the abject poverty and deprivation of the ordinary people of Ireland, are often totally unsuited to modern families or the legitimate expectations of people in the 21 century. (Irish Rural Dwellers Association, 2004: 6)

Therefore, from this perspective, vernacular architectural styles represent an image of rural Ireland characterised by poverty and as 'pre-modern'. Finally, related to the conflicting discourses of rurality among the key stakeholders, are varying perceptions of urban areas also. Urban areas are presented by pro-conservation interests and the IPI as dynamic centres with the potential for developing critical mass for economic development and sustainable patterns of growth. Common terms include 'economies of scale', 'motors of the contemporary economy', and 'growth centres'. This position suggests that 'random' rural housing undermines the ability of urban centres to develop critical mass and the benefits of agglomeration. This analysis is applied throughout the settlement hierarchy, from cities to villages. However, rural lobby groups have employed negative imagery of urban areas as a clear rationale to support rural living. This is illustrated in the following comments by Jim Connelly, Chair of IRDA:

> The blind eye is being turned to the obvious and inevitable downside of urbanisation like traffic congestion, impossible house prices, rising crime, pollution, noise, stress, drugs etc. while the equally obvious upsides to the quality of life of rural living are attacked and denigrated as being unsustainable.

Rural Housing Policy

As outlined in the 2000 Planning and Development Act, the main aim of the planning system is to contribute towards sustainable development, which involves balancing the competing demands of society, the economy and the environment. It is clear from the above assessment that formulating rural planning policies is not a neutral, value-free, technical exercise, but rather involves balancing competing interests in the management of rural land-use involving a vigorous debate about what this balance might be, depending on different viewpoints about what is important. Given the rapidly changing dynamics of rural areas and communities in the Republic of Ireland, the *National Spatial Strategy*, published in 2002, provided a timely opportunity to formulate a national framework for managing rural settlement growth. The *NSS* outlines four broad objectives as a basis for a sustainable rural settlement policy framework:

1   To sustain and renew established rural communities and the existing stock of investment in a way that responds to various spatial, structural and economic changes taking place, while protecting the important assets rural areas possess;
2   To strengthen the established structure of villages and smaller settlements both to assist local economies and to accommodate additional population in a way that supports the viability of public transport and local infrastructure and services such as schools and water services;
3   To ensure that key assets in rural areas such as water quality, the natural and cultural heritage and the quality of the landscape are protected to support quality of life and economic vitality;
4   To ensure that rural settlement policies are appropriate to local circumstances.
    (Department of the Environment and Local Government, 2002: 105)

Encouragingly, the Strategy calls for different responses to managing dispersed rural settlement between rural areas under strong urban influences and rural areas that are either characterised by a strong agricultural base, structurally weak rural areas and areas with distinctive settlement patterns, reflecting the contrasting development pressures that exist in the countryside. This approach is based on a rural typology prepared by NUI Maynooth and Brady Shipman Martin (2000) who based their analysis on demographic structure, labour force characteristics, education and social class, sectoral employment profiles, performance of the farming sector and 'change' variables (e.g. population change, changes in numbers at work, etc). This typology is significant in that it appears to represent a first step towards developing a spatially defined rural policy rather than a sectoral (essentially agricultural) based approach which has predominated in the past. The typology provides the basis for a differentiated policy process which reflects the diversity of rural Ireland, enabling planning policies to be tailored to specific regions or localities. This is a belated recognition that new patterns of diversity and differentiation are emerging within the contemporary countryside (as outlined by Marsden, 1999) and that the key to understanding rural areas is the avoidance of easy assumptions of homogeneity (McDonagh, 2001). Planners at a local authority level must respond to this 'recasting' of rurality in the national spatial framework by avoiding the 'one size fits all' approach which has been prevalent in rural settlement planning and recognise that planning policies for rural areas should reflect the diversity of the challenges facing rural communities.

This is further developed in the Strategy with a distinction made between urban and rural generated housing in rural areas, defined as:

- Urban-generated rural housing: development driven by urban centres, with housing sought in rural areas by people living and working in urban areas, including second homes;
- Rural-generated housing: housing needed in rural areas within the established rural community by people working in rural areas or in nearby urban areas who are an intrinsic part of the rural community by way of background or employment. (Department of the Environment and Local Government, 2002: 106)

In general, the Strategy outlines that development driven by urban areas (including urban-generated rural housing) should take place within built-up areas or land identified in the development plan process and that rural-generated housing needs should be accommodated in the areas where they arise. As a more 'sustainable' alternative to dispersed single housing in the countryside, the Strategy places considerable emphasis on the role of villages in rural areas. The NSS suggests that villages have a key role to play in strengthening the urban structure of rural areas (for example in supporting local services and public transport) and as providing an important residential function for those seeking a rural lifestyle.

While the NSS is careful to avoid detailed policy prescription on rural housing (and thus avoiding additional political controversy at the time of publication), more recently the Department of the Environment, Heritage and Local Government have produced *Planning Guidelines for Sustainable Rural Housing* (2005), ensuring that dispersed rural housing in the countryside remained a high profile issue and a deeply contested feature of the planning policy arena. The Planning Guidelines suggest that the Government has shifted to a less restrictive position on housing in the countryside. In summary, the guidelines provide that: (1) people who are part of and contribute to the rural community will get planning permission in all rural areas, including those under strong urban-based pressures, subject to the normal rules in relation to good planning; and (2) anyone wishing to build a house in rural areas suffering persistent and substantial population decline will be accommodated, subject to good planning. In this context, it is worth noting that the term 'good planning' refers to issues surrounding siting, layout and design, rather than planning in a strategic or spatial sense. The sentiments of the new guidelines can be summarised in the following extract from a speech given by the Minister for the Environment, Dick Roche in July 2005:

> Earlier this year as Minister for the Environment, Heritage and Local Government I introduced some major changes in planning law – the *Guidelines for Rural Housing*. Those who would like to prevent homes being built in the countryside attacked me politically. I suggested at the time that planners in our local authorities and critics in some national organisations, all too often did not value the sense of community that exists in rural Ireland. I asked why was it that planners and some national organisations adopted the attitude 'we know best'. I suggested that this exclusivist attitude was wrong: it smacked of arrogance. The sons and daughters of farmers, men and women who were born and were reared in the countryside, people who live in the countryside and work in the countryside – whatever their following in life – have the same right to have a home of their own and a home in their own place as anybody else. … All too often planning is seen as a way of preventing people building in and living in their own place.
>
> (Department of the Environment, Heritage and Local Government, 2 August, 2005)

Planning Practice: Managing Rural Settlement

Although the *National Spatial Strategy* and the DoEHLG's *Planning Guidelines for Sustainable Rural Housing* now form the broad policy direction and goals for managing housing in the countryside, the local authority scale remains the key level for local land-use decision-making and regulation. Therefore, this section will outline various approaches to managing rural settlement at a local level. Examples will be primarily from Irish local authorities. However, the discussion will also draw on the experiences of elsewhere. The key concept in planning for settlements and the built environment is that planners try to guide and shape development by positive guidance backed up by negative control (Gilg, 1996). The positive tool is represented by land-use plans and policy statements which set out where a local authority would like development to take place. The negative tool of regulatory controls is represented by development control which gives the local authority the power to accept, modify or refuse applications to develop or change the use of land. This section will focus on positive planning tools and rural settlement policies provided by the local authority development plan, which form the framework for development control decisions. The following broad approaches to planning for rural settlement can be identified as follows:

1. *The key settlement approach.* This longstanding approach to rural planning is most commonly adopted in Britain, but has been influential in shaping planning methods in Ireland too. A key settlements policy (increasingly termed a selected villages policy) involves identifying particular towns and villages that are earmarked for expansion, while development elsewhere is tightly restricted (Cloke, 1983). The theory behind this is that economies of scale can be achieved, since there are natural thresholds for certain services. In a critique of the key settlement approach, Gilg (1996) contends that a selected village policy works better in pressured rural areas than in areas of slow growth or decline, suggesting that the policies can only work when they have development proposals to react to rather than proactively encouraging development in areas experiencing depopulation.

An example of a selected villages policy can be found in the *Westmeath County Development Plan 2002-2008* (Westmeath County Council, 2002). Westmeath is under increasing pressure from Dublin-generated housing growth as the commuter belt for the city has continued to expand. In this context, the local authority policy is to channel this new development into identified towns and villages, while allowing residential development outside of these centres only for people employed in agriculture or other rural-based industry or who have close personal, family or economic ties within the area. The primary objectives of Westmeath's rural settlement strategy are outlined in textbox 3 of the Development Plan. In addition to planning controls to achieve this strategy, Westmeath County Council also outlines a number of proactive policies to encourage development to locate in selected villages including the acquisition of strategically placed land within the development areas of villages to provide housing sites at reasonable costs and to facilitate the creation of employment opportunities.

2. *Village or cluster based approach.* This is a variation of the key settlement approach, common in Ireland. Rather than concentrate residential development in a selected number of villages as with a key settlements policy, this approach

is more dispersed and aims to restrict housing in the open countryside by encouraging new housing development to be located in any village or as part of an existing cluster of rural dwellings, with a primary objective of landscape protection. An example of this approach can be found in the *County Meath Development Plan 2001*, which seeks to limit single dwellings in the open countryside though identifying and encouraging development in a tier of smaller settlements, crossroad type villages and clusters (termed locally as 'Graigs') to act as local development nodes for local housing needs (Meath County Council, 2001).

3. *Urban containment approach*. Although urban containment tools, such as greenbelts, are essentially urban policy instruments, this planning approach also has significant implications for rural settlement management. The separation of urban and rural space has been a central principle in planning thought for over 50 years, particularly in the UK (see, for example, Murdoch and Lowe, 2003; Murdoch *et al*, 2003). This has been most notably enforced through the creation of 'greenbelts' around urban centres in highly pressured rural space, in which there is a strong presumption against any development. The downside of this approach is that rather than contain urban centres, greenbelts often displace development, leading to a 'leapfrogging' effect of development into adjacent rural areas (see for example, Gilg, 1996). Urban containment policies are fairly common in Irish development plans, particularly for metropolitan areas – for example, the *Regional Planning Guidelines* for the Greater Dublin Area identifies a 'strategic greenbelt' with the dual aim of restricting development in rural areas and channelling development into designated urban centres (Dublin Regional Authority, 2004b). This approach can also be identified for smaller urban centres. The *County Wexford Development Plan 2001*, for example, identifies a series of 'high pressure rural areas' primarily around Wexford's principal urban centres (Wexford, New Ross, Enniscorthy and Gorey) where more restrictive planning controls are in place (Wexford County Council, 2001).

4. *Landscape based approach*. This approach to rural settlement management is based on relating local land-use decision-making to landscape characteristics, with generally tighter restrictions in the most prized or scenic landscapes. For example, the rural housing policy in the *County Donegal Development Plan 2000* is based on three landscape categories:

- Category 3 landscapes are the 'most sublime landscapes' in the county which have a 'low capacity to absorb new houses'. In these areas, there will be a presumption against planning permission except for immediate members of families established in the local area who may build for their own use.

- Category 2 landscapes are 'uniquely Donegal in character', and there is a presumption for granting planning permission for new housing for the indigenous rural population, but a presumption against building holiday homes and speculative development.
- Category 1 landscapes are 'typically lowland, agricultural areas and do not possess many of the elements essentially Donegal in character'. In these areas, there will be a 'greater degree of flexibility exercised in judging planning applications' (Donegal County Council, 2001).

Therefore, in this case rural areas are defined as a landscape, a visual resource and an environmental amenity. While this approach focuses on protecting scenic landscapes, there appears to be less emphasis given to the social, economic and cultural context of rural areas, often leading to a 'disconnect' between local planning policies and wider rural development objectives (Scott, 2004).

5. *Aesthetic controls*. Local planning policies which emphasise 'site, layout and design' controls are generally formulated to address the issue of quality of rural houses rather than their quantity. This approach recognises that rural housing will continue as a central feature of rural settlement patterns and therefore focuses on design-related issues to reduce the visual impact of new development and to more effectively integrate new dwellings into the landscape. Recent years have witnessed an increasing use of design guidelines for rural housing (for example in counties Cork, Donegal, Galway and Louth) which emphasise local building traditions, including building materials and design, and 'good practice' in terms of siting and layout. This approach is likely to become more commonplace in accordance with the DoEHLG's *Rural Housing Guidelines*. However, drawing on the experience of Northern Ireland, which has adopted a series of rural housing design guidelines since the 1980s, Sterrett (2003) identifies a number of tensions surrounding this approach. Sterrett's analysis suggests there is a major gap between the aesthetic approach adopted in design guidelines and the aesthetic preferences of rural dwellers (or the popular rural aesthetic), which often favours contemporary, suburban style dwellings, but considered inappropriate for the countryside by many professional planners and amenity groups. In this context, aesthetic controls will ensure that rural housing remains a 'highly charged socio-political issue in rural areas' (Sterrett, 2003: 117).

6. *Distinguishing between urban and rural generated housing*. Following the publication of the *NSS* and the *Guidelines for Sustainable Rural Housing*, the distinction between urban and rural generated houses will now also be reflected in development plans at a local level. This will generally be implemented through attaching planning conditions to the granting of planning permission. For

example, in pressured rural areas under urban influence, planning permission will be granted for new dwellings to persons who are an intrinsic part of the rural community. However, variations will exist across planning authorities depending on: how each local authority defines urban and rural generated housing; the controls of occupancy of housing through planning conditions employed by different local authorities; and the level of enforcement of occupancy conditions.

7. Market-based instruments. Although market-based policy instruments such as tax incentives and disincentives are common urban regeneration and environmental policy tools in Ireland, particularly for spatially targeted initiatives, this approach has not been applied to rural planning to date. However, examples of this policy approach are widely used in rural planning in North America and Woods (2005: 200-201) outlines a number of market-based instruments that are commonly applied to rural land-use management:

- Authorities in the United States wishing to control development have introduced schemes to purchase the development rights of agricultural land. Farmland preservation schemes involve payments made to landowners, generally for the difference between the value of the land as farmland and its value for development.
- Tax incentives have been employed to encourage landowners to keep farmland in agricultural use. This type of scheme operates in every US state and Canadian province, where land-owners are offered tax concessions in return for agreeing to maintain land as farmland for a specified period of time.
- An alternative incentive-driven approach involves the collective voluntary agreement of farmers to maintain agricultural land-uses within a defined agricultural district in return for benefits including tax deferrals.

From Wood's summary of North American practice, market-based instruments appear to be most readily employed to preserve agricultural land from development. As farmers in Ireland are familiar with market-based incentives for production, this approach may be a more effective and acceptable method to discourage farmers from selling farmland sites for housing rather than traditional development control and regulatory planning instruments.

Although these various methods for managing rural settlement have been presented as individual approaches, generally local authorities would use a combination of techniques as part of its rural strategy – for example, a development plan may include elements of a landscape-based approach alongside aesthetic controls with occupancy conditions attached to planning permission. However, a key issue regardless of the approach employed is the extent to which policies have been complied with in the development control process. In particular, enforcement of both aesthetic controls and occupancy conditions attached to planning permission is under-resourced in most local planning authorities. Also, elected representatives lobbying on behalf of individual 'clients' can often lead to a more pro-development outlook than the development plan policies may suggest, resulting in a more 'blurred' relationship between planning objectives and actual outcomes.

Conclusion

Fundamental transformations are taking place in Ireland's rural economy and communities, and new demands on rural space have emerged as we shift from a productivist to a post-productivist era, when non-agricultural interests have moved central in the processes shaping rural space. Although the fate of smaller settlements and rural areas has received less than significant attention from physical planners in the past, these changes suggest the importance of a proactive and positive engagement with rural issues. In this regard, the *National Spatial Strategy* and *Planning Guidelines for Sustainable Rural Housing* have provided timely opportunities to debate the rural dimension of planning practice and settlement management.

In terms of policy development, a number of observations can be made. Firstly, at present, there appears to be a common view among rural interests that 'planners stop things happening in rural areas', suggesting a clear need to replace the sense of negativity surrounding rural planning. This could be achieved by adopting a more positive approach to planning for rural areas and for the development plan to evolve into a more proactive strategy. For example, development plans often contain a shallow assessment of rurality (Greer and Murray, 2003), limited to landscape characteristics with no reference to social, economic and cultural contexts. In this regard, the approach adopted in the *NSS* of identifying a rural typology for policy development based on socio-economic indicators should be replicated at a local level, allowing a more nuanced approach to settlement planning. In addition, traditional planning tools for land-use regulation (development plan and control) have been less than successful in achieving spatial policy objectives, suggesting policy-makers could explore the potential of market-based instruments in rural planning and for a more proactive change of emphasis from development control to environmental management. This may include rural design guidelines, village development frameworks, management strategies for environmentally sensitive areas and an enhanced integration of land-use plans and public investment programmes, which could identify what types of development would be beneficial in terms of the local economy, community and environment.

Secondly, ensuring vibrant, sustainable rural communities is a public policy goal (as outlined in the Government's White Paper for Rural Development) and in developing land-use planning policy for rural areas, the economic and social dimensions of rural development must also be included. This suggests a clear need to develop integrated, holistic and multi-dimensional approaches to rural sustainable development. For example, in relation to environmental sustainability (usually cited as a rationale for a more restrictive approach to rural housing), can more environmentally-friendly house designs minimise the impact of rural housing in terms of landscape and energy emissions? Perhaps more significantly, the rural housing debate has increasingly been viewed as a single issue – however, a multi-dimensional and integrative approach suggests that this issue should not be divorced from wider discussions surrounding rural development and a future vision for rural Ireland. This includes the need to consider the economic and social health of rural settlements as aspects of sustainability alongside the environmental dimensions, and to address the evident 'disconnect' between environmental and spatial policy goals and economic and social issues in local policy-making (Scott, 2004). As Healey (1998) argues, this process should explicitly explore 'new storylines' and attempt to create a new discourse for rural policy through collaborative action. In this regard, the planning system should provide a key statutory spatial framework for managing rural change with the potential to produce consensus-driven development strategies or to mediate between conflicting conservation and development goals. However, at present, the role of the planning system as a collaborative arena appears limited. Key rural stakeholders at national and local level, in general, view the planning system as a technical and regulatory process, with planners as 'gatekeepers' of change in rural areas (Scott, 2004). In addition, rural development interests often describe planning officials as 'urban planners' who demonstrate limited affinity with rural communities. This represents a considerable challenge for planners. However, as Murray and Greer (1997) suggest, this challenge can also be viewed as an opportunity to engage in a more interactive style of statutory plan-making partnerships with rural communities, linked to interest group mediation and the building of trust-relations.

Irish Housing in the European Context

Michelle Norris and Patrick Shiels

Introduction

This book has identified the defining characteristics of the system of housing provision in Ireland and examined recent developments in housing markets and non-market provision of housing, housing policy, legislation and regulation, together with the social, economic, and built environment implications of these developments. This final chapter assesses the performance of the Irish housing system over the last decade in comparison with the other European Union member states. This analysis focuses principally on five issues. These are: the context for housing policy making, including economic and demographic trends pertinent to housing; the accessibility of housing; housing quality; recent housing policy developments; and the outcomes produced by the combination of these policy interventions and structural factors, including trends in house prices, mortgage lending, new house building and public expenditure on housing.

This chapter draws on a detailed review of *Housing Developments in European Countries* which was conducted by the authors on behalf of the Department of the Environment, Heritage and Local Government to mark Ireland's presidency of the European Union in 2004 (Norris and Shiels, 2004). This document was compiled from the results of questionnaires which were circulated to Housing Ministries in the 25 countries which were EU members during this year.

Context

Table 18.1 outlines the context for housing policy making, including recent economic and demographic trends pertinent to housing in EU member states, in the latest year for which data are available. In this Table, the Gross National Product (GDP) per capita (in Purchasing Power Standards) is ranked in accordance with the average for all the member states, which is set at 100. Ireland achieves an impressive second place ranking in this category, with an index of 131.4 – surpassed only by Luxembourg which has by far the highest GDP per capita among the countries under examination, at 209.2. In contrast, the ten new member states which acceded to EU membership in 2004 exhibited the lowest GDP per capita among the countries under examination. Moreover, the GPD per capita of this group is significantly inflated by the inclusion of Malta and Cyprus – whereas the GDP per capita of the eight Central and Eastern European countries which joined the EU in 2004 (the Czech Republic, Estonia, Hungary, Latvia, Lithuania, Poland, Slovakia and Slovenia) was only 55.7.

In terms of the rate of economic growth, Table 18.1 indicates that the GDP of the 25 EU countries grew by 3.1 per cent in the latest year for which data are available, with a modest rate of 1.4 per cent for Ireland. The relatively low rate of annual growth in Irish GDP, however, belies the very high rate of recent economic growth this country has enjoyed over the last decade, which has propelled Ireland from the lower end of the EU economic development index to second place in the space of a decade. As mentioned in Chapter 1, for much of the late 1990s and early 2000s, the annual rate of annual GDP growth in Ireland exceeded 7 per cent.

Unemployment and inflation rates in the European Union average 8.2 per cent and 2.8 per cent respectively, the former a major source of concern due to its relatively high level among OECD countries. Ireland, in contrast, is characterised by a very low unemployment rate (4.9 per cent) and a rate of inflation at just below the EU average (2.3 per cent).

Table 18.1 also highlights the demographic trends that have significant implications for housing in the European Union. For instance, in recent years population change has been low in the majority of European countries, and has been negative in several of the new member states. Among the EU as a whole, natural population change per 1,000 inhabitants averages at 0.6, while net migration per 1,000 inhabitants averages at 2.3. As with economic trends, Ireland stands in marked contrast with the EU in general as the country has exhibited a strong rate of population growth in recent years, fuelled by a rate of natural population increase of 7.9 persons per 1,000 inhabitants in combination with an immigration rate of 7.6 per 1,000 inhabitants.

Table 18.1 demonstrates that the average household size in the European Union stands at 2.7 persons per dwelling, with the average household size in Ireland significantly above this level at 2.94 persons per dwelling. Among the longstanding EU members, only Spain has larger average household size. However, in many of the countries where average household size has traditionally been high, it has fallen significantly in recent years due to demographic and social changes. Ireland exemplifies this trend because, as was

Table 18.1: Key Economic and Demographic Trends Pertinent to Housing in European Union Member States, Various Years

Country	Year to which data refer	GDP per capita in Purchasing Power Standards (EU 25=100) (Proj.)	Annual Growth in GDP (GDP) %	Average Annual Inflation (I) %	Unemployment Rate (U) %	Population in 000s (TP)	No. Natural Population Change per 1,000 Inhabitants (NI)	Net Migration (including Corrections) per 1,000 Inhabitants (MI)	Average Number of Persons per Private Household (PH)
Austria	U=2003; I, TP, PH=2001	121.5	Nav	2.3	4.4	8,031	Nav	Nav	2.43
Belgium	GDP, I, U, TP, NI, MI=2002; PH=2001	116.9	0.7	1.6	7.3	10,300	0.5	3.1	2.34
Cyprus	GDP, I, U, TP, PH=2001	83.6	4	2	3	703.6	4.7	Nav	3.06
Czech Republic	GDP, I, U=2002; TP, PH=2001; NI, MI=2000	69	3.7	0.6	9.8	10,232	-1.8	0.6	2.64
Denmark	GDP, I, U, PH=2003; TP, NI, MI=2002	123.9	0.4	2.1	5.5	5,368	1	1.2	2.20
Estonia	GDP, I, U=2001; TP=2002; NI, MI=2000	49	6.5	5.6	11.8	1,360	-3.9	0.2	2.60
Finland	GDP, I, U=2003, TP=2001; NI, MI, PH=2000	110.5	1.9	1.2	9	5,181	1.4	0.5	2.30
France	I, U=2002; TP, PH=2001; NI=2000	113.9	Nav	1.9	8.7	59,188	4.1	Nav	2.40
Germany	GDP, I, U=2001; TP, PH=2002; NI, MI=2000	108.5	0.8	1.9	7.8	82,537	-0.9	2.0	2.20
Greece	GDP, U, TP=2001; I, NI, MI, PH=2000	79.8	4.1	3.2	10.4	10,940	-0.2	2.7	2.70
Hungary	GDP, I, U=2001, TP=2002; NI, MI, PH=2000	61	3.9	5.6	9.1	10,175	-3.7	1.6	2.70

Ireland	GDP, I, U=2003; TP, NI, MI, PH=2002	131.4	1.4	2.3	4.9	3,917.3	7.9	7.6	2.94
Italy	GDP, I, U, TP=2001; NI, MI, PH=2000	107.3	0.4	2.3	9.4	56,757	-0.3	3.1	2.60
Latvia	GDP=2002; U=2003; TP, PH=2001; NI, MI=2000	45.5	7.4	Nav	8.5	2,364.3	-5.0	-0.7	2.40
Lithuania	GDP, I, U=2002; TP, PH=2003; NI, MI=2000	46.1	6.8	-1.0	13.8	3,462.6	-1.4	-5.8	2.55
Luxembourg	GDP, I, U=2001; TP, NI, MI=2003	209.2	1.2	2.4	2.1	448.3	3.6	5.9	Nav
Malta	GDP, I, U=2002; TP=2003, NI, MI, PH=2000	73.7	1.7	2.2	6.8	399.8	3.3	3.4	3.01
Netherlands	GDP, I, U=2001; TP, MI, PH=2002	120.3	1.2	5.1	2.5	16,105	Nav	3.4	2.30
Poland	2002	46.4	1.3	5.5	18.1	38,230	Nav	Nav	2.84
Portugal	GDP=2003, TP=2000	75.2	-0.7	Nav	Nav	10,022	Nav	Nav	Nav
Slovakia	GDP, I, U=2002; TP, NI, MI, PH=2001	51.4	7.8	3.3	18.5	5,379.5	-0.2	0.2	2.59
Slovenia	GDP, I, U=2001; TP, PH=2002	77.3	2.7	8.6	5.8	1,964	Nav	Nav	2.80
Spain	GDP, I, U, NI, MI =2002; TP=2003; PH=2000	95.8	6.9	3.0	2.0	42,600	1.2	10.5	3.03
Sweden	GDP, I, U=2003, TP, NI, MI=2002	115.8	1.5	2.0	4.8	8,900	0.1	3.5	Nav
United Kingdom	GDP, I, U=2002; TP=2001; PH=2000	119.4	1.6	1.3	5.2	59,862.8	Nav	Nav	2.40
Mean (Rounded)	N/a	N/a	3.1	2.8	8.2	N/a	0.6	2.3	2.71

Note: N/a means not applicable; Nav means not available.

Source: Norris and Shiels (2004), with the exception of the data on GDP per capita which were generated from Eurostat data and are projected.

Table 18.2: Housing Availability in European Union Member States, Various Years

Country	Year to which Data Refer	Dwellings		Vacant Dwellings % of Total Dwellings	Dwellings by Tenure			
		No.	Per 1,000 inhabitants		Owner Occupied %	Private Rented %	Social/ Rented %	Other %
Austria*	2002	3,316,000	412.4	Nav	56.9	40.3	2.8	
Belgium	2001	4,095,008	400	Nav	68	25	7	0
Cyprus	2000	286,500	428	Nav	64.3	35.7	0	0
Czech Republic	2001	4,366,293	427	12.3	47	17	17****	12
Denmark	2003	2,541,000	472	Nav	50.6	17.8	27.2	4.4
Estonia	2000	622,600	434	6.2	85	9	3	0
Finland	1999	2478,000	490	8.6	58	17	17	1
France*	2002	24,525,000	413.3	6.8	56.0	19.7	17.2	7.1
Germany*	2002	35,800,000	434.3	Nav	43	51	6	0
Greece	2001	3,657,000	505	Nav	80.1**	19.9**	0**	0**
Hungary	2000	4,076,800,	406.7	Nav	86.9***	10.4***	0***	
Ireland	2003	1,542,321	391	Nav	77.4	11	6.9	4.7
Italy	2001	26,526,000	471	24	80	16	4	0
Latvia	2000	941,000	398.0	Nav	60.1	39.61	0.29	0
Lithuania	2002	1,291,700	367	Nav	87.2	8	3	1.8

Luxembourg*	2001	171,953	391.7	2.33	70	27.5	1.5	1
Malta	1995	155,202	420	23.0	74.1	22.4	3.5	0
Netherlands	2002	6,710,800	419.8	Nav	54.2	10.8	35.0	0
Poland	2002	12,523,600	326.6	6.07	55.2	0	22.8	21.5
Portugal*	2001	3,551,000	346	10.8	75.7	20.98	3.32	0
Slovakia	2001	1,884,846	350	11.63	75.9	0.1	3.7	10.3
Slovenia	2002	777,772	390	14	82.2	2.6	6.5	8.7
Spain	2001	20,800,000	527.98	13.9	81	9.7	1.6	0
Sweden	2002	4,300,000	482.7	Nav	38	22	24	16
United Kingdom	2001	25,456,000	452.2	Nav	69	9.3	20.8	0
Mean (rounded)	N/a	N/a	422.3	11.6	67	17.7	11	3.8

Source: Norris and Shiels (2004).

Note: N/a means not applicable; nav means not available; *: data refer to occupied dwellings only; consequently these countries are not included in the calculation of the mean number of dwellings per 1,000 inhabitants; ** =1994 data; *** =1996 data; **** This figure refers to dwellings rented from municipalities, but dwellings of this type may not necessarily be social rented. Depending on the policy of the individual landlord, some are let at commercial rents. The information on the average per cent of dwellings in each housing tenure is skewed by missing data for some countries. As a result the average values for the four tenure categories exceed 100 per cent.

mentioned in Chapter 1, the average household size has fallen from 3.5 persons per dwelling in 1986 to 2.9 in 2002. Indeed, the size of Irish households is expected to further shrink to converge with the EU average by 2011 (Department of the Environment and Local Government, 2000f).

Housing Accessibility

Table 18.2 examines one of the most important features of the housing stock in the EU – the availability of dwellings. It demonstrates that the number of dwellings per 1,000 inhabitants averages at 422.3 across the 25 countries under examination. However, this mean figure disguises marked variations in availability of housing between member countries. Spain and Greece have the highest numbers of dwellings per 1,000 inhabitants (527.9 and 505 respectively), not unexpectedly, in view of the high numbers of tourists who visit these countries, the proportion of dwellings in these countries which are vacant is also high. Broadly speaking the number of dwellings per 1,000 population is higher in the longstanding EU member states (440.6) compared to the new EU members (394.7). However, the averages for both these groups of countries is skewed by countries with particularly high or low numbers of dwellings per 1,000 population, such as the Czech Republic where the average number of dwellings per 1,000 inhabitants is 427 – well above the average for this region of Europe, and Ireland where average number of dwellings per 1,000 population in Ireland (391) is relatively low by western European standards and indeed closer to the average for the new member states. Among the 15 longstanding EU members only Portugal and Luxembourg have lower levels of housing availability than Ireland.

In relation to housing tenure, Table 18.2 reveals that 67 per cent of the housing stock in the European Union is owner-occupied. With 77.4 per cent of its dwelling stock in this category Ireland is close to the top of the ownership league among the longstanding EU members; indeed in this regard it is surpassed only by Portugal, Greece and Spain. However, the level of owner-occupation is even higher in the new member states in Central and Eastern Europe. Lithuania, Hungary and Slovenia have by far the highest levels of home ownership in the EU – 87.2 per cent, 86.9 per cent and 82.2 per cent respectively. The very high rates of home ownership in these countries is attributable principally to the aggressive programmes of housing privatisation of the formerly state-owned housing stock following their economic and political re-organisation in the early 1990s (Clapham et al, 1996).

As would be expected, in those countries where owner-occupancy rates are very high, the rental housing sector is consequently modest in size and vice versa. On average 17.7 per cent of dwellings in the EU are private rented and only 10.3 per cent are social rented. In this context, Ireland is characterised by lower levels of both private and social rented dwellings, accounting for 11 per cent and 6.9 per cent of the national housing stock respectively. However, levels of social renting are higher in the fifteen longstanding EU members (where an average of 11.3 per cent of dwellings are social rented), in comparison with the ten new EU members (where an average of 7 per cent of dwellings are social rented). The distribution of social rented dwellings is uneven in both groups of countries. The average figure for social rented dwellings in the longstanding EU members is skewed by Sweden, Denmark and the Netherlands where over 22 per cent of dwellings are social rented, whereas, in many other longstanding EU members such as Ireland, Italy, Belgium and Spain less than 7 per cent of the total housing stock is in the social rented sector. In contrast, with the exception of Poland and the Czech Republic, in a majority of the new EU member states under 7 per cent of dwellings are social rented. The variations in social renting in these countries reflect variations in the methods used to privatise the state-owned dwellings in these countries. In most cases this process was carried out in two stages. Ownership of the dwellings was first transferred to the local authorities, which then sold them to occupants generally at large discounts. However, the level of these discounts did vary between the countries in question as did the enthusiasm of municipalities for the sales policy (Clapham *et al,* 1996).

Housing Quality

Table 18.3 examines a second key feature of the housing stock – the standard of dwellings. It reveals that, in European terms, Ireland enjoys relatively high housing standards, but also highlights marked differences between the quality of dwellings in the longstanding EU members and the new members which are greater than the variations in housing availability, highlighted above.

Table 18.3 indicates that dwellings in the 25 EU member states contain an average of 3.9 rooms and have an average floor area of 76.5m^2. The Irish housing stock is characterised by a more generous number of rooms in European terms (5.2 per dwelling) but these are smaller in size than the EU average – the average floor area of Irish dwellings is 70.2m^2.

In terms of the availability of basic facilities, such as running water and central heating, 94.9 per cent of dwellings in the European Union as a whole enjoy the former facility, while 74.4 per cent are equipped with the latter. Again, Ireland fares well in this regard; virtually all (99.7 per cent) of dwellings in the country are served by running water and a significantly higher proportion are supplied with central heating (86.8 per cent) than the EU average.

The average age of dwellings in the EU reflects, to a certain extent, the historic patterns of economic and social development of the various member states. The United Kingdom has one of the oldest housing stocks in Europe; 41 per cent of dwellings in the country were constructed before 1945 which reflects

Table 18.3: Housing Quality in European Union Member States, Various Years

Country	Year to which Data Refer	Date of Construction (DC) (%)				Available Facilities (AF) (%)				Average Number of Rooms (AR)	Floor Area (FA) (in m²)
		Pre 1945	1945-1970	1970-1990	1990-Present	Running Water	Lavatory	Bath/Shower	Central Heating		
Austria	2002	26.8	28	28.7	16.4	99.9	98.7	97.5	87.3	4.3	60-90
Belgium	1996	31.8	29.8	34.1	4.2	Nav	Nav	Nav	Nav	Nav	Nav
Cyprus*	DC, AR, FA=2000; AF-1999	23*	10.7	38.1	28.2	99.2	97.7	94.8	50	5.8	144.8
Czech Republic	DC=1991; AF, FA=2001; AR=2000	41.9	24.6	33.5	0**	98.5	95.4	95.5	81.7	2.7	49.3
Denmark	DC, FA=2000; AF=2003	38.9	29.9	25.9	5.3	99.9	99.9	94.3	99.9	Nav	109.3
Estonia****	DC, AF=2002; AR, FA=2000	18.9	22.8	31.5	4.1	82	72	68	59	3.8	68.9
Finland	DC=1996; AF=2002; AR, FA=2000	12	32.9	46.2	7.9	98	96	99	92	3.8	85.7
France*	2002	29.4*	15.1	32.2	5.7	99.9	99.2	99.2	96.3	4	90
Germany*	DC=2002; FA=1996	27.9*	61		11.1	Nav	Nav	Nav	Nav	Nav	88.4
Greece	N/A	Nav	Nav	Nav	Nav	Nav	Nav	Nav	Nav	Nav	Nav
Hungary*	DC, AF=1996; AR, FA=2000	29.5	27.2	38.9	4	84.4	75.6	79.6	48.2	4.1	52
Ireland*	2002	20.5	17.6	36.2	25.7	99.7	Nav	Nav	86.8	5.2	70.2
Italy	DC=1991; AF=1995; FA=1996	29.5	40.7	29.8		99	99	99	79	Nav	88.3

Country	Year	Notes										
Latvia	2000	DC, AF, AR=2001; FA=2000	25	28	43	4	83.2	77.8	67	64.9	2-3	40-60
Lithuania			27	34	32	7	78.9	76.3	71.8	72	2-3	70.9
Luxembourg		DC, AR=2001; FA=1999	27.3		72.7		100	100	100	100	Nav	81.1
Malta	1995		25.5	22.2	43.1	9.1	99	97.7	96.6	0.7	5	Nav
Netherlands		DC, AF= 2002; AR=2000	20	27	53		100	100	100	90	4.2	Nav
Poland		DC, AF, AR=2002, FA= 1991	23.2	26.9	37	11.6	92.5	80.6	80.8	71.4	3.7	49
Portugal	1991		24.4	31.2	44.2	0	87.2	88.8	82.2	Nav	Nav	Nav
Slovakia	2001		11.5	35.2	46.6	6.7	94.7	60.2	62.2	76.3	3	40-60
Slovenia	2002		23.4	39.8	28.9	7.8	98.5	93	92	78.6	3	Nav
Spain	2001		22	29.8	34.3	13.8	98.6	96.8	Nav	53.2	5	76-90
Sweden		DC=2002; AF=2000, AR=1990; FA=1996	21	43	28	6	100	100	100	100	4.2	71
United Kingdom*	1991		41	22	38	0***	Nav	Nav	Nav	Nav	Nav	Nav
Mean (R)	N/a		25.9	28.7	34.4	11	94.9	86.4	88.3	74.4	3.9	76.5

Source: Norris and Shiels (2004) and United Nations Economic Commission for Europe (2002).

Note: * in these cases the data on date of construction supplied by housing ministries were not originally organised into the categories utilised above. These data were therefore reclassified for the purpose of including it in this table; ** these data only cover the period to 1990; *** these data only cover the period to 1996; **** 22.8% of the housing stock in Estonia is categorised as unknown in terms of age. The information on the average age of dwellings in each housing tenure is skewed by missing data for some countries. Where floor space data refer to a range (e.g. 80-100m²) the interval figure was used to calculate the mean.

its early industrial development compared to many of its European neighbours as well as a comparative lack of war damage during the twentieth century. In European terms Ireland is distinguished by a very young housing stock; 20.5 per cent of the Irish housing stock was built prior to 1945, compared to 25.9 per cent of the EU housing stock, while some 25.7 per cent of the Irish housing stock has been constructed since 1990 – a proportion which, among EU members, is exceeded only by Cyprus. As is explained later in this chapter the atypical age distribution of the Irish housing stock is the result of the comparatively high rate of new house building in this country over the last decade. It is also likely that it has contributed significantly to the relatively high housing standards in this country which were highlighted above.

Housing Policy

Examination of recent housing policy developments in European Union member states reveals that a large number of issues could be categorised as national policy trends insofar as they are the focus of policy interventions in a single European country or very small group of countries. For instance, as part of their negotiations regarding accession to the EU, the Maltese and Czech governments have introduced measures to restrict the purchase of second homes. In Cyprus the Government has introduced a number of measures to house families who are refugees as a result of the partition of the island in 1974. In addition, there are small numbers of pan-European housing policy trends which are common to the majority of the 25 countries under examination, including Ireland, although in some cases the way in which the Irish government has addressed these issues is distinctive in the wider European context. Furthermore, several issues are currently the focus of policy interventions in a relatively large group of countries. Broadly speaking these 'international policy trends' fall into two categories – policies common to the 15 countries which were European Union members prior to 2004, and those which are confined largely to some of all the 10 new member states that joined the EU in 2004. In this regard policy trends in Ireland do not differ dramatically from developments in the other longstanding EU members.

Pan-European Policy Trends

Unbalanced housing demand and supply, and related affordability problems, particularly in the major cities is currently the focus of policy initiatives in the vast majority of European countries. However, the extent and nature of this problem varies between countries as do the policy interventions it has inspired.

This book has revealed that unbalanced housing demand and supply across the housing market as a whole is currently of concern to policy makers in Ireland, but this concern is also shared by policy makers in Finland, the Netherlands,

Luxembourg and Spain. The data on economic and demographic trends pertinent to housing presented in Table 18.1 reveal why this is the case. Spain has enjoyed relatively high annual growth in GDP per capita in recent years, while Ireland, Finland, the Netherlands and Luxembourg have among the highest GPD per capita in the EU. Furthermore, Ireland has the highest rate of natural population increase in the EU. The convergence of these two factors explains the particularly high level of nationwide housing demand in Ireland at the current time. In order to address this problem, the Irish, Dutch and Finnish governments have increased investment in the servicing of building land and have improved the capacity of the spatial planning system in an effort to increase new housing output. In contrast, the Finnish Government has also introduced new types of co-operative ownership housing for households who cannot afford full home ownership, while in Luxembourg a reduced rate of capital gains tax payable on the sale of land or apartment blocks has been introduced for a limited period. If these fiscal measures do not lead to the release of more land for house building, the Government intends to introduce a progressive land tax to penalise the speculative retention of sites by land owners.

In most of the other EU members, housing policy interventions have been introduced to address disequilibrium in specific segments of the housing market or regions of the country. In most countries excess demand is concentrated in urban centres where economic and population growth is centred, although the countries which border the Mediterranean inflated demand in coastal, tourist areas is also an issue. In order to address the former problem, *Sustainable Communities: Building for the Future*, which was published by the United Kingdom government in 2003, aims to increase the provision of high-quality and affordable housing in areas of high demand and to tackle the housing shortage in London and the south east of England by providing for major growth in designated areas (United Kingdom, Office of the Deputy Prime Minister, 2003).

In addition, in several countries the converse problem of vacant and abandoned housing and low housing demand is also the focus of attention from policy makers. Low housing demand in Europe is concentrated principally in rural areas, and to a lesser extent in declining industrial centres. It is a more widespread problem in the new member states, whereas insofar as this problem exists in the longstanding members it tends to be a regional rather than a national problem and is often accompanied by strong demand in other parts of the same country. Sweden is an example of a country in this category. Excess housing demand, particularly the Stockholm region, is accompanied by high levels of vacancies in the social rented stock in areas where the population is in decline. In order to alleviate the burden on municipal housing companies (which provide most social housing in Sweden) with high vacancy rates, the National Board for Municipal Housing Support was set up in 2002. The Board's role is to help municipal housing companies which face this problem to remove surplus housing by recycling it for other uses or demolishing it.

Measures to promote the renovation and improved maintenance of the housing stock have also been introduced in most European countries in recent years. Among the longstanding member states, the refurbishment programmes introduced in Ireland and the United Kingdom are distinctive because both target the social housing sector. Ireland, Luxembourg, Germany and Portugal have also established more refurbishment programmes, which address other housing tenures. However, the various refurbishment grant and tax incentive schemes for owner occupied and private rented accommodation which are available in Ireland are more narrow, targeted on specific groups (older people and disabled people) and designated areas of the country, than those available in these other countries.

As would be expected in view of the problems in relation to housing standards in many of the new member states which were revealed above, policy makers in these countries are particularly concerned about refurbishment of the housing stock, most especially the portion comprised of apartment buildings constructed between the 1950s and 1980s using system building methods. As a result of poor initial construction standards and longstanding neglect of maintenance, these dwellings now require extensive refurbishment (Clapham *et al*, 1996). However, the task of improving them is encumbered by pressures on government finances combined with the fact that after the privatisation measures, many of these dwellings are now in the ownership of private individuals who may lack the means and/or the organisational capacity to arrange the requisite repairs (United Nations Economic Commission for Europe, 1997; 1999). In order to address this problem, compulsory reserve funds were introduced in Slovenia in 2002, which oblige all apartment owners to accumulate funds through monthly deposits for the maintenance and renewal of blocks. The Czech Government has established three programmes to fund the upgrading and repair of the prefabricated panel buildings which are common in its housing stock. At the wider EU level, housing refurbishment does not currently qualify for structural funding and there have been calls for this satiation to be changed during the next round of Structural Funds (covering the 2007-2012 period) (FEANTSA, 2003). Not surprisingly this has proved controversial, because of the significant costs involved, and also because, as Table 18.3 demonstrates, this reform would effect a sharp redistribution of resources from the longstanding members to the new EU members, particularly to those in Central and Eastern Europe.

International Policy Trends

Apart from the above-mentioned issues which are of concern to policy makers across Europe, there is a perceptible difference between the recent housing policy developments in the fifteen countries which were EU members prior to 2004, compared to the ten new EU members. Amongst the latter group, policy makers in the eight Central and Eastern European countries which joined the EU in 2004 share a particularly discrete set of concerns. This phenomenon reflects the distinctive political histories and recent economic and demographic development of these countries in comparison with the fifteen longstanding EU members.

In many of the longstanding EU members, housing policy currently places significant emphasis on expanding the stock of private rented housing, which is recognised as an important resource, particularly in the major cities where rents are high and housing affordability is consequently lower. In response, the Danish, Swedish and French governments have introduced incentives intended to encourage investment in this sector. On the basis of the various tax incentive schemes examined by MacLaran and Williams in Chapter 7 of this volume, Ireland also qualifies for inclusion in this category.

The management of social rented housing and its increasingly residual nature in socio-economic terms is also identified as a key issue in housing policy statements in many of the longstanding EU members. As a result, the governments of the Flanders and Wallonia regions of Belgium, Luxembourg and Denmark are endeavouring to promote a more diverse spatial mix of different housing tenures, in an effort to reduce the socio-spatial segregation of the disadvantaged. Of course, Part V of the Planning and Development Act, 2000, which was examined in Chapters 8, 14 and 15, is also an example of an initiative of this type. Indeed, in comparative terms Part V appears extremely radical, although in Luxembourg recent legislation obliges property developers to include at least 10 per cent rented housing in new housing developments to foster a greater social mix. This measure addresses all types of rented housing, not only social rented housing. However, the social mixing measures introduced in other EU member states in recent years are comparatively modest compared to Part V. For instance, the Government of the Flanders region of Belgium has recently introduced measures intended to facilitate households to buy or refurbish their dwellings in order to ensure a social mix in cities. In Denmark, as a result of recent reforms, pension funds will be permitted to develop mixed tenancy housing developments including rented and owner-occupied housing.

In many longstanding EU members, a range of reforms to arrangements for social housing provision and management has been introduced. In Denmark, for instance, in recent years housing policy has placed increased emphasis on the involvement of the private sector in providing and managing social housing by means of public-private partnership arrangements. The regional governments in

Belgium are working to enhance co-operation between the various associations which provide social housing, and if necessary encourage their geographical relocation in order to ensure that social housing needs in all parts of the country are adequately addressed. In Finland the income limits for access to social housing have recently been increased in order to address the problem of low demand for this type of housing in some parts of the country. The measures of this type which have been introduced in Ireland are examined in Chapter 9.

Socio-economic deprivation and the associated physical dereliction of housing in inner-city areas is also a focus of intervention by governments in several of the fifteen pre-2004 EU member states. Thus, in many of these countries a range of urban renewal measures has been introduced in recent years, typically involving tax incentives to encourage the provision of new and refurbished housing in these locations. The Netherlands is notable for the particularly large number of urban renewal initiatives in operation. Many of these were originally proposed in the Government policy statement *What People Want, Where People Live*, published in 2000 (Netherlands, Ministry of Housing Spatial Planning and the Environment, 2000). In comparison with the Irish urban renewal measures which are examined in Chapter 7, both the Dutch measures and those instituted in many other EU member states are distinguished by their multi-dimensional focus. In other words they target the social, community and economic aspects of urban decline, in addition to addressing the renewal of the built environment, particularly the housing stock, which has been the primary focus of interventions to date in Ireland.

In contrast to their counterparts in the West of the EU, housing policy makers in Estonia, the Czech Republic, Hungary, Latvia, Lithuania, Poland, Slovakia and Slovenia are primarily concerned with responding to the effects of the sale of formerly state-owned housing. One of these effects is a shortage of social rented units in many Central and Eastern European countries, which policy makers are attempting to address by increasing the output of dwellings in this tenure. As revealed in Table 18.2, the private rented sector in many of these countries is also very small and, in the view of many policy makers, its further development has been impeded by rent control measures. Thus, the Slovakian government has recently liberalised the regulation of this sector and the Polish and Estonian governments are also currently considering potential reforms in this regard.

The comparative under-development of the private mortgage lending market is also of concern to policy makers in several of the new EU member states, on the grounds that this deficiency has hindered the provision of new private housing because neither potential property developers nor home buyers can access the requisite finance. In response, the Polish, Slovenian and Slovakian governments have all funded low-interest loan schemes to enable households and social housing providers to build or renovate dwellings. In Estonia government intervention in the mortgage market has taken a distinctive form – the State Bank guarantees a proportion of mortgages raised by specified types of households from commercial lenders.

Outcomes

Public Expenditure on Housing

Table 18.4 details the proportion of Gross National Product devoted to public expenditure on housing policies in the fifteen longstanding European Union member states. Although these data probably underestimate the true level of public expenditure on this area, because they generally exclude revenue forgone as a result of tax exemptions for housing expenditure (see European Central Bank, 2003 for a full exposition of the shortcomings of these data), they provide a useful indication of general trends in this regard. Table 18.4 clearly indicates that this trend is in the direction of stagnant or decreasing public expenditure on housing. The percentage of GDP devoted to housing policies in the countries under examination declined from 0.98 per cent in 1980 to 0.88 in 2000. The European Central Bank (2003: 39) reports that this trend '… appears to reflect a change of policy stance towards more targeted spending' – an analysis which is supported by the discussion of recent trends in housing policy in the pre-2004 EU members, presented earlier in this chapter, which highlights, for instance, increased emphasis on the improvement of the housing stock in declining neighbourhoods, rather than on the stock as a whole.

Table 18.4: Percentage of Gross Domestic Product Devoted to Public Expenditure on Housing Policies in the Fifteen Longstanding European Union Member States, 1980, 1990, 2000

	1980	1990	2000
Austria	1.4	1.3	1.3****
Belgium	Nav	0.8	1.0***
Denmark	1.3	1.3	1.4
Finland	1.4	1.2	1.6
France	Nav	1.1	1.1****
Germany	0.9	0.6	0.9
Greece	0.2	0.2	0.2
Ireland	Nav	Nav	Nav
Italy	0.3	0.14	0.1
Luxembourg	Nav	0.8**	0.6

Netherlands	Nav	0.9	0.7****
Portugal	Nav	0.3	0.8
Spain	1.3*	2.3	1.4****
Sweden	1.0	1.5	0.4
United Kingdom	Nav	Nav	Nav
Mean (rounded)	0.98	0.96	0.88

Source: European Central Bank (2003).
Note: Nav means not available; * = 1981 data; ** = 1992 data; *** = 1997 data; **** = 1999 data; ***** = 1998 data; the figures for Belgium cover the various tax deductions granted by central authorities; the figures for Germany include revenue forgone and public housing allowances; the figures for Portugal refer to revenue forgone due to tax exemptions and interest reliefs as well as to support for public housing; the figures for Sweden include rent and interest allowances.

Although no comparable data are available for Ireland, analysis of the data on housing expenditure and Gross National Product (GNP) presented in Tables 1.2 and 1.3 in Chapter 1 of this volume indicate that the predominant trend in this country is in the opposite direction to that which prevails in the other longstanding members of the EU. Public investment in housing as a percentage of GNP in Ireland grew from 0.846 in 1994, to 9.96 in 2000, to 1.53 in 2003.

Housing Output

These higher levels of public investment are reflected in a higher level of total housing output in Ireland in recent years, compared to most of the rest of the European Union and, more directly, in a higher level of state-subsidised social housing output. The evidence in this regard is set out in Figure 18.1. This graph reveals that Ireland had by far the highest housing output per 1,000 inhabitants in the European Union in 2002 – 14.7 compared to an average of 4.3 among the 25 countries which are currently EU members. During this year Spain and Cyprus had the second and third highest housing output in the EU but their rates of construction were far behind Ireland – 9.4 per and 8.6 dwellings per 1,000 inhabitants respectively. Conversely, among the countries under examination, housing output was lowest in the eight Central and Eastern European states which acceded to EU membership in 2004 (which had an average output of 2.11 dwellings per 1,000 inhabitants in 2002) and in Sweden (where output was only marginally higher at 2.7 per 1,000 inhabitants in 2002). As was mentioned above, housing output in the former group of countries is constrained by the underdevelopment of the commercial mortgage market which inhibits both developers and prospective purchasers of dwellings from lending.

Figure 18.1: Housing Output Per 1,000 Inhabitants and % of Housing Output Completed by Private Investors in European Union Member States, 2002

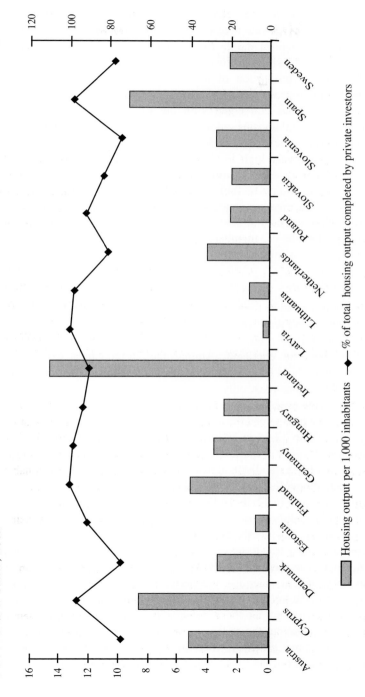

Source: United Nations Economic Commission for Europe (2004).

Note: Data for the following countries are not available: Belgium, Czech Republic, France, Greece, Italy, Luxembourg, Malta, Portugal, Spain and the United Kingdom.

Figure 18.1 also reveals that the proportion of total Irish housing output which is completed by private investors has fallen from 95.8 per cent in 1987 (well above the average for the 25 EU member states which was 84.2 in that year) to 89.9 in 2002 (which is close to the EU average of 89.2). This means, conversely, that the proportion of new house building in Ireland built by government and non-profit agencies, which consists principally of social and affordable housing, has converged with the EU average over this period. Moreover, because total housing output rates in Ireland per 1,000 population are very high in European terms, this also means that Irish rates of social housing output are comparatively high in absolute terms. Trends in relation to non-market house building differ sharply between the old and new EU member states, however. According to Table 17.5, 79.75 of new dwellings built in the fifteen longstanding member states in 2002 were built by private investors, compared to 90.98 per cent in the ten new EU members. Thus when compared with other longstanding EU members the level of output of non-market housing in Ireland appears less impressive.

Housing Affordability

The available information regarding the affordability of housing in European countries is set out in Figure 18.2. This graph highlights a number of significant recent developments in relations to this aspect of the housing system in the different parts of the continent. Among the 25 countries examined, the percentage of household income which is devoted to housing, water, electricity, gas and other fuels has risen only marginally, from 19.13 per cent in 1995 to 19.29 in 2000. However, there are some regional differences in this regard. In the ten countries which joined the EU in 2004, housing costs have risen rapidly, from 12.8 in 1995 to 17.34 in 2000. In contrast, although housing costs have been consistently higher in the fifteen longstanding EU members since 1991, in recent years they have stabilised, albeit at the higher level of 20.29 in 1995 and 20.69 in 2000, although Ireland is an exception to this trend because housing costs here rose from 16.12 in 1995 (well below the average for the fifteen longstanding EU members) to 19.43 in 2000 (just below the average for the fifteen longstanding EU members).

The drivers of these trends are complex and numerous. The data presented in Figure 18.2 include expenditure on all housing costs including rent and mortgages and utility costs such as water, gas and electricity. In the new EU members there is evidence that the utility costs have risen dramatically during the second half of the 1990s as the markets for these commodities were liberalised (Norris and Shiels, 2004). In addition, the ending of controls on private sector rents which were mentioned above probably contributed to inflation in housing for some households in this part of the EU (Norris and Shiels, 2004).

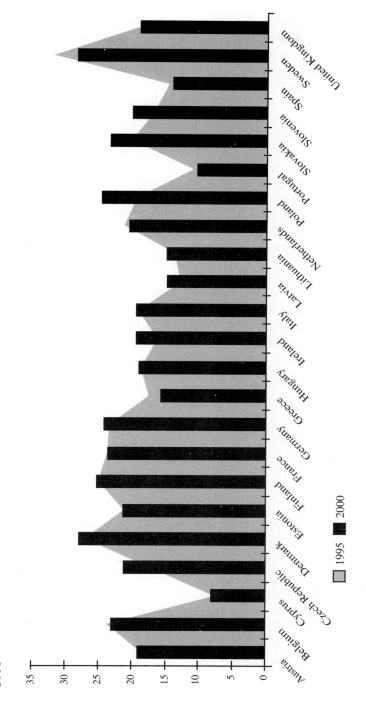

Figure 18.2: Expenditure on Housing Costs as Percentage of Household Income in European Union Member States, 1995, 2000

Source: Eurostat

Note: Data are at current prices and include household consumption expenditure on housing, water, electricity, gas and other fuels. Data for Luxembourg and Malta are not available.

In the fifteen longstanding EU member states the large proportion of home owners who have mortgages (many home owners in the new member states have no mortgage because their dwelling was transferred to them by the state with minimal or no charge) means that mortgage interest rates and house prices are a key determinant of housing affordability. Over the last decade there has been a substantial reduction in interest rates in many of the longstanding EU member states, including Ireland, to the extent that in some cases interest rates are currently at an historic low. The timing of these reductions in mortgage interest rates is coincident with the adoption of the Euro as a single currency by twelve of the longstanding EU members. This development was a key factor in the stagnation of housing costs highlighted above.

At the same time however, falling interest rates have bolstered strong housing demand in some longstanding EU members and, as Figure 18.3 reveals, this has driven a sharp increase in mortgage lending. This growth in residential mortgage debt has been especially marked in Ireland, which helps to explain the marked expansion in housing costs for Irish households which was revealed in Figure 18.2. In addition, as was mentioned in Chapter 1 of this volume, in the Irish case falling interest rates were one of the factors that contributed to an unprecedented increase in house prices since the mid-1990s. Indeed, Figure 18.4 demonstrates that house price growth in Ireland between 1994 and 2003 was by far the highest of the fifteen longstanding EU members. This factor may also explain the increase in the proportion of income which Irish households devote to housing over the same period.

Figure 18.3: Volume and Growth of Residential Mortgage Debt in the Fifteen Longstanding European Union Member States (in € Billion and Annual Percentage Change), 2003

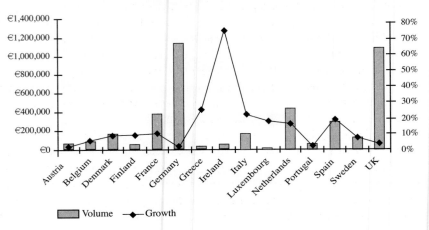

Source: European Mortgage Federation, 2004.

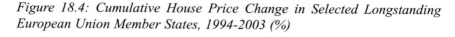

Figure 18.4: Cumulative House Price Change in Selected Longstanding European Union Member States, 1994-2003 (%)

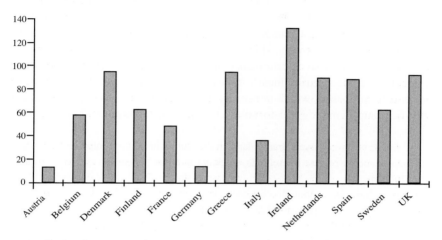

Source: European Mortgage Federation, 2004.
Note: data for Luxembourg and Portugal are not available.

Concluding Comments

This chapter has revealed that, when assessed at the macro level, Ireland's housing system has preformed impressively over the last decade in comparison with many other EU member states. Of particular note is the achievement of the Irish home-building industry in constructing record numbers of new dwellings in recent years, aided no doubt by the comparatively *laissez faire* planning system, as described by Bannon in Chapter 14. Without this dramatic increase in output, it is likely that house price inflation would have been even greater and the accessibility problems in the owner occupied sector, identified by Dáithí Downey in Chapter 3, would have been considerably worse. In addition, this level of output helped to address the historic paucity of the Irish housing stock and to improve housing standards. In contrast, low levels of new house construction are currently of concern to governments in many other EU members, because they are associated with house price booms, and potentially, busts (Chesire, 2004). As a result for instance, the British government recently commissioned a *Review of Housing Supply* in order to ascertain how output can be increased (Barker, 2003).

In European terms, the level of public expenditure on housing in Ireland is also comparatively high, as is social housing output as a percentage of total housing output. Furthermore, some recent housing policy initiatives in this country, such as the tenure mixing provisions of Part V of the Planning and Development Act, 2000, are radical when compared to measures with similar aims instituted by some neighbouring countries. However, it is important to acknowledge that the increased expenditure on housing is a relatively recent development, after severe retrenchment in this area from the mid-1980s and current levels of social housing output are low in historic terms. In addition, Redmond, Williams and Punch argue in Chapter 15 that amendments to the provisions of Part V, introduced in 2002, will substantially reduce its impact.

Despite the impressive performance of the Irish housing system at the macro level, the various contributions to this book have highlighted a multitude of micro-level problems, which negatively affect specific regions or districts and specific groups – mainly, but not solely, low-income households. These include:

- first-time home buyers, particularly in the Dublin area (see Chapter 3)
- low-income private households, particularly those dependent on rent assistance (Chapter 6)
- households on waiting lists for social housing (Chapters 8 and 11)
- homeless people (Chapter 12)
- Travellers (Chapter 13)
- those forced to commute long distances to work in order to access affordable housing or to sit for hours in traffic gridlock caused by unsustainably low development and failure to integrate public transport provision with new housing development (Chapters 14 and 15).

These micro-level failures cannot be attributed to lack of policy initiatives or political priority. Housing was not mentioned in the two key economic policy statements published during the early 1990s (the 1989 and 1993 National Development Plans); nor was it identified as a target in the National Anti-Poverty Strategy (the key contemporary social policy statement); nor addressed in the *Partnership 2000* agreement negotiated in 1996 between government and the 'social partners' (Government of Ireland, 1989, 1993, 1997a, 1996b). The updated versions of these documents, published in the late 1990s, all identified housing as a central issue (Government of Ireland, 2000a, 2000b; 2003; Department of Social Community and Family Affairs, 2002). The Department of the Environment, Heritage and Local Government published only two housing policy statements between 1990 and 1996 (Department of the Environment, 1991, 1995b). However, it has produced nine since the latter year (Housing Management Group, 1996, 1998; Commission on the Private Rented Residential Sector, 2000; Department of the Environment and Local Government, 1998a, 1999a, 1999b, 2000a, 2000d; Department of the Environment and Local Government, Department of Health and Children, Department of Education and Science, 2002). In addition, in 2002 the first national spatial development strategy for over 30 years was published (Department of the Environment and Local Government, 2002).

Furthermore, it is important to acknowledge that some of Ireland's current housing problems would have been difficult to prevent by policy intervention, given the rapid economic and population growth described in Chapter 1. For instance, the National Economic and Social Council (2004) argues that, in view of these factors, the rapid increase in house prices in the late 1990s was, to a significant extent, inevitable.

However, shortcomings in the policy-making and implementation process also contributed to the current housing problems outlined in this book. The following aspects of housing and planning policy were particularly significant in this regard:

- Lack of macro-level analysis of the collective impact of and the interaction between the various policy measures introduced during the last decade, coupled with the fast pace of policy development at the time, led to the introduction of contradictory initiatives. For instance, as Galligan mentions in Chapter 5, the fiscal disincentives to residential property investment introduced to stem house price inflation, were repealed after they contributed to private rent inflation. Similarly, Chapters 14 and 15 also highlight a variety of problems stemming from the failure to integrate housing and planning policy. For these reasons, a white paper, or similar macro-level housing policy analysis is now urgently required from the DoEHLG. A document of this type has not been produced since 1969 (Department of Local Government, 1969).

- The centralisation of housing policy-making in the DoEHLG has led to a tendency to devise nationally orientated housing policies, with relatively minor variations in their terms to reflect local or regional differences. This tendency was no doubt reinforced by the extreme localism of Irish politics, which renders positive discrimination in favour of one locality, over another, practically impossible. Chapters 15 and 16 of this book identify a whole host of problems caused by insufficient regionalism in policy in both urban and rural areas. Admittedly, during the last decade various new housing policy-making arrangements have been established in local authorities, such as local Traveller accommodation consultative committees and housing strategies. However, in the absence of reform of housing finance, which gives local authorities control over revenue generation and spending on this area, the impact of these bodies is likely to be small.

- Failure to address policy implementation has been a key problem. As Silke points out in Chapter 13, this problem is particularly obvious in the case of Travellers as, despite relatively sophisticated policy instruments and generous finding, output of Traveller specific accommodation has fallen far short of target. Similarly in Chapter 14 Bannon makes similar points in relation to the planning system. He relates this 'implementation gap' to lack of implementation guidelines from the DoEHLG which are necessary because of the traditional shortage of professional planning staff in the planning system. In Chapter 9 Norris and Redmond argue that the non-professional, non-specialist staffing system employed in local authority housing departments also necessitates detailed implementation guidance.

The lack of an evidence basis for housing policy-making has been a significant contributor to the above-mentioned problems. Since the abolition of An Foras Forbartha in the mid-1980s, the DoEHLG has lacked a research capacity in planning, while it never had a significant housing research capacity. In addition, the potential of administrative data to inform housing and planning research and review has not been significantly exploited (although see Murray and Norris, 2001 for one example of this type of work in housing). Although non-governmental organisations – principally Threshold, the Simon Community and Focus Ireland – have carried out some very significant housing research projects over the years, the lack of a comprehensive evidence base has made housing policy-making, review and the formulation of implementation strategies very difficult. As was mentioned in the Introduction to this book, in recent years, this shortcoming has begun to be addressed. The Housing Unit has conducted a significant amount of housing research for the DoEHLG and local authorities, the above-mentioned non-governmental organisations have expanded their research programmes, and an increasing amount of research has begun to emerge from the universities and other third-level institutions. However, compared to most other EU countries, particularly the United Kingdom, the Netherlands and Sweden, the discipline of housing studies is still very much in its infancy in Ireland. It is hoped that this book will help contribute to its growth and maturity.

Chapter Notes

Notes to Chapter 4

1   This paper is based on research carried out for the Combat Poverty Agency. A full report of this research is published in Fahey et al (2004a).

2   The median of the distribution is now widely employed in deriving relative income thresholds because the mean can be substantially affected by very high or low reported incomes in which one may not have great confidence. The 60 per cent threshold is arbitrary but often used. The equivalence scale employed at this point attributes a value of 1 to the first adult in the household, 0.66 to each other adult, and 0.33 to each child.

Notes to Chapter 5

1   It should be noted that the increase in privately rented households will be greater than the increase in units, given the prevalence of house sharing arrangements.

Notes to Chapter 6

1   In this context, the term signals an increasing emphasis on housing as an economic or investment good, which provides an opportunity for capital accumulation (exchange values), rather than as a social or merit good meeting fundamental human needs like shelter, home, security, and so on (use values).

2   Rather like the conservative Anglo-American neo-liberal policies which gained momentum through the 1980s, affecting everything from welfare provision to the structural adjustment programmes imposed on the poorest, under-developed countries, neo-liberalism is the doctrine of privatisation, market approaches, deregulation, reducing state intervention and, effectively, promoting the interests of private capital.

3   It is unfortunate that much of the recent debate on housing problems in political and media spheres has been diverted (and almost fully absorbed) by concerns with tenure access for young middle-class households. The real content of any housing crisis has always been the everyday realities of unmet need, displacement, exclusion, vulnerability, overcrowding and homelessness – critical developmental issues, but often lost in the clamour about the (un)affordability of private ownership for relatively advantaged households.

4   It should be noted that this is indicative only since it is based on the total number of cases recorded over the year. This figure is somewhat ambiguous because a significant minority of claimants may be on the scheme for short-term periods only.

Notes to Chapter 11

1   Residualisation of tenants is not synonymous with residualisation of housing estates, and poor tenants may live in former council estates where a majority have bought out their homes, or in flat complexes where the tenant purchase scheme does not usually apply. In general, tenants with a job have been able to buy their house at a subsidised price, while those who have not managed to buy are more likely to have experienced a history of unemployment and low income.

Notes to Chapter 14

1   Any views expressed are the author's and not necessarily those of the National Economic and Social Forum.

Notes to Chapter 17

1   The author wishes to gratefully acknowledge the financial support for this research by the Irish Research Council for Humanities and Social Sciences.
2   In addition, if an organisation had an official policy on rural housing, this was also included in this analysis.

References

Aalen, F. (1997), 'The challenge of change', in Aalen, F., Whelan, K. and Stout, M. (eds), *Atlas of the Irish rural landscape,* Cork: Cork University Press.

Aalen, F. (1990), *The Iveagh Trust: The First Hundred Years – 1890-1990,* Dublin: Iveagh Trust.

Aalen, F. (1992), 'Health and Housing in Dublin c. 1850-1921', in Aalen, F. and Whelan, K. (eds), *Dublin City and County: From Prehistory to Present,* Dublin: Geography Publications.

Aalen, F. (1985), 'The Working Class Housing Movement in Dublin, 1850-1920', in Bannon, M. (ed.), *The Emergence of Irish Planning, 1880-1950,* Dublin: Turoe Press.

Allen, R. and Bowley, A. (1935), *Family Expenditure: A Study of its Variation*, London, P.S. King & Son.

Allgood, S. and Warren, R.S. (2003), 'The Duration of Homelessness: Evidence from a National Survey', *Journal of Housing Economics*, vol. 12, no. 4, pp 273-290.

Anderson, I. and Tulloch, D. (2000), *Pathways Through Homelessness: A Review of the Research Evidence.* Edinburgh: Scottish Homes.

Arnstien, S. (1969), 'A ladder of citizenship participation', *Journal of the American Institute of Planners,* vol. 35, no. 4, pp 216-224.

Atkins and Associates (2004), *Regional Planning Guidelines for the Greater Dublin Area,* Dublin: Dublin Regional Authority.

Bacon, P. (1998), 'The Role of Housing in Creating Sustainable Development', *Proceedings of Joint RIAI /IPI Conference*, Dublin, 19 November.

Bacon, P. and Associates (1998), *An Economic Assessment of Recent House Price Developments*, Dublin: Stationery Office.

Bacon, P. and Associates (1999), *The Housing Market – An Economic Review and Assessment*, Dublin: Stationery Office.

Bacon, P. and Associates (2000), *The Housing Market in Ireland: An Economic Evaluation of Trends and Prospects,* Dublin: Stationery Office.

Baer, W. (1976), 'The evolution of housing indicators and housing standards: Some lessons for the future, *Public Policy*, vol. 24, no. 13, pp 361-393.

Bain, M. and Watt, P. 1999, *Report on Tenant and Resident Participation in Estate Management: The Dún Laoghaire-Rathdown Tenant and Resident Initiative,* Dublin: Dún Laoghaire-Rathdown County Council.

Baker, J. (1998), 'Equality', in Healy, S. and Reynolds, B. (eds), *Social Policy in Ireland: Principles, Practice and Problems*, Dublin: Oak Tree Press.

Baker, T. and O'Brien, L. (1979), *The Irish Housing System: A Critical Overview.* Economic and Social Research Institute, Broadsheet no. 17, Dublin: Economic and Social Research Institute.

Ballymun Regeneration Ltd (1998a), *Integrated Area Plan Under the Urban Renewal*

Scheme: Submitted to the Department of the Environment by Ballymun Regeneration Ltd, Dublin: Ballymun Regeneration Ltd.

Ballymun Regeneration Ltd (1998b), *Masterplan for the New Ballymun,* Dublin: Ballymun Regeneration Ltd.

Banks, J., Blundell, R., Smith, J.P. and Smith, Z. (2003), *Housing Wealth over the Life-Cycle in the Presence of Housing Price Volatility,* London: Institute for Fiscal Studies and University College London.

Bannon, M.J. (1979), 'Urban Land' in Gillmor, D.A. (ed.), *Irish Resources and Land Use,* Dublin: Institute of Public Administration.

Bannon, M.J. (1983), 'Urbanisation in Ireland: Growth and Regulation', in Blackwell, J. and Convery, F. (eds), *Promise and Performance: Irish Environmental Policies Analysed,* Dublin: REPC.

Bannon, M.J. (1999), 'The Greater Dublin Region: Planning for its Transformation and Development', in Killen, J. and MacLaran, A. (eds), *Dublin: Contemporary Trends and Issues for the Twenty-First Century,* Dublin: Geographical Society of Ireland and the Centre for Urban and Regional Studies, TCD.

Bannon, M.J. (2004a), 'Service Activity Concentration in Dublin and its Implications for National Urban Policy and the Regional Development of the Country', paper presented to the City Regions: Economic Change, Technology and Knowledge Research Group, Urban Institute Ireland, UCD, 3 June 2004.

Bannon, M.J. (2004b), Irish Urbanisation: Trends, Actions and Policy Challenges, *Working Paper Number 1,* Dublin: Department of Planning and Environmental Policy, University College Dublin.

Barker, K. (2003), *Review of Housing Supply: Securing our Future Housing Needs,* London: HMSO.

Barlow, J. and Duncan, S. (1988), 'The Use and Abuse of Housing Tenure', in *Housing Studies,* vol. 3, no. 4, pp 219-231.

Bell, J. (1989), *Women and Children First, A Report by The National Campaign for the Homeless on Homeless Women and their Children in Dublin,* Dublin: National Campaign for the Homeless.

Bengtsson, B (1998), 'Tenants' Dilemma – On Collective Action in Housing', *Housing Studies,* vol. 13, no. 1, pp 99-120.

Bergin, A., Cullen, J., Duffy, D., FitzGerald, J., Kearney, I. and McCoy, D. (2003), *Medium Term Review, 2003-2010,* Dublin: The Economic and Social Research Institute, p. 60.

Blackwell, J. (1988a), *A Review of Housing Policy,* Dublin: National Economic and Social Council.

Blackwell, J. (1988b), 'Paying for Policy: Housing Options', in Blackwell, J. (ed.), *Towards an Efficient and Equitable Housing Policy,* Dublin: Institute of Public Administration.

Bluestone, B. and Harrison, B. (1982), *The Deindustrialization of America: Plant Closings, Community Abandonment and the Dismantling of Basic Industry,* New York: Basic Books.

Bluestone, B. and Harrison, B. (1988), *The Great American Job Machine: the Proliferation of Low-Wage Employment in the US Economy,* New York: Basic Books.

Brady Shipman Martin; Kirk McClure Morton, Fitzpatrick Associates, Colin Buchanan and Partners (1999), *Strategic Planning Guidelines for the Greater Dublin Area,* Dublin: Dublin Corporation.

Brennan, B. (2002), *The Sustainable Neighbourhood in New Housing,* Dublin: RIAI Publications.

Brennan, C., McCashin, A. and O'Shea, J. (2001), *Partnership for Housing Renewal* Dublin: Canal Communities Partnership.

Brooke, S. (2001), *Social Housing for the Future: Can Housing Associations Meet the Challenge?* Dublin: Policy Studies Institute.

Brooke, S. and Norris, M. (2001), *The Housing Management Initiatives Grants Scheme: An Evaluation,* Dublin: Housing Unit.

Buchanan and Partners (1969), *Regional Studies in Ireland,* Dublin: An Foras Forbartha.

Burbridge, M. *et al* (1981), *An Investigation of Difficult-to-Let Housing,* three volumes, HDD Occasional paper, 5/80, London: HMSO.

Butler, S. (1997), 'The War on Drugs: Reports from the Irish Front', *Economic and Social Review,* vol. 28, no. 2, pp 157-175.

Cairncross, L., Clapham, D. and Goodlad, R. (1997), *Housing Management, Consumers and Citizens,* London: Routledge.

Callan, T., Nolan, B., Whelan, B.J, Hannan, D.F. and Creighton, S. (1989), *Poverty, Income and Welfare in Ireland*, General Research Series No. 146, Dublin: Economic and Social Research Institute.

Campbell, S. and Fainstein, S. (eds) (1996), *Readings in Planning Theory,* Blackwell: Oxford.

Cantillon, S., Corrigan, C., Kirby, P. and O'Flynn, J. (eds) (2001), *Rich and Poor: Perspectives on Tackling Inequality in Ireland*, Dublin: Oak Tree Press.

Carley, M. (2002), *Community Regeneration and Neighbourhood Renewal: A Review of the Evidence*, Edinburgh: Communities Scotland.

Carlson, H. (1990), 'Women and Homelessness in Ireland', *The Irish Journal of Psychology,* vol. 11, no. 1, pp 68-76

Carmody, P. and McEvoy, M. (1996), *A Study of Irish Female Prisoners*, Dublin: Stationery Office.

Carmona, M. (2001), *Housing Design Quality: through Policy, Design and Review,* London: Spon.

Castells, M. (1983), *The City and the Grassroots: A Cross-Cultural Theory of Urban Social Movements,* London: Edward Arnold.

Castells, M. (1996), *The Rise of the Network Society,* Oxford: Blackwell.

CDP (1977), *The Costs of Industrial Change,* London: Community Development Projects.

Central Bank of Ireland (2004), *Irish Economic Statistics, Autumn 2004*, Dublin: Central Bank of Ireland.

Central Bank of Ireland (2003), *Quarterly Economic Bulletin, Spring 2003*, Central Bank of Ireland, Dublin

Central Statistics Office (1954), *Census of Population of Ireland, 1946, Volume 4: Housing*, Dublin: Stationery Office.

Central Statistics Office (1961) *Census of Population of Ireland, 1961*, Dublin: Stationery Office.

Central Statistics Office (1977), *Household Budget Survey 1973,* Dublin: Stationery Office.

Central Statistics Office (1984), *Household Budget Survey 1980,* Dublin: Stationery Office.

Central Statistics Office (1989), *Household Budget Survey 1987,* Dublin: Stationery Office.

Central Statistics Office (1996) *Census 1991, Volume 10, Housing*, Dublin: Stationery Office.

Central Statistics Office (1997), *Household Budget Survey 1994-95*, Dublin: Stationery Office.

Central Statistics Office (2000), *Quarterly National Household Survey – Housing and Households: 3rd Quarter, 1998*, Cork: Central Statistics Office.

Central Statistics Office (2001a), *Household Budget Survey 1999-2000*, Dublin: Stationery Office.

Central Statistics Office (2001b), *Principal Economic Statistics*, Dublin: Stationery Office.

Central Statistics Office (2002), *Census 2002: Preliminary Report*, Dublin: Central Statistics Office.

Central Statistics Office (2003), *Census 2002: Principal Socio-Economic Results*, Dublin: Central Statistics Office.

Central Statistics Office (2004a), *Census 2002: Volume 8 – Irish Traveller Community*, Dublin: Stationery Office.

Central Statistics Office (2004b), *Census 2002: Volume 13 – Housing*, Dublin: Central Statistics Office.

Central Statistics Office (2004c), *Quarterly National Household Survey: Housing and Households*, Dublin: Stationery Office.

Chapman, M. and Kirk, K. (2001), *Lessons for Community Capacity Building: A Summary of Research Evidence*, Edinburgh: Scottish Homes.

Chartered Institute of Housing (1999), *Resident Involvement in Housing Services: Good Practice Briefing No.15*, Coventry: Chartered Institute of Housing.

Cherry, G. (1995), *Making Sense of Twentieth-Century Planning: A Socio-Political Perspective*, Dublin: Department of Regional and Urban Planning, UCD, Occasional Paper No.1.

Cheshire, P. (2004), 'The British Housing Market: Constrained and Exploding', *Urban Policy and Research*, vol. 22, no. 1, pp 13-22.

Clapham, D. (1997), 'The Social Construction of Housing Management Research', *Urban Studies*, vol. 34, nos 5-6, pp 744-761.

Clapham, D., Hegedüs, J., Kintrea, K. and Tosics, I. (1996), *Housing Privatization in Eastern Europe*, London: Greenwood Press.

Clayton, V. (forthcoming), unpublished PhD thesis, Trinity College, Dublin.

Cleary, A. and Prizeman, G. (1998), *Homelessness and Mental Health: a Research Report*, Dublin: Social Science Research Centre, UCD/Homelessness and Mental Health Action Group.

Clinch, P., Convery, F. and Walsh, B. (2002), *After the Celtic Tiger, Challenges Ahead*. Dublin: O'Brien Press.

Cloke, P. (1983), *An Introduction to Rural Settlement Planning*, London: Methuen

Cole, I. and Furbey, R. (1994), *The Eclipse of Council Housing*, London: Routledge.

Cole, I., Hickman, P., Millward, L. and Reid, B. (1999), *Developing Good Practice in Tenant Participation*, London: HMSO.

Collins, B. and McKeown, K. (1992) *Referral and Resettlement in the Simon Community*, Dublin: Simon Community, National Office.

Collins, M. (2001), 'From Experience to Analysis' in Farrell, F. and Watt, P. (eds) *Responding to Racism in Ireland*, Dublin: Veritas.

Commission of European Communities DG.XI (1990), *Green Paper on the Urban Environment*, Luxembourg: Commission of European Communities.

Commission on Itinerancy (1963), *Report of the Commission on Itinerancy*, Dublin: Stationery Office.

Commission on Taxation (1982), *First Report: Direct Taxation*, Dublin: Stationery Office.

Commission on Taxation (1983), *Report of the Commission on Taxation*, Dublin: Stationery Office.

Commission on the Private Rented Residential Sector (2000) *Report of the Commission on the Private Rented Residential Sector,* Dublin: Stationery Office.

Commission on the Relief of the Poor, including the Insane Poor (1928), *Report,* Dublin: Stationery Office.

Commission on the Status of People with Disabilities (1996), *Report of the Commission on the Status of People with Disabilities: A Strategy for Equality*, Dublin: Stationery Office.

Committee to Monitor and Co-ordinate the Implementation of the Recommendations of the Task Force on the Travelling Community (2000), *First Progress Report*, Dublin: Department of Justice, Equality and Law Reform.

Conroy, E. (1997), 'Centre and Periphery, Housing in Ireland', in Becker, A., Olley, J. and Wang, W. (eds), *Ireland: 20th Century Architecture,* Munich: Prestel.

Conway, B. (2001), 'Democratising the local authority tenant community relationship', *Administration*, vol. 49, no. 3, pp 3-19.

Cooper, C. and Hawtin, M. (eds) (1997), *Housing, Community and Conflict: Understanding Resident Involvement,* Aldershot: Arena Press.

Cooper, C. and Hawtin, M. (eds) (1998), *Resident Involvement and Community Action: Theory to Practice,* Coventry: Chartered Institute of Housing.

Co-ordinating Group of Secretaries (1996), *Delivering Better Government.* Dublin: Stationery Office.

Corbett, J. and Corbett, M. (2000), *Designing Sustainable Communities: Learning from Village Homes,* Washington: Island Press.

Cork County Council (2003), *Cork Rural Design Guide: Building a New House in the Countryside,* Cork: Cork County Council.

Cork Simon (1999), *Homelessness in Cork*, Cork: Cork Simon Community.

Costello, L. (2000), *In from the Cold: Proposals for the Provision of Accommodation for Homeless Street Drinkers in Dublin City*, Dublin: Homeless Initiative.

Costello, L. and Howley, D. (1999), *Under Dublin's Neon: A Report on Street Drinkers in Dublin,* Dublin: CentreCare.

Costello, L. and Howley, D. (2000), *Working Towards Inclusion: A feasibility study on the provision of accommodation for people sleeping rough and using drugs in Dublin City,* Dublin: Dublin Simon Community and Merchants' Quay Project. Unpublished Report.

Crehan, J., Lyons, N. and Laver, M. (1987), *The Effects of Self-Care Skills and Homelessness on the Independent Living Potential of Long-Stay Psychiatric Patients,* Galway: Social Sciences Research Centre, University College Galway.

Cronin, P. (2002) 'Tax Incentives for Property Investment', *The Property Valuer*, Spring, Dublin: IAVI.

Crook, T. and Kemp, P. (1996), 'The Revival of Private Rented Housing in Britain', *Housing Studies,* vol. 11, no. 1, pp 51-68.

Crowley, F. (2003), *Mental Illness: The Neglected Quarter,* Dublin: Amnesty International.

Crowley, N. (1999), 'Travellers and Social Policy', in Quinn, S., Kennedy, P., O'Donnell, A. and Kiely, G. (eds), *Contemporary Irish Social Policy*, Dublin: University College Dublin Press.

Curry, J. (1998), *Irish Social Services*, Dublin: Institute of Public Administration.

Dáil Debates (2000), *Dáil Eireann: Official Report*, Dublin: Stationery Office.

Daly, M. (1997), *The Buffer State: A History of the Department of Environment*, Dublin: Institute of Public Administration.

Daly, M. (1990), 'New Perspectives on Homelessness', in Blackwell, J. *et al* (eds), *Housing, Moving Into Crisis,* Dublin: National Campaign for The Homeless/ Combat Poverty Agency.

Davidson, A. (1999), 'Alternative Models of Social Housing: Tenure Patterns and Cost Renting in New Zealand and Sweden', *Housing Studies,* vol. 14, no. 4, pp 453-472.

Davis, R. and Dhooge, Y. (1993), *Living with Mortgage Arrears,* London Research Centre – Housing and Social Research, London: HMSO.

Dean, G., O' Hare, A., O'Connor, A., Kelly, M. and Kelly, G. (1985) 'The Opiate Epidemic in Dublin, 1979-1983', *Irish Medical Journal*, vol. 78, no. 4, pp 107-110.

Dean, G., O' Hare, A., O'Connor, A., Kelly, M. and Kelly, G. (1987), 'The "Opiate Epidemic" in Dublin: Are we Over the Worst?', *Irish Medical Journal*, vol. 80, no. 5, pp 139-142.

Dean, J. and Hastings, A. (2000), *Challenging Images, Housing Estates, Stigma and Regeneration*, Bristol: Policy Press.

Department of Agriculture, Food and Rural Development (1999), *White Paper on Rural Development*, Dublin: Stationery Office.

Department of Finance (2003), *Public Capital Programme – Revised Estimates,* Dublin: Stationery Office.

Department of Health and Children (2001), *Youth Homelessness Strategy.* Dublin: Stationery office.

Department of Health and Children (2003), *Traveller Health – A National Strategy 2002-2005.* Dublin: Department of Health and Children.

Department of Local Government (1969), *Housing in the '70's,* Dublin: Stationery Office.

Department of Local Government (1973), *Tenant Purchase Scheme for Local Authority Dwellings*, Dublin: Department of Local Government.

Department of Local Government (various years), *Department of Local Government Report,* Dublin: Stationery Office.

Department of Local Government and Public Health (1948), *Housing: A Review of Past Operations and Immediate Requirements,* Housing White Paper, Dublin: Stationery Office.

Department of Local Government and Public Heath (various years), *Annual Reports*, Dublin: Stationery Office.

Department of Public Enterprise (2001), *New Institutional Arrangements for Land Use and Transportation in the Greater Dublin Area,* Dublin: Department of Public Enterprise.

Department of Social and Family Affairs (various years), *Statistical Information on Social Welfare Services,* Dublin: Department of Social and Family Affairs.

Department of Social, Community and Family Affairs (2002), *Building an Inclusive Society: Review of the National Anti-Poverty Strategy Under the Programme for Prosperity and Fairness,* Dublin: Department of Social, Community and Family Affairs.

Department of Social and Family Affairs (various years), *Statistical Report on Social Welfare Services*, Dublin: Stationery Office.

Department of the Environment (1985), *Monograph: Housing in Ireland*, Dublin: Department of the Environment.

Department of the Environment (1991), *A Plan for Social Housing*, Dublin: Department of the Environment.

Department of the Environment (1993), *Memorandum on the Preparation of a Statement of Policy on Housing Management*, Dublin: Department of the Environment.

Department of the Environment (1995a), *Remedial Works Scheme for Local Authority Housing: Memorandum on Procedures, HRT 12/95*, Dublin, Department of the Environment.

Department of the Environment (1995b), *Social Housing: The Way Ahead*, Dublin: Department of the Environment.

Department of the Environment (1996a), *Better Local Government: A Programme for Change*, Dublin: Stationery Office.

Department of the Environment (1996b), *Study on the Urban Renewal Schemes*, Dublin: Department of the Environment.

Department of the Environment and Local Government (1997a), *Housing (Miscellaneous Provisions Act) 1997: Circular H5/97*, Dublin: unpublished circular letter to local authorities.

Department of the Environment and Local Government (1997b), *1998 Urban Renewal Scheme Guidelines*, Dublin: Department of the Environment and Local Government.

Department of the Environment and Local Government (1998a), *Action on House Prices*, Dublin: Department of the Environment and Local Government.

Department of the Environment and Local Government (1998b), *Housing Densities, Ministerial Directive PD. 4/98*, Dublin: Stationery Office.

Department of the Environment and Local Government (1999a), *Action on the Housing Market*, Dublin: Department of the Environment and Local Government.

Department of the Environment and Local Government (1999b), *Administration of Rent and Mortgage Interest Assistance, Report of Inter-Departmental Committee on Issues Relating to Possible Transfer of Administration of Rent and Mortgage Interest Supplementation from Health Boards to Local Authorities*, Dublin: Stationery Office.

Department of the Environment and Local Government (1999c), *Guidelines: Remedial Works Scheme for Local Authority Housing*, Dublin: Department of the Environment and Local Government.

Department of the Environment and Local Government (1999d), *Residential Density: Guidelines for Planning Authorities*, Dublin: Stationery Office.

Department of the Environment and Local Government (1999e), *Social Housing Guidelines: Design Guidelines*, Dublin: Department of the Environment and Local Government.

Department of the Environment and Local Government (2000a), *Action on Housing*, Dublin: Department of the Environment and Local Government.

Department of the Environment and Local Government (2000b), *Part V of the Planning and Development Act 2000, Housing Supply – A Model Housing Strategy and Step-By-Step Guide*, Dublin: Stationery Office.

Department of the Environment and Local Government (2000c), *Part V of the Planning and Development Act, 2000: Housing Supply – Guidelines for Planning Authorities*, Dublin: Department of the Environment and Local Government.

Department of the Environment and Local Government (2000d), *Homelessness – An Integrated Strategy*, Dublin: Stationery Office.

Department of the Environment and Local Government (2000e), *Service Indicators in Local Authorities*, Dublin: Department of the Environment and Local Government.

Department of the Environment and Local Government (2000f), *The Scope and Delivery of the National Spatial Strategy*, Dublin: Department of Environment and Local Government.

Department of the Environment and Local Government (2001), *New Institutional Arrangements for Land Use and Transport in the Greater Dublin Area*, Dublin: Stationery Office.

Department of the Environment and Local Government (2002), *National Spatial Strategy for Ireland 2002-2020 – People, Places and Potential*, Dublin: Department of the Environment and Local Government.

Department of the Environment and Local Government (2003), *Regional Planning Guidelines*, Dublin: Department of the Environment and Local Government.

Department of the Environment and Local Government (23 May 2002), *Dempsey Meets with Traveller Organisations*, Dublin: unpublished press release.

Department of the Environment and Local Government, Department of Health and Children, Department of Education and Science (2002) *Homeless Preventative Strategy: A Strategy to prevent homelessness: Patients leaving hospital and mental health care, adult prisoners and young offenders leaving custody and young people leaving care*, Dublin: Stationery Office.

Department of the Environment, Heritage and Local Government (2004a), *Residential Tenancies Act: A Quick Guide*, Dublin: Department of the Environment, Heritage and Local Government.

Department of the Environment, Heritage and Local Government (2004b), *Sustainable Rural Housing: Consultation Draft Guidelines for Planning Authorities*, Dublin: Stationery Office.

Department of the Environment, Heritage and Local Government (2005), *Planning Guidelines for Sustainable Rural Housing, Consultation*, Dublin: Department of the Environment, Heritage and Local Government.

Department of the Environment, Heritage and Local Government (2 August 2005), 'Minister Roche Praises Community Effort and Calls for less "Dogmatism" in Planning', Dublin: unpublished speech by Dick Roche TD, Minister for the Environment, Heritage and Local Government.

Department of the Environment, Heritage and Local Government (various years), *Annual Housing Statistics Bulletin*, Dublin: Department of the Environment, Heritage and Local Government.

Department of the Environment, Heritage and Local Government, Voluntary and Co-operative Housing Unit (2000), *Circular Letter to all Organisations with Approved Status under the Housing Acts, 11 August 2000*, Dublin: unpublished circular letter.

Department of the Environment and Local Government, Spatial Planning Unit (2001) *Rural and Urban Roles – Irish Spatial Perspectives*. Dublin: Department of the Environment and Local Government.

Dillon, B. *et al* (1990), *Homelessness in Co. Louth. A Research Report*, Dundalk: SUS Research for Dundalk Simon Community and Drogheda Homeless Aid.

Doherty, V. (1982), *Closing Down the County Homes*, Dublin: Simon Community, National Office.

Dollard, G. (2003), 'Local Government Finance: The Policy Context', in Callanan, M. and Keoghan, J., *Local Government in Ireland: Inside Out,* Dublin: Institute of Public Administration.

Donegal County Council (2000), *Donegal County Development Plan 2000*, Donegal: Donegal County Council.

Downey D. (1997), *As Safe as Houses? The Nature, Extent and Experience of Debt in the Irish Housing System*, Dublin: Threshold Housing Debt Project.

Downey, D. (1998), *New Realities in Irish Housing: A Study of Housing Affordability and the Economy,* Dublin: Dublin Institute of Technology.

Downey, D. (2003), 'Affordability and Access to Irish Housing: Trends, Policy and Prospects', *Journal of Irish Urban Studies*, vol. 2, no. 1, pp 1-24.

Downey, D. and DeVilly, I. (1999), 'Changing Circumstances, Latest Consequences: New data on rents, conditions and attitudes in the private rented sector in 1998', in Threshold, *Private Rented Housing – Issues and Options:* Dublin: Threshold.

Drudy, P. (1999), *Housing: A New Approach*, Dublin: The Housing Commission, Labour Party.

Drudy, P. and Punch, M. (2001), 'Housing and Inequality in Ireland', in Cantillon, S., Corrigan, C., Kirby, P. and O'Flynn, J. (eds), *Rich and Poor: Perspectives on Tackling Inequality in Ireland* Dublin: Oak Tree Press.

Drudy, P. and Punch, M. (2002), 'Housing Models and Inequality: Perspectives on Recent Irish Experience', *Housing Studies*, vol. 17, no. 4, pp 657-672.

Drudy, P. and Punch, M. (2004), 'Problems and Inequalities in the Irish Housing System: the Case for Policy Change', Dublin: unpublished paper presented to a TASC seminar.

Dublin Corporation (1993), *Lord Mayor's Commission on Housing* Dublin: Dublin Corporation.

Dublin Corporation (2001) *Regeneration, Next Generation: Looking Forward to a New Future for Fatima,* Dublin: Dublin Corporation.

Dublin Regional Authority (2004a), *Agenda for Dublin,* Dublin: Dublin Regional Authority and the Dublin Employment Pact.

Dublin Regional Authority (2004b), *Regional Planning Guidelines for the Greater Dublin Area,* Dublin: Dublin Regional Authority.

Dublin Simon Community with Focus Ireland and Dublin Corporation (1998), *Report on Street Count,* Dublin: Simon Community.

Dublin Simon Community with Focus Ireland and Dublin Corporation (2000), *Report on Street Count,* Dublin: Simon Community.

Dublin Transportation Office (1998), *Streets as Living Space,* Dublin: Dublin Transportation Office.

Duffy, D. (2002), 'A Descriptive Analysis of the Irish Housing Market', in Economic and Social Research Institute, *Quarterly Economic Commentary*, Summer, Dublin: Economic and Social Research Institute.

Duffy, D. (2004), 'A Note on Measuring the Affordability of Homeownership', in Economic and Social Research Institute, *Quarterly Economic Commentary, Summer,* Dublin: Economic and Social Research Institute.

Duffy, P. (2000), Trends in Nineteenth and Twentieth Century Settlement, in T. Barry (ed.), *A History of Settlement in Ireland*. London: Routledge.

Dunleavy, P. (1981), *The Politics of Mass Housing in Britain 1945-1975: a study of corporate power and professional influence on the welfare state,* Oxford: Clarendon Press.

Dunne, T. (2003), 'High Development Land Prices and the Realities of Urban Property Markets', *Journal of Irish Urban Studies*, vol. 2, no. 2, pp 75-84.

Economic and Social Research Institute (1993), *Quarterly Economic Commentary*, Winter, Dublin: Economic and Social Research Institute.

Economic and Social Research Institute (1999), *National Investment Priorities for the Period 2000-2006*, Policy Research Series No. 33, Dublin: Economic and Social Research Institute.

Elliot, M. and Krivo, L.J. (1991), 'Structural Determinants of Homelessness in the United States', *Social Problems*, vol. 38, no. 1, pp 113-131.

European Central Bank (2003), *Structural Factors in EU Housing Markets*, Frankfurt: European Central Bank.

European Commission (1997), *The EU Compendium of Spatial Planning Systems and Policies*, Brussels: European Commission.

European Commission (1999a), *European Spatial Development Perspective (ESDP)*, Brussels, European Commission.

European Commission (1999b), *The EU Compendium of Spatial Planning Systems and Policies: Ireland*, Brussels: European Commission.

European Mortgage Federation (2004), *Hypostat 2003: European Housing Finance Review*, Brussels: European Mortgage Federation.

European Union (1990), *Green Paper on the Urban Environment*, Luxembourg: European Union.

European Union (2002), *Housing Statistics in the European Union, 2001*, Finland: Ministry of the Environment.

Evans, A. (2004a), *Economics and Land Use Planning*, Oxford: Blackwell.

Evans, A. (2004b), *Economics, Real Estate and the Supply of Land*, Oxford: Blackwell.

Evans, R. and Long, D. (2000), 'Estate-based Regeneration in England: Lessons from Housing Action Trusts', in *Housing Studies*, vol. 15, no. 2, pp 310-317.

Fahey, T. (1998a), 'Housing and Social Exclusion', in Healy, S. and Reynolds, B. (eds), *Social Policy in Ireland: Principles, Practice and Problems*. Dublin: Oak Tree Press and Conference of Religious of Ireland.

Fahey, T. (1998b), *The Agrarian Dimension in the History of the Irish Welfare State*. Dublin: unpublished seminar paper to the Economic and Social Research Institute.

Fahey, T. (ed.) (1999), *Social Housing in Ireland: A Study of Success, Failure and Lessons Learned*, Dublin: Oak Tree Press.

Fahey, T. (1999a), 'Introduction', in Fahey, T. (ed), *Social Housing in Ireland: A Study of Success, Failure and Lessons Learned*, Dublin: Oak Tree Press.

Fahey, T (1999b), 'Recommendations on Policy and Practice', in Fahey, T. (ed.) (1999), *Social Housing in Ireland: A Study of Success, Failure and Lessons Learned*, Dublin: Oaktree Press.

Fahey, T. (1999c), 'Social Housing in Ireland: The Need for an Expanded Role?', *Irish Banking Review*, Autumn, pp 25-38.

Fahey, T. (2001), 'Housing, Social Interaction and Participation among Older Irish People', in *Towards a Society for all Ages: Conference Proceedings*, Dublin: National Council on Ageing and Older People.

Fahey, T. (2002), 'The Family Economy in the Development of Welfare Regimes: a Case Study', *European Sociological Review*, vol. 18, no. 1, pp 51-64.

Fahey, T. (2003), 'Is There a Trade-off Between Pensions and Home Ownership? An exploration of the Irish case', *Journal of European Social Policy*, vol. 13, no. 2, pp 159-173.

Fahey, T. (2004), 'Housing Affordability? Is the Real Problem in the Private Rented Sector?', in Economic and Social Research Institute, *Quarterly Economic Commentary*, Summer, Dublin: Economic and Social Research Institute.

Fahey, T. and Mâitre, B. (forthcoming), 'Home Ownership and Social Inequality in Ireland', in Kurtz, K. and Blossfield, H. (eds), *Home Ownership and Social Inequality in Comparative Perspective*, London: Routledge.

Fahey, T. and Nolan, B. (2003), *Housing Expenditures and Social Inequality in Ireland*, Dublin: Economic and Social Research Institute Interim Working Paper.

Fahey, T. and O'Connell, C. (1999), 'Local Authority Housing in Ireland', in Fahey, T. (ed), *Social Housing in Ireland: A Study of Success, Failure and Lessons Learned.*, Dublin: Oak Tree Press.

Fahey, T. and Watson, D. (1995), *An Analysis of Social Housing Need*, Dublin: The Economic and Social Research Institute.

Fahey, T., Nolan, B. and Mâitre, B. (2004a), *Housing, Poverty and Wealth in Ireland*, Dublin: Institute of Public Administration and Combat Poverty Agency.

Fahey, T., Nolan, B. and Mâitre, B. (2004b), 'Housing Expenditures and Income Poverty in EU Countries', *Journal of Social Policy*, vol. 33, no. 3, pp 437-454.

Fahy, K. (2001), *A Lost Opportunity? A Critique of Local Authority Traveller Accommodation Programmes*, Dublin: Irish Traveller Movement.

Fanning, B. (2002), *Racism and Social Change in the Republic of Ireland*, Manchester: Manchester University Press.

Farrell, N. (1988), *Homelessness in Galway*, Galway: Social Service Council.

FEANTSA (2003), *The Revision of the Structural Funds*, Brussels: FEANTSA.

Feasta (2004), 'Response to Sustainable Rural Housing Consultation Draft of Guidelines for Planning Authorities', Dublin: unpublished submission to the Department of the Environment, Heritage and Local Government.

Feeney, A., McGee, H., Holohan, T. and Shannon, W. (2000), *The Health of Hostel Dwelling Men in Dublin*, Dublin: Eastern Health Board/Royal College of Surgeons in Ireland.

Feins, J. and Lane, T. (1981), *How Much for Housing? New Perspectives on Affordability and Risk*, Cambridge MA: Apt Books.

Fernandez, J. (1995), 'Homelessness: An Irish Perspective', in Bhugra, D. (ed.), *Homelessness and Mental Health*. Cambridge: Cambridge University Press.

Finnegan, M. (1997), Paper delivered at the Foresight Property Seminar, O'Reilly Hall, University College Dublin, 12 November.

Finnerty, S., Guckian, P. and Lough, E. (1995), 'Deinstitutionalisation – The Experience of the Clare Psychiatric Service', *Irish Social Worker*, vol. 13, no. 3, pp 12-13.

Fitzgerald, E. (1990), 'Housing at a Turning Point', in Blackwell, J., Harvey, B., Higgins, M. and Walsh, J. (eds), *Housing: Moving into Crisis?* Dublin: National Campaign for the Homeless/Combat Poverty Agency.

Fitzgerald, E. (2001), 'Redistribution through Ireland's Welfare and Tax Systems', in Cantillon, S. *et al* (eds), *Rich and Poor: Perspectives on Tackling Inequality in Ireland*, Dublin: Oak Tree Press.

FitzGerald, J., McCarthy, C., Morgenroth, E. and O'Connell, P. (2003), *The Mid-Term Evaluation of the National Development Plan (NDP) and Community Support Framework (CSF) for Ireland, 2000 to 2006*, Dublin: Economic and Social Research Institute.

Floyd, D., MacLaran, A. and Williams, B. (1996), *A Report on the Recent Residential Developments in Central Dublin*, Dublin: The Centre for Urban and Regional Studies, Trinity College, Dublin.

Foras Forbartha (1978), *Public Subventions to Housing in Ireland,* Dublin: An Foras Forbartha.

Forrest, R. and Murie, A. (1983), 'Residualisation and Council Housing: aspects of changing social relations of housing tenure', *Journal of Social Policy,* vol. 12, pp. 453-468.

Forrest, R. and Murie, A. (eds) (1995), *Housing and Family Wealth: Comparative International Perspectives*, London: Routledge.

Fraser, M. (1996), *John Bull's Other Homes: State Housing and British Policy in Ireland, 1883-1922,* Liverpool: Liverpool University Press.

Frehill, J. (2003), *Clustered Housing: The View of the Rural Community,* Unpublished Master of Regional and Urban Planning Thesis, Dublin: University College Dublin.

Frobel, F., Heinrichs, J. and Kreye, O. (1980), *The New International Division of Labour.* Cambridge: Cambridge University Press.

Gallent, N., Shucksmith, M. and Tewdwr-Jones, M. (2003), *Housing in the European Countryside, Rural Pressure and Policy in Western Europe,* London: Routledge.

Galligan, C. (2001), *Estate Management Pilot Project: Final Review*, Donegal: Donegal County Council.

Galway County Council (2003), *Galway County Development Plan 2003-2008*, Galway: Galway County Council.

Gavin, C. (2000), 'Swings in Property Prices: A Global Perspective', *Central Bank of Ireland Bulletin,* Winter, pp 73-78.

Geddes, P. (1913), 'Evidence' quoted in the *Report of the Departmental Committee on Housing Conditions of the Working in the City of Dublin,* London: HMSO, 1914.

Gehl, J. (1996), *Life Between Buildings: Using Public Space,* Copenhagen: Architeckteus Forlag.

Geoghegan, P.B. (1983), *Voluntary Housing in Ireland*, Dublin: The Housing Centre.

Gilg, A. (1996), *Countryside Planning,* London: Routledge.

Gkartzios, M. and Scott, M. (2005), 'Urban-generated rural housing and evidence of counterurbanisation in the Dublin city-region', in Moore, N. and Scott, M. (eds), *Renewing Urban Communities: Environment, Citizenship and Sustainability in Ireland.* Aldershot: Ashgate.

Golland, A. and Blake, R. (2004), *Housing Development: Theory, Process and Practice*, London: Routledge.

Goodbody Economic Consultants (2001), *Review of the National Anti-Poverty Strategy: Framework Document, Dublin.*

Goodbody Economic Consultants (2003), *Rationale for and Impact of a Use it or Lose it Scheme*, Dublin: Department of the Environment, Heritage and Local Government.

Goodbody Economic Consultants *et al* (1997), *Mid-Term Evaluation of the Local Urban and Rural Development Operational Programme,* Dublin.

Goodlad, R. (2001), 'Developments in Tenant Participation: Accounting for Growth', in Cowan, D. and Marsh, A. (2001) (eds), *Two Steps Forward: Housing Policy Into the New Millennium,* Bristol: The Policy Press.

Government of Ireland (1964), *Second Programme for Economic Expansion*, Dublin: Stationery Office.

Government of Ireland (1984), *The Psychiatric Services – Planning for the Future:*

Report of a Study Group on the Development of the Psychiatric Services, Dublin: Stationery Office.

Government of Ireland (1989) *Ireland: National Development Plan 1989-1993,* Dublin: Stationery Office.

Government of Ireland (1990), *Programme for Economic and Social Progress,* Dublin.

Government of Ireland (1993), *Programme for Competitiveness and Work,* Dublin.

Government of Ireland (1996a) *Delivering Better Government,* Dublin: Stationery Office.

Government of Ireland (1996b), *Partnership 2000 for Inclusion, Employment and Competitiveness, 1997-1999,* Dublin.

Government of Ireland (1997a), *National Anti-Poverty Strategy: Sharing in Progress,* Dublin: Stationery Office.

Government of Ireland (1997b), *Sustainable Development: A Strategy for Ireland,* Dublin: Stationery Office.

Government of Ireland (2000a), *Ireland: National Development Plan: 2000-2006,* Dublin: Stationery Office.

Government of Ireland (2000b), *Programme for Prosperity and Fairness,* Dublin.

Government of Ireland (2003a) *National Anti-Poverty Strategy: National Action Plan Against Poverty and Social Exclusion 2003-*2005. Dublin: Stationery Office.

Government of Ireland (2003b), *Sustaining Progress: Social Partnership Agreement 2003-2005,* Dublin.

Government of Ireland (2004), *The All-Party Oireachtas Committee on the Constitution, Ninth Progress Report: Private Property,* Dublin: Stationery Office.

Gray, J. (2000), 'The Common Agricultural Policy and the Re-Invention of the Rural in the European Community', *Sociologia Ruralis,* vol. 40, no. 1, pp 30-52.

Greer, J. and Murray, M. (1993), 'Rural Ireland – Personality and policy context', in Murray, M. and Greer, J. (eds), *Rural Development in Ireland, A Challenge for the 1990s.* Aldershot: Avebury.

Greer, J. and Murray, M. (2003), 'Rethinking Rural Planning and Development in Northern Ireland', in Greer, J. and Murray, M. (eds), *Rural Planning and Development in Northern Ireland.* Dublin: Institute of Public Administration.

Gribbin, E. (1998), 'Increasing Housing Densities: The Path to Sustainability', paper presented to the joint Royal Institute of Architects of Ireland/ Irish Planning Institute Conference, Dublin, November 19.

Guerin, D. (1994), *Claiming Rent Supplement,* Cork: Threshold.

Guerin, D. (1999), *Housing Income Support in the Private Rented Sector: A Survey of Recipients of SWA Rent Supplement,* Dublin: Combat Poverty Agency.

Gunne Residential (2002), *An Analysis of the Facts on the Residential Property Market,* Dublin: Gunne Estate Agents.

Gunne Residential (2004), *The Residential Property Market 2003 – An Analysis of the Facts,* Dublin: Gunne.

Gunne Residential and ICS Building Society (2002), *Market Research,* Dublin: Gunne.

Hadjimichalis, C. (2003), 'Imagining Rurality in the New Europe and Dilemmas for Spatial Policy', *European Planning Studies,* vol. 11, no. 2, pp 103-113.

Halfacree, K. (1997), 'Contrasting Roles for the Post-Productivist Countryside, A postmodern perspective on counterurbanisation', in Cloke, P. and Little, J. (eds), *Contested Countryside Cultures, Otherness, Marginalization and Rurality,* London: Routledge.

Hall, P. (1996), *Cities of Tomorrow: An Intellectual History of Urban Planning and Design in the Twentieth Century,* Oxford: Blackwell.

Halpenny, A.M., Greene, S., Hogan, D., Smith, M. and McGee, H. (2001), *Children of Homeless Mothers: The Daily Life Experience and Well-being of Children in Homeless Families.* Dublin: Children's Research Centre/ The Royal College of Surgeons in Ireland.

Halpenny, A.M., Keogh, A.F. and Gilligan, R. (2002), *A Place for the Children? Children in Families Living in Emergency Accommodation: The Perspectives of Children, Parents and Professionals.* Dublin: Children's Research Centre/ Homeless Agency.

Harloe, M, (1995), *The People's Home: Social Rented Housing in Europe and America,* Oxford: Blackwell.

Hart, I. (1978), *Dublin Simon Community 1971-1976: An Exploration.* Dublin: Economic and Social Research Institute.

Harvey, B. (1985), 'Administrative Responses to the Homeless', *Administration,* vol. 33, no. 1, pp 131-140.

Harvey, B. (1990) 'Counting the Homeless', in National Campaign for the Homeless, *Small Change for the Homeless: Annual Report of the National Campaign for the Homeless.* Dublin: National Campaign for the Homeless.

Harvey, B. (1995), 'The Use of Legislation to Address a Social Problem: The Example of the Housing Act, 1988', *Administration,* vol. 43, no.1, pp 76-85.

Harvey, B. (1998), *Homelessness and Mental Health – Policies and Services in an Irish and European Context,* Dublin: Homelessness and Mental Health Action Group.

Harvey, B. and Higgins, M. (1988), 'The Links between Housing and Homelessness', *Administration,* vol. 36, no. 4, pp 33-40.

Harvey, D. (1990), *The Condition of Postmodernism,* Oxford: Blackwell.

Harvey, D. (2000), *Spaces of Hope,* Edinburgh: Edinburgh University Press.

Health Research Board (2002), *Trends in Treated Drug Misuse in the Eastern Health Board Area 1996-1999,* Health Research Board: Dublin. Occasional Paper No. 8.

Healey, P. (1998), 'Collaborative planning in a stakeholder society', *Town Planning Review,* vol. 69, no. 1, pp 1-21.

Helbling, T. and Terrones, M. (2003), 'When Bubbles Burst', in *International Monetary Fund World Economic Outlook,* April 2003, IMF, Washington DC.

Helleiner, J. (2000), *Irish Travellers: Racism and the Politics of Culture,* London: University of Toronto Press.

Hickey, C. (2002), *Crime and Homelessness,* Dublin: Focus Ireland and PACE.

Hickey, C., Bergin, E., Punch, M. and Buchanan, L. (2002), *Housing Access for All? An Analysis of Housing Strategies and Homeless Action Plans,* Dublin: Focus Ireland, Simon Communities of Ireland, Society of St Vincent de Paul and Threshold.

Higgins, M. (2001), *Shaping the Future: An Action Plan on Homelessness in Dublin, 2001-2003,* Dublin: Homeless Agency.

Higgins, M. (2002), 'Counted in 2002', *Cornerstone:* The Magazine of the Housing Agency, no. 14, pp14-15.

Hill, M. (ed.) (1997), *The Policy Process: A Reader,* Hemel Hempstead: Prentice Hall/ Harvester Wheatsheaf.

Hobsbawm, E. (1995), *The Age of Extremes: the Short Twentieth Century,* London: Abacus.

Holohan, T. (1997), *Health Status, Health Service Utilisation among the Adult Homeless Population of Dublin,* Dublin: Eastern Health Board.

Horner, A. (1995), 'The Dublin Region, 1880-1982: An Overview on Its Development and Planning', in Bannon, M., *The Emergence of Irish Planning 1880-1920,* Dublin: Turoe Press

Houghton, F.T. and Hickey, C. (2000), *Focusing on B&Bs: The Unacceptable Growth of Emergency B&B Placement in Dublin,* Dublin: Focus Ireland.

Housing Inquiry (1914), *Report of the Royal Commission appointed to inquire into the housing conditions of the working classes in the city of Dublin,* British Parliamentary papers, vol. 19, 1914, cd. 7272/7317-xix, London.

Housing Management Group (1996), *First Report,* Dublin: Department of the Environment.

Housing Management Group (1998), *Second Report* Dublin: Department of the Environment.

Housing Policy and Practice Unit (1994), *Good Practice in Housing Management: Tenant Participation,* Edinburgh: Scottish Office.

Housing Unit (2000), *Good Practice in Housing Management: Guidelines for Local Authorities – Repair and Maintenance of Dwellings,* Dublin: Housing Unit.

Housing Unit (2001a), *Good Practice in Housing Management: Guidelines for Local Authorities – Enabling Tenant Participation in Housing Management,* Dublin: Housing Unit.

Housing Unit (2001b), *Good Practice in Housing Management: Guidelines for Local Authorities – Managing Voids: Coordinating the Monitoring, Repair and Allocation of Vacant Dwellings,* Dublin: Housing Unit.

Housing Unit (2001c), *Good Practice in Housing Management: Guidelines for Local Authorities – Rent Assessment, Collection, Accounting and Arrears Control,* Dublin: Housing Unit.

Housing Unit (2003a), *Good Practice in Housing Management: Guidelines for Local Authorities – Housing Refugees,* Dublin: Housing Unit.

Housing Unit (2003b), *Good Practice in Housing Management: Guidelines for Local Authorities – Preventing and Combating Anti-Social Behaviour,* Dublin: Housing Unit.

Housing Unit (2004), *Good Practice in Housing Management: Guidelines for Local Authorities – Training and Information for Tenants,* Dublin: Housing Unit.

Howley, D. (2000), *An Analysis of the Dublin Simon Outreach Contacts for the Year ended December 1999,* Dublin: Simon Community.

Hulchanski, J.D. (1995), 'The Concept of Housing Affordability: Six Contemporary Uses of the Housing Expenditure-To-Income Ratio', *Housing Studies,* vol. 10, no. 4, pp 471-491.

Hulchanski, J.D. and Michalski, J.H. (1994), *How Households Obtain Resources to Meet Their Needs: The Shifting Mix of Cash and Non-Cash Sources,* Toronto: Ontario Human Rights Commission.

Hunt, T. (2000), *Portlaw, County Waterford, 1825-76: portrait of an industrial village,* Dublin: Irish Academic Press.

Hunter, J. and Dixon, C. (2001), 'Social Landlords' Responses to Neighbour Nuisance and Anti-Social Behaviour: From the Negligible to the Holistic', *Local Government Studies,* vol. 27, no. 4, pp 89-104.

Inspector of Mental Hospitals (2002), *Report for the Year Ending 31 December 2001,* Dublin: Stationery Office.

Inter-Departmental Committee on Future Rental Arrangements (1999), *Administration of Rent and Mortgage Interest Assistance,* Dublin: Stationery Office.

Irish Auctioneers and Valuers Institute (2000), *Annual Property Survey,* Dublin: IAVI.

Irish Auctioneers and Valuers Institute (2001), *Annual Property Survey,* Dublin: IAVI.

Irish Auctioneers and Valuers Institute (2002), *Annual Property Survey,* Dublin: IAVI.

Irish Auctioneers and Valuers Institute (2003a), *Annual Property Survey,* Dublin: IAVI.

Irish Auctioneers and Valuers Institute (2003b), 'Planning and Rural Housing', Submission by the IAVI to DoEHLG, Dublin: from unpublished submission to the Department of the Environment, Heritage and Local Government.

Irish Council for Social Housing (1997), *Tenant Participation in Housing Management,* Dublin: Irish Council for Social Housing.

Irish Council for Social Housing (1999), 'Achieving a More Mainstream Role for Housing Associations: Building Output to 4,000 Dwellings a Year', unpublished submission to Mr Robert Molloy TD, Minister for Housing and Urban Renewal.

Irish Home Builders Association (1999), 'IHBA Response to the Planning and Development Bill 1999', Dublin: unpublished press release.

Irish National Committee for the European Year against Racism (1997), *European Year against Racism: Ireland Report,* Dublin: Department of Justice.

Irish National Co-Ordinating Committee for the European Year Against Racism (1997), *Travellers In Ireland: An Examination of Discrimination and Racism,* Dublin: Irish National Co-ordinating Committee for the European Year Against Racism.

Irish Planning Institute (2003), 'Policy on Housing in Rural Areas, IPI Submission to the DoEHLG', Dublin: unpublished submission to the Department of the Environment, Heritage and Local Government.

Irish Rural Dwellers Association (2004), *Positive planning for rural houses, seeking radical changes in rural planning policy,* Clare: Irish Rural Dwellers Association.

Irish Traveller Movement (2002), *Charting a Future for the Delivery of Traveller Accommodation,* Dublin: Irish Traveller Movement.

Irish Traveller Movement (2003), *An Analysis of the use of the Housing (Miscellaneous Provisions) Act, 2002,* Dublin: Irish Traveller Movement.

Irwin, G. (1998), *Linking to Meet the Needs of the Homeless: A Cross-Border Research Study into Homelessness in Counties Armagh, Cavan, Donegal, Fermanagh, Leitrim, Monaghan and Tyrone,* Dublin: Simon Community Republic of Ireland and Simon Community Northern Ireland.

ISIS Research (1998), *Subvention and the Private Rented Sector: Access to Rent Allowance Accommodation in Inner City Dublin,* Dublin: Dublin Inner City Partnership.

Jacobs, J. (1961), *The Death and Life of American Cities,* New York: Random House.

James, O. (2003), 'The Residential Decline of Medium Sized Irish Towns', Unpublished Master of Regional and Urban Planning, Thesis, Dublin University College Dublin.

Jencks, C. (1994), *The Homeless,* Cambridge: Harvard University Press.

Johnson, J. (1994) *The Human Geography of Ireland.* Chichester: Wiley.

Kearns, K. (1994), *Dublin Tenement Life: An Oral History,* Dublin: Gill & Macmillan.

Kearns, K.C. (1984), 'Homelessness in Dublin. An Irish Urban Disorder', *American Journal of Economics and Sociology,* vol. 43, no. 2 April pp 217-233.

Kearns, N., Norris, M. and Frost, L. (2000), *Homelessness in Cork,* Cork: unpublished report for Cork City Council and the Southern Health Board.

Kelleher, C., Kelleher, P. and McCarthy, P. (1992), *Patterns of Hostel Use in Dublin and the Implications for Accommodation Provision,* Dublin: A Focus Point Publication.

Kelleher, P. (1990), *Caught in the Act. Housing and Settling Homeless People in Dublin*

City. The Implementation of the Housing Act 1988, Dublin: A Focus Point Report.

Kelleher, P. *et al.* (1995), *Making the Links: Towards an Integrated Strategy for the Elimination of Violence against Women in Intimate Relationships with Men,* Dublin: Women's Aid.

Kelleher, P., Kelleher, C. and Corbet, M. (2000), *Out on their Own: Young People Leaving Care in Ireland,* Dublin: Oaktree Press.

Kelly, C. (1997), 'Eviction Plans for Drug Pushers are Flawed', *Poverty Today,* no. 25 (April).

Kelly, S. and MacLaran, A. (2004), 'Incentivised Gentrification in Central Dublin', unpublished paper to the Conference of Irish Geographers, NUI Maynooth, May 2004.

Kemeny, J. (1995), *From Public Housing to the Social Market: Rental Policy Strategies in a Comparative Perspective,* London: Routledge.

Kemp, P.A., Lynch, E. and McKay, D. (2001), *Structural Trends and Homelessness: a Quantitative Analysis,* Homelessness Task Force Research Series. Scottish Executive Central Research Unit.

Kennedy, S. (1985), *But Where Can I Go? Homeless Women in Dublin,* Dublin: Arlen House.

Kenny, B. (1998), 'Tenant participation and Estate Management: A Local Authority Perspective', in Community Workers Co-operative, *Strategies to Encourage Tenant Participation,* Galway: Community Workers Co-operative.

Kenny, Justice (1973), *Report of the Committee on the Price of Building Land,* Dublin: Stationery Office.

Keogh, F., Roche, A. and Walsh, D. (1999), *'We Have No Beds...': An Enquiry into the Availability and Use of Acute Psychiatric Beds in the Eastern Health Board Region,* Dublin: Health Research Board.

Keohane, K. (2002), 'Model Homes for Model(ed) Citizens: Domestic Economies of Desire in Prosperity Square Cork', *Space and Culture,* vol. 5, no. 5, pp 387-404.

Kirby, P. (2001), 'Inequality and Poverty in Ireland: Clarifying Social Objectives', in Cantillon, S. *et al* (eds), *Rich and Poor: Perspectives on Tackling Inequality in Ireland,* Dublin: Oak Tree Press in association with Combat Poverty Agency.

KPMG *et al* (1996), *Study on the Urban Renewal Schemes,* Dublin: Department of the Environment.

Landt, J. and Bray R. (1997), *Alternative Approaches to Measuring Rental Housing Affordability in Australia.* Discussion Paper No. 16, National Centre for Social and Economic Modeling, University of Canberra.

Layte R., Maître, B., Nolan, B. and Whelan, C. (2001), 'Explaining Deprivation in the European Union', *Acta Sociologica,* vol. 44, no. 2, pp 105-122.

Layte, R., Maître, B., Nolan, B., Watson, D., Whelan, C. Williams, J. and Casey, B. (2001), *Monitoring Poverty Trends and Exploring Poverty Dynamics in Ireland,* Dublin: Economic and Social Research Institute, Policy Research Series, No. 41.

Lee B., Price-Spratlen T. and Kanan J.W. (2003), 'Determinants of Homelessness in Metropolitan Areas', *Journal of Urban Affairs,* vol. 25, no. 3, pp 335-356.

Lee, P. and Murie, A. (1997), *Poverty, Housing Tenure and Social Exclusion,* Bristol: Policy Press.

Lee, P. *et al* (1995), *The Price of Social Exclusion,* London: National Federation of Housing Associations.

Leon, C. (2000), 'Recorded Sexual Offences 1994-1997: An Overview', *Irish Criminal Law Journal,* vol. 10, no. 3, pp 2-7.

Leonard, L. (1992a), 'Official Homelessness Figures Show only Tip of Iceberg', *Simon Community Newsletter* no. 180, Dublin: Simon Community National Office.

Leonard, L. (1992b), 'Voluntary-Statutory Partnership in the Housing Area: The Experience of the Simon Community', *Co-Options – Journal of the Community Workers Co-Operative,* Spring, pp 79-84.

Leonard, L. (1994), 'Official Homelessness Results Published – Simon Questions New Assessments', *Simon Community Newsletter* no. 198. Dublin: Simon Community National Office.

Llewelyn-Davies (2000), *Urban Design Compendium,* London: The Housing Corporation / English Partnerships.

Llewelyn-Davies and the Bartlett School of Planning (1998), *The Use of Density* in *Urban Planning,* London: Department of the Environment Transport and the Regions.

Lynch, C. (2002) 'Capacity and Community – The balance between the social and the environmental in a specific cultural context', paper presented to the 6th Annual Conference of the Nordic Scottish Network, Sustainability in Rural and Regional Development.

Lynch, K. (1990), *The Image of the City,* Massachusetts: MIT Press.

Lynch, K. (1999), *Equality in Education*, Dublin: Gill & Macmillan.

Lynch, R. (1999), *Subvention and the Private Rented Sector,* Dublin: Larkin Centre.

Mac Neela, P. (1999), *Homelessness in Galway: A Report on Homelessness and People Sleeping Rough in Galway City*, Galway: Galway Simon Community.

MacCabe, F. (2003), 'Supply constraints and serviced land development supply in the Dublin region: A Review of the Projections and Recommendations of Bacon III', *Journal of Irish Urban Studies,* vol. 2, no. 1, pp 55-64.

MacLaran, A. (1993), *Dublin: The Shaping of a Capital,* London: Belhaven Press.

MacLaran, A. (2001), 'Middle-Class Social Housing? Insanity or Progress?', in Drudy, P.J. and MacLaran, A. (eds), *Dublin: Economic and Social Trends,* vol. 3, Dublin: Centre for Urban and Regional Studies, Trinity College Dublin.

MacLaran, A. (1996), 'Private-Sector Residential Development in Central Dublin', *Dublin: Economic and Social Trends*, vol. 2, Dublin: Centre for Urban and Regional Studies, Trinity College Dublin.

MacLaran, A., MacLaran, M. and Williams, B. (1994), *Residential Development as an Engine for Inner-city Renewal in Dublin: Commentary and statistical appendices,* Dublin: Centre for Urban & Regional Studies, Trinity College Dublin.

MacLaran, A., Emerson, H., Williams, B., Brew, A., Floyd, D., Punch, M. and Smith, É. (1995), *Residential development in central Dublin: a survey of current occupiers,* Dublin: Centre for Urban & Regional Studies, Trinity College Dublin.

MacLaran, A. and Hamilton Osborne King (1993), *HOK Offices, 1993,* Dublin: Hamilton Osborne King.

MacLaran, A. and Floyd, D. (1996), *A Report on the Recent Residential Developments in Central Dublin,* Dublin: The Centre for Urban and Regional Studies, Trinity College.

MacLaren, A. and Murphy, L. (1997), 'The Problems of Taxation Induced Inner City Housing Development – Dublin's Recipe for Success?' *Irish Geography,* vol. 30, no.1, pp 31-36.

MacLaran, A. and Killen, J. (2002), 'The Suburbanisation of Office Development in Dublin and its Transport Implications', *Journal of Irish Urban Studies*, vol. 1, no. 1, pp. 21-36.

Maclennan, D., Muellbauer, J. and Stephens, M. (2000), *Asymmetries in Housing and*

Financial Market Institutions and EMU:www.housingoutlook.co.uk/papers/oxrep.pdf

Maclennan, D. and Pryce, G. (1996), 'Global Economic Change, Labour Market Adjustment and the Challenges for European Housing Policy', *Urban Studies*, vol. 33, no. 100, pp 1849-1866.

Madden, M. (2003), 'Braving Homelessness on the Ethnographic Street with Irene Glasser and Rae Bridgman', *Critique of Anthropology*, vol. 23, no. 3, pp 289-304.

Malos, E. and Hague, G. (1997), 'Women, Housing, Homelessness and Domestic Violence', *Women's Studies International Forum*, vol. 20, no. 3, pp 397-409.

Malpass, P. (1990), *Reshaping Housing Policy: Subsidies, Rents and Residualisation*. London: Routledge.

Malpass, P. and Murie, A. (1999), *Housing Policy and Practice*, Fifth Edition, Basingstoke: Macmillan.

Mansur, E.T., Quigley, J.M., Raphael, S. and Smolensky (2002), 'Examining Policies to Reduce Homelessness using a General Equilibrium Model of the Housing Market', *Journal of Urban Economics*, vol. 52, no. 2, pp 316-340.

Marinetto, M. (1999), *Studies of the Policy Process: A Case Analysis*, London: Prentice Hall Europe.

Marsden, T. (1999) 'Rural Futures: The Consumption Countryside and its Regulation', *Sociologia Ruralis*, vol. 39, no. 4, pp 501-520.

Marsden, T., Murdoch, J., Lowe, P., Munton, R. and Flynn, A. (1993), *Constructing the Countryside*. London: UCL Press.

Massey, D. (1995), *Spatial Divisions of Labour: Social Structures and the Geography of Production*, London: MacMillan.

McCabe, F., O'Rourke, B. and Fleming, M. (1999), *Planning Issues Relating to Residential Density in Urban and Suburban Locations*, Dublin: Department of the Environment and Local Government.

McCarthy, C., Hughes, A. and Woelger, E. (2003), *Where Have all the Houses Gone?* Dublin: Davy Stockbrokers.

McCarthy, P. (1988), *A Study of the Work Skills, Experience and Preferences of Simon Community Residents*, Dublin. Simon Community (National Office).

McCashin, A. (2000), *The Private Rented Residential Sector in the 21st Century: Policy Choices*, Dublin: Threshold and St. Pancras Housing Association.

McDonagh, M. (1993), 'The Plan for Social Housing and the 1992 Housing Act: New Thinking on Social Housing?', *Administration*, vol. 41, no. 3, pp 235-248.

McDonagh, M. (2000), 'Origins of the Travelling People' in Sheehan, E. (ed) *Travellers: Citizens of Ireland*, Dublin: The Parish of the Travelling People.

McDonagh, J. (1998), 'Rurality and Development in Ireland – the need for debate?', *Irish Geography, v*ol. 31, no. 1, pp 47-54.

McDonagh, J. (2001), *Renegotiating Rural Development in Ireland*. Aldershot: Ashgate.

McDonald, F. (1997), 'Irelands Suburbs', in Becker, A., Olley, J. and Wang, W. (eds), *Ireland: 20th Century Architecture,* Munich: Prestel.

McGettrick, G. (2003), 'Access and Independent Living', in Redmond, B. and Quin, S. (eds), *Disability and Social Policy in Ireland,* Dublin: UCD Press.

McGrath, B. (1998), 'Environmental Sustainability and Rural Settlement Growth in Ireland', *Town Planning Review*, vol. 3, no. 3, pp 227-290.

McKeown, K. (1999), *Mentally Ill Homeless in Ireland: Facing the Reality, Finding the Solutions*. A Report for Disability Federation of Ireland. Dublin: Disability Federation of Ireland.

McKeown, K. and Hasse, T. (1997), *Audit of Services,* Dublin: Homeless Agency.

McKeown, K. and McGrath, B. (1996), *Accommodating Travelling People,* Dublin: Crosscare.

McLoughlin, D. (1994), 'Ethnicity and Irish Travellers: Reflections on Ní Shúinéar', in McCann, M., Ó Síocháin, S. and Ruane, J. (eds), *Irish Travellers: Culture and Ethnicity,* Belfast: The Institute of Irish Studies.

McManus, R. (2002), *Dublin 1910-1940: Shaping the City and Suburbs,* Dublin: Four Courts Press.

McNulty, P. (2002), 'The Emergence of the Housing Affordability Gap', *Journal of Irish Urban Studies,* vol. 2, no. 1, pp 83-90.

Meath County Council (2001), *Meath County Development Plan,* Meath: Meath County Council.

Memery, C. (2001), 'The Housing System and the Celtic Tiger: the State Response to a Housing Crisis of Affordability and Access', *European Journal of Housing Policy,* vol. 1, no.1, pp 79-104.

Memery, C. and Kerrins, L. (2000a), 'Investors in the Private Rented Residential Sector', *Threshold Findings,* no. 1, March.

Memery, C. and Kerrins, L. (2000b), *Estate Management and Anti-Social Behaviour in Dublin. A Study of the Impact of the Housing (Miscellaneous Provisions) Act 1997,* Dublin: Threshold.

Merchants' Quay Project (2000), *Annual Report 1999,* Dublin: Merchants' Quay Project, Dublin.

Minister for Local Government (1964), *Housing – Progress and Prospects,* Dublin: Stationery Office.

Moore, J. (1994), *B&B in Focus: The Use of Bed and Breakfast Accommodation for Homeless Adults in Dublin.* Dublin: Focus Point.

Moughton, C. (1992), *Urban Design: Street and Square,* London: Architecture Press.

Mullins, D., Niner, P. and Riseborough, M. (1993), 'Large Scale Voluntary Transfers', in, Malpass, P. and Means, R., *Implementing Housing Policy,* Third Edition, Buckingham: Open University Press.

Mullins, D., Rhodes, M.L. and Williamson, A. (2003), *Non-Profit Housing Organisations in Ireland, North and South: Changing Forms and Challenging Futures,* Belfast, Northern Ireland Housing Executive.

Murdoch, J. and Lowe, P. (2003), 'The preservationist paradox: modernism, environmentalism and the politics of spatial division', *Transactions of the Institute of British Geographers,* vol. 20, no. 3, pp 368-380.

Murdoch, J., Lowe, P., Ward, N. and Marsden, T. (2003), *The Differentiated Countryside.* London: Routledge.

Murphy, A. and Brereton, F. (2001) 'Modelling Irish House Prices: A Review', paper presented at the Irish Economic Association Annual Conference, April.

Murphy-Lawless, J. and Dillon, B. (1992), *Promises, Promises. An Assessment of the Effectiveness of the Housing Act, 1988 in Housing Homeless People in Ireland,* Dublin: Nexus and the National Campaign for the Homeless.

Murray, K. and Norris, M. (2002), *Profile of Households Accommodated by Dublin City Council: Analysis of Socio-Demographic, Income and Spatial Patterns, 2001, Dublin,* Dublin City Council and the Housing Unit.

Murray, M. (1993), 'Paradigm redundancy and substitution: rural planning and development in Northern Ireland', *Pleanáil, Journal of the Irish Planning Institute,* pp. 195-218.

Murray, M. and Greer, J. (1997), 'Planning and Community-Led Rural Development in Northern Ireland', *Planning Practice and Research,* vol. 12, no. 4, pp 393-400.

National Building Agency (1989), *Annual Report,* Dublin: National Building Agency.

National Building Agency (2003), *Sligo and Environs Draft Development Plan,* Dublin: National Building Agency.

National Council on Ageing and Older People (2001), *Towards a Society for all Ages: Conference Proceedings,* Dublin: National Council on Ageing and Older People.

National Economic and Social Council (1977), *Report on Housing Subsidies,* Dublin: National Economic and Social Council.

National Economic and Social Council (1981), *Urbanisation: Problems of Growth and Decay in Dublin,* Dublin: National Economic and Social Council, Report no. 55.

National Economic and Social Council (1988) *Redistribution Through State Social Expenditure in the Republic of Ireland: 1973-1980,* Dublin: National Economic and Social Council, Report no. 85.

National Economic and Social Council (1991) *The Economic and Social Implications of Emigration,* Dublin: National Economic and Social Council, Report no. 90.

National Economic and Social Council (2004), *Housing in Ireland: Performance and Policy,* Dublin: National Economic and Social Council, Report no. 112.

National Economic and Social Forum (2000), *Social and Affordable Housing and Accommodation: Building the Future.* Dublin: Dublin: Stationery Office, Report no. 18.

National Economic and Social Forum (2001), *Lone Parents.* Dublin: Stationery Office, Report no. 20.

National Economic and Social Forum (2002), *A Strategic Policy Framework for Equality Issues,* Dublin: Stationery Office, Report no. 23.

National Traveller Accommodation Consultative Committee (2000), *Evaluation of Local Traveller Accommodation Consultative Committees,* Dublin: Department of the Environment and Local Government.

National Traveller Accommodation Consultative Committee (2002), *Annual Report 2002,* Dublin: Department of the Environment, Heritage and Local Government.

National Traveller Accommodation Consultative Committee (2004), *Review of the Operation of the Housing (Traveller Accommodation) Act 1998: Report of the National Traveller Accommodation Consultative Committee to the Minister for Housing and Urban Renewal,* Dublin: Department of the Environment, Heritage and Local Government.

Neale, J. (1997) 'Homelessness and Theory Reconsidered', *Housing Studies,* vol. 12, no. 1, pp 47-61.

Neale, J. (2001), 'Homelessness Amongst Drug Users: A Double Jeopardy Explored', *International Journal of Drug Policy,* vol. 12, no. 4, pp 353-369.

Netherlands, Ministry of Housing Spatial Planning and the Environment, (2000), *What People Want Where People Live,* The Hague: Ministry of Housing, Spatial Planning and the Environment.

Ní Nualláin, E. (2003), 'The Context of the Single Rural House', Unpublished Master of Regional and Urban Planning Thesis, Dublin: University College Dublin.

Ní Shúinéar, S. (1994), 'Irish Travellers, Ethnicity and the Origins Question', in McCann, M., Ó Síocháin, S. and Ruane, J. (eds), *Irish Travellers: Culture and Ethnicity,* Belfast: The Institute of Irish Studies.

Nixon, J. and Hunter, C. (2001), *Tacking Anti-Social Behaviour,* Coventry, Chartered Institute of Housing.

Nolan, B. (1991), *The Wealth of Irish Households: What Can We Learn from Survey Data?* Dublin: Combat Poverty Agency.

Nolan, B., (2004), *The Social Situation in the European Union,* Dublin: The Economic and Social Research Institute.

Nolan B., Maître, B., O'Neill, D and Sweetman, O. (2000), *The Distribution of Income in Ireland,* Dublin: Oak Tree Press.

Nolan, B. and Whelan, C. (1996), *Resources, Deprivation and Poverty,* Oxford: Clarendon Press.

Nolan, B. and Whelan, C. (1999), *Loading the Dice? A Study of Cumulative Disadvantage,* Dublin: Oak Tree Press.

Nolan, B., Whelan, C. and Williams, J. (1998), *Where are Poor Households? The Spatial Distribution of Poverty and Deprivation in Ireland,* Dublin: Oak Tree Press.

Nolan, B., Gannon, B., Layte, R., Watson, D., Whelan. C. and Williams, J. (2003), *Monitoring Poverty Trends in Ireland: Results from the 2000 Living in Ireland Survey,* Policy Research Series Paper no. 45, Dublin: Economic and Social Research Institute.

Nolan, B., O'Connell, P. and Whelan, T. (eds) (2000), *Boom to Bust: The Irish Experience of Growth and Inequality,* Dublin: Institute of Public Administration.

Norris, M, (1999), 'The Impact of the Built Environment', in Fahey, T. (1999) (ed), *Social Housing in Ireland: A Study of Success, Failure and Lessons Learned,* Dublin: Oaktree Press.

Norris, M. (2000), *Managing in Partnership: Developing Estate Management in Limerick,* Limerick: Limerick Corporation and the PAUL Partnership.

Norris, M. (2001), 'Regenerating Run-Down Local Authority Estates: A Review of the Operation of the Remedial Works Scheme Since 1985', *Administration,* vol. 49, no. 1, pp 25-45.

Norris, M. (2004), 'Developing, Designing and Managing Mixed Tenure Estates: Implementing Planning Gain Legislation in the Republic of Ireland', unpublished paper presented to the Housing Studies Association Conference, Belfast.

Norris, M. and Kearns, N. (2003) 'Local Government Anti-Poverty Initiatives in the Republic of Ireland: A Critical Review of Policy, Practice and Prospects for Future Development', *Administration,* vol. 51, no. 3, Autumn 2003, pp 90-109.

Norris, M and O'Connell, C (2002), 'Local Authority Housing Management Reform in the Republic of Ireland: progress to date – impediments to further progress', *European Journal of Housing Policy,* vol. 2, no. 3, pp 245-264.

Norris, M. and Shiels, P. (2004), *Regular National Report on Housing Developments in European Countries: Synthesis Report,* Dublin: Department of the Environment, Heritage and Local Government.

Norris, M. and Winston, N. (2004), *Housing Policy Review 1990-2002,* Dublin: Stationery Office.

NUI Maynooth and Brady Shipman Martin (2000), *Irish Rural Structure and Gaeltacht Areas,* Dublin: Department of the Environment and Local Government.

O'Brien, J. (1979), 'Criminal Neglect – Some Aspects of Law Enforcement as it Affects the Single Homeless', unpublished submission from The Simon Community (National Office) to The Commission of Enquiry into the Irish Penal System.

O'Brien, L. and Dillon, B. (1982), *Private Rented: The Forgotten Sector,* Dublin: Threshold.

Ó Cinneide, S. and Mooney, P. (1972), *Simon Survey of the Homeless,* The Simon Community of Ireland supported by the Medico-Social Research Board. August.

Ó Cofaigh, E. (1998), 'Housing Densities', unpublished paper to the Joint Royal Institute of Architects of Ireland/Irish Planning Institute, Conference, Dublin, 19 November.

O'Connell, C. (1999), 'Local Authorities as Landlords', in Fahey, T. (ed.), *Social Housing in Ireland: A Study of Success, Failure and Lessons Learned,* Dublin: Oak Tree Press.

O'Connell, C. (1994), 'The Dynamics of Tenure in Ireland, 1922-1994', unpublished PhD thesis, Cork: University College, Cork.

O'Connell, C. (1998), 'Tenant Involvement in Local Authority Estate Management: A New Panacea for Policy Failure?', *Administration*, vol. 46, no. 2, pp 25-46

O'Donnell, I. (1998), 'Crime, Punishment and Poverty', in Bacik, I. and O'Connell, M. (eds), *Crime and Poverty in Ireland*, Dublin: Round Hall Sweet and Maxwell.

O'Donnell, I. and O'Sullivan, E. (2001), *Crime Control in Ireland: The Politics of Intolerance,* Cork: Cork University Press.

O'Donnell, I. and O'Sullivan, E. (2003), 'The Politics of Intolerance – Irish Style', *British Journal of Criminology*, vol. 43, no. 1, pp 41-62.

O'Flaherty, B. (1996), *Making Room: The Economics of Homelessness,* Cambridge: Harvard University Press.

O'Flaherty, B. (2002), *'Causes' of Homelessness: Understanding City- and Individual-level Data,* New York: Columbia University, Department of Economics, Discussion Paper #:0102-59.

O'Flaherty, B. (2004), 'Wrong Person and Wrong Place: For Homelessness, the Conjunction is What Matters', *Journal of Housing Economics*, vol. 13, no. 1, pp 1-15.

O'Gorman, A. (1998), 'Illicit Drug Use in Ireland: An Overview of the Problem and Policy Responses', *Journal of Drug Issues*, vol. 28, no. 1, pp 155-166.

O'Gorman, A. (2000), *Eleven Acres, Ten Steps* Dublin: Fatima Groups United.

Ó Grada, D. (2004), 'Some Hidden Costs of Irish Rural Housing', Paper to the National Planning Conference, Irish Planning Institute.

O'Kelly, R., Bury, G., Cullen, B., and Dean, G. (1988), 'The Rise and Fall of Heroin Use in an Inner City Area of Dublin', *Irish Medical Journal,* vol. 157, no. 2, pp 35-38.

O'Mahony, P. (1997), *Mountjoy Prisoners: A Sociological and Criminological Profile.* Dublin: Stationery Office.

Ó Riain, S. (2000), *Solidarity with Travellers*, Dublin: Roadside Books.

O'Sullivan, E and Higgins, M. (2001), 'Women, the Welfare State and Homelessness in the Republic of Ireland', in Edgar, B., Doherty, J. and Mina-Couell, A. (eds), *Women and Homelessness in Europe,* Bristol: Policy Press.

O'Sullivan, E. (1998a), 'The State, Voluntary Agencies, Housing and Homeless Services in the Republic of Ireland', 1997/1998 Annual Report from the Republic of Ireland to the European Observatory on Homelessness, unpublished.

O'Sullivan, E. (1998b), 'The Other Housing Crisis: The Contribution of Social and Voluntary Housing', paper presented at the Foundation for Fiscal Studies' Conference on Housing, October 1998.

O'Sullivan, E. (2001), *Access to Housing: The Case of the Republic of Ireland,* Brussels: FEANTSA.

O'Sullivan, E. (2004), 'Welfare Regimes, Housing and Homelessness in the Republic of Ireland', *European Journal of Housing Policy*, nol. 4, no. 3, pp 323-343.

O'Sullivan, E. (2006), 'Homelessness in Rural Ireland', in Cloke, P. and Milbourne, P.

(eds), *International Perspectives on Rural Homelessness,* London: Routledge.

O'Sullivan, E. and O'Donnell, I. (2003) 'Imprisonment and the Crime Rate in Ireland', *Economic and Social Review,* vol. 34, no.1, pp 33-64.

O'Sullivan, T. and Gibb, K. (eds.) (2003), *Housing Economics and Public Policy,* Oxford: Blackwell Science Ltd.

ODEI – The Equality Tribunal (2003), *Annual Report 2002,* Dublin: ODEI – The Equality Tribunal.

Office of An Tanáiste (1997) *Report of the Task Force on Violence against Women.* Dublin: Stationery Office.

Office of the Revenue Commissioners (various years) *Annual Reports,* Dublin: Stationery Office.

Organisation for Economic Co-operation and Development (1998), *Integrating Distressed Urban Areas,* Paris: OECD.

Organisation for Economic Co-operation and Development (1999), *Ireland: Origins of the Economic Boom – Sustaining High Growth,* Paris: OECD Economic Surveys.

Oswald, A. (2002), *The Great 2003-2005 Crash in Britain's Housing Market,* Warwick: University Of Warwick.

Oxley, M. (2004), *Economics, Planning and Housing,* Basingstoke: Palgrave.

Pacione, M. (1990), 'The Ecclesiastical Community of Interest as a Response to Urban Poverty and Deprivation', *Transactions – Institute of British Geographers,* vol. 15, pp 193-204.

Passaro, J. (1996), *The Unequal Homeless: Men on the Streets, Women in their Place.* New York: Routledge.

Patricios, N. (2002), 'Urban Design Principles of the Original Neighbourhood Concepts', *Urban Morphology,* vol. 6, no.1, pp 21-26.

Pavee Point Travellers' Centre (2002), *Traveller Proofing – Within an Equality Framework,* Dublin: Pavee Point Travellers' Centre.

Pearn Kandola Occupational Psychologists (2003), *Travellers' Experiences of Labour Market Programmes,* Dublin: Equality Studies Unit, Equality Authority.

Permanent TSB and the Economic and Social ResearchI (2002), *Permanent TSB/ESRI House Price Index,* Dublin: Economic and Social Research Institute.

Pfretschner, P. (1965), *The Dynamics of Irish Housing,* Dublin: Institute of Public Administration.

Pinto, R. (1993), *The Estate Action Initiative: Council Housing Renewal, Management and Effectiveness,* Aldershot, Avebury.

Pooley, G. (ed.) (1992), *Housing Strategies in Europe, 1880-1930,* Leicester: Leicester University Press.

Power, A. (1987), *Property Before People: the Management of Twentieth-Century Council Housing,* London, Allen and Unwin.

Power, A. (1997), 'A Portrait of Ballymun, Ireland, 1966-95', in *Estates on the Edge: the Social Consequences of Mass Housing in Northern Europe,* London: Macmillan.

Power, A. (1993), *Hovels to High Rise: State Housing in Europe Since 1850,* London: Routledge.

Power, A. (1999), 'High-Rise Estates in Europe: Is Rescue Possible?', *Journal of European Social Policy,* vol. 9, no. 2, pp 139-163.

Power, S. (2000), 'The Development of the Ballymun Housing Scheme, Dublin: 1965-1969', *Irish Geography,* vol. 33, no. 2, pp 199- 212.

Punch, M. (2001), 'Inner-City Transformation and Renewal: the view from the grassroots', in MacLaran, A. and Drudy, P. (2001), *Dublin: Economic and Social Trends,* vol. 3, Dublin: Centre for Urban and Regional Studies, Trinity College Dublin.

Punch, M. (2002), 'Local Development Issues on the Urban Periphery: Tallaght from Bottom-Up', *Journal of Irish Urban Studies*, vol. 1, no.1, pp 61-77.

Quigley, J.M. and Raphael, S. (2001), 'The Economics of Homelessness: The Evidence from North America', *European Journal of Housing Policy*, vol. 1, no. 3, pp 323-336.

Ravetz, A. (1980), *Remaking Cities: Contradictions of the Recent Urban Environment,* London: Croom Helm.

Reddy, P. (2002), 'Creating Residential Communities in the Twenty First Century', *Irish Architect,* vol. 173, pp 46-48.

Redmond, D. (2001), Social Housing in Ireland: Under New Management? *European Journal of Housing Policy,* vol. 1, no. 2, pp 291-306.

Redmond, D. and Walker, R. (1995), 'Housing Management in Ireland: Transition and Change', *Regional Studies,* vol. 29, no. 3, pp 312-316.

Registrar of Friendly Societies (various years) *Annual Report*, Dublin: Stationery Office.

Rent Tribunal (various years) *Annual Report*, Dublin: Rent Tribunal.

Revenue Commissioners (2002), *Effective Tax Rates for High Earning Individuals*, Dublin: Stationery Office.

Review Group on the Role of Supplementary Welfare Allowance in Relation to Housing (1995), *Report to the Minister for Social Welfare*, Dublin: Stationery Office.

Reynolds, F. (1986), *The Problem Housing Estate: An Account of Omega and Its People,* London, Gower.

Roche, D. (1982), *Local Government in Ireland,* Dublin: Institute of Public Administration.

Rottman, D., Tussing, D. and Wiley, M. (1986), *The Population Structure and Living Conditions of Irish Travellers: Results of the 1981 Census of Traveller Families,* Dublin: Economic and Social Research Institute.

Rourke, S. (2001), 'Research Project on People Evicted from Dublin Corporation Housing Units in 1997 and 1998 for Anti-Social Behaviour', Dublin, unpublished report for Dublin Corporation and the South Western Area Health Board.

Royal Institute of Architects of Ireland (2004), 'RIAI Strongly support proposed introduction of national Guidelines on Rural Housing', Dublin: unpublished press release.

Ruddle, H., Donoghue, F. and Mulvihill, R. (1997*), The Years Ahead Report: A Review of the Implementation of its Recommendations,* National Council on Ageing and Older People, Report No. 48, Dublin: National Council on Ageing and Older People.

Rudlin, D. and Falk, N. (1998), *Building the 21st Century Home: The Sustainable Urban Neighbourhood,* Oxford: Butterwork-Heinemann.

Scott. M. (2004), 'Managing rural housing and contested meanings of sustainable development: insights from planning practice in the Republic of Ireland', paper presented to *Planning and Housing: Policy and Practice, Housing Studies Association Conference*, 9-10 September 2004, Belfast.

Scott, M. (forthcoming), 'Strategic spatial planning and contested ruralities: insights from the Republic of Ireland', *European Planning Studies*, in press.

Scott, S (ed.) (2001), *Good Practice in Housing Management: a Review of the Literature,* Edinburgh: Scottish Executive Central Research Unit.

Shannon, D. (1988), 'The History and Future of the Housing (Miscellaneous Provisions) Bill, 1985', in Blackwell, J. and Kennedy, S. (eds), *Focus on Homelessness*. Dublin: Columba Press.

Sheahan, J. (1992), 'Development Dichotomies and Economic Strategies', in Teitel, S. (ed.), *Towards a New Development Strategy for Latin America*, Washington DC: Inter-American Development Bank.

Sherry FitzGerald (2003), *Irish Residential Market,* Dublin: Sherry FitzGerald Estate Agents.

Simon Community (1992), *Still Waiting for the Future,* Dublin: unpublished submission from the Simon Community to the Minister and Department of Health.

Smith, M., McGee, H., Shannon, W. and Holohan, T. (2001), *One Hundred Homeless Women: Health Status and Health Service Use of Homeless Women and their Children in Dublin,* Dublin: Royal College of Surgeons in Ireland/ Children's Research Centre.

Smith, N. (1984), *Uneven Development,* Oxford: Basil Blackwell.

Smith, N. (1996), *The New Urban Frontier: Gentrification and the Revanchist City,* London: Routledge.

Society of St Vincent de Paul (1999), *Housing Policy: Mixed Housing and Mixed Communities,* Dublin: St. Vincent de Paul.

Somerville, P., Steele, A. and Hale, J. (1998), *Assessment of the Implementation of the Right to Manage,* London: Department of the Environment, Transport and the Regions.

Somerville, P. (1998), 'Empowerment Through Residence', *Housing Studies,* vol. 13, no. 2, pp 233-258.

Somerville, P. and Steele, A. (1995), 'Making Sense of Tenant Participation', *Netherlands Journal of Housing and the Built Environment,* vol. 10, no. 3, pp 259-281.

South Dublin County Council (2003), *Adamstown Strategic Development Zone Planning Scheme,* Dublin: South Dublin County Council.

Stephens, M., Burns, N. and McKay, L. (2002), *Social Market or Safety Net? British Social Rented Housing in Comparative Context,* Bristol: Policy Press.

Sterrett, K. (2003), 'The countryside aesthetic and house design in Northern Ireland', in Greer, J. and Murray, M. (eds), *Rural Planning and Development in Northern Ireland.* Dublin: Institute of Public Administration.

Stewart, M. and Taylor, M. (1995), *Empowerment and Estate Regeneration: A Critical Review,* Bristol: Policy Press.

Stone, M.E. (1990), *One Third of a Nation: A New look at Housing Affordability in America,* Washington DC, Economic Policy Institute.

Stringer, R. (1971), 'The Importance of Survey for Development Plans', in Bannon, M.J. (ed), *The Application of Geographical Techniques to Physical Planning,* Dublin: An Foras Forbartha.

Study Programme on European Spatial Planning (2000), *Final Report,* Brussels and Stockholm.

Suffren, P. (1974), *Clustered Rural Housing: An Alternative to Sprawl,* Dublin: An Foras Forbartha.

Sweeney, J. (2003), 'Planning, Climate Change and Culture Change: Theory and Practice in Shaping the Future of Ireland', Paper presented to SIPTU/LAPO conference, September 2003.

An Taisce (2001), *An Taisce Policies on the Rural Built Environment,* Dublin: An Taisce.

An Taisce (2004), 'Submission on DoEHLG's Sustainable Rural Housing Guidelines – Draft', Dublin: unpublished submission to the Department of the Environment, Heritage and Local Government.

Task Force on the Travelling Community (1995), *Report of the Task Force on the Travelling Community,* Dublin: Stationery Office.

Taylor, M. (1995), *Unleashing the Potential: Bringing Residents to the Centre of Regeneration* York: Joseph Rowntree Foundation.

Taylor, M. (2000), 'Communities in the Lead: Power, Organisational Capital and Social Capital', *Urban Studies*, vol. 37, nos 5-6, pp 1019-1035.

Tenant Participation Advisory Service (1994), *Tenant Information: A Good Practice Guide,* Glasgow: TPAS (Scotland).

Thompson, B. (1988), 'Social Housing', in Blackwell, J. and Kennedy, S. (eds), *Focus on Homelessness: A New Look at Housing Policy*, Dublin: The Columba Press.

Thornley, A. (1993), *Urban Planning Under Thatcherism: the Challenge of the Market,* London: Routledge.

Thorns, D. (1989), 'The Production of Homelessness: From Individual Failure to System Inadequacies', *Housing Studies*, vol. 4, no. 4, pp 253-266

Threshold, (1987), *Policy Consequences: A Study of the £5000 Surrender Grant in the Dublin Housing Area,* Dublin: Threshold.

Town Tenants Commission (1927), *Interim Report on the Working of the Small Dwellings Acquisition Act 1899*, Dublin: Stationery Office.

Townsend, P. (1970), *The Concept of Poverty*, London: Heinemann.

Treacy, L. (2002), 'Occupant Satisfaction with the Design of Speculative Housing', Unpublished Master of Regional and Urban Planning Thesis, Dublin: University College Dublin.

Travelling People Review Body (1983), *Report of the Travelling People Review Body,* Dublin: Stationery Office.

Tribal HCH (2004), *The Irish Planning System and Affordable Housing*, Edinburgh: Scottish Executive.

United Nations Economic Commission for Europe (1997), *Strategies to Implement Human Settlements Policies on Urban Renewal and Housing Modernization,* Geneva: United Nations Economic Commission for Europe.

United Nations Economic Commission for Europe (1999), *Guidelines on Condominium Ownership of Housing for Countries in Transition,* Geneva: United Nations Economic Commission for Europe.

United Nations Economic Commission for Europe (2002), *Bulletin of Housing and Building Statistics,* Geneva: United Nations Economic Commission for Europe.

United Nations Economic Commission for Europe (2004), *Bulletin of Housing and Building Statistics,* Geneva: United Nations Economic Commission for Europe.

United Kingdom, Audit Commission (1999) *Listen Up! Effective Community Consultation* London: Audit Commission.

United Kingdom, Department of the Environment, Transport and the Regions (1998a) *National Framework for Tenant Participation Compacts* London: HMSO.

United Kingdom, Department of the Environment Transport and the Regions (1998b), *The Use of Density in Urban Planning*, London: ETR Publications.

United Kingdom, Department of the Environment, Transport and the Regions (1999), *Tenant Participation Compacts: Consultation Paper* London: HMSO.

United Kingdom, Department of the Environment Transport and the Regions and Commission for Architecture and the Build Environment (2000), *By Design, Urban Design in the Planning System – towards better practice,* London: Thomas Telford Publishing.

United Kingdom, Department of the Environment, Transport and the Regions (2001), *Tenant Participation in Transition: Issues and Trends in the Development of Tenant Participation in the Local Authority Sector in England* London: Department of the Environment, Transport and the Regions, Housing Research Summary, no. 147.

United Kingdom, Department of Work and Pensions (2002) *Households Below Average Income 2000/01*, HMSO: London.

United Kingdom, Office of the Deputy Prime Minister (2003), *Sustainable Communities: Building for the Future,* London: Office of the Deputy Prime Minister.

Urban Design Group (2000), *The Community Planning Handbook,* London: Earthscan.

Urban Task Force (1999), *Towards an Urban Renaissance,* London: Spon.

van Dam, F., Heins, S. and Elberson, B. (2002), 'Lay discourses of the rural and stated and revealed preferences for rural living. Some evidence of the existence of a rural idyll in the Netherlands', *Journal of Rural Studies,* vol. 18, no. 4, pp 461-476.

Walker, B. and Murie, A. (2004), 'The Performance of Social Landlords in Great Britain: What Do We Know and What Does It Show?' *Housing Studies,* vol. 19, no. 2, pp 245-268.

Wallich-Clifford, A. (1974), *No Fixed Abode*, London: Macmillan.

Wallich-Clifford, A. (1976), *Caring on Skid Row,* Dublin: Veritas.

Walsh, D. (1997), 'Mental Health Care in Ireland 1945-1997 and the Future', in Robins, J. (ed), *Reflections on Health: Commemorating Fifty Years of the Department of Health,* Dublin: Department of Health.

Watson, D. (2003), 'Sample Attrition between waves 1 and 5 in the European Community Household Panel' *European Sociological Review,* vol. 19, no. 4, pp 361-378.

Watson, D. and Williams, J. (2003), *Irish National Survey of Housing Quality 2001-2002*, Dublin: Economic and Social Research Institute and Department of Environment, Heritage and Local Government.

Watt, P. (1998), 'The Development of tenant participation in estate management', in Community Workers Co-operative (1998), *Strategies to Encourage Tenant Participation,* Galway: Community Workers Co-operative.

Weafer, J. (2001), *The Education and Accommodation Needs of Travellers in the Archdiocese of Dublin*, Dublin: Crosscare and Travelling People Awareness.

Westmeath County Council (2002), *Westmeath County Development Plan*, Westmeath: Westmeath County Council.

Wexford County Council (2001), *Wexford County Development Plan*, Wexford: Wexford County Council.

Whelan, C., Layte, R., Maître, B. and Nolan, B. (2001), 'Income, Deprivation and Economic Strain: An Analysis of the European Community Household Panel', *European Sociological Review,* vol. 17, no. 4, pp 357-372.

Whitehead, J. and Carr, C. (2001), *Twentieth-Century Suburbs: a morphological approach,* London: Routledge.

Whyte, G. (2002), *Social Inclusion and the Legal System: Public Interest Law in Ireland,* Dublin: Institute of Public Administration.

Wilcox, D. (1994), *The Guide to Effective Tenant Participation,* Brighton: Partnership Books.

Williams, B. (1997), 'Taxation Incentives and Urban Renewal in Dublin', *International Journal of Property Tax Assessment,* vol. 2, no. 3, pp 69-88.

Williams, B. (2001), 'Recent Work on Affordable Housing in Ireland', *Economic and Social Review,* vol. 32, no.1, pp 81-101.

Williams B. and Shiels P. (2000), 'Acceleration into Sprawl: Causes and Potential Policy Responses', Economic and Social Research Institute, *Quarterly Economic Commentary,* June 2000, Dublin: Economic and Social Research Institute.

Williams, B. and Shiels, P. (2001), *An Assessment of the Development Potential of Public Open Space in North Dublin*, Dublin: the North Dublin Development Coalition.

Williams, B. and Shiels, P. (2002), 'The Expansion of Dublin and the Policy Implications of Dispersal', *Journal of Irish Urban Studies*, vol. 1, no. 1, pp 1-20.

Williams, B., Shiels, P. and Hughes, B. (2002), *SCS Housing Study 2002 – a Study on Housing Supply and Urban Development issue in the Greater Dublin Area*, Dublin: Society of Chartered Surveyors and Dublin Institute of Technology.

Williams, B., Shiels, P. and Hughes, B. (2003), 'Access to Housing: the role of housing supply and urban development policies in the Greater Dublin Area', *Journal of Irish Urban Studies*, vol. 2, no. 1, pp 25-52.

Williams, J. and Gorby, S. (2002), *Counted in 2002: The Report of the Assessment of Homelessness in Dublin*, Dublin: Homeless Agency and the Economic and Social Research Institute.

Williams, J. and O'Connor, M. (1999), *Counted In: The Report of the 1999 Assessment of Homelessness in Dublin, Kildare and Wicklow.* Dublin: Economic and Social Research Institute and the Homeless Initiative.

Woods, M. (2003), 'Deconstructing rural protest: the emergence of a new social movement', *Journal of Rural Studies,* vol. 19, no. 3, pp 309-325

Woods, M. (2005), *Rural Geography*, London: Sage.

Woods, M. and Humphries, N. (2001), *Statistical Update: Seeking Asylum in Ireland*, Dublin: Social Science Research Centre.

Working Group on Security of Tenure (1996), *Report of the Working Group on Security of Tenure,* Dublin: Stationery Office.

WRC Social and Economic Consultants (2003), *Accommodating Diversity in Labour Market Programmes,* Dublin: The Equality Authority.

Wulff, M. and Maher, C. (1998), Long Term Renters in the Australian Housing Market, *Housing Studies,* vol. 13, no. 1, pp 83-98.

Zimmerman, C.C. (1936), *Consumption and Standards of Living*, New York: Van Nostrand.

Index